A Century of South African Theatre

CULTURAL HISTORIES OF THEATRE AND PERFORMANCE

The Bloomsbury series of *Cultural Histories of Theatre and Performance* recognizes that historical knowledge has always been contested and revised. Since the turn of the twenty-first century, the transformation of conventional understandings of culture created through new political realities and communication technologies, together with paradigm shifts in anthropology, psychology and other cognate fields, has challenged established methodologies and ways of thinking about how we do history. The series embraces volumes that take on those challenges, while enlarging notions of theatre and performance through the representation of the lived experience of past performance makers and spectators. The series' aim is to be both inclusive and expansive, including studies on topics that range temporally and spatially, from the locally specific to the intercultural and transnational.

Series editors:

Claire Cochrane (University of Worcester, UK)
Bruce McConachie (University of Pittsburgh, USA)

George Farquhar: A Migrant Life Reversed
David Roberts

The Polish Theatre of the Holocaust
Grzegorz Niziołek

Forthcoming titles

Alternative Comedy: 1979 and the Reinvention of British Stand-Up
Oliver Double

A Century of South African Theatre

Loren Kruger

methuen | drama
LONDON · NEW YORK · OXFORD · NEW DELHI · SYDNEY

METHUEN DRAMA
Bloomsbury Publishing Plc
50 Bedford Square, London, WC1B 3DP, UK
1385 Broadway, New York, NY 10018, USA

BLOOMSBURY, METHUEN DRAMA and the Methuen Drama logo are
trademarks of Bloomsbury Publishing Plc

First published in Great Britain 2020

Cover image: Chuma Sopotela and Mdu Kweyama in *Karoo Moose* by Lara Foot.
Photograph © Ruphin Coudyzer; FPPSA; www.ruphin.co.za

A catalogue record for this book is available from the British Library.

A catalog record for this book is available from the Library of Congress.

ISBN: HB: 978-1-3500-0800-7
        PB: 978-1-3500-0801-4
        ePDF: 978-1-3500-0803-8
        eBook: 978-1-3500-0802-1

Series: Cultural Histories of Theatre and Performance

Typeset by Integra Software Services Pvt. Ltd.

To find out more about our authors and books visit www.bloomsbury.com
and sign up for our newsletters.

Contents

Illustrations

Figures

Maps

Acknowledgments

A Century of South African Theatre documents more than a hundred years of theatre and performance, drawn from research on print, video, and aural material on the years from 1910 to 2017, and personal observation of performance since the 1970s. In that time, I have garnered many debts, from the teachers who took high school girls to plays probably not intended for their eyes and ears, to the theatre practitioners in Johannesburg, Pretoria, Cape Town, Durban, Grahamstown, and other places who have enlightened and entertained me over decades, and to colleagues in Africa, North America, Europe, and Australasia, for stimulating discussion about performance and politics at home and abroad.

I would like to begin by acknowledging the South African practitioners and critics who have engaged with my work, especially since the publication of my first book on this subject in 1999: David Coplan, Cynthia Kros, Greg Homann, Lwazi Mjiyako, and Samuel Ravengai at the University of the Witwatersrand (Wits), as well as Maishe Maponya and Liz Gunner, who have moved on elsewhere; Marisa Keuris, Lydia Krüger, Andries Oliphant, Andile Xaba, and others at the University of South Africa; Anton Krueger at Rhodes University; Ismael Mahomed at the Market Theatre Foundation; Dom Gumede, Liza Key, Gcina Mhlophe, Eliot Moleba, Paul Slabolepszy, Adrienne Sichel, and Malcolm Purkey in Johannesburg; Kriben Pillay in Durban; Mark Fleishman, Lara Foot, Gay Morris, Jennie Reznek, and Mike van Graan in Cape Town; Temple Hauptfleisch in Stellenbosch, Lynn Dalrymple and Hazel Barnes in KZN, and Clive Evian, Shirley Ngwenya, Helene Schneider, Mhlalabesi Vundla, and Jane Doherty, variously involved in theatre and/or health education. I would also like to honor those whose lives and contributions to this book and many other projects have passed into history: Tim Couzens, Lewis Nkosi, Sipho Sepamla, and Barney Simon, among many.

Several archives and individuals provided me with print and visual material. Thanks are due to the National Library of South Africa (Cape Town); Rhodes University Cory Library; the Western Cape Archive; the Johannesburg Public Library; the State Archive (Pretoria); Market Theatre Publicity Office and the Killie Campbell Library in Durban. Gabriele Mohale at Wits University Library, and Crystal Warren at the National English Literary Museum (Grahamstown) have been particularly helpful, as have Ruphin Coudyzer and John Hogg, whose images have greatly enhanced this book. Visits to archives, theatres, and other venues in South Africa were partially enabled by funds from the US Dept of Education Fulbright-Hays Fund, and by research leave from the University of Chicago.

Many colleagues and friends at Chicago and elsewhere have offered valuable criticism: at the University of Chicago: Ralph Austen, Emily Osborne, and others at the African Studies Workshop; Cathy Cohen, Marcus Lee, and others at the Reproductions of Race Workshop; Sarah Wells, Tejumola Olaniyan. Aparna Dharwadker, Laurie Beth Clark, Matthew Brown, and other respondents at the University of Wisconsin-Madison; numerous participants at conference presentations at the American Society for Theatre Research, International Federation for Theatre Research, African Studies Association, and the Modern Language Association. I would also like to thank Christopher Balme (Munich), Rose Bank (Kent), Johann Buis (Wheaton), Catherine Cole (Seattle), Joachim Fiebach (Berlin), Neville Hoad (Austin), Tsitsi Jaji (Durham, NC), Laurie Frederik Meer (Maryland), Megan Lewis (Amherst), Mark Sanders (New York), Gerhard Schutte (Chicago), and David Graver (Chicago).

Since the publication of my previous book on South African theatre, *The Drama of South Africa* (Routledge 1999), my essays on this and related topics have appeared in the following journals—*Modern Drama* (2000); *Theatre Journal* (2001, 2008, 2012); *Scrutiny2* (2001, 2004, 2007, 2009); *Theatre Research International* (2002, 2015); *The Drama Review* (2007); *Research in African Literatures* (2006, 2011, 2017); *Theater* (2006, 2008, 2015); *Journal of Southern African Studies* (2009); *Comparative Drama* (2012); *Critical Stages* (2017)—and edited volumes—*Cambridge History of South African Theatre* (2012); *Playing Culture* (2013); *Performance and the Global City* (2013); *Methuen Guide to Contemporary South African Theatre* (2015); *Reconfiguring South African Theatre and Performance* (2015); and *Cambridge Companion to International Festivals* (forthcoming). Thanks are due to the editors and publishers for their critical contributions to improving these essays. The present book thoroughly revises and updates all of the above and includes as yet unpublished analysis of current theatre and performance as well as engagement with new research on historical work, and will, I hope, provide a foundation for more investigation by colleagues in the field.

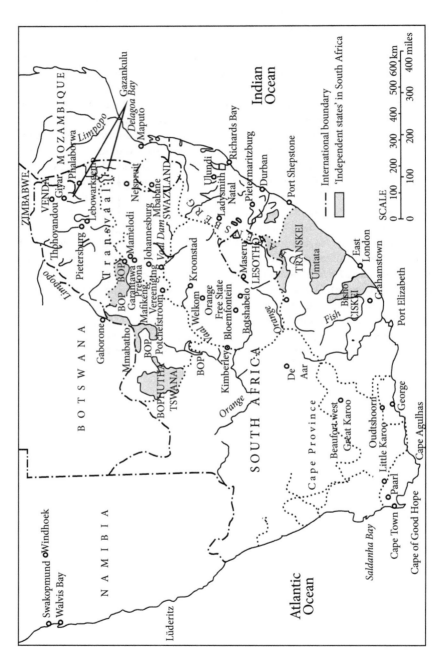

Map 1 South Africa immediately prior to 1994, showing four provinces and Bantustans.

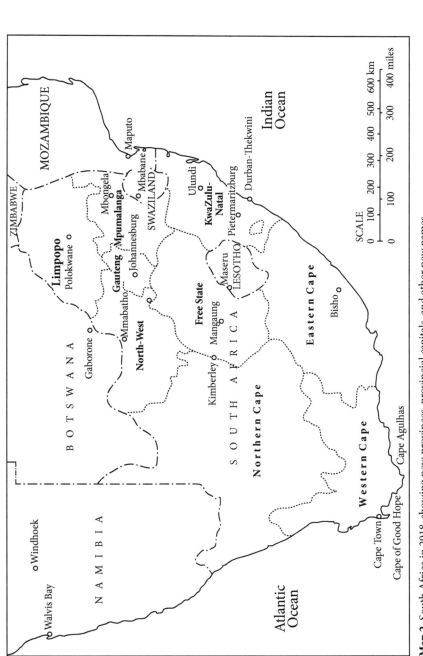

Map 2 South Africa in 2018, showing new provinces, provincial capitals, and other new names.

Introduction: Theatre and South African Public Spheres

Texts, Performances, Archives, and Audiences

"'Theatre' is not part of our vocabulary." This assertion by Sipho Sepamla (1932–2007) seems at first downright contrary. Sepamla had been writer and later editor at *S'ketsh* (1972–79), subtitled "South Africa's popular theatre and entertainment magazine," and he made this assertion in Johannesburg's major daily paper *Rand Daily Mail* in an article entitled "Towards an African Theatre" (Sepamla 1981) that showcased his knowledge of African performance history as well as current political theatre.[1] His assertion seems even more astonishing when we remember that 1981 was the year of *Woza Albert!* [Albert Arise], the ground-breaking play whose virtuoso fusion of African comedy sketches, experimental techniques from Brecht and Grotowski, and satirical treatment in English, Zulu, and Afrikaans of an imagined visit by Jesus Christ to apartheid South Africa earned it enduring acclaim as *the* anti-apartheid classic, prompting revivals and worldwide sales of the text to this day. Created by Percy Mtwa, Mbongeni Ngema, and Barney Simon, founding director of the Market Theatre, and published in 1983, *Woza Albert!* delighted black audiences while entertaining and discomfiting whites, and became the key exemplar of the testimonial play that is at once South Africa's distinctive theatrical genre and the syncretic product of multiple influences transnational and local. *Syncretic* best describes performance practices in South Africa because the term highlights the agency of practitioners to appropriate conventions, scripts, and behaviors to their own ends and is thus more precise than the biological metaphor "hybrid," which, despite its habitual use in postcolonial theory, reminds South Africans of apartheid claims to ground identity in supposedly biological "race."[2]

Sepamla was not the first intellectual to seek distinctive modes of African performance. Herbert Dhlomo (1904–56), active from the 1930s to 1950s but largely forgotten until his collected work was published in 1985, argued for a theatre that would combine European and African influences (Dhlomo 1933). Fifty years later Mafika Gwala (1946–2014) of the Black Consciousness Movement (BCM) argued against colonial influences in favor of an as yet unrealized African national theatre (Gwala 1973). But, where Dhlomo and Gwala advocated serious drama about African history and struggle, Sepamla argued for the potential of popular entertainment. Drawing on his experience with Union Artists, an organization that offered partial support to black entertainers, Sepamla made two important points. First, like Gwala and other Black Consciousness activists (Chapter 5), he critiqued as neocolonial the education that he had received from church-sponsored schools, while acknowledging that this instruction—including the liberal tradition of civil rights along with Shakespeare and the social drama of George Bernard Shaw and John Galsworthy—had shaped Nelson Mandela (1918–2013) and his generation before the apartheid government closed these schools in 1953 and left the British Commonwealth in 1961.[3] English touring productions offered the reflected glow of London glamour and bolstered the white Anglophile desire to see the Union of South Africa (1910–60) as a "European" dominion but with heightened black awareness of segregation (Chapters 1 and 2). Second and more unusually, Sepamla challenged black intellectual promotion of serious drama in English by arguing that multilingual variety shows enjoyed a wider audience. These entertainments had since the 1920s included a broad range of forms from "sketches" to "concerts" to "musicals." If popular producers did not see "theatre" as part of African vocabulary, even when their shows included drama of interest to Africans, it was because these shows and their audiences had limited institutional support and thus little attachment to the aura of theatre. While intellectuals crafted new words to describe dramatic performance—such as Dhlomo's *izibongelo* [performances for an audience] (1977d) or Credo Mutwa's *umlinganiso* [living imitation] (1974–5)—popular audiences tended, as Sepamla argued, to favor English words that highlighted the modernity of urban variety shows: "concert," "sketch," or in Nguni articulation, *isiketshi* or *S'ketsh* (Kavanagh 2016: ix).

The changing institutional determination of theatre that attracted Africans and Afrikaners as well as English-speaking migrants reminds us that urban venues provided key places and occasions for contesting public spheres. Building on Habermas's conception of *Öffentlichkeit* [publicity or *public-ness*] and my own work on national and transnational theatre, I take *public sphere* (the usual translation) to mean not only public sites for performance but also the public significance of performance especially theatre understood by participants to constitute a place and occasion for contestation in societies where debate is otherwise not free and, in the absence of a democracy, operates in a restricted rather than expanded field of play.[4] In neocolonial and apartheid South Africa, people seeking modern agency found on stage and in audience assembly the articulation of *aspirational* nationhood that might constitute an alternative public sphere in anticipation of the struggle for full participation in a *legitimate* public sphere. While white English-speakers often copied trends from London or occasionally New York and thus reproduced an *ersatz* public sphere marked by the neocolonial deference to metropolitan tastes that Australians dub the "cultural cringe" (Minogue 1995), Afrikaner intellectuals favored performances that promoted *volkseie*—the unique character of the *volk*. Events such as the Tercentenary of the Dutch East India Company (VOC) official Jan van Riebeeck's arrival at the Cape (1652/1952), which featured the Afrikaner nationalist play *Die Jaar van die Vuur-os* [The Year of the Fire-Ox] by W.A. de Klerk, set the pattern: Afrikaans writers enjoyed state support for publication, even if some plays such as *Die Verminktes* [The Maimed] (1962) by Bartho Smit, proved too controversial to stage (Chapters 3 and 4). Whatever their differences, English- and Afrikaans-speaking whites were largely united in the belief that the public sphere was the domain of "civilized Europeans" and tended to assume that Africans were limited by "traditional" custom. Nonetheless, the actual tastes of urbanizing Africans defied simple oppositions between European and African, white and black, in part due to a third set of influences: the entertainment and educational initiatives of African Americans, whose achievements inspired educated Africans to follow their example.

In black urban spaces, new performance practices emerged from the encounters between commercial entertainments of European, American, and African-American vintage and *ingoma*—music or performance in ritual or play. *Ingoma ebusuku* [music by night], or shows performed as after-work entertainment in interior spaces for cash, became known from the 1920s as variety concerts or simply "concerts" to a wide range of urban and urbanizing audiences (Ballantine 2012). In their anticipation of ticket income for a marketable commodity, these concerts, performed in venues from the refined Bantu Men's Social Centre (BMSC) in central Johannesburg through the 1940s to informal township halls thereafter, reflected on a modest scale the culture of capitalism (Coplan 2008). African variety was refined by impresarios such as Griffiths Motsieloa (1896–1950), who drew on a range of models including the Eisteddfod and the church choir imported by the British to local modes of storytelling—*izinganekwane* (Zulu) or *iintsomi* (Xhosa)—and praises, such as *izibongo* (Zulu) and *lithoko* (Sotho), spirituals, minstrelsy, and African-American hit revues such as *Shuffle Along* (1921), which ran in New York until 1924 and inspired many imitators, including Motsieloa's own "Lost in the Shuffle" (Chapter 1).

These genres appealed to black urban audiences from educated English-speakers to migrant workers not so much because they were black but because they were modern. They demonstrated their creators' control over their own labor, and, in the hands of entrepreneurs like Motsieloa, who financed his shows by working as talent scout for local record company Gallophone, attempted to match aspirations to agency with urban prosperity (Chapter 1). Motsieloa's successors include Todd Matshikiza (1922–68), composer of the "jazz opera" *King Kong* in 1959 (Chapter 3), Gibson Kente (1932–2004), master writer-composer of musicals (Chapter 5), Mbongeni Ngema (1955–), co-creator of *Woza Albert!* but best known for *Sarafina* (1986; Chapter 6), and Aubrey Sekhabi (1969–), creator of *Marikana—the Musical* (2014; Chapter 8). All of these and more have made the "concert," or its offspring the "township musical," the most durable form of theatre in South Africa, even if their sentimental plots tend to soften the critical edge of political drama in, for example *Sarafina*'s treatment of the Soweto uprising of 1976 or *Marikana*'s of the police massacre of miners in 2012. The lineage from Motsieloa through Kente and Ngema to Sekhabi, as well as their debts to African-American traditions, highlights the complexity of transnational black cultural transmission; it also decolonizes the Eurocentric habits of critics who, apparently unaware of this lineage, overemphasize Kente's affinity with European musical theatre (Solberg 2011).

Any investigation of South African theatrical "vocabulary," to return to Sepamla's term, thus requires attention to African variety alongside the overtly political drama often identified with South African theatre per se, whichever label—protest, resistance, defiance—is applied to plays that bear witness to struggle against injustice.

As outlined in the sole entry on theatre in *The Cambridge History of South African Literature* (Kruger 2012a), *testimonial theatre* is the most useful umbrella term since it not only covers the different rhetorical emphases signaled by "protest" or "resistance" (Chapters 5 and 6) but also stresses the *act* of testifying more directly than the less active phrase "theatre of witness." Testimonial theatre includes too many plays to cover in an introduction but the following list demonstrates its rich diversity: Athol Fugard (1932–) and Serpent Players' collaborative work from *The Coat* (1966) to *The Island* (1973), more demonstrative defiance in Matsamela Manaka's *Egoli* (1979) or Maishe Maponya's *Gangsters* (1985), workshop productions directed by Simon, above all *Born in the RSA* (1985), or women's autobiographical pieces such as Gcina Mhlophe's *Have You Seen Zandile?* (1986) or Thembi Mtshali [Jones]'s *Woman in Waiting* (1988) (Chapter 6). More recently, techniques inherited from anti-apartheid testimony, from terse direct address to mime and other expressive deployment of the human body, have enlivened post-apartheid plays such as Omphile Molusi's anti-corruption *Itsoseng* (2008) or Eliot Moleba's quiet but telling indictment of the Marikana massacre in *The Man with the Green Jacket* (2014) (Chapter 8). While post-apartheid stages have featured spectacular fusions of local and transnational themes and forms in, for instance, William Kentridge and Handspring Puppet Theatre's experimental collaborations from *Woyzeck on the Highveld* (1993) to *Ubu and the Truth Commission* (1997; Chapter 7), Yaël Farber's *Molora* (2007), which adapts the *Oresteia* to explore the tragic dimensions of reconciliation, Brett Bailey and company's Third World Bunfight's mash-ups of classical legend and racial masquerade in, for example, *Orfeus* (2007), which relocated the legend of Orpheus and the underworld to an eerie abandoned quarry outside the university town of Grahamstown, the annual venue for the National Arts Festival, Magnet Theatre's multilingual migrant plays (Reznek et al. 2012), or Lara Foot's lyrical fusion of physical dexterity and social critique in plays like *Karoo Moose* (2007; Chapter 8), testimonial plays and musicals remain the definitive models for new work as well as the revivals of anti-apartheid classics that predominate in the subsidized theatres. Commercial houses in South Africa as elsewhere favor comedy or local productions of imported hits, which are evidently more profitable than new drama.

The distinctive character of theatre in South Africa and its national and transnational influences and impacts will be taken up in the chapters that follow. For the moment, the preliminary list of texts above—a small sample of the rich archive—should counter ahistorical demands for "decolonization." In response to similar demands twenty years ago, Nigerian Professor Biodun Jeyifo cautioned against Africanist "ontologisation" of an essential identity allegedly fully expressed by precolonial practices against which "theatre" would be a mere colonial import (Jeyifo 1990: 37). He argued that this ontologization inverted rather than critiqued "neocolonial essentialism" (1996: 155), which diminished African practices by finding them incompatible with European norms. While some South Africans might join Gwala in the pursuit of Africanization, others such as S'khumbuzo Mngadi describe this quest as a "new exoticism" (1997: 18). Theatre in South Africa is not *essentially* African or European; rather it *takes place* between and within practices, forms, and institutions, sometimes pointedly local, at others evidently transnational, but always engaged with combinations that may include

European, African, American, African-American, or Indian influences. As Tsitsi Jaji suggests in *Africa in Stereo* (2014), these combinations have generated stereophonic and stereoscopic repertoires and innovations in theatrical and musical performance that confound appeals to purity, including those made in the name of decolonization.

The historical and formal range of even the small sample mentioned so far indicates that the global resonance of South African theatre is not simply a recent product of "South African theatre in the age of globalization" (Kruger 2012b), although the reopening of cultural trade routes since the 1990s has given some companies and individuals (Handspring, Magnet, Kentridge, Bailey, Farber) worldwide acclaim, and provided emerging practitioners with international exposure. Going beyond my earlier book *The Drama of South Africa* (1999a), *A Century of Theatre in South Africa* shows that theatre and other performances have registered transnational influences and resonances at least since the inauguration of Union in 1910; the identification of practices and forms as South African has depended on the institutional frames determining the impact of text, performances, and archives on audiences

Subjunctive Enactments: Theatre as Aspirational, Ersatz, or Legitimate Public Sphere

The institutional determination of what may be identified, on different *occasions*, commemorative, creative, or recreational, and in a variety of *places* including but not limited to theatre buildings, as theatre art as Raymond Williams defines the emphasized terms (1995: 130–33), suggests that aesthetic value—value vested in complex form, imaginative content, artistic autonomy—may not be the most relevant criterion for distinguishing theatre, especially avowed political or testimonial theatre, from other forms of political performance such as *izibongo* declaimed at activist funerals. In South Africa and even in those European states with stable national theatres, the theatre institution is characterized by the *relative autonomy* (Bourdieu 1993) of its practices from social, political, and economic forces, and its power to attract an engaged public, especially in times of political turbulence, may depend on its engagement with competing public spheres. The relative autonomy of theatre in this expanded field of play means that it may approach but does not fully become an autonomous artwork. As a syncretic practice, theatre combines aesthetics and politics, autonomy and heteronomy, imagined plots and social representations. Both more and less than art, it straddles the border between the aesthetic and political state on stage where the contradictions between them can be enacted.

What is at issue in plotting the differences between theatre and related practices is not the definitive delineation of aesthetic norms or "vocabulary" but rather the *productive friction* of different conventions, scripts, or "twice-behaved" behaviors, as Richard Schechner defines performance (1985: 36–37) on the occasions of their enactment and reception as "theatre," as cultural practice judged to offer a compelling if imagined representation of conflict while also eliciting pleasure. Elements absorbed from Western scripts (for instance, the nuanced development of character through dialogue) matter less to practitioners and audiences than theatre's capacity for subjunctive enactment, for dramatizing scenarios that may be fictional but also depict persuasive as well as entertaining possible worlds. This relative autonomy of the cultural field enabled theatre to contest or to confirm dominant ideologies, whether the "civilization" of British colonial rule or the "separate development" of apartheid. Its capacity for subjunctive enactment, which in my reading revises Williams's distinction between the indicative character of formal political acts and subjunctive cultural practices (Williams 1979; Kruger 1993) to highlight the dialectic that complicates this opposition, lends an aspirational and thus deeply imagined rather than just imaginary aspect to political acts while allowing cultural practices to open space for effective and thus indicative dissident agency in repressive societies like apartheid. Whether formal, such as the act of inaugurating the president, or informal but forceful, such as the speeches and songs at anti-apartheid funerals, often contrasting *Nkosi sikelel' iAfrika* [God Bless Africa]—banned at the time, now the national anthem—with the militant *Siyaya ePitoli* [We are marching to Pretoria], the power of performances depends on representing effective links between performers and potential action in the world beyond.[5] Conversely, while participating in institutional structures as distinct as literary drama performed by professional actors in a specially designed house, and role-playing to analyze conflicts in a workplace, theatre's power is not completely determined by institutional contexts or their stated aims. The friction between structure and enactment, the force of law and the play of imagination is thus productive not only when it produces a harmonious outcome, as in the inauguration of Mandela in 1994 but also when it articulates outright conflict, as members of parliament (MPs) interrupted then-president Jacob Zuma's State of the Nation Address on February 11, 2016, or avowedly "theatrical" protesters called out Zuma's apparent indifference to gender violence in the run-up to National Women's Day.

The dialectic between formal ceremony and informal improvisation shaped Mandela's inauguration on May 10, 1994 as South Africa's first democratically elected president. Taking place in the amphitheatre courtyard of the Union Buildings, the complex designed by Sir Herbert Baker in 1910 to house the pro-British Union of South Africa on a hill outside the capital Pretoria, whose name—after Voortrekker Andries Pretorius—reflected its history as bastion of Afrikanerdom, this event was understood by participants and observers to inaugurate the new nation along with the new president. The act of inauguration—the oath of office by which Mandela swore "in the presence of all those assembled" to "uphold the Constitution" and to devote himself "to the wellbeing of the Republic" (Mandela 1994: 4)–was preceded by *Nkosi sikelel' iAfrika* and *Die Stem van Suid-Afrika* [The Voice of South Africa], the Afrikaner anthem. Two *izimbongi* [praise poets] vied with each other with *izibongo* [praises] for the new nation and its leaders and, following the oath of office, prayers from representatives of South Africa's international religions began with Hinduism and proceeded through Judaism and Islam to Christianity, the last represented by renowned Archbishop Desmond Tutu. Celebrating this diversity, Mandela nonetheless hailed the people as a whole: "we the people of South Africa ... have at last achieved our political emancipation ... we shall build a society in which all South Africans will be able to walk tall, without any fear in their hearts, assured of their inalienable right to human dignity—a rainbow nation at peace with itself and the world" (1994: 5).[6]

The official enactment of the new state in the privileged space of the Union Building amphitheatre was refracted by performances outside. These other performances may have lacked the indicative force of law but carried nonetheless the subjunctive power of prayer, prophecy, play or, occasionally, doubt about the resolution of conflict as they animated people and material from the many cultures of South Africa. Mandela's official speech did not obliterate the reality of "poverty, deprivation, suffering, and gender and other discrimination" but acknowledged the work to be done to "assure" the people of their "inalienable rights" (1994: 2–3). His acknowledgment of the labor needed to build on the "miracle of unity" (1994: 4) recognized the struggle history embedded in the militant language invoked by new *imbongi yeSizwe* [national praise poet] Zolani Mkhive; his call to arms—*A luta continua* [the struggle continues]—recalled the Portuguese phrase from ANC guerrilla camps in Angola.[7] Mandela went on after the official speech to modify that legacy in words spoken on the lawn outside in Afrikaans, the language associated with apartheid, calling for the overcoming of the past—"Laat ons die verlede vergeet. Wat verby is, is verby" [Let us forget the past. Bygones are bygones]. In the eyes, ears, bodies, and minds of those present, and in reports in all but the most extreme separatist media, this was no mere "imagined community"—as Benedict Anderson categorizes the notion of nation in the "mind of each citizen" all of whom cannot be literally present to each other (1983: 15)—but an experience of simultaneous presence as national belonging. Understood in temporal as well as spatial terms, the space between the Union Buildings and the lawn marked the threshold between the limited imagination of the restricted Union and the generous enactment of the democratic republic.

After Mandela's remarks, a series of performances continued on the lawn. While these acts may not have been obviously theatrical, they nonetheless enacted scripts that recalled the aspirational or *theatrical nationhood*—nationhood performed in the subjunctive—of the anti-apartheid movement. The opening act, the African Jazz Pioneers, recalled in personnel—black and white— and in repertoire—jazz laced with *jikela* [African swing]—the integrationist politics and syncretic aesthetics of 1950s Sophiatown, the intercultural "bohemia" destroyed by apartheid, while also resonating with the memorial boom that had started with the revival of Junction Avenue Theatre Company's *Sophiatown* (1986) just before the inauguration in April 1994. Others included the band Savuka [we are waking up], whose leader "white Zulu" Johnny Clegg sang of Mandela's time in prison—*Asimbonanga* [we did not see him] Mandela-fusing rock and *maskanda* (from Afrikaans *musikant*; Zulu migrant guitar music), together with Suria Govender's Surialanga Dance Company, whose name combined the words for "sun" in Sanskrit and Zulu. The range of musical styles, from the *boeremusiek* of Nico Carstens to the *isicathamiya* harmonies of Ladysmith Black Mambazo, was matched by diversity in movement from Indian *Bharata Natyam* [national dance] to *tiekiedraai* (Afrikaans square dancing [turning on a threepenny piece]). And on the lawn, South Africans celebrated in ways that upended apartheid notions of ethnic purity—a black woman danced the *tiekiedraai* declaring: "I am black, I am white, I am Coloured, I am Indian" (Gevisser 1994a: 9) while an Afrikaans woman wearing and selling T-shirts claimed to identify both with ANC and the National Party. "Traditional" and "modern" elements were thus mediated by personal engagement as well as public broadcasting and marketing.[8]

Informal improvisations in response to Mandela's emphasis on reconciliation prompted journalist Mark Gevisser to call this complex "political theatre," which "blurred the distinction between audience and players to such an extent that … the … event became a living enactment of this country's possibilities" (1994a: 9). This celebration of blurred boundaries may seem *anti-theatrical* to the extent that it posits an unmediated experience of collective belonging that cuts through theatrical fabrication and that transforms the democratic hope that had long seemed a fiction into political reality. As Gevisser and his readers knew, however, "political theatre" had a local positive referent: the anti-apartheid drama which represented a counter-public sphere contesting the censored culture of apartheid, and thus provided the place and occasion for representing an alternative nation, whose achieved legitimacy in 1994 translated aspiration into authority. In inaugurating the new nation, these performances were seen by citizens to "actualize" a "potential" action (Bauman 1989: 3, 262–63). In other words, these enactments were felt to have the force of rites of passage or what Victor Turner calls *liminal* performances (1982: 54), in that they marked a collectively acknowledged breach in the life of a community, as well as the resolution of that breach in the reassembly of the nation. At the same time, the combination of the legally binding act of inauguration and the idiosyncratic responses of individual participants suggests performances of a *liminoid* character (Turner 1982: 54) not only because the latter were playful but also because they introduced an ostentatious, theatrical pause in the visual and narrative representation of collectivity and drew attention to the mediation of this immediate experience by the exchange of commodities such as T-shirts.[9]

This series of events signifies theatrical nationhood because it purports to summon the nation, its unofficial as well as official representatives, to ratify the event (Kruger 1992: 3); it does so theatrically because it is a performance for an audience at a designated site, and because this performance follows scripts that call on the actors to take on roles not quite their own, from Mandela speaking in Afrikaans to the *tiekiedraai*-dancing black woman. The power of these scripts arises out of their embodiment in "twice-behaved behavior": the "symbolic," "reflexive" representation of behavior in a new context (Schechner 1985: 36–37). As Schechner notes, this restoration may have an ambiguous relationship to its source, or, as Williams might add, it may restore residual practices understood as exclusionary, or outline an emergent practice that challenges traditional legitimacy (Williams 1995: 203–05). The Union Buildings recalls the neocolonial Union of 1910 for which they were erected and the legacy of the apartheid government until 1994, but they have accommodated Mandela and his successors since 1994.

From the perspective of 2018, the *izibongo* that mixed historic praise of chiefs with the imperative to honor the universally admired Mandela prompt comparison with the divisive figure of Zuma (president 2008–18) whose State of the Nation address to Parliament on February 11, 2016 might invite more negative views of political theatre as deceptive display.[10] The *imbongi* who introduced Zuma ended his praises with a punch line—*Uboholi kabu fundelwa MaAfrika / Ubuholi buse gazini kuwena Msholozi* [Leadership is not a matter of being educated, fellow Africans / Leadership is in your blood, Msholozi (Zuma's epithet)]—that played on the repeated assertions by ANC spokesmen that Zuma's education in the field of struggle made up for his limited schooling.[11] Reading these praises in light of previous events—Zuma's indictment by the Public Protector for misappropriating public funds for his homestead at Nkandla, an otherwise poor part of KwaZulu, his replacement of a seasoned Treasurer with a lackey favored by allies who enjoyed government contracts, and the consequent collapse of the currency and stock markets, Tinyiko Maluleke, professor of African theology, suggested that the *imbongi*'s "linguistic overstatement and dramatic exaggeration" connoted "suspicious vehemence" if not outright "doubt" about Zuma (2016: 23).

Whether Maluleke is right to detect doubt in these praises is open to question but the ensuing contest on live television between the House Speaker and MPs from opposition parties who deployed points of order to delay Zuma's speech for an hour, staged political theatre in the sense of improvised challenges to Zuma's claim to represent the state. The interruptions—from the volatile Economic Freedom Front (EFF) to the official opposition Democratic Alliance (DA)—began even before Zuma started speaking, as Julius Malema and other EFF members in their trademark red workers' overalls or domestic worker uniforms opened not with the belligerence often attributed to them but with apparently modest questions from the parliamentary rulebook, and continued with assertions that Zuma's speech or even his presence at the presidential podium contravened procedure for reasons that varied from the EFF observation that the speech was praising past heroes rather than addressing the current crisis and thus not a state of the nation speech, to accusation that his conduct made him "unfit for office" from spokesman for Congress of the People Mosiuoa Lekota. It culminated in the Speaker's ejection of all EFF members, who danced out of the chamber chanting "Zupta must fall," while DA leader Mmusi Maimane, normally a sharp critic of the ANC, played peacemaker, asking his colleagues, with more courtesy than the Speaker could muster, to respect the wishes of the "eight million South Africans" who might want to "know where their jobs went."[12] In the shifting roles adopted by Maimane and his rival Malema to challenge Zuma's legitimacy, the friction between constitutionally mandated protocols and the performance of dissent exposed the real state of the nation beyond the disorder in the house.

The 1994 inauguration bears comparison both with the Pageant of Union in 1910 and its theatrical legacy in staged fictions of empire and nation embedded in performances announced as pageants by English, Afrikaans, and African players until 1940 (Chapter 1) and with its opposite, the disruption of the State of the Nation Address in 2016 and the silent protest against the president's cavalier response to gender violence and the charge of rape brought against him by the woman known as Khwezi, staged by four young women at Zuma's speech in Pretoria (a.k.a. Tshwane) after municipal elections in August 2016.[13] What is at issue in these performances is not just the citation of tradition—itself a site for invention—or of the historical record, but the transformation of inherited material that might provide the basis not only for the future construction of a new history but also for critical vigilance to counter its potential manipulation by powerful interests. The analogy between theatre and inauguration draws attention both to the power of theatre as aspirational public sphere in South Africa and to the difficulty of securing a singular definition of "theatre" and "South Africa," and thus highlights the issues at stake in this book. To unpack the meanings of "South African," we should look briefly at a site of contention that has not yet been explicitly examined, the question of language.

The Languages of South African Theatre

South Africa has eleven official languages: Zulu has the most native speakers at over 23 percent of a population of about 57 million, followed by Xhosa, also a Nguni language, at 17 percent, then Afrikaans at 13 percent. Native speakers of English number around 10 percent but close to half the population speaks some English as a second (ESL) or third language (ETL).[14] Whereas elites elsewhere in Africa have sometimes promoted one language, South African theatre practitioners treat the questions of indigenous or endo-glossic (locally spoken) languages pragmatically. Black urban theatre has tended to use English dialogue, with jokes and songs in a range of vernaculars, which may change on tours to different regions. The argument for indigenous authenticity or, in Ngũgĩ wa Thiong'o's phrase "decolonizing the mind" (1986), promotes local languages in countries, including Ngũgĩ's Kenya, where English is the language of education and government. It does not take full account, however, of the range of transformations undergone by English-language and dramatic conventions in South Africa, or the history of Afrikaans, whose evolution from colonial Dutch was shaped by enslaved people from South and Southeast Asia and their lingua franca Malay-Portuguese, and borrowings from indigenous Khoe (Khoi) but for decades denied by Nationalist claims for the "European" character of suiwer [pure] Afrikaans (February 1990; Roberge 2002). Nor does it address the risk, ignored by Ngũgĩ, that the promotion of one local language whether Gikuyu in Kenya or Zulu in South Africa, might provoke a backlash from speakers of other languages, or, if nothing else, the low-level grumbling that I and other learners of Zulu have encountered, for example, from Sotho speakers.

Moreover, the insistence on absolute distinctions between European and African, imported and indigenous, repeats, as Jeyifo argues in the citation earlier, the neocolonial essentialism that it purports to critique. The promotion of endoglossic language education was for decades linked with the apartheid policy of divide and rule to reinforce boundaries between languages using radio and later television in addition to school texts. While Bantu Education reached more Africans than did the church schools, the policy of linguistic apartheid limited African access to English and thus to the world. Even if associated historically with British hegemony, English today is the lingua franca of government and commerce and the vehicle of aspiration for black students and their parents.[15] While the South African Broadcasting Corporation (SABC) meets government quotas for local language programs mostly with soap opera and occasionally with documentaries, and while many who aspire to act in theatre or television are not native English-speakers, paying audiences for theatre remain small and for endoglossic language theatre even smaller. This discrepancy between the numbers of aspirant performers and the lag in the development of audience culture led Malcolm Purkey (1950–) to suggest that "theatre in South Africa could disappear and no-one would notice" (2008: 18). Speaking at the time as artistic director of the Market, he said this not to disparage work at his or at other theatres, but to remind theatre fans that most South Africans prefer broadcast and social media or live music and that theatre in English or other languages has to acknowledge this asymmetry between production and reception if it is to contribute to building the national "vocabulary" not only for theatre-making but also for "audiencing."[16]

While acknowledging the value of English on South African stages, we should be cautious about celebrating postcolonial "englishes" as evidence of resistance to empire (Ashcroft et al. 1989: 41–44), since such celebrations generalize from ex-settler colonies where English has marginalized native languages. Even if English is the lingua franca in South Africa, publications that for convenience presume that theatre here is essentially English speaking (e.g. Middeke et al. 2015) miss the actual diversity of languages that take the stage with English. At the same time, commentators cannot lose sight of the fact that while only a minority speaks English as mother tongue, many actors and writers speak English as a second language. The local transformation of English (see Buthelezi 1995, Mesthrie 2002b, Branford/Claughton 2002, and Posel/Zeller 2015) is clear today in everyday speech as well as testimonial drama and public poetry, but it was already evident in the 1930s in the arresting combination of literary drama, *izibongo*, and African hymns in plays such as Dhlomo's *Moshoeshoe* (1938; Chapter 2) and has taken on regional flavor such as the "Indian" English in Ronnie Govender's *The Lahnee's Pleasure* (Durban 1972; Chapter 5).

Although not the first to create "political theatre in the Western mode," despite this assertion by Zakes Mda (1995: 35) among others—that honor goes to leftists in the 1930s (Kruger 2004: 222–37)—Fugard has made a unique contribution to South African English. This is so not just because he was the most widely produced playwright from South Africa for decades but also because he was the first to create fully colloquial dialogue, as opposed to the self-conscious literariness that affected black writers such as Dhlomo and whites such as Guy Butler. Furthermore, his best collaborative work absorbed the idiom and subtexts of other languages. Shaped by his mother's Afrikaans, the language that many of his characters would likely speak, especially in the "Port Elizabeth plays" *The Blood Knot* (1962), *Hello and Goodbye* (1966), and *Boesman and Lena* (1972), Fugard's English can be both political and intimate, locally resonant and globally understood. His collaborations with the African Theatre Workshop in 1950s Johannesburg, the Serpent Players in Eastern Cape townships in the 1960s, and most famously with John Kani and Winston Ntshona in the 1970s, drew on their experience of African variety concerts and in the Eastern Cape on the players' native Xhosa to create the testimonial plays that would later define anti-apartheid theatre. The syncretizing character of *Sizwe Banzi is Dead*, their signature collaboration, shows not only in its formal combination of anti-apartheid testimony, naturalistic dialogue, and African variety gags—especially in Kani's impersonation of characters ranging from his white boss to a township cockroach—but also of a more subtle engagement with the little-known history of photographic as well as dramatic depiction of African aspirations (Chapter 6; Kruger 2013). Testimonial theatre from *Sizwe* through *Woza Albert!* and *Born in the RSA* to Paul Noko's *Fruit* (2016), reflects ongoing negotiation with forms and practices, whether identified as modern or traditional, imported or indigenous.

Even if the transformations of the 1990s and the disappointments of the 2000s have dissipated the righteous conviction that sustained generations of activists since the 1930s, and the uncertain transition that I called the "post-*anti*-apartheid" era (1999a: 191) has given way to a turbulent present, theatre in South Africa today is more diverse in terms of language and the occasions and places of performance in township and rural venues as well as central urban spaces. Whether this theatre should be described as "post-apartheid" is a question for debate but several companies have created multilingual theatre that shifts register for different audiences and locations as well as theatre rooted not only in particular languages but in the cultural ground that sustains them.

We will discuss these developments in Chapters 7 and 8 but two examples that stage the productive friction between inherited language and cultural practices and the pressures of modernity in its harsh neoliberal form can be sketched here. At the 1996 Grahamstown Festival, *Zombie* by Brett Bailey and Third World Bunfight combined the theatrical skills of trained actors with the religious fervor of church elders and community choirs on the one hand and animist diviners or *sangomas* on the other to capture the tensions in precarious rural communities bypassed by liberation euphoria and by the investments in housing and infrastructure that had improved urban areas. The play dramatizes the struggle of the Xhosa-speaking community Bhongweni (twinned with the formerly white town Kokstad on the border of the impoverished former Bantustan Ciskei) to cope with the death of twelve schoolboys in a mini-bus crash in 1995. Using the local knowledge of Bhongweni citizens, aided by singers and sangomas from Rini, Grahamstown's township twin, this cast of dozens captured the conflict that ensued in Bhongweni (and could have occurred in similar places across the country) between young "comrades"—would-be activists, motivated in part by resentment at the new government's apparent indifference to them, who accuse old women of witchcraft and stealing the souls of the dead—or the undead, and the church elders who try to end the witch-hunt and give the deceased a Christian burial (Figure I.1). In its original form, *Zombie* captured this complex social matrix even if some elements—such as the male actor playing the girl who denounces her grandmother as a witch (a common casting practice in communities reluctant to allow girls to act), and surreal touches like black umbrellas flapping like wings to evoke the community's sense of supernatural forces around them—may seem exotic to some.[17] These actions highlighted the uncanny intensity of the performance, whether in the throbbing drums and chants of the sangomas dueling with the choir or the quieter conclusion: "near the end, a rousing cleansing ritual suddenly stops when a comrade straddles a coffin and hacks at a corpse made of wood and feathers, All we hear are the umbrellas opening and closing … the blows of his ax, and his growing sobs" (Graver 1997: 59). Against this vivid picture of profound frustration, the young men playing female roles also conveyed in gesture and voice the problematic but persistent view that women hold community power, and thus cast light on the tangled roots of the gender violence saturating South Africa.

Thirteen years later, in 2009, *Ingcwaba lendoda lise cankwe ndlela* [The man's grave is next to the road] (Mbothwe 2012) also illuminated aspiration and dislocation in the Eastern Cape. Due in large part to Magnet Theatre's development of the talents of residents in Western Cape informal settlements, many of whom were Eastern Cape migrants, this play, created by Mandla Mbothwe and the cast, treated these themes with more delicacy than *Zombie*, using the nuances of Xhosa dialogue to explore the customs of home birth and home burial that pull migrants back to ancestral lands, and the forces, including the exhaustion of the land after centuries of overcrowding

Figure I.1 *Zombie* by Brett Bailey and Third World Bunfight.
Photograph courtesy of the National Arts Foundation, Grahamstown.

and overgrazing precipitated by the expropriation of good pasture from the colonial to apartheid periods, forces that push migrants from home to look for work in the wealthier Western Cape. While English-only theatre-goers may miss meaning accessible to Xhosa-speakers, the performers' capacity to speak to a broad audience, using precise body techniques as well as evocative language with projected images and text in English and Xhosa, demonstrates the potential for theatre attentive to both roots and routes.[18] As these two pieces show, theatre in South Africa traces shifting terrain on multiple maps. Even plays that deal with pressures on people's lives today call up unfinished business from the past. So, while we may for convenience call the current period "post-apartheid" or "postcolonial" if we use the latter term to imply with Mandela that 1994 inaugurated "political emancipation" from the neocolonial legacy, we need to keep in mind the competing claims across the last century for emancipation or decolonization and thus for the history as well as immediate appeal of these concepts.

When Was Postcolonial?

As a liminal event marking the moment of national renewal after the "country [tore] itself apart in a terrible conflict" (Mandela 1994: 4), the first democratic inauguration laid claim both to uniqueness, in that it marked the threshold of South Africa's belated passage into the postcolonial era that is usually understood to have begun in Africa with Ghana's independence in 1957, and to exemplarity, as *the* definitive moment in the struggle for liberation, which it claimed to surpass and thus to end. Notwithstanding the power of the inauguration to transform the Union Buildings into the government seat, in Mandela's words, of a "non-racist, non-sexist, democratic South Africa," the structure contains layers of meaning inherited from 1910—the place and occasion at which four colonies became one dominion "under the shield of Britannia and the civilised nations of the world," as the Pageant of Union had it (*Historical Sketch* 1910: 8) and thus alludes to an earlier partially postcolonial moment that was neither democratic nor non-racist.[19] In 1994, four score years and four more later—to borrow from Abraham Lincoln—this legacy had been revised but not obliterated. Multiple claims—the achievement of what the ANC calls the "national democratic revolution" over the old regime, or the incremental modification of earlier occasions on the same spot, or the inauguration of a coming African Renaissance—are all present here, but none triumphs unequivocally. What emerges from this event and other instances of South African theatrical nationhood is not an authoritative teleology of performance terminating in single national identity defined by the ruling party. Instead, performances of theatrical nationhood enact multiple genealogies whose ends remain undecided, the analysis of which might, as Joseph Roach suggests, clarify the place of the past in the present (1996: 25), or, as Ernst Bloch had it, the "non-synchronic dialectic" between different Nows—and Thens (1977: 22).

This combination of modernizing and archaizing impulses resists assimilation into an old but still prevalent idea of postcolonial culture as "all the culture affected by colonization from imperialism to the present day" (Ashcroft et al. 1989: 2). In its day, this formulation did well to stress the irrevocable impact of colonization and the significance of resistance, whether as anti-colonial rebellion or as negotiation with neocolonial hegemony, where strategic appropriation of imported practices may be postcolonial in orientation if not yet in fact. The problem with this generalized postcolonial condition and its corollary, the notion that postcolonialism is a mode of "textual/cultural resistance" (Gilbert and Tompkins 1996: 2), is that it "suspends" history, including the history of cultural imperialism and the past and present of uneven development (McClintock 1992: 88). The attribution of political force to textual complexity also tends to promote forms that represent metropolitan modernism and postmodernism, while neglecting those, from "tribal sketches" to "historical pageants," which, despite association with colonial and neocolonial institutions such as mission schools, have been used by Africans to assert their own modernity by syncretizing transnational with national formations and modes of expression. "Transnational" joins "syncretizing" in my analysis to highlight the agency of practitioners and audiences in South Africa and the dynamic character of transnational exchanges that challenge simple oppositions between center and periphery. Although the 1994 inauguration represents a *political* break from white supremacism, the difference between this event and earlier instances of theatrical nationhood masks *pragmatic* and *aesthetic* links to an under-investigated genealogy of national enactments. This history juxtaposes the performance of white rule in the pro-British Pageant of Union (1910) and its Afrikaner Nationalist rival, the Voortrekker Centenary (1938), with the inauguration of majority rule in 1994 and the contestation of political power at Zuma's State of the Nation Address in 2016. It ought also to include performances of unrealized freedom, such as the Emancipation Centenary Celebration (1934), which featured the Gettysburg Address—hence my allusion to Lincoln at the top of this section—or the ANC's Defiance Campaign, which started on the same day as the Van Riebeeck Tercentenary, April 6, 1952. As Chapters 1 and 3 show, these quite different enactments had in common the attempt to remember the past in the present, and so to enact a desirable South African future, not just through declarations and documents but above all through their embodiment by citizen performers.

These processes of imposing, reclaiming, or transforming the scripts and behaviors of the past in the present enactment of the nation deploys what Roach has called *surrogation*. The enactment of collective memory, enacted in pageants, plays, historical sketches, or contemporary celebrations responds to "perceived vacancies in the network of social relations" (1996: 2), attempting to fill gaps, inconsistencies, or outright contradictions in the record or its recollection with figures who act as surrogates for absent agents. As Roach suggests, the act of surrogation draws attention to itself when it succeeds only partially, leaving a deficit, or excessively, creating an unmanageable surplus. Interpreting the difference between deficit and surplus or between the recuperative and provocative moments raises questions of agency, intent, and control. At its most direct, surrogation may proceed literally, with the authorized impersonation of a historical figure by his kin. In the 1910 Pageant of Union, for instance, Sokobe, son of the legendary Sotho King Moshoeshoe whose wisdom as a peacemaker was acknowledged by British and Basotho, played his own late father in the episode when Moshoeshoe made a pact with the president of the Orange Free State at the sacred site of Thaba Bosiu [Mountain at Night] and so lent the authority of his person to the legitimation of the white Union. This surrogation could sustain the Union's ideology of benevolent rule because the pageant ended in 1854, omitting the subsequent annexation of Basutoland and the part of the Free State where diamonds were discovered in 1867 and its massive transformation by the mining industry.

Shadowed by these crucial omissions, Sokobe's surrogation of the mighty Moshoeshoe might seem tame, in contrast to John Wilkes Booth's deadly citation of his role as Brutus in Shakespeare's *Julius Caesar* while actually assassinating Lincoln in 1865 but, no less than this example in Rebecca Schneider's excavation of the "performance remains" of the American Civil War (2011: 1), African acts of surrogation revivify the past for the present. Motsieloa reciting the Gettysburg Address—"Four score years and seven years ago our fathers brought forth …"—at the Emancipation Centenary in 1934 may not have matched Lincoln exactly, but the surrogation of Lincoln by a black intellectual infused the British colonial emancipation of 1834 and its centenary celebration in 1934 with American emancipation scripts to inspire South African audiences. At the 1994 inauguration, Mandela's Afrikaans supplement to his English speech enacted reconciliation through translation, an act that may have reassured Afrikaners but that doubtless disturbed some ANC supporters. Clegg's performance as a "white Zulu" has been generally seen as a benign homage to the culture of South Africa's largest ethnic group, but it does not erase the ambiguous historical legacy of this figure, exemplified by nineteenth-century landowner John Dunn, who manipulated his marriage alliances with Zulu clans for his own gain (Chapter 2). Conversely the young African women in black protesting Zuma's indifference to the rights of women and other citizens in 2016 recall the silent protests outside apartheid institutions enacted by the Black Sash, founded by white women in 1955 but today an integrated human rights organization. These performances mark the breaches and the links between bondage and freedom, tradition and modernity, subordination and sovereignty, revising earlier scripts and constructing new genealogies of performance.

If the term "postcolonial" is to apply to theatre in South Africa, we should entertain the notion that the term could fit 1910 in addition to 1994. Even if only partially, the idea of 1910 as a postcolonial moment illuminates the history of asymmetrical and asynchronic enactments of South Africa and the serial appropriations whose surrogations draw on the scripts, behaviors, and sites of apparently incompatibly South African occasions, and thus highlight, as Homi Bhabha has it, the "disjunctive" character of the "enunciative present of modernity" (1991: 195), even though many observers may miss layers of reference to little-known archives or repertoires.[20] In its juxtaposition of apparently incompatible conventions from European, American, and African practices, theatre has syncretized South African culture, even in 1910, when the not-quite-postcolonial elite reinforced racial hierarchy in the name of Union.

The Shape of this Book

A Century of South African Theatre documents more than a hundred years of theatre and performance, drawn from research on print, video, and aural material from 1910 to 2017. My personal observations of performance from the 1970s to the present have therefore been mediated and revised by rigorous investigation of historical precedents and have prompted me to cultivate a healthy skepticism towards recent claims of novelty or transformation, and to refine my appreciation of what is truly new. Beginning Chapter 1 with the 1910 Union may imply a conventional chronological order, but my sketch above of Sokobe's surrogation of his father Moshoeshoe and the critical potential of this and other elements in the Union Pageant introduces a counter-current in the official progress of "European civilization," reminding us that history is more complicated than chronology. Moments that appear to interrupt chronological order do not negate the importance of history but, as Walter Benjamin reminds us (1980/2006), signal its contested character and thus invite the critical examination of

"invented traditions" that have been marshaled to support "usable pasts" (Hobsbawm/
Ranger 1982) or to challenge such recollection in the name of revolution. This critical
examination must, however, rest on historical evidence. While active recollection
does matter—it has enabled me to share with readers close to half a century of South
African performance—the habit of relying on memory as if it were an unmediated
source of fact has led too many accounts to rely on unreliable recollection or myths of
origin rather than on research in multiple archives and repertoires. Recollection alone
does not qualify as a research "method": depending on "personal memories as much
as archival documentation" as one writer has claimed, tends to justify rather than
correct "subjective bias" and to ignore inevitable memory gaps, let alone decades of
production before the critic in question was born.[21] To counter this selective amnesia,
A Century of Theatre in South Africa animates archives and repertoires of performance
and the experience of spectatorship—mediated by critical analysis—so as to encourage
the rediscovery of theatre's roles in South Africa.

With both newcomers and seasoned researchers in view, this book follows a
chronological plan but modifies it to highlight continuity and comparison as well as
change across time. The contestation of the nation in public confrontations as well
as mediated representations in 2016 is illuminated in comparison not only with the
inauguration of 1994 but also with the national pageants of 1910 and 1936 (Chapter
1). Dhlomo and contemporaries in the 1930s (Chapter 2) tapped European historical
and avant-garde forms and African music and storytelling to provide a more complex
legacy than usually acknowledged for anti-apartheid theatre and for enduringly
popular township musicals in the 1970s (Chapters 5 and 6), as well as immediate
inspiration for the 1950s, when the tension between enforced separation and embattled
sites of cultural integration shaped the early work of Fugard. Chapter 3 shows how the
Sophiatown bohemia in the 1950s inspired emulation in anti-apartheid practitioners
seeking a usable past for urban integration in the 1980s but acknowledges the struggle
by tracking the Afrikaner ascendancy in official events from the Van Riebeeck
Tercentenary, and the violence of white supremacy buried in domestic drama, which
in turn provided material for Afrikaner dissidents from the 1960s to the 1990s and
beyond (Chapter 4).

Thus, the first half of the book reminds readers of the foundational work that
took place decades before the world awoke to South African theatre with *Sizwe
Banzi* (1972) and *The Island* (1973). These plays certainly heralded an anti-apartheid
reawakening but, as the second part shows, this resurgence took inspiration not only
from Fugard but also from the BCM, which inspired political theatre before Soweto
while anticipating debates about race in the twenty-first century. These debates in turn
invite critical scrutiny of anti-apartheid theatre from *Survival* (1976) through *Woza
Albert!* to *Born in the RSA* (1985) (Chapter 6). Committed to bearing witness to the
anti-apartheid struggle, this testimonial form may seem insufficient to treat themes
beyond apartheid but the plays of Mda from *We Shall Sing for the Fatherland* (1979)
on, drew on the critical distance of exile in Lesotho to depict people struggling with
postcolonial corruption and underdevelopment, and to suggest that the post-apartheid
future might be blighted by similar problems.

From the perspective of the recent past, when corruption and impunity enabled state violence against citizens at Marikana in 2012 and other protest sites, and inspired compelling performances such as *The Man with the Green Jacket* (2014) and *MARI+KANA* (2015), Mda's dramas ring retrospectively of prophecy. The power of Marikana mourning plays should not, however, eclipse the dazzling diversity that has flourished despite economic and political obstacles after apartheid. To better encompass this diversity, Chapters 7 and 8 modify the chronological order to distinguish between institutions and players that have tackled the crises and opportunities that emerged in the 1990s but are still with us, from criminal violence dramatized in Paul Slabolepszy's *Mooi Street Moves* (1992) and Paul Grootboom's *Foreplay* (2009) to the more famous theatre inspired by the Truth and Reconciliation Commission (Chapter 7), and those that respond to conditions that have emerged more clearly since 2000, from local concerns about the collusion between state actors and crony capitalists, to South Africa's transnational impact as a destination for migrants and competitor for global resources, all of which animate the work of Lara Foot and of Magnet Theatre (Chapter 8). The final chapter tracks theatre that expresses the hopes raised by the 1996 Constitution for well-being as well as democracy, while acknowledging the alarm sounded by studies of political failure such as *Betrayal of the Promise* (Bhorat et al. 2017) and shows how the texts and performances of the twenty-first century weave together elements drawn from the archives, memories, repertoires, and other traces of a century of South African theatre at home and in the world.

Commemorating and Contesting Emancipation

Pageants and Other Progressive Enactments

On Sunday June 3, 1934, an audience of African artists, American Board Missionaries, liberal whites in the Joint European/African Council movement, and "New Africans" (educated and to a degree Europeanized) gathered at the Bantu Men's Social Centre (BMSC) in central Johannesburg for an Emancipation Centenary Celebration, commemorating the abolition of slavery in the British Empire in 1834. This celebration, subtitled a National Thanksgiving, was framed by speeches by American missionaries and leading New Africans, members of a small but influential class of clergymen, writers, teachers, and other professionals, such as R.V. Selope Thema, editor of *Bantu World*, and Dr. A.B. Xuma, physician and later ANC president. It included extracts from Handel's *Messiah*, Elgar's *Land of Hope and Glory*, European, African, and American hymns, including "Negro spirituals," and Lincoln's Gettysburg Address, delivered by Trinity College (London) graduate, Griffiths Motsieloa. This event, organized by Africans rather than the brown or Coloured descendants of enslaved people who had commemorated emancipation in the nineteenth century, culminated in a "dramatic display," whose text, compiled from sources including Harriet Beecher Stowe's *Uncle Tom's Cabin*, did not focus on the abolition of slavery in the British colonies in 1834 or the official end of unpaid servitude in 1838, but rather on the enslaved in the United States.[1] The evening concluded with Enoch Sontonga's well-known hymn *Nkosi sikelel' iAfrika* [God Bless Africa] (1897).

Despite research on this event (Erlmann 1991; Kruger 1999a; Peterson 2000) and renewed interest after apartheid in the commemoration of emancipation, the Emancipation Centenary Celebration itself remains largely invisible. Nonetheless it deserves attention for linking aspirations of Africans at home and in the diaspora, and highlighting Africans' syncretic repurposing of American emancipation discourse and, less obviously, challenges to the British Empire, as hinted in another hymn on the program, Reuben Caluza's *Silusapo or iLand Act* (Caluza 1992), whose title alluded not only to the 1913 Land Act restricting African access to land but also to Sol Plaatje's 1914 *Native Life in South Africa*, which was both a study of colonization and a petition for justice addressed to the British Crown. It also merits comparison with Mandela's inauguration in 1994. The differences are obvious: the 1934 commemoration was staged by and for an educated but embattled minority conscious of their precarious hold on political rights, economic security, or happiness, while the 1994 inauguration ushered in South Africa's first democratic government; the latter event was legally binding, the former only aspirational. And yet—while the millions who celebrated in 1994 were likely unaware of the modest event of 1934–these events have common elements. *Nkosi sikelel' iAfrica* is now part of the composite national anthem and Mandela's choice to call the inauguration the achievement of "our political emancipation" (1994: 4) acknowledged South Africans' abiding interest in global as well as local struggles that began well before his birth. Reviewing these connections in 2018, the centenary of Mandela's birth in 1918, highlights the unfinished project of emancipation, which in the terms of the South African constitution, calls for social well-being as well as political rights. The participants in 1934 were concerned about losing the franchise but those celebrating full enfranchisement in 1994 doubtless remembered the attempts to sabotage democracy by Afrikaner and Zulu nationalists barely months before the elections, as Mandela recalled—"we saw our country tear itself apart in violent conflict." From the vantage point of 2018, after former president Zuma's promises to bridge the widening inequality gap between the poor majority and the tiny rich minority were exposed as cover for corruption and impunity, the promises of 1994 seem likewise fragile, aspirational, subjunctive. The achievement of freedom for political assembly, housing, and the right to work are enshrined in the constitution but the executive disregard for these rights prompts vigilance as well as hope.

For the moment, the genealogy of performance and the productive friction of syncretic practices that link the Emancipation Celebration to the inauguration of 1994 call us to look at the 1934 response to the 1910 Pageant of Union, which unified British colonies and Boer republics at the expense of the black majority. While it commemorated emancipation, the Emancipation Centenary also reproached the Union for disenfranchising Africans and for the racialist ideology that shaped the Historical Pageant in 1910. This pageant, which began in Table Bay and continued before the Cape Town City Council, Parliament, and British dignitaries, employed five thousand performers. Borrowing its form from pageants staged in Canada and other British dominions (Merrington 1997), it depicted the European (Portuguese, Dutch, and British) "discovery" of the natives and the conquest of their lands but avoided the sensitive topic of the Anglo-Boer War (1899–1902). By ending with the meeting between King Moshoeshoe I and President Hoffmann of the Orange Free State in 1854 before the discovery of diamonds in 1867, the pageant elided the coercion that forced Africans to work in the diamond and later gold mines, and instead reenacted the imperial teleology of the "Progress of Prosperity" over "hordes of ignorance, cruelty, savagery, unbelief, war, pestilence, famine and their ilk" (*Historical Sketch* 1910: 93), whereby Europe brought "civilization" to what G.W.F. Hegel called the "unhistorical, undeveloped Spirit of Africa" (1956: 99). Despite this presumption, the pageant acknowledged the historical role of some people of color. In addition to Moshoeshoe who was played by his son, the pageant featured an actor playing Sheik Yusuf, a Muslim cleric exiled by the VOC in 1696 and credited today with bringing Islam to the Cape. Yusuf was both slave-owner and anti-colonial rebel but the script identifies him merely as "a Javanese teacher" (*Historical Sketch*: 78). Although the pageant thus included a few black roles and mute "maidens in white" (94), the "historical heroes" (95) were white men (Figure 1.1).

Figure 1.1 Boer and Briton before Britannia in *The Pageant of Union*, Cape Town, May 1910.
Photograph: courtesy of the National Library of South Africa, Cape Town; artist unknown.

The Emancipation Celebration shared with the Union Pageant a homage to the value of European civilization, represented by the music of Handel and the Gettysburg Address but exposed the subordination of even elite Africans, who depended on liberal white patrons of their project. Even Africans who criticized the savagery of whites in Africa and who sought therefore to "provincialize Europe" (Chakrabarty 1992: 20) by relativizing its claim to represent universal values used the language of the European enlightenment to defend universal human rights. The1934 script cast the participants as New Africans, as opposed to the "tribal" figures in the Union Pageant. By including Lincoln's 1863 text and African Nationalist songs, the program pointed toward an as yet utopian democratic future. More concretely, the representation of New Africans in this modest event led to appearances at official events staged by whites, such as the Empire Exhibition (1936), as well as other events staged by Africans, such as "Africa—a revel pageant" (1940), "depicting the march of progress of the Bantu." While New Africans could not operate on the scale of the Union, they could appropriate the forms of these enactments while borrowing other elements from African Americans to represent themselves as modern agents. Taking into account the precarious nature of New African aspirations between the prospect of emancipation by "European civilization" in the abstract and the actual constraints on African freedoms, this chapter investigates the ways in which the flexible formats of variety and the pageant created space for the representation and negotiation of these contradictions.

New Africans, New Negroes, and the Paradoxes of Neocolonial Modernity

This Emancipation Centenary Celebration negotiated multiple political meanings that may seem contradictory to present-day observers but which managed nonetheless to express critical opinions about the present as well as the past conditions of Africans. Written by noted Zulu writer R.R. [Rolfes] Dhlomo and directed by his brother H.I.E. [Herbert] Dhlomo, the "dramatic display" (Dhlomo et al. 1934) quoted the subtitle and several scenes from *Uncle Tom's Cabin*'s depiction of what the novel's subtitle called "The Life of the Lowly." As suggested in *Bantu World* and *Umteteli wa Bantu*—newspapers edited and read by blacks even if funded by whites—"the suffering of the American Negroes on the slave market, in the cotton fields and at home, until the joyful news of the liberation" highlighted the pathos of enslaved people and their gratitude for the act of emancipation.[2] This pathos was modified, however, by the inclusion of such thoroughly modern songs as *Sixotshwa emsebenzini* [We are being fired (expelled from work)] by Reuben Caluza, Zulu composer, cousin to the Dhlomo brothers, and visiting fellow at Columbia University, New York (Erlmann 1991: 119–47). While white spectators may have missed the full import of the songs, Africans would have been familiar with this and others on the program such as *iLand Act*. For New African participants, the historical references to emancipation and the Land Act called up the immediate threat posed by the Hertzog Bills (named for J.B.M. Hertzog, Nationalist minister in the ruling United Party), which became law in 1936. The Native Representation Act abolished African rights to the general franchise in favor of voting only for white representatives, and the Native Trust and Land Act (Couzens 1985: 139) slightly revised the 1913 Act to put land in the reserves under the jurisdiction of compliant chiefs.

Caught in the contradiction between the European rhetoric of emancipation and the South African reality of segregation, New Africans, like the subjects of British India, had to negotiate what Shula Marks calls the "ambiguities of dependence" (1986: 54). Even if the white establishment that Indian sociologist Ashis Nandy calls the "intimate enemy" (1983) of native intellectuals betrayed these ideals, the ideals of liberal individualism offered them arguments to challenge segregationists. Selope Thema enjoined *Bantu World* readers to "honour the great emancipators" such as Lincoln who show the way to "rescue [the world] from the thralldom of nationalist and racial passions."[3] In pointing to racial discrimination despite formal freedoms, however, he drew on W.E.B. Du Bois, whose *Souls of Black Folk* (1903) vividly described the oppression of African Americans *after* emancipation (1989: 28–29). Selope Thema wrote "it is true that Natives can no longer be bought and sold ... but they are still in bondage as a people and there is a determined stand by Europeans against the grant to them [*sic*] of that full liberty to which all men are entitled ... Natives are not slaves, but they are not freemen."[4] Quoting Du Bois, his editorial challenged white segregationists with the example of African-American achievements. Although not themselves descendants of enslaved people, New Africans found in the progress of African Americans a crucial point of reference for criticizing the curtailment of civil rights for black South Africans. As teacher S.V. Mdhluli wrote, "the Negroes on the other side of the Atlantic have made gigantic progress; all the same we are making a steady advance to the same goal … They have shown … that this much debated 'arrested development' is practically unknown among the Negroes" (1933: 48–49). Like New Negro Alain Locke who challenged white society's "sentimental interest" in black traditions and the "double standard" of the "philanthropic attitude" (1992: 8–10), New Africans were suspicious of whites whose concern for "Native" traditions masked indifference to black aspirations for citizenship. In this respect they joined Du Bois's challenge to African conservatives who, like Booker T. Washington, supported separate development.[5]

While New Africans held on to the idea of universal rights, conservatives in the ANC, led by its president Pixley ka Seme and president of the Zulu-dominated Natal branch John Dube, saw in the state's program of separate development an opportunity for maintaining African autonomy through what Ali Mazrui calls *re-traditionalization*.[6] Just as tradition has less to do with the "persistence of old forms" than with the "ways in which form and value are linked together" (Erlmann 1991: 10), re-traditionalization implies not a return to pre-modern custom but instead a re-appropriation of customary practices for present purposes. This project aimed to consolidate the limited power of the chiefs eroded by the migration of peasants to the cities; they welcomed laws such as the amended Land Act that allotted land in the reserves to be supervised by themselves.[7] Unlike "neo-traditionalism," a de-historicized view of tradition as timeless and immune to present politics, re-traditionalization appropriated aspects of modernity, such as vernacular literacy and the refashioning of precolonial remains into national heritage, so as to reinvent loose clan affiliation as obligatory respect for traditional authority within the confines of the white state.

New Africans by contrast held to the belief that modern citizenship would ultimately outweigh the disruption of traditional authority. Selope Thema defended African appropriation of elements of European civilization, such as literacy and individual rights, and, while acknowledging the value of precolonial communal organization, lambasted tribal custom as the weight of the "dead … on the living."[8] Profoundly suspicious of European interests in "development along the Native's own lines," New Africans such as the Dhlomo brothers did not, however, abandon tradition. Rather, by participating in networks established by mission schools such as Lovedale (founded 1832), Amanzimtoti—later Adams—College (1855), and Marianhill (1884), as well as cultural institutions such as the Gamma Sigma debating societies (1918), the BMSC (1924) or the Eisteddfodau (1931)—festivals of song and dramatic sketches based on British versions of the Welsh original—they hoped to enrich African culture. The mission school syllabus, which supplemented Shakespeare and the European musical repertoire with imperial writers such as Rudyard Kipling and John Buchan, provided material for New Africans but they drew also on African-American sources. The abolitionist melodrama and "Negro spirituals" in the Emancipation Centenary program competed with vaudeville, ragtime, jazz, and local *marabi* music, which reached a wider audience in the dance halls frequented by growing numbers of plebeian *abaphakathi* (the people in between, neither fully assimilated nor fully at home with indigenous custom).

New African admiration for the New Negro elite made them ambivalent towards plebeian culture, but they acknowledged that the appeal of black popular music flowed in part from African-American assertions of pan-African affiliation and in part from local *marabi* music's pan-ethnic appeal to urbanizing Africans.[9] The influence of black American music could be traced from Orpheus MacAdoo's Virginia Jubilee Singers touring in the 1890s to local minstrel groups such as the African Darkies who borrowed coon songs and skits from imported recordings and sheet music (Coplan 2008: 148).[10] By the 1930s, some local bands had become polished troupes such as the Darktown Strutters, whose repertoire mixed jazz, ragtime, and comic sketches with jubilee and *amakwaya* [choir] music favored by mission-educated blacks (Erlmann 1991: 60). Women's groups, though less common, were also popular and, as names such as Emily Makanana's Dangerous Blues imply, did not limit their repertoire to "respectable" music. New African negotiation of these African-American currents was well underway by the 1930s and was more independent than the later Sophiatown scene, even if the latter may be better known thanks to the photographic record of Jürgen Schadeberg, Bob Gosani, and others in *Drum* magazine. New Africans in the 1930s still had some control over the means of their production—thanks to exemptions to the pass laws for educated Africans—which allowed the relative autonomy of impresarios such as Motsieloa, which would become impossible in the 1950s, when African impresarios were losing ground to European managers and apartheid law. If African modernity merits comparison to the Harlem Renaissance, we should explore the New African dawn, however, darkened by neocolonial clouds, before the twilight of Sophiatown (Chapter 3).

New African exploration of African, American, and European cultural flows involved passionate but variable appropriations of English culture, popular entertainments, and indigenous traditions, as they knew that entertainment could function as social control. Missionary Ray Phillips hoped to curb unrest and the "swaggering, sweeping claims of Communism" by "moralizing the leisure time of the natives" (1930: 51, 58), encouraging mining managers to see that organizing their workers' leisure time with dancing or film shows was a "good business investment" (Koch 1983: 167). R.W.H. Shepherd, director of the Lovedale Mission and one of a few presses publishing Africans, argued that literature should not only "equip the Bantu for the demands of the new day" but also offer a "substitute of a satisfying kind to take the place of so much that has passed from them" (1935: 76). This experience of culture as refuge from politics could give New African performance culture an affirmative cast, in Herbert Marcuse's sense of an imaginary refuge from oppressive political power (1968: 116) but unlike whites attached to "European" culture, New Africans escaped the cultural cringe by striving to create their own framework for the subjunctive enactment of free African agency; the Emancipation Celebration and other public commemorations in the New African calendar such as Moshoeshoe Day offered occasions for public claims to self-representation. Marginalized from a public sphere defined in racially exclusive terms, New African theatre articulated a virtual public sphere. At stake in the subjunctive enactments of this New African publicity was the attempt to seize the idea of modernity—citizenship, emancipation, individual and collective agency— from its colonial representation, the attempt, in other words, to "deploy, deform, and defuse" neocolonial institutions so as to make "many modernities" out of colonial modernization (Comaroff and Comaroff 1993: xi, xii).

The Modernity of the Tribal Sketch

The re-traditionalist road to African self-representation may have been paved with colonial materials but this did not mean that all vehicles on it served the missionary project. Nowhere was the ambiguity of re-traditionalization more vividly staged than in the "tribal sketch," exemplified by the Mthethwa Brothers, whose mastery of "dance, mime, sketches and songs," mostly in Zulu, expressed the intention, as Bhekizizwe Peterson argues, to "assert the social cohesiveness of traditional African societies" (2000: 170). Despite their creators' traditionalist intent, these sketches of customary rituals reflected a re-traditionalist reaction to modernization by people who had themselves received a modern education. The key institution shaping re-traditionalization was paradoxically also the crucible for modernization: the mission school, Lovedale, Adams, or the Ohlange Institute, Dube's Zulu counterpart to Washington's Tuskegee Institute in Alabama. One of the first performances in what a contemporary observer dubbed "redefined Zulu folk idiom" took place at the Hampton Institute in Virginia in 1913 where, as a white American noted, Madikane Cele, Dube's nephew and graduate of Ohlange, "acquainted his black American students with Zulu folklore and music" (Curtis 1920: 58), culminating in the presentation of "For Unkulunkulu's Sake" (Erlmann 1991: 72). Madikane was named for the founder of the Cele clan, who were stigmatized by the ascendant Zulus and, for this reason, among the first to adopt Christianity. As Carolyn Hamilton notes, he would have encountered the story in its missionized form that rendered *Unkulunkulu* as God the Creator, but in the oral tradition this figure could be used to respond to new contexts and challenges from conservative chiefs as well as European missionaries (Hamilton 1985: 474–84).

This ambiguous mix of "salvaging" precolonial tradition and the limited modernization of the mission school shaped African performance into the 1950s. The Lucky Stars (1929–37), aptly illuminate the modernity of this re-traditionalizing enterprise. Founded by Esau and Isaac Mthethwa at Adams College, the group performed dances and sketches in reconstructed Zulu costume and in the Zulu language.[11] The titles—*Ukuqomisa* (courting) and especially *Umthakathi* (sorcerer, trickster)—allude to the ambiguous legacy of these sketches, which included the "smelling out" of the diviner as an imposter impeding the civilizing mission, an interpretation favored by the missionaries.[12] However, the several parts of this show, sketches, dancing, and choral singing of Zulu songs, and its varied places of performance suggest a more complex matrix of occasion and meaning. An account by white observer T.C. Lloyd is illuminating:

> This new departure among the black races is valuable in presenting to the public scenes of native domestic life with a realism that would be otherwise unattainable. Such education of the white man is a necessary preliminary to his understanding of Bantu problems … these plays are presented with a naiveté which would be impossible for the white man to imitate. The style of acting is much more free than we have been accustomed to see on the more civilized stage. The producer is an educated Zulu [Isaac Mthethwa] but the players have only a rudimentary knowledge of reading and writing. Consequently, the parts are learned by word

of mouth and no strict adherence to the original wording is insisted on ... This
induces a freshness and vigor of presentation, which is a welcome relief from the
too conscious presentation of our own stage. (Lloyd 1935: 3)

Lloyd rehearses the familiar colonial opposition between jaded European culture—
"at the hotels and socials in Durban" or the "too conscious" artifice of the "civilized"
actor—and the apparent naiveté of the "black races." At the same time, he concedes
the artifice of this native naiveté; Mthethwa trained mission school performers
to reproduce traditional scenes. Furthermore, Lloyd suggests that the "education
of the white man" might be the object and not merely the incidental result of the
performance. Even the natural setting, "the lush sub-tropical bush," is framed by the
modern contrivance of the illusionist set: "The scene was set by ... a canvas sheet
with a painting of a Zulu hut" (3). The "historical songs" that ended the performance
emphasized the modern concerns framing the "tribal" content. Lloyd's description
of the songs—"they traced the record of the Zulu nation through their kings" (3)—
suggests the historical consciousness of *Elamakosi* [Of the Kings], by Caluza, which
appealed to modern Zulu audiences.

Although led by educated Africans, the Lucky Stars were well received by black
workers and rural Africans, especially in less industrialized Natal, where audiences
apparently found these "idealized images of a rural past" a welcome escape from
their alienation from "civilization" (Coplan 2008: 150). Nevertheless, claims that
the Lucky Stars anticipated protest theatre of the 1970s (Kavanagh 1985: 45) should
be read with caution. The fact that they came from Adams College did not prevent
the sketches from appealing to diverse audiences, but they expressed first of all the
Zulu pride of the performers. As the sketches were performed in the Zulu language
and in reconstructed rural costume rather than the mixed attire worn by working
Zulus, any critical intent would have been only partially accessible to speakers of
other Bantu languages, whose response may have been affected as much by the
music and the stage presence of African actors, as by the authentic details of attire
or speech.

While groups such as the African Own Entertainers (founded like the Lucky
Stars in 1929) and the Darktown Strutters (active by 1931) were taking their variety
shows of music, comedy, and sketches on the road through the Union, the Lucky
Stars performed only in Natal until "discovered" by Bertha Slosberg, the Jewish South
African impresario and later talent scout for British film productions such as Robert
Stevenson's *King Solomon's Mines*, starring African-American Paul Robeson as an
African prince (Slosberg 1939: 194). With her backing, they performed to diverse
audiences at the Durban City Hall in March 1936, the BMSC in Johannesburg in
May, and to whites at the Empire Exhibition in October, accompanied at the last two
venues by the avowedly modern Darktown Strutters in "An African Entertainment."[13]
Slosberg's claim to have discovered both groups testifies not only to the arrogance
of the white impresario but also to an ambiguous desire to give Africans their due.
Slosberg insisted that she paid the performers well and that she socialized with them
despite scandalized responses from the white press (1939: 210–13), but her aspirations
to honorary Zulu status (Figure 1.2) have to be matched against the privileges

[*Photo—General Photographic Agency*

"In Town Tonight," Coronation Week, 1937

Figure 1.2 The Mthethwa Lucky Stars and the Honorary Zulu, Johannesburg Empire Exhibition, 1936.

Source: Bertha Slosberg, *Pagan Tapestry*, London: Rich and Cowan, 1939; photographer unknown.

conferred by her place in white society. Isaac Mthethwa's acquiescence to this arrangement testifies above all to the obstacles faced by Africans attempting to make a living as artists. Although Mthethwa and Motsieloa had worked as professionals for more than half a decade, they could not maintain full control. Segregation law made hiring a hall difficult, the pass laws inhibited evening rehearsals, and lack of capital made African producers dependent on white benefactors. The dependence of Africans reinforced the appeal of primitivist nostalgia to whites in London as well as Johannesburg.[14] In this scenario, the spectacular elements overlap with the folkloric, and the reason "to salvage from European influence, the remaining power, the native simplicity, the splendid savage grandeur of a dying pagan land" (Slosberg 1939: 192). The authenticity of the spectacle depends on its difference from the self-proclaimed modernity of the white spectators because a clear distinction between "native simplicity" and the "progress of the Union" confirms their identity as "Europeans." Only when the "splendid savage grandeur" is seen to be "dying" can the neocolonial Union be modern. In the name of the Union, the Empire Exhibition, which incorporated African entertainers as well as the Pageant of South Africa, could not erase the contradictions in that modernity.

Empire and its Discontents: Archaism, Modernity, and the Progress of the Pageant

Whereas Africans faced with the ambiguous benefits of "civilization" sought alternative routes to modernity that led sometimes through re-traditionalization, whites who identified with Britain were keen to assert their European affiliation. The organizers of the Johannesburg Golden Jubilee (1886–1936) and Empire Exhibition—the first held outside Britain—saw themselves as celebrants of Africa's most modern city. This modernity was represented not only by gold mines but also by dozens of commercial and residential high-rises springing up in the central city (Chipkin 1993: 94–95), designed by both local and immigrant architects, including Herman Kallenbach, a Berlin-trained modernist known today as a patron of Mohandas Gandhi during his two decades in South Africa. The Exhibition's official poster, which featured a white farmer gazing up at a skyscraper, possibly Johannesburg's ESCOM (Electric Supply Company) building in the art deco style pioneered in Chicago and New York, captured this aspiration (see Kruger 2013: 32). Whereas pavilions at the Greater Britain Exhibition (1899) and the Empire Exhibition of 1924 had represented South Africa as a source of raw materials and exotic "natives," Johannesburg emphasized its achievement as "Africa's Wonder City."[15] Foregrounding the city's "resources and potentialities," as expressed in the *South African Mining and Engineering Journal*, the organizers hoped "to present a striking picture of the history, development and progress of the Union."[16]

Although Exhibition manager B.M. Bellasis demurred, Chicago architecture rather than British imperial styles shaped the design of the exhibition halls, including *art moderne* structures celebrating mining and manufacture and a Tower of Light that copied a tower at the Chicago Century of Progress (1933) and is still on the site, now Wits University's west campus.[17] The description of the site as a "white city" (Empire Exhibition 1936: 1) borrowed the moniker from the Chicago Columbian Exposition of 1893, while the full-scale models of Van Riebeeck's three ships mimicked those of Columbus at the Chicago event. These elements did not disguise the uneasy relationship in Johannesburg as in Chicago between the products of progress displayed in the pavilions and the indigenous people housed in "native villages." Just as Chicago officials were reluctant to admit black visitors to the Columbian Exhibition, the organizers of the Johannesburg Jubilee limited access to Africans, initially demanding the same entrance fee as whites, modified only under pressure from the press. Both the Century of Progress and the Johannesburg Exhibition did better in employing blacks and including some displays reflecting black modernity, such as a facsimile of the cabin built by Chicago's founder Jean-Baptiste Point Du Sable in the former, and a demonstration in the ESCOM pavilion of ancient African methods of iron-smelting in the latter.[18] The Johannesburg Native Commissioner Geoffrey Ballenden thanked the "the city's great army of native workers" for erecting high-rises in the city itself as well as the temporary exhibition structures.[19]

Despite this acknowledgment of African labor and the three-mile long procession following African miners carrying gold ingots to the Chamber of Mines pavilion, the exhibition poster features a Boer, identifiable by the covered wagons in the frame, and, in the skyscraper, the power of Anglo capital. The Boer in the poster may be in awe of the City of Gold but Afrikaans drama in this period, such as *As die Tuig Skawe* by J.F.W Grosskopf (1885–1948) regarded the city with fear and loathing. The display at the exhibition of a model of the Voortrekker Monument that was to be erected outside Pretoria for the centenary of the Great Trek of 1838 suggested further dissent, which took spectacular form when thousands of Afrikaners congregated to celebrate the centenary and lay the foundation stone in December 1938. The sheer scale of this gathering would overshadow the Pageant of South Africa even though the Johannesburg event attempted a show of white unity.

The Pageant of South Africa at the Empire Exhibition was intended to reconcile the differences between Anglo and Afrikaner interpretations of history. Although the pageant was formally performed only four times in December 1936, its rehearsal nonetheless commanded attention for over a year, from the initial plans in mid-1935 to build an amphitheatre that would seat 12,000 people, through the selection of André van Gyseghem (1906–79, born in Britain to Belgian parents), who traveled to Europe's theatre capitals and worked in the Soviet Union and the United States, as a suitably bilingual Pageant Master in February 1936, to the recruitment of the provincial pageant leaders in the mid-year winter and the performance the following summer. Although his methods had more in common with the European avant-garde than with the drawing room comedy that dominated the stage in Johannesburg as in London, and despite his later involvement with African theatre groups such as the Bantu Peoples Theatre, Van Gyseghem was fêted more as a metropolitan bearer of the latest fashions from abroad.[20] Like the 1910 pageant, the 1936 event depicted scenes from South African colonial history but, extending the chronology to 1910, attempted to combine the achievement of Union with the representation of modernization that had transformed South Africa. The script was written by populist Afrikaans chronicler Gustav Preller (1875–1943), whose vivid accounts of the Voortrekkers in print and in film played a central role in shaping Afrikaner Nationalist mythology. The planned scenes published in *Pretoria News* listed the episodes as follows [dates and other information added in brackets].[21]

1. Zimbabwe the Magnificent
2. The Bushmen, at one time sole owners of the Continent
3. The Hottentots
4. The Beginning of History
5. The Landing of van Riebeeck [1652]
6. Simon van der Stel welcomes the Huguenots [1690]
7. The British occupy the Cape [1806]
8. The arrival of the British settlers in 1820
9. Chaka, King of the Zulus, presents the Charter of Natal to Lt. Farewell [1824]
10. Piet Uys and his trek party are presented with a Bible by the citizens of Grahamstown
11. Nagmaal [communion] after the Battle of Vegkop [1836]
12. Arrival of Louis Trichardt's trek party in Lourenço Marques
13. The Vow taken to build a Church should the Boers be victorious over Dingaan [1838]

14. Dingaan's Day: [Andries] Pretorius and Mpande [Dingaan's successor] on the Rock
15. [Cape governor Harry] Smith's Soldiers and the Lady Kenneway Girls [1840s]
16. Discovery of Diamonds [1867]
17. The Discovery of Gold on the Rand [1886]
18. Rhodes's indaba [conference] with Lobengula [King of the Matabele] [1889]
19. The Arrival of the first train in Bulawayo [1897]
20. Election of Paul Kruger as President [South African Republic] in 1898 [third term]
21. Final Tableau—Union—The National Convention Assembly in Cape Town [1910]

As might be expected, these episodes rested on the assumption that South African history began with European arrival at the Cape. Indigenous inhabitants appear either in prehistoric preludes or in capitulation to the imperial plan, as in Rhodes's indaba with Lobengula, or the defeat of the Zulus at "Blood" (Ncome) River. To emphasize the importance of this last episode, the pageant opened on December 16—the date commemorated by Afrikaner Nationalists as the Day of the Vow, and today in the post-apartheid calendar as the Day of Reconciliation. Despite the final tableau of Union, the penultimate episode on Paul Kruger could not but remind spectators of Afrikaner Nationalist dissent from the unity narrative.

The Voortrekker March beyond the Pageant

This dissent erupted in the Afrikaner counter-pageant whose scale surpassed that of the Empire Exhibition. The reenactment of the Great Trek in 1938 commemorated both the centenary of the vow taken at the Battle of Blood River in 1838 and a century of Boer resistance to the British. The *Afrikaner Taal- en Kultuurvereniging* [Afrikaans Language and Cultural Union] (hereafter: ATKV) began by organizing a trek of two wagons from Cape Town but gained enough contributions from its parent union, the South African Railways and Harbours Union, dominated by Afrikaners, as well as from nationalist intellectuals, to support nine ox-wagons retracing the trekkers' journey along what the official *Gedenkboek van die Voortrekker-Eeufees* [Commemoration Book of the Voortrekker Centenary Celebration] called the "path of South Africa" (*Gedenkboek* 1938: 57; trans. LK), the route from Cape Town northwards to Pretoria. Men in *boere* [farmer]-*kommandos* and women in *kappie* [bonnet]-*kommandos*—attire and formations that recalled the Anglo-Boer War era—gathered at points along the route. In Pretoria, two hundred thousand people assembled to welcome the wagons, and, on December 16, amassed on the hill opposite the Union Buildings to witness the laying of the cornerstone of the Voortrekker Monument, the "altar of Afrikanerdom" (*Gedenkboek* 1940: 815). The days leading up to this climax featured speeches by ATKV and National Party leaders, *boere*-sport, folk singing, dancing, prayer, a film, *Die Bou van 'n Nasie* [They Built a Nation] (script: Preller, dir. Joseph Albrecht), and a play, *Die Dieper Reg* [The Deeper Right] written by well-known poet N.P. van Wyk

Louw (1906–70). Although he called the play an allegory, Louw's preface called for Voortrekker costume (1938: 7) and his dramatization of national loss and recovery drew on the Voortrekker narrative. Directed by Anna Neethling-Pohl (1906–92), with elements such as marchers carrying torches borrowed from Nazi rallies she had observed at Nuremburg, *Die Dieper Reg* reinforced the claim articulated in *Die Bou van 'n Nasie* that Afrikaners had primary rights to South Africa.[22]

The tension between Preller's populist script, which was intended to inspire landless farmers as well as satisfy ATKV intellectuals, and the aesthetic aspirations of *Die Dieper Reg* suggested, as Louw admitted in a contemporary essay on "nationalism and art" (1939: 23), that the festival had not eliminated "sharp class consciousness" among Afrikaners (12). Nonetheless, Louw asserted that "perfect [*volkome*] beauty" rather than "fiery rhetoric" was the best way to support the "struggle of the volk" (35), *volkseenheid* [Afrikaner unity] had "middle-class support" (Grundlingh/Sapire 1989: 24) but it was contested from above and below. On the one hand, liberal internationalists such as Jan Smuts disdained this spectacle as a consolation for disaffected "poor whites" (Moodie 1975: 175); on the other, Afrikaners who identified with the international class struggle, such as the garment workers who wished to organize a socialist *kappiekommando*, were rejected by the ATKV as dupes of the "communist Sachs" (E.S. Sachs, Garment Workers Union secretary: citations and image in Kruger 2004: 226–31). Despite these tensions, this "Second Great Trek" revivified the "sacred history" of Boer suffering and regeneration (Moodie 1975: 180): it was able to link the memory of misery, especially of women and children in British-run concentration camps during the Anglo-Boer War, the wretchedness of Afrikaners in the "English" city, and the promise of restoration as the Chosen People. As the *Gedenkboek* put it, in the nationalist pathos dear to Preller, "the covenant was sealed at Blood River … The continued existence of our Volk is a miracle … Our Volk was frequently in deep grief and divided, but will always unite again" (1938: 55). This reenacted *Voortrek* [progress] offered Afrikaners a compelling alternative to the British Empire, which would be enacted by the purified National Party, once it won the election in 1948 (Chapter 4).

This Nationalist current had already emerged in disputes around some scenes in the 1936 Pageant. Due partly to political pressure and partly to logistical difficulties, the premiere of this "magnificent historical spectacle" (as advertised by the organizers) offered only twelve episodes. Others were deemed too controversial such as the Anglo-Zulu War of 1879 or the Day of the Vow, or too complex for visual representation, such as the gold and diamond fields and the miners who worked them. These omissions also allowed a return to colonialist nostalgia, which, as in 1910, was projected on the bodies of women. Although not on the initial list, the reenactment of a ball supposedly held by Lady Anne Barnard, wife of the first British colonial secretary, which had appealed to 1910 audiences, was revived in 1936. This scene had less to do with historical reconstruction than with the pleasures of neocolonial prestige, reflected in the liveried footmen and debutantes in period dress admired in the press (image: Kruger 1999a: 41).[23] Staging the past as a beauty pageant, this spectacle stole the show from history, as it were, but also reminds present-day readers of what Roach calls the "surplus of surrogation" (1996: 2). In this case, the expropriation of African land and labor was displaced by the display of leisured white women. This picture of civilization as the leisure of "English ladies" contrasts with the *kappiekommando* in the Second Great Trek, whose lack of ornament reflected not only Calvinist custom but also readiness for the battle around *volkseie* (Hofmeyr 1987).

The "Real Africa" and the African National Pageant

Anglophone critics of the Empire Exhibition who favored "a pictorial representation of a period in history with a minimum of verbal comment" (Linscott 1937b: 16) took little notice of urban blacks, except when performing "evening entertainments" that Africans were not allowed to attend. Although accounts of the Empire Exhibition in African papers were overshadowed with concern about imminent disenfranchisement, reporters stressed African visibility despite these restrictions. Amid articles noting that about 500 Africans attended daily as opposed to tens of thousands of whites, one reporter noted the city's thanks to African workers but concluded ironically that Africans "look forward to the day they will be granted the freedom of the city."[24] Another remarked that, while the pavilions celebrated the "pulsing life of modern commerce" rather than "the mysteries of the past," Africans with permission to visit would have no access to evening entertainment except the amusement park.[25] While no African critic matched Frederick Douglass's condemnation of the 1893 Chicago Columbian Exposition as a "white sepulcher" (Douglass 1999: 9), all regretted the Empire Exhibition's neglect of African visitors.

The evening entertainments from which Africans were barred included ballroom dancing and ballet but most popular were the African entertainments, which ranged from the urban sophistication of the Darktown Strutters and the Merry Blackbirds, through the Lucky Stars, to Zulu dancing orchestrated by Van Gyseghem himself. This last show, *Amangabeze* [exhortations]—but glossed as "the dancing place"—was billed as "the Real Africa" and performed at least a dozen times, more often than the Pageant. Van Gyseghem took pains to preserve what he understood to be the authenticity of the dances—often against the wishes of the dancers. As Mary Kelly, representative of the British Drama League noted:

> He toured native territories, but original ritual dances untouched by European influence could not be witnessed by Europeans and those dances that he did see definitely bore traces of White contact. The original costumes had been added to by brilliantly coloured cheap silks and other trimmings easily available at village and city stores.
>
> Eventually a troupe ... was gathered together and before they appeared in the arena, a man, employed for the purpose, removed the superfluous apparel. (Kelly 1938: 2)

This battle for the authenticity of the dance waged against the preferences of the dancers reveals the mix of modernity, capitalism, and neocolonial anxiety about both. The African dancers act as consumers as well as performers of a living syncretic culture but their promoters seem consumed by the encroachments of modern life on "native territory." The Native Affairs Department's role as expert advisor on traditional custom should remind us of New African suspicion about white enthusiasm for African "tradition." As one African commentator wrote, "there is no objection to war dances provided they are staged by the enlightened Bantu. When they are staged by the uncivilised Native, it is a sign of retrogression," and, as another reiterated more than a decade and a half later, "the proper people and place for modernising this primitive art are the Zulu Cultural Society, " not white experts.[26]

At stake here is not the authenticity of the African object, but rather the legitimacy of African agency in determining the character of tradition. New Africans were particularly concerned that the revival of traditional custom did not cast them in a primitivist light: "The joy that a civilised man gets when watching Zulus dance is the same kind of joy that he gets when looking at monkeys."[27] If the interest of sympathetic liberals such as Lloyd or Slosberg differed in tone from the man viewing Africans as monkeys, the white liberal view speaks as much of anxious insistence on European identity as of interest in African tradition. Slosberg's case is once again illuminating; she insisted repeatedly on preserving the specifically Zulu character of the Lucky Stars' performance but when her plan to present a Zulu show to London audiences was thwarted by the South African government's refusal to grant passports to the group, she devoted the same enthusiasm to a curtain-raiser for *The Sun Never Sets*, a stage adaptation of Zoltan Korda's *Sanders of the River* (1935, filmed in South Africa, performed mostly by Nigerians and British blacks whom she had trained herself (Slosberg 1939: 312–20). Like Slosberg, Van Gyseghem was unwilling to acknowledge the modernity of this reproduction of tradition, even if the place and occasion of the show at the Empire Exhibition confirmed its place on a modern stage.

The African entertainments at the Empire Exhibition may have been closed to African spectators, but this did not prevent the event from "influenc[ing] Johannesburg location performances" (Vilakazi 1942: 273). This influence was spread by performances in township halls and enhanced by the prestige garnered from appearances at the Empire Exhibition. Even though they did not get the same publicity as *Amangabeze*, the Darktown Strutters portrayed an actual Africa more complex than the "real Africa." The skill of leader Motsieloa and the patronage of Gallophone—later Gallo—Records, which employed him as a talent scout from 1938 (Coplan 2008: 163), gave the group a rare measure of economic independence. Motsieloa was a friend of Peter Rezant, leader of the Merry Blackbirds, and the husband of Emily Makanana, a talented pianist who had led the Dangerous Blues (Matshikiza 1956). He qualified as a teacher at Lovedale College and studied at Trinity College of Music, where he earned a reputation as "London's Favourite Bantu Actor" (Skota 1931: 215). He ran a series of groups, from the African Darkies in the 1920s to the Darktown Strutters to the Pitch Black Follies in the 1940s, which can perhaps be characterized as "middle-class" (Coplan 2008: 156) but their repertoires mixed *amakwaya* with *marabi* music—as demonstrated by Motsieloa's songs on the CD accompanying *Marabi Nights* (Ballantine 2012)— and minstrel gags with more sustained dramas on the modern African and African-American condition, using Sotho and Zulu as well as English. In places far away from their Johannesburg base—Queenstown in the Eastern Cape, Serowe in Bechuanaland (Botswana) and Lourenço Marques (Maputo) in Mozambique—they had to offer a broadly appealing program that crossed class lines and ethnic boundaries.[28] African reviews suggest that performers and audience alike celebrated the African, European, and African-American aspects of the show without regarding them as separate elements. A reviewer in Xhosa-speaking Queenstown praised the comic Petrus Qwabe as the "Zulu king of laughter and mirth" and tap-dancer Johannes Masoleng—like Motsieloa, of Sotho origin—as "South Africa's Stephen [*sic*] Fetchit."[29] While Stephin Fetchit might disturb readers wary of American minstrel stereotypes, this allusion is complimentary. In so far as Stephin Fetchit was the image of a "successful and self-conscious urban black," he represented a positive role model (Erlmann 1991: 63). At the very least, the virtuoso *impersonation* was worthy of emulation.

Renamed the Pitch Black Follies in 1938, after Motsieloa started earning money from Gallo, the group began to include more ambitious dramatic material, as one program indicated:

1. The Xhosa prophet Ntshikana: Ntshikana's vision, tribal dance, Ntshikana sees the coming of the white man (led by Victor Mkhize)
2. Jim Utakata Kanje [Jim the Trickster] (Petrus Qwabe)
3. Die Oorlams Mense van Vrededorp [The Clever People of Vrededorp]
4. The Recruiter, a two-act play by J. Mathews [*sic*], written by a Negro during the early days of the USA's entry into the Great War (SAIRR, AD843/Kb28.2.2).

This line-up was complemented by "Native hymns," likely including Tiyo Soga's "Lizalis' idinga lakho/Thixo Nkosi yenyaniso [Fulfill your promise/Lord God of Truth]" in John Knox Bokwe's 1915 setting, which would feature in the Truth and Reconciliation hearings seventy years later.[30] "The Recruiter," or "'Cruter," by the African-American folklorist John Matheus (1887–1983) dramatized the recruiting of rural blacks for work in Northern cities that prompted the Great Migration of African Americans:

> At that time the Negroes on the plantations were bound on contract to the cotton plantation owners, and the recruitment of labour for the factories was in consequence illegal. Led by promises of emancipation and riches, scores of Negro youth left their homes where their forebears lived as "Squatters" for many generations.
>
> This play serves to illustrate the antagonisms of the Negro youth to the superstitions and willing subjection of their parents (SAIRR, AD843/Kb28.2.2).

Motsieloa's use of the word "squatters" offers an oblique comparison between Negro sharecroppers and South Africans displaced by the Land Act, while the final sentence is more hopeful, as it equates the urbanization of the youth with their emancipation from superstition. These were clearly issues of interest to Africans at a time when the government was placing greater constraints on their mobility. Equally important, however, was the institutional status of this text. Published in *Opportunity*, the organ of the National Urban League (USA), the play addressed the pressing questions of urban migration and economic self-sufficiency for blacks while showing that this modern theme could be couched in folk idiom.[31]

This point/counterpoint between the modern and the folk formed the leitmotif of Pitch Black Follies shows. A description of "Africa—a revel pageant" (1940) recalls a show "depicting the march of progress among the Bantu, from the primitive stage right up to that of the 'Upper Tenth,'" with a didactic climax—the necessity of "Unity in Diversity in Bantudom."[32] Calling the show a "pageant," the reviewer emphasizes its affinity with British imperial trends while also noting the influence of African Americans. At the same time, he draws attention to the mix of high and low elements with comic sketches and variety numbers like "Lost in the Shuffle." Since this particular performance took place in the state-administered "community hall" in Western Native Township, today reinvented as the suburb of Westbury, its audience in 1940 would have included industrial and service workers as well as intellectuals; the combination of uplift and self-mocking exaggeration addressed an audience that could interpret this show as a pageant of a nation in the making even as they laughed at the gags.

Over the next decade, however, the relationship between the Pitch Black Follies and their audience would be subject to strain. On the one hand, the rapid expansion of urban industry due to the Second World War brought in a new generation of Africans who did not share the cosmopolitan tastes of the New Africans. On the other, overseas service with the troops brought the Pitch Black Follies and other variety groups in closer contact with whites who aspired like Slosberg to "discover" the "real Africa." Thus, while the Liberty Cavalcade for American soldiers in Cape Town in 1944 gave the Pitch Black Follies and Merry Blackbirds the opportunity to perform for people who bandleader Rezant called representatives of "Harlem and Chicago," it also gave Lt. Ike Brooks, a white South African, the chance to put together a "large variety company from the South African Native Military Corps" (Coplan 2008: 182). Brooks went on to produce the show *Zonk* in 1946, which absorbed members of the United Bantu Artists and Jabulani Concert Party as well as the Pitch Black Follies, and to claim that he had trained them from scratch (Coplan 2008: 183), despite ample evidence of their performance experience. Dhlomo commented on this appropriation: "After seeing the Nu-Zonk revue many Europeans were amazed at so much African talent ... On the African side, there have been some heart-searchings [*sic*]. Why do we neglect our talent? Why cannot we organize and efficiently manage ourselves? Why must there always be a European behind us?"[33] The answer lies in part in the state's restrictions on African entrepreneurs, which were to become a stranglehold under apartheid after 1950. White preference for "tribal sketches" over modern depictions of the African "march of progress," persists today in tourist shows in Gold Reef City and other theme parks.

Despite the tourist cliché, the diverse formats of African variety and its happy appropriation of musical, comic, and dramatic elements from Europe, America, and African America, as well as African practices, gave rise to the "concert," which is still the term favored by black audiences in the twenty-first century, demonstrating the durability of this syncretic form and its wide appeal for different classes. We will return to the "concert" and its cousin, the musical, in later chapters. The New African generation, however, remained ambivalent about popular entertainment. On the same page as the favorable review of "Africa—a revel pageant" cited above, Walter Nhlapo challenged the popularity of jazz and vaudeville, which "deafen our appreciation for art," and called instead for the "greater beauty" of drama.[34] His contemporary Herbert Dhlomo was to spend the next two decades promoting African drama. Regarded by New Africans as a "capable interpreter of the desires and ambitions of his people" (Skota 1931: 143) and self-appointed spokesman for an "African tradition grafted onto the European," Dhlomo criticized the commodification of traditions as "exotic crudities" (Dhlomo 1977a: 7) but also resisted embalming these traditions in "static museum-like plays" (1977e: 39). Instead, he proposed a new theatre that would harness the best of European and African forms. That project, its achievements and contradictions, brings us to Chapter 2.

Neocolonial Theatre and "An African National Dramatic Movement"

Modern drama is not a mere emotional entertainment. It is a source of ideas, a cultural and educational factor, an agency for propaganda and, above all, it is literature. What part will the new African play in modern drama? On its physical side, he can contribute strong, fast rhythm, speedy action, expressive vigorous gesture and movement, powerful dramatic speech–no small contribution when modern plays drag so tediously ... We want African playwrights who will dramatize ... African History. We want dramatic representations of African Serfdom, Oppression, Exploitation, and Metamorphosis ... The African dramatist ... can expose evil and corruption and not suffer libel as newspapermen do; he can guide and preach to his people as preachers cannot do. To do this he must be an artist before a propagandist; a philosopher before a reformer, a psychologist before a patriot; be true to his African "self" and not be prey to exotic crudities.

This passage from Herbert Dhlomo's essay, "The Importance of African Drama" (1933: 17), marks a key point for South African theatre not only because it argues for plays on African aspirations but also because it outlines the developments that shaped theatre by Africans and their articulation of national identity.

As a playwright, critic, and impresario, Dhlomo saw the friction between elite and popular, imported and indigenous, literate and oral practices which shaped New African culture as productive friction. Although his career was marred by the contradictions between his liberal formation at Adams College and the illiberal policies of the segregationist state, his contribution to South African culture was considerable. He directed the Emancipation Centenary Celebration, served as vice-president of the Bantu Dramatic Society (BDS), and published essays over two decades in *Bantu World* and *Ilanga lase Natal*. His plays feature historical protagonists from prophetess Nongqause to kings Moshoeshoe and Cetshwayo, and in the latter especially critiqued the violence of colonialism. In formal terms, Dhlomo's "modern drama" drew on models from African oral history and song to English social drama and German expressionism, and on the musical and thespian talents of his fellow New Africans. These endeavors inspired black activists to found a Dhlomo Theatre in 1983, *before* the editors of his collected—but not complete—works confirmed his status as "the pioneer of modern black drama" (Visser and Couzens 1985: xv). While the neglect that lasted from his death until the publication of his works may encourage the view that "we have no script" (Coplan 2008: 151) of plays such as *Moshoeshoe*, or that "for more than half a century" Dhlomo's reputation rested on his first play *The Girl Who Killed to Save* (Wenzel 2009: 76), these omissions slight the Africans who read his published essays (Masilela 2007) and who saw other plays staged in his lifetime: *Moshoeshoe* and *Ruby and Frank* in 1939 and *Dingana*—published by the University of Natal—in 1954, all more ambitious than his first. These performances linked the drama to key events, such as Moshoeshoe Day celebrated at home and in neighboring Basutoland (Lesotho) to dramatize African history and legacy for a pan-ethnic African audience.

Dhlomo's articulation of New African aspirations also challenged neocolonial theatre institutions. In the 1930s commercial managements such as African Consolidated Theatres run by the Schlesinger family who controlled African Consolidated Mines sponsored touring companies from London, while local amateurs such as the Johannesburg Repertory (hereafter Rep.) and the Cape Town Little Theatre followed a slightly bolder program, including modern drama from London and New York, and English classics from Sheridan to Wilde. Local drama on controversial topics was not entirely absent, however. Lewis Sowden's *Red Rand* (1937) dealt with the 1922 Rand Revolt, which captured international attention for its impact on the gold industry and for state violence against strikers, and continues to resonate in comparisons to the Marikana massacre of 2012. Black groups, the BDS and the Bantu Peoples Theatre (BPT), were hampered by insufficient capital and lack of access to venues, but nonetheless attempted to stage plays that would speak to urban African audiences, drawing on seasonal celebrations and workers agitprop, the European avant-garde and English drawing-room comedy. While research since Tim Couzens's (1944–2016) pioneering study *The New African* (1985)—by Peterson (2000); Masilela (2007), and Wenzel (2009)—has looked more closely at New African culture, none, apart from Martin Orkin (1991) and my previous study (1999a), has compared black and white practitioners and institution and the shifting meanings of "theatre," "amateur," and "national" in the early twentieth century. Understanding the contexts of neocolonial theatre is essential before we can evaluate New African negotiation, let alone outright resistance to neocolonial pressures.

Amateurs and Dissidents in Neocolonial Theatre

South African theatre in the decades after Union (from 1910 to the 1950s) was neocolonial to the extent that it was dominated by touring groups, or by local productions of plays that had premiered in London or New York, but the assertion that theatre in this period should be evaluated as to the degree to which it "displaced the colonial centre" (Orkin 1991: 7) misses the diversity of the repertoire. The Johannesburg season of 1911, sampled from the Strange Theatre Collection at the Johannesburg Public Library, included Shakespeare's *Richard III, The Girl Who Lost Her Character, The Pageant of Great Women*—Cicely Hamilton's emancipation pageant staged in London by Edy Craig, Ellen Terry's daughter—and *Love and the Hyphen* (1984 [1902]), a popular satire on Cape Town's would-be gentry, by Stephen Black (1879–1931), local playwright and editor of the magazine *The Sjambok* [meaning a leather whip from the era of slavery].[1]

The Girl Who Lost Her Character and *Great Women* both came from the "colonial centre" but that label ignores the difference between the formulaic "woman with a past" plot of the former and the suffragist message of the latter. Unlike the imports, *Love and the Hyphen* was frequently revived from 1902 to the 1920s. Although Orkin dismisses the play because it was not published (1991: 6), Stephen Gray (1941–), editor of Black's *Selected Plays*, notes that by withholding plays from print in an era of weak copyright law, Black kept rights and revenue firmly in his hands (Gray 1984: 21).

Love and the Hyphen's satire of pretentious masters and cheeky servants at the Cape did not break any neocolonial norms but Black adapted other, more controversial plays. His 1929 production of *Damaged Goods*, Eugène Brieux's drama about the social impact of syphilis, exposed this taboo issue to public debate. The Johannesburg Rep.'s staging of Brieux's *The Red Robe* in 1930 drew the remark from Black that "smug lawyers will no doubt reassure themselves (and their clients) by saying 'well, of course, it isn't like that here.' But my own experience has been rather that French law is more … *merciful* than English or Roman Dutch law."[2] The black-cast production of Eugene O'Neill's *The Hairy Ape*, produced in 1936 by the BPT and André van Gyseghem, drew on the company's very different experience of day-to-day oppression but it also reflected the pageant master's experience with international avant-gardes for its portrayal of the alienation of workers. This last production in particular shows that distinctions between the center and the periphery, between imported and indigenous production, between affirmative and critical culture were far from clear-cut and that practitioners drew on a variety of local and transnational sources to achieve their aims to represent themselves and South Africa.

The first three decades of the twentieth century saw a few producers such as Black and Leonard Rayne (1869–1925) penetrate a field dominated by tours from London managed above all by Schlesinger's African Consolidated. By the 1930s, Schlesinger had moved into film distribution, opening up space for repertory companies run by white amateurs in regional centers from Pretoria to Cape Town. Whereas Afrikaans theatres staged drama on nationalist themes such as Grosskopf's plays about displaced rural Afrikaners or patriotic tearjerkers like *Sarie Marais* (see Kannemeyer 1988: 90–91), English-language groups, in particular the Johannesburg Rep. (1928–78; the longest running), showed little interest in local playwrights, preferring to balance the comedies of Wilde and Coward with Shakespeare and Shaw and, somewhat more boldly, modern playwrights such as Karel Čapek along with Chekhov, Pirandello, Giraudoux, and O'Neill.

In contrast to this cultural deference, the Repertory Reading Group staged *Red Rand* by Lewis Sowden (1903–74), critic for the *Rand Daily Mail* and later for the *Jerusalem Post*, which dealt with the Rand Revolt, still a controversial memory in 1937. Measured against other local plays that deal indirectly with mining capital, such as Black's *Helena's Hope Ltd.* (1910), which satirizes rapacious land-sharks but follows a classic melodramatic plot in which the genteel Helena outwits the capitalists—cast as Jewish stereotypes—to reclaim her inheritance, or *Where the Money Goes* (1925) by Jewish South African Bertha Goudvis, about a woman's love for a gambling man who embezzles money from the company that employs them both, *Red Rand* is remarkable for its serious engagement with mining capital's exploitation of workers and with the still potent memory of the 1922 revolt, recalled by commentators on the Marikana massacre of 2012 (Alexander at al. 2013). The 1922 revolt began as a strike by white miners against the threat that lower-paid blacks allegedly posed to their wages but ended in a massacre of black as well as white miners and bystanders after Prime Minister Jan Smuts used the army to suppress the uprising. Historian Jeremy Krikler uses theatrical terms, "heroic and cruel, ambiguous and doomed," to describe the revolt as a "tragedy" (2005: 295). The funerals of leaders were accompanied by parades under the international socialist banner and accompanied by *The Red Flag* anthem (written by Jim Connell in 1887), and commemorated on a scale that would not be repeated until the anti-apartheid 1980s—but the red flag was banned in 1950 until the return of the South African Communist Party (SACP) in 1990.[3] The "people's flag of deepest red" that "shrouded oft our martyred dead" took the stage again much later, in the soundtrack for Harry Kalmer's solo play *The Bram Fischer Waltz* (2012; published 2016), which dramatized scenes from the life (1908–75) of the advocate who was the scion of a storied Afrikaner family and the head of the clandestine SACP, as he looks back from prison, where he served a life sentence for opposition to apartheid.[4]

Directed by Elsie Salomon in the new Johannesburg Public Library's chamber theatre in December 1937, *Red Rand* was a more restrained event than the protest that inspired it.[5] While drawing on eyewitness accounts by Johannesburg writers such as Bernard Sachs (Kruger 2013: 46–47), Sowden's treatment of strikers and their families remains within the bounds of "social concern"—in the Edwardian manner of John Galsworthy—rather than revolution. Like Galsworthy's *Strife* (1910), which was hailed as a play of national importance at its London premiere (Kruger 1992: 101–24), *Red Rand* portrays the strikers as heroic but misguided laborers, whose grievances against the Chamber of Mines are justified but whose armed resistance is shown to be the last resort of desperate men. *Red Rand* also shares with *Strife* predominantly domestic settings for the public drama that occurs off stage. In both plays, the single public scene—a workers' meeting—reeks of suppressed violence. The character of Taylor, marked in the stage directions as a rabble-rouser, uses violent language similar to the talk that Sachs recorded of the historical agitator Percy Fisher (Sachs 1959: 119): "I've got no time for moderate men ... Those who know history know that it is only by force that great reforms are effected" (Sowden 1937: I, 70). Salomon directed this scene to intensify the threat, deploying what one reviewer called "the new device of using the entire body of the hall" so that the "strike leaders harangued the audience and the strikers at the back of the hall" until the strikers "rushed down the aisles to join their fellows" on stage.[6] The army's violence, on the other hand, remains off stage, a shadowy but powerful force whose machinations are impenetrable. This dramaturgy may have generated sympathy for the underdog miners, but it also evaded the question of the state's responsibility for the escalation of violence.

Despite the play's ostensible focus on the labor struggle, the protagonist is not the strike leader Will Mullins, but his educated brother John. After John is shot by mine security men while trying to retrieve his books, Will reiterates his brother's plea for education rather than direct action:

That's the trouble with you strikers. You go about shouting and waving the Red Flag but you don't know the first thing about the force you set in motion ... You've got to know as much as the other side know before you can beat them ... And they've learnt a good deal from books. Without geometry, you couldn't sink a shaft, without knowledge of history, you wouldn't know how to govern. You've got to learn and learn before you can have power. (Sowden 1937: II, 48)

The action thus endorses an alliance between intellectual and manual labor, while saying little about state violence and next to nothing about the fate of black workers caught between white state and white labor. The miners' defense of the Colour Bar is glossed over, as are occasional references to the deaths of black miners. The only black speaking part, Mrs. Mullins's servant Samuel, is portrayed as loyal but naive. He works for only room and board and is killed by a bomb while watching the airforce planes from the roof. Thus, while this play gives attention to conflicts among the workers and offers a relatively sympathetic portrayal of their grievances, racism remains its structuring absence. Africans were also excluded from the audience, since black spectators were admitted to the Library Theatre only by special permit.

This play deserves attention for vividly dramatizing the conflict between workers and intellectuals responding to the Rand Revolt and invites comparison with commemoration miners' actions against both apartheid and post-apartheid governments, but it is not surprising that it received little attention in its day. Although some amateur theatres hoped to challenge audiences with dramas about social conflict at home or abroad, most white audiences, like others in the British orbit, preferred the genteel norms of the English drawing room. In Canada and Australia, as in South Africa in this period, neocolonial tastemakers favored the idea of theatre as art while aspiring to enjoy metropolitan culture.[7] As Harley Granville Barker, chief sponsor of an English National Theatre, wrote: "Leisure is not so much an opportunity as a quality of mind … But the mass of the world's work is too highly specialized to call for well-balanced faculties. So much the worse for … workers (1922: 286–87). "Amateur" should be understood here as the activities of those who love theatre rather than those who sell it, and as the informal association of leisured patrons who express disdain for workers in the culture industry but remain oblivious to the menial work that supported their leisure. Even productions of experimental plays succumbed to English norms of gentility. The Johannesburg Rep.'s revival of *R.U.R–Rossum's Universal Robots*, Čapek's apocalyptic vision of a future robot revolt, was produced in 1936 while the Empire Exhibition was celebrating modern technology, more than a decade after it hit the New York stage, but was allegedly so "uninspired," playing "like men's football on a Sunday afternoon" (Linscott 1936: 15), that the critic felt moved to quote expatriate Roy Campbell's indictment of neocolonial gentility: "We note the great restraint with which you write / We're with you there, of course / You use the snaffle and the curb all right / But where's the b—y horse?" In deflecting Campbell's attack on critics who praise restraint as well as writers who submit to it, this quotation authorizes gentility even as it criticizes it.[8]

The BDS and New African Aspirations

Neocolonial metropolitan aspirations also affected New African groups who were exposed to English drama as part of mission school education. The first production of the BDS, Oliver Goldsmith's eighteenth-century comedy *She Stoops to Conquer* reflects that influence. The most likely reason for this choice was not, as has been claimed, a production of the play by "a visiting English company at His Majesty's Theatre" (Hoernlé 1934: 224; repeated: Orkin 1991: 25), but the input of members such as Dan Twala, who had performed in a production at Lovedale College (Couzens 1985: 51) and had seen a production by the Johannesburg Rep. at His Majesty's in 1932.[9] *She Stoops to Conquer* opened at the BMSC on April 28, 1933, ran for two weekends, and included after each show a dance party to music by the Merry Blackbirds. African critics thought the event worthy of front-page news, in part because it marked African acquisition of European modernity but chiefly because of BDS's aim to "to encourage Bantu playwrights and to develop African dramatic and operatic art," as noted by Mary Kelly (1934: 2), secretary of the British Drama League that sponsored the BDS.[10] Local white critics treated the event with condescension: Alfred Hoernlé, Wits professor of African languages, commended the players' "natural aptitude for acting" (1934: 225) and J.D. Rheinallt Jones, director of the Institute for Race Relations, asserted: "the group would benefit from guidance from an experienced European."[11] "Experienced Europeans" apparently preferred drawing-room comedy such as Wilde's *Lady Windermere's Fan* (staged in 1934; image: Kruger 1999a: 56). *Abraham Lincoln* by John Drinkwater (1882–1937) (Drinkwater 1925), proposed for 1935, did not reach the stage, despite support from Kelly (1934: 3). Sybil Thorndike, visiting from London's Old Vic Theatre, was more generous, "in holding the black man back, we are holding back the best in ourselves … We are not so clever that we cannot learn from him."[12] Van Gyseghem proposed American social dramas such as O'Neill's *Hairy Ape* or *Stevedore* by Paul Peters and George Sklar but these were rejected because they were "not sufficiently genteel" (Kelly 1938: 3). The "experts" were, however, willing to criticize neocolonial propaganda such as *uNongqause* by the missionary Mary Waters, the second BDS production, which treated the cattle killing that the prophetess prescribed in 1856 and that led to starvation among the Xhosa as an opportunity to praise Christian missionaries, who dominate the play despite the title. Hoernlé dismissed it as a "harangue" (1934: 226), while Kelly regretted Waters' "lack of dramatic knowledge" and noted the indifference of African audiences (1934: 2). The appearance of *uNongqause* renewed African suspicion of missionary versions of "Native idiom" and prompted Dhlomo to write his own play on Nongqause, *The Girl Who Killed to Save* in English, published by Lovedale Mission Press.[13] Where Waters portrayed Xhosa custom as primitive and therefore doomed, Dhlomo's play treats the nineteenth-century prophet as a figure who staged "the dynamic of retrieval, loss and recovery," and thus expressed his generation's "ambivalence about the prospect of assimilation and the necessity of a new kind of nationalism" (Wenzel 2009: 72).[14]

The Girl Who Killed to Save begins by juxtaposing Nongqause's doubts about her visions with her desire to help her people repel the invaders, and ends with a dying convert, Daba, who translates Nongqause's divination into Christian prophecy. The end of the play casts Nongqause in the role of "Liberator from Superstition and the rule of Ignorance" (Dhlomo 1985: 29) but these words are first uttered by Hugh, a white missionary, who endorses the most radical kind of social engineering:

Nongqause may accomplish in a short time … what in the ordinary course of events would have taken generations of Christianity and education … The only thing to ask is whether or not the price she has asked the people to pay is not too costly … If we believe in the doctrine of the survival of the fittest then we may excuse her by saying that those who survive her purging and liberating test will be individuals physically and intellectually superior to the others. (18)

The edge of cruelty in the speech cuts against the promise of liberation and reminds the audience of the brutality of colonization. At the same time, Hugh's reference to those who "have already shown their intellectual independence by being sceptical and refusing to kill their cattle" allows for those Xhosa that later generations called the "unbelievers," whose independence of mind looks forward to a critical appropriation of the tools of modernity—skepticism, rational thought, improvisation—which may be used against the neocolonial modernity that reduced Africans to subjects of European tutelage.

Neocolonial modernity may have shaped the salvation plot of *The Girl Who Killed to Save* but it did not entirely determine its meaning. To be sure, the key moments of crisis—the private confrontation between Nongqause and her skeptical suitor Mazwi, the showdown between paramount chief Kreli and unbelievers among his subjects, the debate between intervention and inaction among the British—as well as the confrontations between white settlers and the Xhosa on the colonial frontier, are rendered in a language that recalls the heightened realism of contemporary English writers such as Drinkwater and Shaw and, for one reviewer of Dhlomo's published play, even the expressionist intensity of Ernst Toller's portrayal of collective anguish and individual alienation in *Masses and Man* (1921).[15] Yet dialogue between autonomous agents, the signature of modern European drama, is not the only convention operating here. The five songs that accompany the original manuscript shift the mode of performance; the first four, written by Dhlomo, are interspersed in the first two scenes; introducing the customs and activities of the Xhosa, they recall the folk melodies disseminated by Dhlomo's cousin, Reuben Caluza. Like Caluza's songs, these draw from an African/European syncretic practice.[16] The last song introduces a more complex note, however; the opening "Nkosi kawu sikelele" [God bless you] quotes the tradition of *amakwaya*—church hymns—established by Tiyo Soga (1829–71), who makes a silent appearance in this play. While the tonic-solfa sheet in the Lovedale Collection attributes music and text to Dhlomo, the music is John Knox Bokwe's setting of Soga's 1865 hymn "Lizalis' idinga lakho, Thixo Nkosi yinyaniso [Fulfill your promise, Lord God of Truth]" (Bokwe 1915) and the title "Nkosi kawu sikelele" recalls Sontonga's 1897 hymn that was by 1935 the ANC anthem "Nkosi sikelel' iAfrika." Inserted in the final scene of the play as the converts gather at Daba's deathbed, Dhlomo's quotation praised the Christian God but the line also recalls the ANC anthem's expression of national longing and nationalist struggle (Chapter 1), and Bokwe's melody sings of hope that would resonate in the Truth and Reconciliation Commission whose hearings it would open in 1996 (see Chapter 7).

Despite the genteel norms of Anglophile institutions, BDS members were keen to stage plays such as *The Hairy Ape*, which combined metropolitan prestige—O'Neill had just won the Nobel Prize for Literature—with more robust social critique. Although "European experts" had previously blocked its production, Twala approached Van Gyseghem on behalf of a new group, the BPT, and Van Gyseghem directed Twala in the role of Yank at the BMSC in December 1936, and at Wits University's Great Hall in June 1937.[17] Although set in America, *The Hairy Ape's* depiction of the gulf between rich and poor resonated in Johannesburg and was praised for its "stark, symbolic treatment of the action" by the same critic who had mocked the timidity of the Johannesburg Rep's *R.U.R* (Linscott 1937a: 15). *The Hairy Ape* depicted the exploitation of urban workers rather than the lives of precolonial Africans; it used language that matched the urban milieu—the "American slang was rendered in the idiom of Bantu English" (Kelly 1938: 3), and the performance used staccato delivery and expressionist gesture quite different from English decorum.

This project was noteworthy, but it did not automatically put the BPT in the vanguard of a new political movement, as Kavanagh suggests (1985: 16). Its members were careful to reassure prospective patrons such as Rheinallt Jones that they were "entirely dissociated from political movements and parties" and the company's draft constitution states its goal as the cultivation of art rather than politics:

(a) The Bantu Peoples Theatre stands for the cultivation of Bantu Art and Drama.
(b) It aims at improving the undiscovered talents of Bantu Art in Drama.
(c) To be non-political.[18]

This statement was probably designed to deflect queries from white patrons as to the political complexion of plays like *The Hairy Ape*. The very terseness of the final clause suggests dissonance between the nationalist potential of the first two clauses and the disavowal at the end. In the political context of 1936, the BPT draft constitution looks like a defensive manoeuver. The Hertzog Acts of 1936, the impotence of the All-African Convention (AAC) to halt this legislation and the loss of the franchise, and the spectacle of European barbarity in Italy's invasion of Ethiopia undermined the authority of "European civilization." As the convener of the AAC, D.D.T. Jabavu had it:

> All Africans as well as other non-White races of the world have been staggered by the cynical rape of Italy of the last independent State belonging to indigenous Africans. After hearing a great deal for twenty years about the rights of small nations, self-determination, Christian ideals, the inviolability of treaties, ... the glory of European civilization, and so forth, the brief history of the last eight months [since the first Convention in December 1935] has scratched this European veneer and revealed the white savage hidden beneath. (quoted: Kabane 1936: 187)

Despite the attack on white savagery, Jabavu keeps faith with the ideal of civilization that has been betrayed by particular Europeans rather than by Europe as such. By stripping the "European veneer" from the face of the "white savage," he can criticize the brutality of colonization while appropriating the values of modernity. The more conservative Selope Thema makes a related though softer point when he writes that: "tribal life is not a peculiarity of the African race; it is a stage through which all the great nations of today have passed ... we have a right to decide our own destiny and to make our distinctive contribution to the world's civilizations."[19] While these statements do not resolve the contradictory impulses of colonial modernization, they reiterate the idea of modernity as progress and enlightenment, even if Europeans fall short of the ideal.

"History ... and Metamorphosis": Dhlomo's Africa

Dhlomo's later work was influenced by this skeptical regard for "European civilization" but he was energized by the ongoing project to "graft African tradition on to the European" (1977a: 7). In a series of essays written between the founding of the BDS in 1932 and the performance of one of his more ambitious plays, *Moshoeshoe*, in 1939, Dhlomo moved closer to the kind of syncretic theatre of "history and metamorphosis" that he had proposed in "The Importance of African Drama," the 1933 essay cited at the top of this chapter, while criticizing "African Entertainments" for white audiences as "exotic crudities"(1977a: 7). These essays, many prominently placed in the African papers, chart Dhlomo's navigation of fault-lines between and within African, European, and American cultural practices, while his plays of this period, grouped together in a collection that he hoped to publish as "This is Africa," plot a way forward, building on these traditions. Even the 1933 essay offers a trenchant critique of simple oppositions, while examining the prospects and pitfalls of an African National Theatre. Dhlomo defends the value of literary drama, yet he insists that the strong performative qualities of the oral traditions should inform the theatre. He calls for the dramatic representation of social injustice—"African serfdom, Oppression, Exploitation, and Metamorphosis"— but also argues that the modern African dramatist should be artist before propagandist. This tension between liberal education, which affirmed autonomous art against the contingencies of politics may push him and his peers towards commitment, but he holds on to the idea of art as a negative critique of the status quo.

The appeal to art above propaganda does not entail a capitulation to gentility, however. Rather, it attempts to use artistic autonomy to negotiate space for contesting oppression in a public sphere in which direct political mobilization was curtailed. Framing the revitalization of tradition in terms of African legacies, Dhlomo challenges both white and black separatists; he argues in "Why Study Tribal Dramatic Forms?" (1939), that this revitalization should transform not only African forms but also modern drama as a whole by "infus[ing] new blood into the weary limbs of the older dramatic forms of Europe" (1977e: 35). The deference in the question is offset by the critical reference to the "weary limbs" of Europe and to the "tedium" of modern (by implication, genteel English) plays. This disdain for gentility echoes the advocates of the "new social drama"" in Britain, who criticized the drawing room comedy that dominated the commercial stage, but does not merely imitate it. Whereas Dhlomo's themes, exposing corruption and representing metamorphosis as well as oppression, may suggest the influence of Shaw and Galsworthy, his ideal institution of theatre differs from that of the "new drama" in England, whose producers, such as Barker, operated within a modified version of the commercial theatre institution.

Dhlomo calls instead for linking the occasion of performance and the commemoration of rites of passage, seasonal festivals, and the like (1977d: 28–35) and argues in this essay "The Nature and Variety of Tribal Drama,"(1939) that African drama shares with the classical Greek its integration into the social fabric (1977d: 30). This evocation of ritual power does not entail a nostalgic revival of tribal community, but rather the reverse: "The African artist cannot delve into the Past unless he has first grasped the Present. African art can grow and thrive not only by ... excavating archaical [sic] art forms, but by grappling with present-day realities" (1977e: 40). Instead of "static museum-like drama based on primitive tradition and culture"(1977e: 39)—veiled censure of the Lucky Stars—Dhlomo envisaged an African National Theatre that would use those African performance forms that lent themselves to a critical engagement between past and present. While highlighting the public character of these forms, he insists that they be evaluated as "ends in themselves," in aesthetic as well as functional terms (1977d: 27). He appropriates the courtly tradition of *izibongo*, which suggests a desire to legitimate African traditions as potentially universal as Greek tragedy in the European pantheon but his appeal to tradition rests on a distinctly modern invention—*izibongelo*—to bolster his claim that the panegyric form contains elements of dramatic structure and that its function, like that of drama is to "tell the story of the nation" (1977d: 24, 35).[20]

These essays record the impact of re-traditionalist rhetoric but do not submit to it. They appeal to a "sacred inheritance" (1977e: 37) as the "ground on which a great original African drama can be built" (1977d: 35), even as they echo New African skepticism of the "museum-like" construction of ethnicity. They also register the strain on New African faith in modernization at a time when African resistance to "Serfdom, Oppression, and Exploitation" was confronting explicitly segregationist legislation. As arch-racialist George Heaton Nicholls argued, the policy of separate development "along the Native's own lines" defended the chiefs as a bulwark against the "native proletariat" (quoted Dubow 1987: 86). New Africans responded to this trend by insisting on full citizenship. As Jabavu wrote in response to the Hertzog bills: "There are Black men today fully capable of representing their people in the House of Assembly … These bills were framed on the assumed basis that the Black race is a race of children who will continue to be children for all time" (1935: 25–26). Both apologists for and opponents of segregation emphasized the continuity between Hertzog's program in the 1930s and the policy, implemented by Theophilus Shepstone (1817–93), Natal colonial secretary for Native Affairs, of maintaining tribal custom under British authority (Hamilton 1998: 72–129)). Admirers such as Sarah Gertrude Millin called Shepstone "the greatest native administrator South Africa has ever had" (1924: 47). Shepstone's participation in Zulu politics from the reign of Mpande to Cetshwayo (1826–84), the last autonomous Zulu king, earned him the honorific Somtsewu after a famed Zulu hunter (Hamilton 1998: 75), even before his attempt to choreograph Cetshwayo's coronation in 1873. All sides in this debate acknowledged his ambiguous but forceful synthesis in his dealings with Zulu leaders, of the interests of imperial supremacy, and the preservation of indigenous institutions but critics such as Jabavu and Dhlomo argued that Shepstone's policy was the cornerstone of contemporary segregation (Couzens 1985: 138).

Dhlomo's most developed history play *Cetshwayo* (written 1936–37) speaks both to the historical conflict and contemporary debates about African rights. The play focuses on the betrayal of Cetshwayo by Shepstone after the Anglo-Zulu War of 1879 but also articulates Dhlomo's indictment of disenfranchisement in the name of civilization. The representative of the British Empire, Governor Lord Chelmsford, and the ambiguous figure of John Dunn, English adventurer and "white Zulu," speak of imperial power as the irresistible force of modernization as well as conquest, while Cetshwayo and his followers evoke the utopian image of Africa for the Africans.

Dhlomo's Shepstone is more than a mere agent of imperialism, however. On the one hand, Dhlomo incorporates Shepstone's role as kingmaker from the tradition cultivated not only by Shepstone and his friend, imperial writer Henry Rider Haggard in his purportedly documentary account *Cetywayo and His White Neighbours* (1882) but also by Cetshwayo's predecessor Mpande, who called Shepstone Somtsewu. He also modifies Mpande's endorsement to highlight Shepstone's cunning manipulation of Zulu ceremony and thus to heighten the conflict between Cetshwayo and Shepstone.

Dhlomo readily exploits the theatrical potential of Shepstone's king-making as well as the idea of history as the struggle of great men, drawn from Shepstone's mentor Thomas Carlyle and Carlyle's student, Drinkwater, but he also modifies the historical record by fusing two events: the nomination of Cetshwayo as heir in 1861, at which Shepstone arrived to a tense reception which he turned to his advantage, and the coronation, to which Cetshwayo invited him, only to conduct a secret ceremony ahead of time and to keep Shepstone waiting for his appearance (Hamilton 1998: 80–85). The investiture scene in the play incorporates the tension of the nomination scene; it begins with the rivalry between the declining Mpande and his heir Cetshwayo, which is in turn amplified by the contest between Mpande's advisor who stresses the authority of the past and the Bard who praises Cetshwayo as a new light (Dhlomo 1985: 121). While Shepstone's praise of the king and proclamation of himself as the king's servant (123–25) replay the role of kingmaker, Cetshwayo's anger at his presumption marks Dhlomo's resistance to this tradition. At the same time, using Haggard's admiring account to critical effect, he makes his Shepstone an overt imperialist by having him insist not only on the power of the British army: "Like waves, the men roar and charge, ... can never be exterminated" but also on the divine supremacy of the Empire: "Why do you refuse to obey the sacred Voice?" (125; cf. Haggard 1882: 7–8).[21]

In the final silent action of the scene, when Mpande drapes Cetshwayo with a royal robe while Shepstone crowns him with a headdress of "brass and leather" (Dhlomo 1985: 125–6), Dhlomo vividly depicts Shepstone's power as well as his disruption of Zulu rule, but also attempts to redeem Cetshwayo's authority from conflicting accounts that threaten to denigrate it. Dhlomo's headdress appears to correspond to the curious hybrid of Zulu, British, and Roman elements fashioned by the tailor of the Natal regiment at Shepstone's request but his image of the royal robe departs sharply from the small cloak worn by Cetshwayo in a photograph of the proceedings (image: Hamilton 1998: 129), which Shepstone apparently borrowed from "the Natal Society's amateur dramatic group" (Dominy 1991: 73). The fictional transformation of this diminutive garment into "a huge tiger skin," and the transfer of the task of draping it from Shepstone to Mpande (Dhlomo 1985: 125) suggest that Dhlomo was drawing his devious Shepstone in part from *A History of the Zulu War* by Frances Colenso, daughter of Bishop Colenso, Shepstone's ardent antagonist. Colenso records Shepstone wrapping the king in a "little scarlet mantle—formerly a lady's opera cloak" and crown him with a "pasteboard, cloth and tinsel crown" which Cetshwayo tolerated so as to maintain the alliance with Britain (Colenso 1881: 11). This scene shows that colonial legitimation is more complex than imperial conquest. When Shepstone claims in

Dhlomo's play that "the Native" should "develop along his own lines," his assistant Park exposes the contradiction in this policy:

> You want Natives to develop on their own lines. Yet, even now, you are compelled to dictate those lines. For the truth is that they are developing along their own lines at present ... You intend creating many petty Chiefs, who will have no real power ... [who] will be your police and puppets under a Native Affairs Dept. That will see that they never get absolute liberty or full rights or enter the centre of the maelstrom of progress. (Dhlomo 1985: 143–4)

Despite his defense of rights, Park concedes that Shepstone's policy is a "most ingenious and effective instrument for maintaining white supremacy" because it will "advance European interests ... under the guise of ... benevolent guidance" while appearing to "give them recognition and [to] preserve their racial integrity" (145). In other words, it underpins hegemony as *consent* to domination (Gramsci 1971: 12).

The conclusion exposes this benevolence as "protection that is destruction" (Dhlomo 1985: 149). The "sunset of Zulu power" that Chelmsford celebrates as Ulundi burns (165) is reflected in the deterioration of cultivated land and in the squabbles between Cetshwayo's would-be successors exploited by Dunn. Where Shepstone covers the fist of domination with the glove of diplomacy, Dunn speaks plainly to the audience like a Vice in a morality play: "What conflicting forces! Shepstone and the Government, Mpande and the old tribal order, Cetshwayo a new revolutionary force ... there must be an explosion soon and it must blow up poor Dunn to some mighty position"(122). As a settler who had secured alliances by marrying Zulu wives, all the while retaining white privilege, the historical Dunn straddled two worlds but ultimately supported British imperial interests.[22] In the play, he serves as a foil to Cetshwayo's tragic failure to maintain his kingdom. Whereas the historical Cetshwayo lived to plead his case to Queen Victoria in 1882 and to be reinstated, under British control, in 1883, Dhlomo gives his protagonist a dignified death and suggests the struggle for freedom yet to come. He does not resolve the discrepancy between Cetshwayo's defeat—"Now that I am lost, I know that ... [n]o man can live for others before living in himself" (175)—and the promise of a future when "Black kings shall watch over vast dominions" (176) but ends the play nonetheless with the prospect of emancipation: "We shall be free" (176).

Dramatic Agency and the Limits of Colonial Modernity

For all Dhlomo's arguments in favor of African forms, the dramaturgy of *Cetshwayo* is mostly Aristotelian or, more precisely, Schillerian, in that it focuses on a national hero, whose unwillingness to act decisively against the machinations of his enemies brings about his tragic defeat. Although there is no evidence that Dhlomo read Friedrich Schiller (1759–1805), he was familiar with relevant material in the BMSC library: Drinkwater's history plays and Carlyle's essay *On Heroes, Hero-Worship and the Heroic in History* (1841), which show the influence of Hegel and Schiller. Drinkwater's *Mary Stuart* (1925) follows Schiller's play of the same name (1800), emphasizing the individual inner conflicts of Mary of Scotland and Elizabeth I of England, and copying Schiller's famous if fictitious confrontation between the two queens, but even a play of his on a very different subject, *Abraham Lincoln*, shares with Schiller's historical dramas—such as *Wilhelm Tell* (1804)—the focus on a self-conscious protagonist, whose heroism emerges in critical reflection as well as conclusive action. Cetshwayo's final words on the discrepancy between leadership and personhood draw from this tradition.

This focus on subjective doubt in conflict with decisive agency was for Schiller's contemporary Hegel the hallmark of modern drama (1974: 1224–25). Hegel's idea of drama as the "product of a … developed national life" (1159) resonates in Schiller's plays as in Dhlomo's, in which the struggle for national identity at a time when the nation is not yet established is embodied in the person of the protagonist (1224). The historical conflicts with which Schiller and Hegel were concerned—the French Revolution and its impact on German national aspirations—were different from the situation in which New Africans found themselves but the tension between the promise of self-determination embodied by the French Revolution, and the actual conditions of subjection to a paternalist state merit comparison. Dhlomo's essay on "African Drama and Research" reflects an interest in a theory of history which suggests at least the imprint of Hegelian philosophy: "Our ideas of Past, Present and Future do not rest on an unchangeable rock of finality, but on the plastic wax of time, conditions, progress … Man's life is an unfolding, a revealing of new colours and designs … It is this process of birth and revelation that writers should record" (1977c: 19–20). He also shares the conviction that these ideas are embodied by individuals, through their desires and actions in human society, so their passionate confrontations of individuals with each other become the principal site of historical change (Hegel 1956: 23; Dhlomo 1977c: 20).

This emphasis on agency and critique in the drama of history does not make Dhlomo's dramaturgy "Brechtian" (Orkin 1991: 42). Bertolt Brecht and Augusto Boal, both of whom influenced South African theatre a generation later, objected to Hegel's emphasis on individual subjectivity as a form of bourgeois individualism that overemphasizes the protagonist's interiority as the driving force of the action (Boal 1979: 87) and Schiller's prioritizing of the subject's idealism over the realistic portrayal of the social conditions that undermine that idealism (Brecht 1998: 23, 167). In this untranslated note on "controlling 'stage temperament,'" Brecht takes Schiller to task for encouraging histrionics. Dhlomo's depiction of Cetshwayo follows Drinkwater to encourage empathy with the historical protagonist, while highlighting Cetshwayo's heroism as a "great African genius" (Dhlomo 1977c: 19). At the same time, he modulates his version of great man history by stressing the necessity of "historical and anthropological research" into the life of "the masses," (21) who appear in the rousing warrior choruses that punctuate the action and in scenes of everyday life and its disruption by war. When Dunn comments on the repercussions of his actions, this gesture emphasizes rather than critiques his power to manipulate his action and thus owes more to the medieval Vice or perhaps to the Victorian villain than to the techniques—historicization, acting in the third person, critical demonstration rather than the embodiment of character—of *Verfremdung* [estrangement] that Brecht proposed in the "Short Description of a New Technique of Acting" (2014: 184–8).[23] While Dhlomo could be said to share Brecht's view that history should be critically revised by actors fighting for present revolution, his treatment of Dunn's manipulation of Cetshwayo makes Dunn a foil to highlight the king's heroism and to encourage audience identification with the his goals of national emancipation. This tactic is closer to Schiller by way of Drinkwater than to Brecht, whose work did not reach South Africa until the 1950s (Kruger 2004: 215) but we can only speculate on *Cetshwayo's* impact, since it was not performed or published in Dhlomo's lifetime.[24]

However, Dhlomo was able to stage *Moshoeshoe* in 1939, in part because King Moshoeshoe was less controversial than Cetshwayo. While *Cetshwayo* may have stirred up memories of the 1905 Zulu rebellion, *Moshoeshoe* portrayed the wise Sotho statesman whose likeness had already appeared in the Pageants of 1910 and 1936. The king was revered not only for his ability to resolve conflicts between his subjects and refugees from the *mfecane*—the mass migration caused in part by Shaka's expansionism in the 1820s—but also as a model African leader whose perspicacity was sadly missed a century later. The play's emphasis on Moshoeshoe's statesmanship highlighted the Basutoland Protectorate's successful resistance in the 1930s of the South African government's attempts to wrest it from British control. By placing at the center of his play a *pitso* or people's assembly, Dhlomo also called to mind the disputes of the ANC and AAC at the time and thus implied that the wise advice of the great leader could not heal African disunity without community support in the council of elders.[25] Since the performance of the play by the Bantu Dramatic and Operatic Society at the BMSC in May 1939 honored Moshoeshoe Day, these links to current politics would have been explicit.[26]

The significance of *Moshoeshoe* does not lie solely in an aspirational representation of a modern African state. Equally important is the play's attempt to forge a new combination of form, content, and occasion of performance. Although the manuscript used European dramatic conventions, *Moshoeshoe* drew also on African oral narrative motifs that recall and re-present the origin and progress of the clan (Vail/White 1991) or what Coplan calls *auriture* (1994: 8–10), the performance of narrative that can be fully realized only in the ears of the participants. Chief among these motifs would have been the opposition between Shaka, represented in Sotho oral narratives as a Lord of Chaos or a "cloud of red dust" that would "devour our tribe" (1), and Moshoeshoe, who not only maintained peace among Basotho but also gave refuge to people displaced by the *mfecane*. Dhlomo also included in his play the figure of Mohlomi, a diviner of the Bakoena clan who is said to have advised Moshoeshoe to make peace even with the migrants "devouring" Sotho livelihood, and to have prophesied the *mfecane*, though he did not live to see it (1). By including a character whom the historical record marks as already dead, Dhlomo use the creative prompts of the African oral tradition as well as Shakespeare. He telescopes events in the record to intensify the power of the play as subjunctive enactment of "African history ... and metamorphosis" and so to amplify the historical resonances of the present commemoration of Moshoeshoe.

Contemporary reviews noted these resonances but also reflected the influence of modern notions of antiquarian authenticity. Shepherd, at the Lovedale Press, had the previous year judged *Moshoeshoe* "artificial" and, although the performance was praised in the African press for portraying an exemplary leader and for its evocation of Sotho "legend and reality, action and philosophy," the attempt to render Sotho in English received a mixed response.[27] Whereas the *Bantu World* reviewer praised it as the first drama combining the efforts of Zulu–Dhlomo and Caluza–Sotho, choreographer A.P. Khutlang and songwriter, Salome Masoleng, and justified the flowery verse and choppy syntax by claiming that the play's "chief charm lies in the dialogue which is a literal translation from the language in which it was originally spoken," his counterpart at *Umteteli wa Bantu* maintained that "there was too much of the refined" in the dialogue and accused the actors of not being "typically Masotho."[28] Songs in Sotho rather than English, the latter argued, "would have contributed much to making the play a strong living drama of a significant episode in our national life." This dispute reflects the pressure on New Africans to write in African languages rather than English.[29] It spotlights the tension in the play between a desire for idiomatic authenticity and an aspiration to poetic language that might, as Aristotle enjoined, "find the changeless in the changing, the fundamental in the ephemeral" (Dhlomo 1977c: 20) and also shows that the question of authenticity could not be resolved in terms of timeless literary value but rather the significance of the occasion of performance.

The occasion of the performance was likewise subject to strain. The play was performed at the BMSC and not, for instance, at Thaba Bosiu, King Moshoeshoe's high Lesotho stronghold at 1,800 m, now a UNESCO heritage site, or at its modest namesake in Pimville in what is now Soweto, where political meetings and spiritual gatherings have invested both places with the power to inspire if not quite to rebel.[30] Nonetheless, its loosely linked scenes—the *pitso* at the center, framed by suitors' quarrels and encounters between the Basotho and the refugees, mediated by the bard Mohlomi, and ending with a harvest festival (Dhlomo 1985: 229–66)—suggests the logic of commemoration rather than dramatic climax, and the form of a pageant, incorporating varied accounts of past events of ongoing significance. The music for the performance, like that for the Emancipation Centenary, would have alluded to Caluza's songs of national sorrow such as *iLand Act* and *Elamakosi*. Dhlomo attempted to legitimate his play in African eyes by drawing on the Moshoeshoe Day rallies that took place over the two months prior to the premiere in May but this legitimation was under threat by1939. The authority of Moshoeshoe might be considerable, but the political transformation of his nineteenth-century leadership into a pan-African rallying point in the twentieth century was hampered by British imperial interests and the consolidation of white power.

While reviewers made the connection between the *pitso* and the rallies, the harvest festival that concludes the play does not quite bring in the yield. The festival envelopes but cannot incorporate the missionaries who praise Moshoeshoe's genius only to cast doubt on his legacy: "Moshoeshoe ... a man consumed by the smouldering and devastating fire of ... great expectations unfulfilled, of plans and ambitions whose very attainment would give birth to plans and ambitions never to be attained" (Dhlomo 1985: 260–1). This ambiguous praise strikes a cautionary note against the soaring *izibongo* at the end; the allusion to Thaba Bosiu and to "Moshoeshoe the man-mountain, the mountain-mind" (265) invokes his historical example but not the force of historical inevitability. In this juxtaposition of a nourishing if fragile inheritance and a still-born emancipation, *Moshoeshoe* struggles to express New African conviction in "African Evolution and Emancipation" (Dhlomo 1977e: 40), while enacting the constraints on that conviction. Even as it raises the modern standard of "Emancipation from the tyranny of custom and taboo," the play appeals to a precolonial "sacred inheritance, which, as Dhlomo argues in "Why Study Tribal Dramatic Forms?"(1939), should provide "contact with the culture, the life, the heart of forefathers" (1977e: 37). The performance attempted to treat this contact as the simultaneous presence of ancient custom and modern evolution: "The *izibongelo* ... are, as it were, an extensive, dense forest, where we may go to gather sticks to fight our literary and cultural battles, timber to build our dramatic genres, wood to light our poetic fires, leaves to decorate our achievements ... They are the essence of our being, the meaning of our name."[31] By summoning the "sacred inheritance" as a present resource, Dhlomo implies that the spirit of harvest gathering infuses the celebrations of Moshoeshoe Day with an invocation of a past and future national unity in the face of its actual absence.

This invocation of the future as the symbolic presence rather than the developmental result of the past does not turn *Moshoeshoe* into a ritual act to conjure the nation through "sympathetic magic" (1977d: 35), nor does it revive the ancestor worship shunned by Selope Thema as the "iron hand" of the dead. It does nevertheless speak to faith in the simultaneous presence of current experience and ancestral memory and in the embodiment of that memory in surviving forms and institutions that escape modern distinctions between secular history and religious divination. As researchers on *izibongo* argue, this kind of drama is "history with the metaphysics included" (Vail/White 1991: 73). It wields metaphysics with a skeptical edge, however. Showing contemporary audiences Moshoeshoe's struggle against encroachments on his country's autonomy, and the image of this contradictory legacy in the Moshoeshoe Day celebrations, the performance of the play *Moshoeshoe* gives voice and body to the inheritance of King Moshoeshoe, while staging the gap between that inheritance and limited agency for Africans going forward. In 1934, the Emancipation Centenary Celebration was still able to sustain the conviction of the promoters, participants, and audience in the necessary conjunction of emancipation, modernity, and European civilization. In 1939, however, this conviction was evaporating in the white heat of European savagery.

In the decades to come, a revitalized African nationalism would galvanize resistance to the segregationist state and its even harsher successor—apartheid. *Moshoeshoe*, with its juxtaposition of incompatible elements, its lack of resolution, in short, its inauthenticity, does not offer a model for the anti-apartheid protest and resistance that many at home and abroad equate with performance of and in South Africa. Nonetheless, the flaws and fissures in this play and the occasion of its performance speak more truly than a resounding fictional triumph to the realities of the historical moment: the contradictions of colonial modernity extolling the benefits of civilization while restricting civil rights, and the aspirations of New Africans to freedom from both. From a twenty-first-century perspective, the refusal of Dhlomo and his contemporaries to put tribal affiliation ahead of aspirations for universal freedom draws attention once again to the generosity of the New African worldview that might better sustain us in this era of resurgent ethnic parochialism. In order to understand the twenty-first-century variant of this phenomenon, we should look first at apartheid's cultivation of ethnic separatism—and anti-apartheid resistance in the name of non-racial nationalism—and the impact of this conflict on the middle years of the twentieth century. That is the subject of Chapter 3.

City against Country

(Anti-)apartheid Theatre in the Shadow of Sophiatown

Country, as Raymond Williams notes, comes from *contra*, "against." City, on the other hand, comes from *civitas* or "citizenship" (Williams 1973: 307). This etymology complicates the familiar opposition between the city as a "place of light" and the country as a "place of backwardness" or conversely between the country's "natural way of life" and the city's "worldliness, ambition" (1973: 1) and possibly decadence. In the South African context, at a time of rapid urbanization around the Second World War, the contrasting meanings of country and city emerge not only out of the contest between competing ideas and practices of citizenship, progress, and tradition but also out of the paradox of the global periphery in which both country and city are "in the country," the "hinterland of the metropolitan center" (Skurski and Coronil 1993: 232).

This paradox inhabits the hole in the heart of neocolonial modernity, the gap between the promise of emancipation in the city and the practice of retribalization in the country. At the end of the Second World War, Africans in the cities outnumbered whites for the first time.[1] With numbers swelled by the temporary relaxation of influx control to recruit workers for war industries and severe drought that pushed more people off the land, urbanized blacks resisted apartheid with bus boycotts and miners staged a massive strike, spurred by a newly militant ANC Youth League led by Anton Lembede, Walter Sisulu, and Mandela (Thompson 2014: 177–83).[2] When the Afrikaner Nationalists took power in 1948, they tightened residential segregation, reinforced labor discrimination, and forced Africans onto reserves that later became Bantustans. Supported by Afrikaner farmers and displaced "poor whites," the Nationalists spoke an anti-urban language, asserting a primal link between blood and soil for the Afrikaner and in debased form for Africans as well. In practice, however, apartheid subsidized Afrikaner capitalists as well as workers, and depended on African labor even as they restricted African residence in the cities. While English-speaking whites may not have embraced Afrikaner *volk* mythology, their attachment to an imaginary green and pleasant land—which had shaped English identity (Williams 1973: 31–32) and persisted in South Africa despite arid terrain—encouraged a similar distaste for urban life. In a reversal of the classic modern paradigm where urbanity represents progress and enlightenment, the city, especially Johannesburg, came to signify the threat of barbarism. This threat appeared most vividly to anxious whites in the black workers massing in city streets but it also took shape in the figure of the educated "native." Discomfited by "native" cosmopolitans, Afrikaner Nationalists and English fellow-travelers proposed a perverse modernity defined not by urbanity but by rural retreat.

Identifying themselves as *Boere*—meaning both farmers and Afrikaners—Nationalists saw urban enclaves such as Sophiatown as a threat to Western civilization. Settled by blacks since the turn of the century, Sophiatown was the last remaining Johannesburg suburb in which Africans held freehold property but it accommodated people of many colors. Although increasingly overcrowded as blacks were pushed in from other districts designated "white" and although troubled by the symptoms of enforced poverty from unsanitary housing to gangsterism, Sophiatown boasted a vibrant cultural life. Its rebellious urbanity defied apartheid norms of racial purity. The attitude of many Sophiatown writers, from Can Themba (1924–68) to Lewis Nkosi (1936–2010), was ironic, even cynical, rather than politically committed (Chapman 1989: 186; Gready 1990: 152–53), but their attachment to cosmopolitan cultural practices, from jazz to journalism, theatre, and film nonetheless challenged the official reverence for land and race. The threat of Sophiatown's destruction, enacted into law by 1953 and finished by 1959, prompted the late flowering of an integrated urban milieu, which has become the object of nostalgia in the post-apartheid years. We can understand this nostalgia only once we examine Sophiatown in its own time.

In contrast to those whites that claimed to represent civilization while shunning the city, the educated "native" aspired to be more cosmopolitan than the "European." Indeed, the ensemble of practices that made up "Sophiatown" absorbed influences from Africa, Europe, America, and African America in a milieu that was as free as apartheid would allow. In contrast, Afrikaners, self-appointed guardians of European civilization in Africa, imposed a culture of retreat that was at once postcolonial in its anti-British republicanism, and pre-modern in its ideological insistence on rural belonging despite the fact of Afrikaner conquest of African land. Afrikaners also looked to performance, national pageants as well as literary drama, to provide place, occasion, and form to promote their worldview and manage the contradictions lurking in the concept of "country."

African National Theatre and Transnational Modernity

The urban natives most disliked by Afrikaner Nationalists were those who took an interest in international socialism. African theatre had in the 1930s only rarely portrayed urban life but in 1940 the members of the Bantu Peoples Theatre (BPT) described their program in socialist terms: "Here [in South Africa] the economic disintegration, the breakdown of tribal economy, and the impoverishment of Europeans, with the massing of classes in their trade unions and employer organizations, is enriched by the emotional complications of race and colour."[3] They explicitly linked anti-colonial and class struggle: "our situation is symptomatic of the world-wide travail of all repressed communities and dominated classes" (Kabane 1936: 188). The African National Theatre (ANT) saw no contradiction between African nationalism and international socialism. Stressing in the1940 program that the BPT constitution was modeled on the Unity Theatres in Britain, they linked their endeavors with similar projects abroad. Like Unity Theatres in Manchester, Liverpool, and Glasgow, as well as London, and the Theatre Union in New York (which had staged Paul Peters' *Stevedore*, one of the plays suggested by Van Gyseghem), the ANT targeted urbanized workers and intellectuals. But, where their English counterparts could expect support from well-established unions, the South Africans had to endure state harassment and lack of funds, along with the "pressures of war" (Routh 1950b: 23). The paucity of literate members is also significant, especially since the BPT, like the Unity Theatres, favored plays with dialogue in a domestic setting rather than the agitprop sketches of the Workers Theatre Movement whose mass choreography did not depend on learning written lines (Samuel et al. 1985).

Alongside *The Dreamy Kid* by Eugene O'Neill set "in the Negro quarter of New York," the BPT festival at the BMSC included two plays by trade unionist Guy Routh (1916–93), who later left for Britain after the passing of the Suppression of Communism Act (1950)[4]: *The Word and the Act* indicted the hypocrisy of the Native Representatives Act, while *Patriot's Pie* exposed the contradictions in Union policy on African soldiers. Setting both in the township home of *Sonke* [all of us], Routh used a domestic frame but situated the action in an urban environment. Performing the following year in Gandhi Hall in inner-city Fordsburg as the ANT, the group was hailed by communist paper *Inkululeko* [Freedom] as a theatre with national aspirations.[5] The program included *The Rude Criminal* by Gaur Radebe (1908–72), later leader of the Alexandra bus boycotts and mentor to Mandela (Mandela 1995: 85–90), which dealt with the pass laws. The play opened with a "policeman" striding into the hall, demanding passes from the audience, which so alarmed African patrons (Routh 1950b: 23), that some left abruptly, anticipating by two decades the staged assault on audiences in Workshop '71's *Survival* (1976). *Inkululeko* focused on *Tau* by Ivan Pinchuk, also a unionist, which used an actual case to show the "cruel way in which Africans are treated on the farms," and to suggest that, "when a tribe is united, it can fight for its rights and win."[6] This play in Sotho and English featured Dan Twala, who had played Yank in O'Neill's *Hairy Ape* but was better known for organizing soccer; he later became a radio sports reporter. In the plight of African farmers, the ANT showed the tension between country and city, rural expropriation and urban poverty, which would not take the stage again until Zakes Mda's plays in the 1970s.

Yet, brief as the South African experiment was, its national aspirations and topical themes inspired others. Dhlomo's unperformed plays *The Workers* (1941) and *The Pass* (1943) engage more directly with apartheid capitalism than his earlier drama on African kings but portrays working conditions too abstractly "to develop proper unions as well as tactics for strike action" (Orkin 1991: 48). *The Workers* resembles expressionist drama like Georg Kaiser's *Gas* in its attempt to depict a mechanized society and the alienation of labor (Dhlomo 1977f). The chauffeur for the "Nigger-Exploitation Slave Crookpany" calls for union organization but the massed workers are described in mystical terms: "Don't speak of the close of day. It is here and now!" (Dhlomo 1985: 213). The Manager's defense of machines over men—"The machines must not stop ... even if men die like flies. Machines are rare and costly, men are cheap and common ... we no longer believe in the myth of the soul and the dignity of Man but we know that machines have a soul" (216)—recalls Čapek's *R.U.R.* (from the Johannesburg Rep.'s 1936 revival), rather than naturalist strike plays such as Galsworthy's *Strife*. The final scene in which the workers overwhelm the police only to die in an explosion (227) suggests expressionist apocalypse rather than disciplined revolutionary action.

The Pass in contrast is more "rooted in a more clearly defined political vision" (Steadman 1990: 216). Compressed into twenty-four hours, the action tracks the impact of the pass laws and arbitrary police power on a group of Africans arrested in a sweep one night in Durban. The strength of the play lies not merely in its graphic depiction of police brutality but also in the portrayal of different people, including an elderly woman shamed by the arrest, a burglar whose scorn for the police earns him some respect from other prisoners, and Edward Sithole, an educated man and the playwright's surrogate. Although Sithole is acquitted thanks to the legal loophole that exempted educated Africans from the obligation to carry passes, he asserts that the pass laws will radicalize the population: "The pain and hate in our hearts will ... be suckled by our children of the next generation. When these children grow up, the white man will regret [it]" (Dhlomo 1985: 200). With this prediction, *The Pass* looks forward to the Defiance Campaigns of the 1950s and to the "children's" revolt and political theatre of the 1970.

Tribal Cultures and the Battle for a New South Africa

In the 1950s, however, black mobilization was effectively curtailed. State-subsidized institutions, such as the South African Broadcasting Corporation (SABC), which programmed in seven African languages under Radio Bantu from 1962 (Coplan 2008: 199), were harnessed to the production of tribal identities. The Bantu Education Act in 1953 closed the mission schools whose liberal instruction was dismissed by Bantu Affairs Minister Hendrik Verwoerd, who declared that "Bantu had no place in the European community above certain forms of labor" (1966: 83). Bantu Education met with resistance in the Cape and Transvaal but the situation in Natal was complicated by the history of negotiation between Native Affairs and the Zulu Cultural Society, and reflected in debates about the legacy of Shaka. Well aware of the state's manipulation of this legacy to secure apartheid, Dhlomo and contemporaries regarded with ambivalence the promotion of Shaka as "nation-builder" as against the bloodthirsty tyrant of European legend (Couzens 1985: 321–23). Dhlomo worried that those invoking Shaka defended the glories of the past rather than civil rights in the present, to favor a "new kind of tribalism [that] ... encourages non-progressive institutions among the people and made the government the supreme chief and dictator."[7]

Dhlomo's play *Dingane*, about Shaka's assassin and successor, dramatizes this ambivalence. Directed by (white) William Branford, with "African music" by Charles Marivate, the play was performed as *Dingana* by students at the University of Natal Medical School ("Non-European" section) in May 1954, almost two decades after its composition, and revived at the Durban City Hall in August as a "milestone in the indigenous theatre of this century."[8] The stage version revised Dhlomo's 1937 manuscript at several points.[9] The most obvious addition was a prologue performed by Branford, which was part homage to oral tradition and part condescending explication:

> My work tonight is to tell you what cannot be shown. It is a story of the kings of long ago, ... written in books, ... but that is not the real story. The real story is in darkness, ... there is no-one left to show us the truth. But some of the old men tell the story like this, and we must not contradict them. (Dhlomo 1954: 1)

Most important were changes to the confrontation between Boers and Zulus. The 1937 text has a prelude to the Boers' arrival—a discussion among the *indunas* [elders], in which they impersonate Boers and comment on their disrespect for royalty (Dhlomo 1985: 85). Piet Retief's audience with Dingane in which he evades questions about cattle and land theft confirms this disrespect (88–89). Only after Dingane hears that the Boers have broken Zulu taboo by talking to virgins in the *isigodlo* [enclosure], does he authorize punishment. Although the killing is not staged, the text describes a dance designed to dazzle the Boers, followed by Dingane's signal (raising his shield; 97), suggesting but not enacting the assassination to follow. The stage version had the violation of taboo following the elders' discussion lead directly to the ambush, but diluted the climactic assault by having the narrator remind the audience of white power: "Dingane did not get rid of all the white men by killing a few of them ... The gun and horse of the white men were too much for Zulus armed only with assegais and shields, and thousands of warriors were sent to battle, never to return" (Dhlomo 1954: 21). Delivered under houselights, this speech acknowledged the outcome of the Ncome (a.k.a. Blood) River battle without naming it, but spells out the white victory only hinted in the original text, where Shaka's ghost prophesies ruin like Brutus in Shakespeare's *Julius Caesar*. The final comment—"There is nothing left but to mourn for the wreck of Zululand, and there are not words for that" (36)—speaks of the 1950s as well as the 1830s but does so equivocally. Although the narrator's interpretation, as well as the stage presence of the white teacher, reinforces white supremacy, the drama suggests limits of apartheid's idea of "tribal culture" in the gaps between the narrator and the action.

If the term "tribal culture" applies directly to culture sanctioned by Bantu Education, it also describes the ideology of *volkseie* [ethnic uniqueness] that underlay Afrikaner nationalism. The wretchedness of displaced *bywoners* [tenant farmers] in city slums—by 1948, more than half the Afrikaner population lived in urban areas—fanned anti-English and anti-capitalist sentiment and prompted the invention of a divine pact between Afrikaners and the land. This pact recast Afrikaners as the *natural* if not original inhabitants, thus erasing the history of Dutch expropriation of African farmers on the one hand, and recent Afrikaner urbanization on the other. In the conflict between civilization and barbarism, modernity and backwardness, Afrikaners appeared to occupy both positions. They claimed as the descendants of white settlers to represent European manifest destiny, while at the same time cast themselves in the role of autochthonous, indeed *African*, victims of British imperialism.[10]

This potent ideological mix expressed itself in the reenactment of the Great Trek in 1938 (Chapter 1) but was rehearsed already in earlier drama. Despite the claim that the Afrikaans repertoire was more serious than the English (Bosman 1969: 11), it included sentimental comedy and melodrama, as in Andre Huguenet's adaptation of Jochen van Bruggen's country boy *Ampie* (1930) or J.F.W. Grosskopf's *As die Tuig Skawe* [When the Harness Chafes] (1926), which blamed the failures of Afrikaans farmers on Jewish money-lenders, a scapegoating gesture characteristic of this period (Coetzee 1988: 79), as well as dramas of martyrs for Boer freedom.[11] After the electoral victory of 1948, the Tercentenary of Jan van Riebeeck's landing at the Cape on April 6, 1652 offered an apt occasion for representing a triumphant *volk*. The organizers, led by the Federasie vir Afrikaner Kultuur (FAK), recast Van Riebeeck—a servant of the imperial VOC on whose behalf he set up a refreshment station for trading ships—as *volksplanter* or founding father of an *anti*-imperialist Afrikanerdom. In this national drama—or what Leslie Witz calls "apartheid's festival" (2003)—Van Riebeeck stood for whites generally but asserted Afrikaner priority. Pageant Mistress Anna Neethling-Pohl (Chapter 1), author Gerhard Beukes (1913–98), and FAK public relations officer Willem Adriaan (W.A.) de Klerk (1917–96; author of *The Puritans in Africa* [1975], a history of Afrikaners for English readers) reinforced Afrikaner claims to represent European civilization in Africa. The pageant included ideologically mixed motifs from the Pageants of 1910 and 1936, such as the replay of Lady Anne's ball even though it had historically celebrated the British seizure of the Dutch colony, and cast the liberal Huguenet in the role of Van Riebeeck. Nonetheless, the overall mission was to secure Afrikaner supremacy. The pageant began with the masked figure of Africa conquering "Beauty, Righteousness, Prosperity and Faith," reducing all to "spiritual darkness" (Beukes 1952: 100; trans. LK). The second part used the Great Trek to assert that only the Voortrekkers' occupation of the land could reverse this barbarism and build the nation. It treated the Peace of Vereeniging that ended the Anglo-Boer War in 1902 as a defeat and the recognition of Afrikaans as the second official language in 1925 as the moment in which "the Boer was once again at home [*tuis*] in his own land") (145).

Like the Voortrekker Centenary, the Van Riebeeck Tercentenary drew on Preller's populist myth-making to represent Afrikaners as a nation born of struggle on two fronts, against British imperialism and "native" barbarism (Naudé 1950: 10). Unlike the earlier event, which was staged when Afrikaners were still a subaltern group, the Van Riebeeck pageant was produced by a state committed to the *volkseenheid* [ethnic unity] promoted by Geoffrey Cronjé (1945) and P.J. Meyer (1942), who encouraged the Afrikanerization of all "Europeans." The English South African elite, represented by the Chamber of Mines, who had sponsored the Empire Exhibition, responded by attacking the pageant as a "second Voortrekker monument" (quoted: Witz 2003: 114). The Non-European Unity Movement and the ANC, who launched the Defiance Campaign on the very day—April 6, 1952—of the tercentenary, indicted white domination, but targeted what they saw as an Afrikaner variant of Nazi ideology, in "the orgy of Herrenvolkism" in the festival (152).

The Tercentenary appealed to Afrikaners first but cultural support for apartheid came from other quarters as well. The National Theatre Organization (NTO; 1947–62) aspired to link South Africa to metropolitan theatre. Its multilingual organizers—Huguenet, educator P.B.B. Breytenbach, and international director Leontine Sagan—hoped the NTO would combine literary quality and state subsidy on the European model to produce metropolitan classical and modern drama, while making a place for local talent (Huguenet 1950: 200).[12] Although the organizers insisted that they had a "people's theatre ... within reach of the poorest," they acknowledged tensions between the aspirations of urban audiences and the tastes of rural Afrikaners (Stead 1984: 66). They did not acknowledge black theatres nor the black majority excluded from this "people's theatre." As the first season in 1948 shows, NTO offered on the one hand English imports and on the other drama in Afrikaans, including translations of European classics. The English company opened with J.M. Barrie's *Dear Brutus* and continued with J.B. Priestley's *An Inspector Calls*, while the Afrikaans company opened with *Altyd, my Liefste* [Always, My Love], an adaptation of G.E. Lessing's eighteenth-century comedy *Minna von Barnhelm*, and continued with De Klerk's *Nag het die Wind Gebring* [Night Brought the Wind] (De Klerk 1947), which portrayed the conflicting loyalties of an Afrikaner family in the British Cape Colony during the Anglo-Boer War.

The NTO's participation in the Van Riebeeck Tercentenary thus confirms consent to Afrikaner hegemony. The plays for this occasion, *Die Jaar van die Vuur-os* [The Year of the Fire-ox], by De Klerk and *The Dam*, by poet and advocate of South African English Guy Butler (1918–2001), explore the historic tensions between Boer and Briton and their resolution in the marriage plot. While *The Dam* had little impact, the influence of *Vuur-os*, directed by Hermien Dommisse, was magnified by the Hertzog Prize, awarded to both De Klerk and Beukes in 1952, and by the book's assignment in Afrikaans high schools until the 1990s. Published less than two years after the Group Areas Act, which evicted blacks en masse from land coveted by whites, *Vuur-os* rewrites this apartheid legislation as the government's allocation of *white* land to Africans, here the Van Niekerk farm in South West Africa, then controlled by South Africa under United Nations mandate. Kemp, a member of parliament, appears to speak for African interests but the claims of Ngondera, son of deceased servant Kasupi, are marginalized, variously interpreted by Kemp and the Van Niekerk men. After the eldest son Pieter kills Ngondera, his brother Martin—the *verlore seun* [prodigal son] returned from medical service among displaced persons in post-war Germany—promises to make right "wat verkeerd is" [what is wrong] (De Klerk 1952: 91) but that promise is not fulfilled.

The family farm in this tribal drama functions not only as a stand-in for the nation but also as its structuring principle. In his critique of "white writing," J.M. Coetzee describes the fiction of the farm as a "kingdom ruled over by a benign patriarch" (1988: 6) and the Afrikaner view of the nation as an assembly of patriarchs speaking on behalf of dependents who cannot—or should not—speak for themselves. Located on an imaginary frontier, even if in fact in the midst of indigenous communities, the farm marks white dispossession of Africans, even as it claims to represent the natural rights of the Afrikaner. Orkin argues, following Mikhail Bakhtin, that the frontier is the *chronotope* in which "time ... thickens, takes on flesh ...; likewise, space becomes charged and responsive to the movements of time, plot, and history" (Bakhtin 1987: 84–85); the family creates the frontier by treating colonial possession as natural right (Orkin 1991: 59–60). The juxtaposition of wilderness and homestead intensifies the sense of the latter as a citadel formed by the bonds of kinship in which individuals must meet the claims of the tribe.

Vuur-os takes Afrikaner patriarchy as its point of departure but it is not just a family drama. The tensions among family members reflect the contradictory character of Afrikaners as pre-modern postcolonial, simultaneously native to Africa and defenders of European civilization. Although the old father, a Boer General, appears in some ways out of touch with modern times, his dramatic authority is secured at the outset by his "Chair, which dominates the stage," (De Klerk 1952: 1), by stage directions that insist that despite his age "his sun still shines high in the sky," and by his assertion of land rights:

> You know how the first Van Niekerks came here to cleanse the world [die wêreld hier kom skoonmaak het] and, with greatest suffering, paid for it with their life ... Can you now imagine that Okonjenje belongs to anyone other than our descendants, especially since the disturbing things that happen these days on the reservation? (27)[13]

Spoken in rebuttal to Kemp's appeal to "human rights" (25), this claim of ownership rests on blood sacrifice while also uses the language of realpolitik to enforce Afrikaner order against black "disturbances." It also reinforces the myth of Afrikaner identity forged through mastery of the land, in which "the family fathers pay for the farm in blood, sweat and tears, not in money; they hack it out of primeval bush, they defend it against barbarism; they leave their bones behind in its soil" (Coetzee 1988: 85) but also, in claiming to "cleanse the world," asserts the right to set a global example for civilization.

In this scenario Afrikaners play both aggrieved victims and rightful owners, critics of transnational modernity and the bearers of civilization. Pieter is the most tribal of the General's three sons, and fits Kemp's scathing description (in English) of "those desperate Dixiecrats under Capricorn" (27) who treat Africans as "half-people"(71), but he also boasts of his scientific agriculture (27). The youngest, Alexis, vows to abandon small-minded nepotism but still extols the "great renewal" of the nation (45). Martin sympathizes with Alexis, yet defends white rule by asserting the Afrikaner's unique claim to represent Europe in Africa: "I got to know Europe, yes, but also my own country, precisely because over *there* I perceived for the first time what was after all unique in our national life, ... that we are a nation with a *history*, perhaps alone in our hemisphere" (50). This link between the rational authority of history and the attachment to the land soaked with blood borrows from European myths of identity and like them is both modern and primitive, grounded in the written record and steeped in primal blood-ties.[14] What is peculiar in the Afrikaner mix of race and reason is the claim to be both European and, in a limited but enduring sense, African as well. In this white patriarchy, women play helpmeets and blacks little more than specters. Emma, Pieter's long-suffering wife, makes coffee, tends to the children, and cautions her husband against action that might threaten family stability. Gillian, the widow of Desmond Hammond, brother to the Van Niekerk's English neighbor, is the lure that will secure Martin's return to the land and the device which will ensure the unity of Boer and Briton in white South Africa. Where white women have a partial voice, blacks are heard only in incomprehensible song in the background. The Africans, loyal but dead Kasupi and his militant son Ngondera, remain at an unbridgeable distance.

But, more than threats of violence, it is the whites' casual presumption that they control black lives that pervades this play. Emma's apologies for slow maid service and Martin's assurances to his father that he will do what is right for "their" people share an assumption that the patriarchal homestead is the natural basis for social order. Vividly painted in the final tableau—Martin and Gillian on the *stoep* facing the rising sun (92)—this homestead is the foundation on which the "new South Africa" of the apartheid era is ostensibly to be built.[15]

The Dam, directed by expatriate Marda Vanne who returned from Britain for the occasion, also draws analogies between marriage and national unity. Its protagonist Douglas Long, English South African farmer, aspires to shape the land "as he himself has been shaped by it" (Orkin 1991: 60), sharing with Martin van Niekerk the desire to harness this pre-rational intuition to modernity. By damming the river, Long aims to compel the Karoo's "too hard sun" and "intruding stone" (Butler 1953: 8) to contribute to progress. His daughter Susan, like Gillian Hammond, feels that she too belongs to "this land" (69) despite her English heritage. But, while the union between Boer and Briton in *Vuur-os* had securely attached this sense of belonging to land ownership, *The Dam* is less certain. Long's quest to master the land is beset by doubts about his legitimacy and the objections of his Afrikaner neighbor Jan de Bruyn to his disruption of the natural order. Susan is unable finally to accept the proposal of De Bruyn's son Sybrand, and the marriage resolution is scuttled by her preoccupation with the slums where she does charity work, but she also registers a pervasive unease about the impact of modernization on black people.

This uneasiness permeates Long's most heroic vision. While the Christian motifs of the play may suggest the themes of doubt and redemption articulated by T.S. Eliot (Orkin 1991: 60), Long's desire to risk all in bold action—"All men must choose–to risk themselves or not" (Butler 1953: 19)—recalls Goethe's Faust, whose quest for mastery is matched only by his fear of his own weakness, represented in *Faust* by Mephistopheles and in *The Dam* by masked choral figures (Figure 3.1). Long's project recalls Faust's attempt to harness the "unfettered elements" (Goethe 1981: 3:309; translation LK). Faust pursues technological mastery of the environment by attempting to reclaim land from the sea. At its most seductive, Faust's vision conjures the transformation of the sand dunes into a "green and fertile meadow" (3:348; l.11565), cultivated by a "free people [*volk*] on free ground" (l.11580). This vision of desert made fertile by imagination—aided by laborers—recurs in Long's celebration of the finished dam: "What I ... / Find so very precious is the sense / Of a larger, freer world" (Butler 1953: 63). Freedom appears to emanate from the creative combination of mind and hands. But this freedom is not universal; the mind of one controls the hands of many. In "Faust the developer" Marshall Berman (1988: 64) hears Faust extolling the liberation of human energy from the bondage of "unfettered elements" even as he reduces his workforce to tools—"One mind is enough for a thousand hands" (Goethe 1981: 3:346; l.11510). At first glance, Long seems more compassionate, as he appeals to God to "touch these semi-savage things that sweat for me" (Butler 1953: 62), but this paternalist concern grants the laborers no voice other than, as in *Vuur-os*, incomprehensible song, "[w]ide and moaning at the indifferent stars" (67). In contrast, Faust's instrumentalization of his workforce calls forth eloquent dissent from one of his victims who protests against the sacrifice:

Figure 3.1 The dam-builder meets his nemesis: Rolf Lefevre (L) as Douglas Long and Gerrit Wessels as the chorus in *The Dam* by Guy Butler, National Theatre Organization, 1952.

Photograph courtesy of the National Archive, Pretoria; photographer unknown.

> Human sacrifices had to bleed
> Tortured screams would pierce the night
> Where from the sea blazes spread
> A canal would greet the light (Goethe 1981: 3:335, ll.11127–30)

Faust confronts directly the brutality of exploitation in this nightmarish vision of industrial production as well as in Mephisto's blunt exposure of Faust's idea of rational development and efficient labor as "colonization" (3:339; l.11273) but *The Dam* camouflages the realities of colonization with appeals to God's grace and, as an aside to the celebration of a "freer world," a rather disingenuous worry about who "the next employer" of these temporary workers might be (Butler 1953: 62).

The *Dam* is too burdened by liberal doubts to match the clash of forces in *Faust* or even the faith in the paternalist modernization that granted *Vuur-os* authority in the eyes of its target audience. But where *Vuur-os* does not leave the farm, *The Dam* acknowledges urban life in South Africa, especially the conditions of the most rapidly urbanizing section of the population in the 1950s: Africans in search of work:

> It can't be told, it must be met with all
> Five senses; the violence, and smells,
> Degradation, the lurid colours, the dark
> Of a primitive human storm–How sweet

The air is here, how spacious, how secure ...
Into space one-tenth the size of this farm;
A horde of hovels, hedged between a white
And well-lit suburb ...
And mine dumps ... on the other (Butler 1953: 65)

Despite Susan's compassion, the "primitive human storm" suggests not only the "paternalist aspects of assimilationist discourse" (Orkin 1991: 60) but also the alacrity with which paternalism shifts under pressure to fear of "hordes" supposedly at the gates. Black laborers, like Faust's "hands," may enable modernization but, despite examples such as the 1946 strike of 70,000 miners, are not supposed to be modern agents.

Sophiatown Scenes: Defiance, Nostalgia, and Repair

In *The Dam*, individual blacks may be objects of pity but collectively they appear either as a threatening mass or as helpless migrants. Butler's depiction of Sophiatown, in 1952 an overcrowded but still stable mixture of brick houses and backyard shacks, hesitates between the pity that permeates Paton's *Cry the Beloved Country* (1946) and the fear expressed in Verwoerd's *swart gevaar* [black peril] rhetoric, but shares with both an unwillingness to accept black urbanization. Far from streaming into the city without constraint, blacks were being forced *out* into Orlando, Meadowlands, and other tracts of veld that would become Soweto, while whites were taking over central districts like Vrededorp and eventually Sophiatown. The picture of the black horde ignores Sophiatown's thoroughly urban denizens, including professionals such as Dr. Xuma, writers such as Themba, entrepreneurs of all sorts from owners of *shebeens* [speakeasies] to city workers, and a floating population including rural migrants, whose search for work was made illegal by the pass laws, and tsotsis, who openly defied the law. It also paints out the fascination of the place for white intellectuals and tourists and for blacks from all over the country.[16]

This image of Sophiatown, an embattled but vibrant urban settlement living on the edge, persists today, often in nostalgic hues. Looking back from exile, Lewis Nkosi remembered Sophiatown as "on the verge of ... a new and exciting cultural Bohemia" (1983: 24). Part ghetto, part meeting place of black radicals, bohemians of all colors, and organized and disorganized criminals, Sophiatown was an actual but thoroughly *imagined* place that came, despite the violence perpetuated by police as well as tsotsis, to symbolize a utopia of racial tolerance and cultural diversity crushed by apartheid for the "Sophiatown set" (Gready 1990: 140), writers who habituated the place even if they did not inhabit it, and late apartheid writers looking for an intercultural legacy that might nourish urban culture in a post-apartheid future (Stein/Jacobson 1986; Chapman 1989). Its appeal as a model, however imperfect, of an urban bohemia made sense to progressives in the twilight of apartheid but in its twenty-first-century recycled form, as we shall see at the end of this chapter, risks becoming *merely* a set, a backdrop for nostalgic marketing.[17]

Despite Nkosi's optimism about the "fabulous fifties" (1983: 3), Sophiatown signaled the end rather than the beginning of an era: as Nick Visser had it, it was "the renaissance that failed" (1976: 42). Apartheid law undermined the precarious aspirations of New Africans by ending the exemption from the pass laws that had allowed them to enjoy cultural events in the city center.[18] In Sophiatown, gang activity made life dangerous; tsotsis may have embodied outlaw glamour in their American suits and in their mockery of Afrikaans in *tsotsitaal* ([tsotsi lingo; a.k.a *flaaitaal*]; Makhudu 2002). Their defiance of authority earned admiration from urban Africans, much as African Americans in the Chicago ghetto treated the "shady" entrepreneurs among them (Drake/Cayton 1993), but they also preyed on ordinary people and extorted money from entertainers, kidnapped their favorites, such as Miriam Makeba, to bolster their prestige, and even killed those, such as Solomon "Zuluboy" Cele of the Jazz Maniacs, for allegedly playing for a rival gang (Matshikiza 1953). Established impresarios such as Motsieloa and Wilfred Sentso (leader of the Synco Fans and composer of township musicals) were reluctant to play there, while aspiring producers could not match the capital of whites such as Alfred Herbert, who organized *African Jazz and Variety* (Coplan 2008: 213–14) and the Union of South African Artists, which helped African performers secure royalties and rehearsal pay—for a share of the takings.[19] Like the monthly magazine *Drum*, Union Artists attempted to fuse "African native talent and European discipline and technique" (Nkosi 1983: 19) at a moment when both groups by and large acquiesced to this division of labor. The white managers of Union Artists claimed, like Slosberg before them, that they had "discovered" African talent. The pressure of the "white hand," in the words of Job Radebe, one of *Drum*'s "African advisers" (Sampson 1983: 21), was a combination of handshake and manipulation, well-meaning liberalism and pursuit of profit. Nonetheless, Union Artists was able to marshal capital and legal skills to secure royalties and benefits for the families of deceased associates, such as Pitch Black Follies comedian Victor Mkhize. The organization also lent rehearsal space to Athol Fugard and the African Theatre Workshop for *No-Good Friday* (1958), and sponsored the "jazz opera" *King Kong* (1959), based on the life of "Non-European" heavyweight boxing champion, Ezekiel Dhlamini.

No-Good Friday was not the first play on urban African life but it received more mainstream attention than the BPT had done. In addition to Fugard and Nkosi, the workshop included William "Bloke" Modisane, later author of *Blame Me on History* (1963), Nat Nakasa who like Nkosi and Dhlomo had come to Johannesburg via Adams College and *Ilanga Lase Natal*, and actors Zakes Mokae, Stephen Moloi, Ken Gampu, Cornelius "Corney" Mabaso, and two women, Gladys Sibisa and Sheila Fugard. Although shielded by white privilege, Fugard had a visceral reaction to black urban life, especially the "horror" of the Native Commissioner's Court, where Africans accused of "pass offenses" were summarily judged and expelled from the city (Benson 1997: 78). Nkosi argued that Fugard "was interested in learning about how we lived and in practising his art. The politics of the South African situation touched him on these two levels" (Nkosi 1983: 139). He shared Fugard's "concern with the trapped individual," especially the alienated intellectual, dubbed a "situation" by tsotsis mocking Africans seeking white-collar "situations vacant" (140) but faulted the play for sensationalizing township violence. While acknowledging the daily humiliations of Africans by white employers and the police, *No-Good Friday* shies away from direct representation of these conflicts. It dwells instead on residents in a Sophiatown slum-yard, including a waiter, a musician, an ANC activist, and Willie Seopelo, B.A. student by correspondence and "situation," a part written for Nkosi but performed by Moloi (Vandenbroucke 1986: 33). The action focuses on confrontations between these people and tsotsis who are portrayed as gratuitously violent rather than the regrettable products of apartheid structural, but resistance appears futile. The ANC activist Watson is portrayed as an opportunist, and those who resist the tsotsis end up dead. Tobias, a rural migrant, is killed for refusing to pay up, and Willie, the *raisonneur* of the drama, who is finally outraged enough to tell the police, waits at the end for the tsotsis to come for him too.

Although set in Sophiatown at the moment of its destruction, *No-Good Friday* places more weight on individual integrity in the face of defeat than on political action against its causes. When Willie attacks his neighbors' fatalism—"You think we're just poor, suffering, come-to-Jesus-at-the-end-of-it black men and that the world's all wrong and against us" (Fugard 1993a: 50)—and argues instead that "my world is as big as I am. Just big enough for me to do something about it" (51), all he can propose is a private act of conscience. Despite his disdain for the "simple man" from the reserves, Willie ends by praising the values that apparently enabled Tobias to defend his manhood against the decadent city that has made life "cheap" (52). But Tobias's dignity is not an innate aspect of his "simple nature," as argued by Sophiatown pastor, Father Higgins—modeled by Fugard on Father Trevor Huddleston, anti-apartheid pastor of the Church of Christ the King in Sophiatown—but rather an idealistic view of rural life. This idealization is striking because it ignores the reality of brutal farm labor tracked by *Drum* and known to Fugard and because it follows a literary example roundly rejected by urban blacks: *Cry the Beloved Country* (Kruger 2013: 65–71).[20] Alan Paton's story of the pious rural pastor Stephen Kumalo, his odyssey to Johannesburg in search of his son and sister who have fallen on evil ways, and his return to rebuild the church with the help of English farmer-patriarch Jarvis, is whispering in the wings of *No-Good Friday*. Although this play is set in the city, its moral center lies in a lost rural idyll; the reticent Tobias and his spokesman Father Higgins rather than the activist or the intellectual, point the way beyond the "B-type Gangster film" milieu of the tsotsis (Nkosi 1983: 141). As in Paton's novel, the rural characters in *No-Good Friday* are in Nkosi's view projections of white desires for "simple Africans" rather than plausible migrants (1983: 5–7).

The performance of *No-Good Friday* only reinforced this equivocation. Staged initially at the BMSC in August 1958, it garnered enough attention for a one-week run at the Brian Brooke Theatre. Since Brooke did not allow an integrated cast, Nkosi played Fugard's part Father Higgins. Noting his improbable appearance—"a thin hungry black cat in a white priest's robes exhorting the 'natives' to stand up to the criminal elements"—Nkosi nonetheless avows a "surprised nostalgia" for this moment (1983: 141). Modisane, who played the tsotsi Shark, claimed that the group acquiesced to please Fugard (Modisane 1986: 291) yet laments his exclusion from "white society": "I want to listen to Rachmaninoff, Beethoven, Bartok, and Stravinsky ... I am the eternal alien between two worlds"(218). These outbursts articulate the "fantastic ambiguity, the deliberate self-deception" in the African's enactment of figments of a white imagination (Nkosi 1983: 7) that W.E.B. Du Bois dubbed "double consciousness" (1989: 3).They express the volatile ambivalence of the "situation" in the situation, of the African intellectual faced, in the demolition of Sophiatown, with the destruction not simply of his environment, but of his access to the world beyond.

King Kong, the musical intended to showcase African singers and musicians, reflected the showbiz ambitions of Union Artists more than the collaborative method of the African Theatre Workshop. Its creation was nonetheless more equitable than a brief glance suggests, even if an influential critic has argued that the spectacle of multiracial harmony reflected the interests of the show's powerful sponsor, the Anglo-American Corporation, whose chairman claimed that the "disintegration of traditional African society" was a necessary step in the development of a "modern state and society built on European foundations" (Harry Oppenheimer; quoted Kavanagh 1985: 89). It is true that the Anglo-American Corporation sponsored African entertainment but not the African franchise and that it provided scholarships for individuals but no political pressure for universal education. But it is also true that the largely Jewish group—intellectuals, philanthropists, and amateur and professional artists—who collaborated on *King Kong* constituted a dissident class faction at one remove from the Anglo-Saxon economic elite and several from the Afrikaner political class. This dissidence sometimes meant open revolt, as in the case of communists Joe Slovo and Ruth First. More often, as with *King Kong* producer Leon Gluckman (1922–78), musical director Stanley Glasser (1926–2018), writer Harold Bloom (1913–81), and colleagues Clive Menell (1931–96) and Irene Menell (1932–), it meant commitment to the "tenuous liberalism and humane values" that "tempered the harsh social order of apartheid" (Nkosi 1983: 19). While the differences in privilege that separated Jewish patrons from Africans such as Nkosi are undeniable, they shared an affinity for the cosmopolitan potential that made "Johannesburg alive and absorbent in a way no other city in the Republic was" (Nkosi 1983: 19) and an aversion to the anti-urban myths that had captured the Anglo-Saxon as well as the Afrikaner imagination.

If Jewish South Africans were the "catalyst" that brought about "the fusion of Africa and Europe""(Nkosi 1983: 19), America was the base. The Manhattan Brothers followed groups such as the Pitch Black Follies in borrowing from African-American bands like the Ink-Spots, while the white producers drew on the American musical. *West Side Story* (music: Leonard Bernstein; book: Stephen Sondheim, 1957) and *Threepenny Opera* (music: Kurt Weill; Mark Blitzstein's American adaptation of Brecht's 1929 text; 1956) were also discussed.[21] The most telling model was *Porgy and Bess* (1935). Composed by George Gershwin, based on a play by white Southerners Dorothy and Du Bose Heyward, *Porgy* was hailed in *Drum* as "the Negro show sweep[ing] the world."[22] *King Kong* uses Gershwin's subtitle "jazz opera," and echoes of "Summertime" in the overture, but was not a simple imitation. Its musical numbers and the Nguni lyrics were written by Todd Matshikiza, composer, journalist, and musician steeped in African-American and European music as well as African styles from *amakwaya* to *kwela* street music; the English lyrics by journalist Pat Williams (1932–) and the book by Bloom—based on a synopsis by Williams, the Menells, and Matshikiza—drew on the *flaaitaal*-inflected English favored by *Drum*.[23]

In a context where Africans were barred from specialized training, the issue of expertise should be treated skeptically. At its crassest, the comments of Bloom, an avowed amateur (1961: 9), on actors such as Moloi and Gampu, whose performances in *No-Good Friday* and in films like *The Magic Garden* (Donald Swanson 1951), had given them more experience than he, reflect the limitations of the writer rather than the performers. Bloom's characterization (Bloom/Williams et al. 1961: 8) of Matshikiza as an "unknown musician" reveals more than ignorance, however. Matshikiza was not only an accomplished pianist but also *Drum's* Music Editor, writing reviews, social commentary, "How Musicians Die" (1953), and a history of African jazz, "Jazz Comes to Jo'burg" (1957). Unlike colleagues Nkosi or Themba, who professed indifference to African traditions, Matshikiza combined "Music for Moderns," the title of his *Drum* column, with Xhosa lyrics, as in his musical praise poem, *uMakhalipile* [The Undaunted One] (1953), in honor of Father Huddleston, and *Uxolo* [peace], a cantata for 200 voices and a 70-piece orchestra, commissioned for the seventieth anniversary of Johannesburg in 1956 but largely forgotten (Kruger 2013: 58–61). The misrecognition of Matshikiza's contribution to South African culture is less a matter of individual oversight than a symptom of the tension between African aspirations to modern agency and white tendency to naturalize Africans as merely natives.

This tension structures the relationship between text and performance. Nakasa's account in *Drum* of Dhlamini's life follows him from mission school and petty crime to triumph as a powerful if undisciplined boxer, and on to his murder conviction and subsequent suicide by drowning; he also mentions Dhlamini's humiliation by the white champion and the violence of the police (Nakasa 1959: 27). Although Bloom agrees that Dhlamini was a "symbol of the wasted powers of the African people" (1961: 17) and has King Kong's manager Jack comment bitterly about discrimination against African champions (77), his script focused on the decline of a glamorous legend, from "the winner" (31) to "a man [with] writing on him–bad, rubbish, gangster" (78) (image: Kruger 1999a: 953). The performance of Nathan Mdledle, lead singer for the Manhattan Brothers, complicated this melodramatic image of a muscle-man gone bad, however. A "tall rangy man with expressive hands" (Glasser 1960: 21), Mdledle used his supple baritone and deft movement to give his character more subtlety than the text implied. Jack as played by Moloi had a reflective quality that muted the swagger of the stereotypical boxing manager and provided contrast with the other parts, particularly the outlaw glamour of gangster Lucky (Joseph Mogotsi) and shebeen queen Joyce (Miriam Makeba), displayed in their duet "Back of the Moon," named after a real Sophiatown shebeen.

Although not written into the published book, the actors' interpretation of their roles and of African dramatic and musical resources beyond the bounds of the dialogue and the initial sketch of the "jazz opera" enliven the original cast recording. Most overt in Jack's bitter comment and in the chorus of washerwomen, who point to the discrepancy between King Kong's legend and the shabbiness of township life, social criticism surfaces in the ironic use of musical themes. During King Kong's prison term, Joyce throws a party to a flashier version of "Back of the Moon," while Jack trains a substitute for King Kong to a "ragged version" of "Marvellous Muscles" (Bloom 1961: 56–58). While this critical comment through comic gesture and musical phrasing may have been prompted by some actors' struggle with English lines (Glasser 1960: 17), it also borrowed the comic style of the Pitch Black Follies, which the Manhattan Brothers would have known. The variety format did not reflect African ignorance of "proper theatre" (Bloom 1961: 15). It suggests rather that the repertoires—from the American musical and European drama to African variety and African-American vaudeville— available to cast and production team were too intertwined with one another to be reduced to a single "dramatic line" (Glasser 1960: 13).

The performance of *King Kong*, rather than its musical or textual notation, put the American musical in contact with African variety; it also revealed the syncretic character of the African forms that Bloom's text marks flatly as "traditional." The songs with Nguni lyrics by Matshikiza are important not simply because the first uses Xhosa and the second Zulu to speak to African audiences who might be put off by "talky" theatre (Kavanagh 1985: 109), but because the music and lyrics draw on layered practices of *Africanizing* performance that absorb transnational elements without being overwhelmed by them. The overture, for instance, despite its English title "Sad Times, Bad Times," is a Xhosa saying sung to a jubilee choir melody with a swing beat, as the gangsters disrupt the morning routine:

Ityala lalamadoda	It's the fault of these men
nguAndazi noAsindim'.	It's "I don't know" and "it's not me" ...
Alaziwa-mntu	Nobody knows (Bloom 1961: 27)

While the lyrics allude to township passivity against gangsters, the music resembles less the *kwela*-inflected jazz of the 1950s than the national laments written a generation earlier by composers like Caluza whose music combines *amakwaya* with ragtime. The second song *Hambani madoda* registers the gloomy mood after Joyce dismisses King as "rubbish" but speaks also to the trials of urban Africans, as did Caluza's *Sixotshwa emsebenzini* (Chapter 1), mixing lament and work song:

Hambani madoda	Keep moving, men.
Siy' emsebenzini	We are going to work
Sizani bafazi	Stand with us, women
Siyahlupheka	We are suffering
Amakhaza nemvula	cold and rain
Ibhas' igcwele	the bus is packed
Sihlutshwa ngotsotsi	we are preyed on by tsotsis
Basikhuthuza	they rob us of what we have
Siyaphela yindhlala	we are half-dead with hunger
Nemali ayikho	there is no money
Hambani madoda	keep moving, men
Isikhathi asikho	time is short
Hambani madoda	keep moving, men
Isikhathi asikho	time is short.

(Bloom 1961: 82–83; trans. modified: Kavanagh 1985: 111; and LK)

Although it opens with the staccato rhythm and masculine bass of the work song, this is not the "thousand [male] voices" that Kavanagh associates with mass struggle.

The expression of longing has more in common with *isicathamiya* (soft-shoe dance from Solomon Linda to Ladysmith Black Mambazo) than the rallies of the Defiance Campaign. Combined with the women sopranos, an addition unlikely in 1950s *isicathamiya*, it expresses an intimate quality reminiscent of the women and men in Caluza's Double Quartet. Even though this song is not repeated and the finale has a conventional reprise of King Kong's theme, the note struck by this restrained lament gives Kong's death an element of celebration as well as mourning.

Matshikiza's appropriation of New African *amakwaya* does not mean that these songs have nothing to do with protest; on the contrary, they mine a long tradition of singing resistance against the grain of genteel choir melody, but they suggest tenacious survival rather than heroic defiance. The locus for this survival is not in the first instance the ANC, but the subdued subversion by migrants, or, to a certain degree, women. By including these songs in a musical environment (jazz) that is otherwise modern and transnational, Matshikiza extends the boundaries of the modern by suggesting ways of representing Sophiatown's cultural complexity that includes women and men, lament and celebration, European, African, and American influences. The originality of this combination, the challenge of cross-cultural work under apartheid, and the death of Dhlamini who inspired it, made this production memorable but unrepeatable: neither the 1979 nor the 2017 revival had much to offer apart from nostalgic spectacle, even if the latter was enhanced by the choreography of Gregory Maqoma.[24]

"Music for Moderns": Playing Sophiatown in the Twenty-First Century

Matshikiza's motto "music for moderns" and the idea of Sophiatown as the crucible of a modern South Africa found its most vital expression in the historically informed *Sophiatown*, which was produced in 1986 and revived in 1994 and again in 2016, but feeling for the place resonated already in the shows produced in the years directly after the district's demolition. Before he left South Africa for good, Matshikiza composed *Mkhumbane*, a cantata for 200 voices, with text by Paton. It dealt with life in Cato Manor, a township outside Durban slated for demolition, in an idiom close to *Hambani madoda*.[25] As contacts with whites declined with police harassment under the Group Areas Act, African impresarios worked on their own. *Washerwoman* (1959) and *Frustrated Black Boy* (1961) by Wilfred Sentso were performed at the Johannesburg City Hall but did better in Soweto. *Back in Your Own Backyard* (1962), by Ben "Satch" Masinga—who had played Jack's flashy sidekick Popcorn in the London revival of *King Kong*—was performed in Soweto with Union Artists support, as a vehicle for Masinga and singers such as Letta Mbulu.[26] This combination of star turns and a melodramatic plot of love thwarted, often by female infidelity, held together by the dominant personality of the actor-manager-composer, was to become the successful formula of popular theatre in the townships, developed above all by Gibson Kente (Chapter 5).

Nostalgia saturates many depictions of Sophiatown on post-apartheid stages, such as Mothobi Mutloatse's musical adaptation of Modisane's *Blame Me on History* in *Bloke*,

Zola Maseko's film *Drum* (2004), or celebrity impersonations like Sello Maake ka Ncube as Can Themba in *House of Truth* (2016; an adaptation of his stories and essays). All of these borrowed from Lionel Rogosin's 1960 docudrama *Come Back Africa* (2010), the clip in Johannesburg's Museum Afrika that features Themba holding forth in his bedsit the House of Truth, his famous wit muffled by alcohol. In contrast *Sophiatown*, created by the Junction Avenue Theatre Company (JATC) in 1986, may have seemed nostalgic in 2016, the year of its thirtieth-anniversary revival, but its original production during the apartheid "emergency" dramatized place and people in ways both playful and critical. Produced at a time when looser censorship allowed for the selective screening of Rogosin's film and the publication of interviews and memoirs of formerly banned writers, the play kept nostalgia in check by drawing not only on memoirs by Modisane and Don Mattera but also on research by the South African History Workshop. Their example in turn prompted other thoughtful adaptations of Sophiatown writing such as the stories by Themba, *The Suit* (1993) and *Crepuscule* (Gumede 2014).

Before looking at these post-apartheid treatments, we should briefly review JATC's work. From its inception, JATC collaborated with historians to unearth competing South African pasts so as to better understand its presents.[27] *Randlords and Rotgut*, JATC's second play but the first with an integrated cast, opened the second History Workshop in 1978. Like the paper by historian Charles van Onselen whose title it borrowed, *Randlords and Rotgut* exposed the hypocrisy of mining magnates who denounced worker drunkenness while profiting from the sale of liquor, and showed how such moralizing served to rationalize the interests of capital in a labor force sober enough to work but drunk often enough to be dependent on wages. The satirical impersonation of capitalists Sammy Marks, owner of the Hatherley Distillery, and Lionel Philips, chairman of the Chamber of Mines, recalled in dress, gesture, and singing delivery the politicians and arms merchants of the London Theatre Workshop's *Oh! What a Lovely War* (1963) and the stockbrokers in Brecht's *St Joan of the Stockyards* (1932).[28] Following Brecht, JATC illuminated the legacy of the past in the present and reminded its (predominantly white dissident) audience that they inherited the evils as well as benefits of apartheid capitalism. If JATC's depiction of capitalism was Brechtian, their workers owed more to anti-apartheid marches or plays such as *Survival* by Workshop '71, some of whose members joined JATC. This combination highlighted public rather than private action, and men rather than women; the only female character is a white prostitute, and cross-gender casting of some roles in the 1989 revival (Orkin 1995: 78) did not alter the masculinist cast of Van Onselen's historiography.

Where *Randlords and Rotgut* was satirical, *Sophiatown* was reparative. The premiere of the play, along with the publication of interviews (Stein/Jacobson 1986), and the republication of banned texts such as Modisane's *Blame me on History*, encouraged the rediscovery of a historical model of an integrated Johannesburg. The plot was based on a serious prank: Nakasa and Nkosi advertised in *Drum* for a Jewish girl to stay with them (Purkey 1993: xii). Out of the interaction between the visitor Ruth and members of a Sophiatown household—the matriarchal owner, Mamariti and her daughter Lulu, the gangster Mingus and the "situation" Jakes—JATC recreated a microcosm of the suburb while also probing the connections between 1950s bohemia and the tentative integration of the 1980s. The situation of the "situation" Jakes (played originally by

Patrick Shai) and Ruth (Megan Kriskal) articulated the mixture of alienation and celebration in urban life (image: Kruger 1999a: 88). As Jakes remarks after Ruth brings Jewish Sabbath wine:

> God is One and God is Three and the ancestors are many. I speak Zulu and Xhosa and Tswana and English and Afrikaans and Tsotsitaal and if I'm lucky Ruth will teach me Hebrew ... And this Softown is a brand new generation and we are blessed with a perfect confusion. (JATC 1995: 180)

This celebration honors a moment suspended in time, hope for solidarity thwarted by apartheid, which engineered this place and would demolish it. Fahfee, numbers-game man and ANC activist—played by Ramolao Makhene (1947–2003), a founding member of Workshop '71 (Chapter 6) who went on to act and direct in the 1990s—reminds the audience of links between 1955 and 1985: "This year is the year of the Congress of the people ... What's the number? It's 26. 26 June 1955." (49) As director Malcolm Purkey remarks, the association of dates in the anti-apartheid calendar (June 26, 1955 launched the Freedom Charter) with the numbers game constitutes a key structuring principle of the play (1993: xii). Implying that predicting an imminent ANC victory at that time had something of a magic spell about it, this invocation bears witness to the intensity of the desire for change as well as the difficulty of achieving it.

Sophiatown participates not only in historical repair but also in critical debate about the legacy of the 1950s. The play uses the anti-apartheid moment of the Defiance Campaign (1952) and the post-apartheid utopia anticipated in the Freedom Charter as counter-narratives to the 1986 "emergency" but also suggests the limits of this utopia. The mass resistance to the removals summoned by the Defiance Campaign never materialized, in part because Sophiatown's poorer tenants saw the Meadowlands houses as an improvement on their overpriced backyard shacks. Nonetheless, *Sophiatown* emphasizes the value of memory for healing as well as agitation. The songs that punctuate the domestic scenes with comments on the struggle link the self-aware but insufficient rebellion of the *Drum* era with the militant politics of the 1980s. The final song, *Izinyembezi Zabantu* [Tears of the People], juxtaposes pathos and militancy, as the play concludes with a litany of those who, like Matshikiza, died in exile:

> And out of this dust Triomf rises. What triumph is this? Triumph over music? Triumph over meeting? Triumph over the future? ... I hope that the dust of that triumph ... covers these purified suburbs with ash. Memory is a weapon. Only a long rain will clean away these tears. (JATC 1995: 204–05)

Invoking Mattera's recollection of the Sophiatown rubble as a prediction of its revival—"Memory is a weapon" (1987: 151)—the song is a both a lament and a call to arms to revive Sophiatown buried under Triomf, the name that apartheid planners gave the white suburb that replaced it.

In the twenty-first century, Triomf is once again Sophiatown and its gentrification has led boosters in neighboring Westbury—Mattera's birthplace formerly known as Western Native Township—to promote this suburb as an intact version of the "old"

Sophiatown. Reread in the context of the play's thirtieth-anniversary revival in 2016, the invocation of healing rain invites a certain skeptical regard. If the dominant tone of *Sophiatown* was Jakes's mixture of irony and hope in the spirit of Mattera, the better turn-of-the-century adaptations of Sophiatown material drew more from Themba. B.A. graduate and Sophiatown wit, Themba saw himself as South Africa's Underground Man on the model of Dostoyevsky, by turns corrosively cynical and intensely emotional.[29] The productions at the Market of two adapted stories by Themba, *The Suit* (1993) and *Crepuscule* (2014), illuminate the contradictory impulses pulling at South African society after 1990. While other adaptations in the 1990s like Muthobi Mutloatse and Corney Mabaso's musical riff on *Baby, Come Duze* (1991), Themba's photo-novella of flirtation and betrayal (1957), seem like *Bloke* (1994), Mutloatse's sentimental version of Modisane's self-lacerating autobiography, both nostalgic and casually misogynist. Barney Simon's direction of Mutloatse's adaptation of *The Suit* conveyed precisely the tension between high melodrama and sharp irony that animated Themba and his subjects—lively, self-aware, and sometimes self-destructive ghetto denizens.[30]

The story is simple—and peculiar. Philemon discovers his wife Tilly with another man who escapes, leaving behind his suit. To punish his wife, Philemon insists that she treat the suit as an honored guest, but his elaborations on this torment—culminating in a party in which she has to perform this cruel charade for the guests—hastens her death. The story's debt to melodrama is clear but closer reading reveals the complex combination of the penny-dreadful, the profound torment of Dostoyevsky's *Gentle One*, and the naturalistic depiction of the daily trials of urban blacks. Under Simon's direction, the shifting third person narration juxtaposed with dialogue additions by Mutloatse, Simon, and the cast, highlighted different views of the action, not only that of husband and wife but also the interventions of friends and comments of passers-by. The high melodramatic color of Themba's aggrieved husband was complicated by the actors' delivery: Sello Maake kaNcube and Stella Khumalo were angry, ironic, and pathetic by turns (Figure 3.2). Their performances suggested the allure but also the limits of gender typing in ghetto melodrama, while the narrative reminded the 1990s audience of the wretched environment that prompted this story. In *The Suit*, as in the best moments of *Sophiatown*, the past offers neither an explanation for the present nor a refuge from it. Instead, it uses the cruelty of this Sophiatown story to sharpen the corrosive edge of the interregnum, tracing the effects of violence and disorder on post-anti-apartheid Johannesburg, which has escaped the forms and gestures of anti-apartheid theatre but cannot yet imagine a post-apartheid stage.

Crepuscule, Themba's fictionalization of his relationship with Jean Hart, an Englishwoman who left South Africa thereafter, invokes the twilight between historical eras and thus offers an apt conclusion to this chapter.[31] The story was written in the early 1960s, after Themba left his position as deputy editor of *Drum* for exile in Swaziland. Themba's first-person narrative opens with the crush of black people leaving the "morning township train" merging into the stream of white commuters. He homes in on "young ladies" whose "colourful frocks" in the sunlight "articulate the silhouettes beneath," teasing the male observer (Themba 1972: 2). This scene juxtaposes a vivid picture of the city commute with the narrator's ironic reflections on the Immorality Act—repealed in 1985—that prohibited interracial sex but here prompts him to defy

Figure 3.2 Can Themba's corrosive melodrama *The Suit*: Sello Maake kaNcube and Stella Khumalo in the stage adaptation by Barney Simon and Mothobi Mutloatse, Market Theatre Johannesburg, 1993.

Photograph and permission by Ruphin Coudyzer, FPPSA: www.ruphin.co.za.

the law, declaring that he can still "feast for free" on the street looking at white women whom he might get to "know for real" in Johannesburg's cosmopolitan district of Hillbrow (3). Themba's story is more complex than this voyeuristic opening suggests, however. While the narrator's interest in Janet may have been prompted by political protest—"I insist on my right to want her"—and flavored by quotations from Dickens's *Tale of Two Cities*—"It was the best of times, it was the worst of times" (3)—and impish mockery of Dickens's taste for melodrama—"in the superlative degree of comparison only" (4)—his account of the affair is enlivened by humor, from his recollection of the "sisters" in his favorite Sophiatown shebeen tying a *doek* [scarf] over Janet's blonde hair in "the current township style" (4), to his inner debate about the relative power of the *amadhlozi* [ancestors] and the half-jack of brandy to wake him up and send him to Janet's apartment in a narrow escape from the police who raid his bedsit on a tip from his previous lover Baby (6). Despite the ironic distance, the recollection of the "crepuscular shadow life" of those who break apartheid law in search of love or meaning "for ourselves" (8) poignantly points to the author's life after Sophiatown, to isolation—and death by alcohol—in exile.

Khayelihle Dominic Gumede's adaptation of *Crepuscule* follows *The Suit* in that it uses the songs of Sophiatown to frame the action and puts the narration in productive tension with scenes in which Sophiatown denizens who appear only indirectly in the story so as to insert playful ripostes to Can's perspective. He does so first by adding Themba's self-deprecating laughter, which he recalled from the museum clip from *Come Back Africa* (Gumede 2014: 9), underneath the protagonist's opening comments about young ladies in colorful frocks, and thus using Can's laughter to puncture his bravado. Second, he gives more dialogue to women who challenge Can. These include characters from the story, Can's aunt Mam' Dora and former lover Baby, as well as women performers playing men—Lerato Mvelase played both Baby and Can's sidekick Kleinboy. Gumede also adds new characters, Janet's husband Malcolm and her housekeeper Ousie Lethabo, whose blunt comments puncture the romantic haze around Can's recollection of his affair. While these changes do not make a feminist out of the rake, the role that Themba affected in life and writing, they portray the couple's deep affection while acknowledging the context, a society deeply scarred by violence against women and men. As Robyn Sassen wrote of the Market production with Kate Liquorish as Janet and Leroy Gopal as Can in 2015, Gumede's adaptation was more than a "doomed love story"; the play opened up the story's "social underbelly with a sharp tool."[32] The penultimate scene, which brings Baby to Janet's suburban house (rather than the Hillbrow apartment in Themba's story) as she is preparing to return to England, tries awkwardly to transform the vitriol with which Baby treats Janet in the story into a kind of reconciliation, but the last scene ends on a more sober note. Gopal as Can, swaying as if on the train to Swaziland, singing "Ifikile le min'" [My [day] has come], is overtaken by former student and fellow writer Stan [Motjuwadi], who represents those who survived exile to return home. Alone again after Stan leaves, Gopal lingered in the spotlight with a letter pulled from his pocket, dropping it behind him as he left. Liquorish entered and read Janet's words: "thank you for the crepuscule" (2014: 103–4). These vignettes suggest not only regrets for love suppressed by apartheid but also the shadow cast by those who died in exile. Performed half a century since the story, the play *Crepuscule* prompts reflection about "brooding clouds" on the horizon—as Phaswane Mpe painted the turn of our century—the consequences for women, men, and others of endemic gender violence that lurks beneath the glamour of stage and screen.

In the long view, these adaptations of *Crepuscule* and *The Suit*, which have prompted feminist revisions by Makhozasana Xaba (2013) and others, bring together Nkosi's skeptical regard of his "surprised nostalgia" (1985: 141) for Sophiatown in the 1960s, and, as indexed by *Native Nostalgia* (2009) by the much younger Jacob Dlamini (1973–), current debates about nostalgia and the demands of critique and repair of the fractured state of South Africa today. More immediately, the exile of Themba and kindred writers marked the death of Sophiatown as the apartheid regime state attempted to bury the district and with it the threat posed to white supremacy by educated natives. The drama of that state, its *Triomf* and *Retreat*, is the subject of Chapter 4.[33]

Dry White Seasons

Advance and Retreat of the Afrikaner Ascendancy

In May 1961, the year after the apartheid government banned the African National Congress (ANC) and the Pan-African Congress (PAC) and with them mass resistance to apartheid, Prime Minister Hendrik Verwoerd took South Africa out of the British Commonwealth. Although the all-white referendum on the republic was promoted as national self-determination, the idea appealed little to English-speaking voters (Moodie 1975: 285) and the celebration at the Voortrekker Monument, where Verwoerd invoked God's will before a crowd dressed in Voortrekker garb (1966: 32), left no doubt as to the priority of Afrikaner interests. The reprise of Boer themes and theatrics in 1961 went beyond the Voortrekker Centenary of 1938 and the Van Riebeeck Tercentenary of 1952 to insist that the *tuiste vir die nageslag* [home for posterity] proposed in 1945 by Geoffrey Cronjé, racial eugenicist and member of the Nazi-inspired Ossewa Brandwag [Ox-wagon Sentinel], strive for an ethnically exclusive *volkstaat* rather than a liberal democracy (Meyer 1942). This legacy may discomfort twenty-first-century Afrikaans-speakers who identify with a democratic South Africa but the yearning for a *volkstaat* still animates a vocal minority at home and white nationalists abroad.

In order to understand the Afrikaner ascendancy, we need to track the consolidation of Verwoerd's republic, which proceeded by abolishing or capturing institutions that had supported liberal culture. In 1962, the relatively cosmopolitan National Theatre Organization (NTO) was replaced by provincial Performing Arts Councils: Performing Arts Council of the Transvaal (PACT), Cape Performing Arts Board (CAPAB), Performing Arts Council of the Orange Free State (PACOFS), and the Natal Performing Arts Council (NAPAC). The Performing Arts Councils were supposed to promote the "vitality of the artistic life of the country" and express its "cultural aspirations" toward European standards (Dept. of Information 1966: 1) but their repertoires reflected the Nationalist agenda. Afrikaans plays dominated, supplemented by translations of European classics. Until the mid-1970s, only CAPAB produced South African English drama, including Fugard's *People are Living There* (1969) but not his more controversial *Blood Knot* (1961) and *Hello and Goodbye* (1965).[1] In the same

---

Mongane Serote's poem *Dry White Season* (1973) uses the image of frost on dry grass to evoke apartheid.

period, PACT, CAPAB, and PACOFS produced over a dozen Afrikaans plays, from N.P. van Wyk Louw's Anglo-Boer War drama, *Die Pluimsaad waai ver* (PACT 1966) to P.G. Du Plessis's white prole tragicomedy *Siener in die Suburbs* (PACT 1971) and Chris Barnard's dark farce about a misfit clerk *Die Rebellie van Lafras Verwey* (PACT 1974). Even after the Soweto uprising challenged the compulsory use of Afrikaans in schools, the Commission of Inquiry into the Performing Arts insisted that "national education is the cardinal task of the theatre, to establish language, national sentiment, ... and the entire life of the nation" (Commission of Inquiry 1977: 19) while favoring institutions that employed Afrikaners.[2] In this respect, cultural institutions joined bodies like the Land Bank, the Volkskas, and the Handelsinstituut to further *volkskapitalisme* (O'Meara 1983)—advancement of the volk through capital subsidy. This integration of state and culture impeded the development of a public sphere, in Habermas's sense of a realm of civic debate outside the state, as the Nationalist state sought to curtail dissidence by appealing to *volkseie*.[3]

Ironically, the very success of the Afrikaner ascendancy caused concern. The PACs so effectively promoted Afrikaans theatre that they completely absorbed the private groups that had been in operation since the 1930s (Commission of Inquiry 1977: 6). The Publications and Entertainment Control Board (PCB, 1963–93) tended to allow the publication of Afrikaans texts even when it censored live performances.[4] Worrying that Afrikaans theatre might not survive without state support (Commission of Inquiry 1977: 20), the PCB appealed to Afrikaner ethnic loyalty by allowing the publication of plays deemed too provocative for performance such as *Die Verminktes* [The Maimed] whose author Bartho Smit (1924–86) ran the subsidized Afrikaanse Pers's literary division. Ethnic loyalty was no guarantee of state favor, however. No less a national figure than N.P. Van Wyk Louw defied Verwoerd's call to praise "Afrikaner patriots" (quoted: O'Meara 1996: 128). Commissioned for the first Republic Festival in 1966, Louw's play *Die Pluimsaad waai ver* [The Plumed Seed Blows Far] challenged the sacred history of the Anglo-Boer War, named by Boers the "Second War of Independence." Whereas Preller's 1938 pageant had favored the intransigent President Kruger of the then South African Republic (Chapter 1), Louw foregrounded the moderate President Marthinus Steyn of the Orange Free State, acknowledged the indiscipline and even cowardice of the troops, and earned the ire of the Prime Minister.[5] After Verwoerd's assassination, his followers proposed a Verwoerd prize for "patriotic literature" but were rebuked by Louw, who compared the proposal to the Stalin Prize (O'Meara 1996: 129).

Disputes between *verkrampte* [narrow-minded] and *verligte* [enlightened] Afrikaners were conducted in the press but ultimately adjudicated by the Afrikaner Broederbond, the secret society (founded 1918) that promoted Afrikaner interests in politics and economics and kept dissidents in line. While independent theatres tackled interracial drama like *The Kimberley Train* by Lewis Sowden (1958) or Fugard's *Blood Knot*, the PACs rejected the Afrikaans equivalent, Smit's *Die Verminktes*, published in 1960 but performed locally only in 1977. Smit's next play to expose Afrikaner hypocrisy, *Putsonderwater* (1962) had an invitation-only production (PACOFS, 1969) seven years after its publication. Moreover, the promotion of Afrikaans did not extend to subsidizing plays by Coloured writers, even if most were native speakers (Goldin 1987: 164–68). Although published by an Afrikaans press, *Kanna Hy Kô Hystoe* (1965) by Adam Small (1936–2016), a drama of a native son returning to Cape Town from Canada, received a student staging by DRAMSOC at Small's base at the University of the Western Cape (UWC) in 1971 and a short run by the Cape Flats Players at a nurses' residence in nearby Athlone in 1972, followed by a subsidized production by an all-white cast (PACT 1974). Praised by internationally known André Brink (1935–2015), the play was nonetheless distorted by white attempts to distinguish "Coloured" from "pure" Afrikaans, so as to uphold the official denial of the *taal*'s hybridization of Asian and African as well as European elements (February 1990; Roberge 2002).

Although operating within very different institutions, Fugard shares with Smit a desire to portray intimacy between white and brown people deemed undesirable by apartheid. Their challenge to racist law takes most blatant form in the drama of miscegenation, but it also animates plays that depict people from one group—*Hello and Goodbye* portrays poor whites who were supposed to join the middle class with *volkskapitalisme*, while *Kanna* depicts the effects of poverty and segregation on Coloureds. By probing the contradictions in the Calvinist precepts of (sexual) self-control and (economic) self-reliance fundamental to Afrikaner *volkseie* (De Klerk 1975) and thus exposing the alienation of poor Afrikaans speakers in the Afrikaner Republic, some plays such as Smit's *Putsonderwater* and in milder form Du Plessis's *Siener in die Suburbs* pushed the limits of official tolerance. While these plays revel in the excessive sentiment, emphatic conflicts, and sudden reversals associated with melodrama on racial themes since Dion Boucicault's *The Octoroon* (1861), they share with this unacknowledged American ancestor the obsessions of a not-so-master-race, especially the twin specters of "poor whites" and "passing whites" haunting white supremacy. The Southern gothic of *The Octoroon* found local expression in Reza de Wet's dark farces; her breakthrough play *Diepe Grond* (1985; published 1991) acknowledged this legacy belatedly in her English title "African Gothic" (2005).

The obsession with white purity and divine destiny that characterized Afrikaner nationalism at its height may seem far away in 2018 but Afrikaans drama since 2000 has reformulated these themes to address Afrikaners who see themselves as an embattled white minority in black Africa. Although not the only writer to dramatize aggrieved white men—Paul Slabolepszy has done so vividly in several plays in English—Deon Opperman (1962–) has become the dramatist of this generation, most controversially in *Ons vir jou* [We for thee] (2008) a musical wrapped around the emotional appeal of the historic anthem *Die Stem van Suid-Afrika* and the new and controversial song *De La Rey* by Bok van Blerk (Louis Pepler), which called in 2006 for Boer general Koos de la Rey (d.1914) to come back to lead the Boers.[6] Opperman's earlier plays—the anti-military *Môre is 'n Lang Dag* [Tomorrow will be a long day] (1984) and the anti-clerical *Die Teken* [The Sign] (1985) published in 1986—challenge Afrikaner patriarchy, its glorification of blood sacrifice, and its reduction of women to the bearers of progeny, but his post-apartheid drama appears to redeem Afrikaner patriarchs fighting against alleged marginalization. In the epic *Donkerland* (1996) and the television series *Hartland* (2011), Opperman explores the new reality in which women and black people assert their rights in ways discomfiting to Afrikaner men used to calling the shots. The chapter will conclude with this recent drama but begins with one of its key sources, the melodrama of miscegenation, articulated both by Fugard, who writes in English but draws on his mother's Afrikaans, and Smit, who combined European influences with local inspiration to expose sanctimonious hypocrites in dramas both domestically relevant and globally resonant.

Although Fugard's plays from *The Blood Knot* (1961) to *Boesman and Lena* (1969), produced mainly by independent or university theatres, are not generally associated with Afrikaans drama, produced mainly by the state from 1960, his work belongs in this chapter. First, as Fugard himself noted, his characters would plausibly be speaking Afrikaans (Fugard/Simon 1982: 48); second, his plays share with their Afrikaans counterparts the sentimental garrulity and the underdog types of melodrama. Both encourage empathy for suffering, without directly indicting the social agents causing that suffering. In a decade of political repression, from the police state established in the early 1960s to the rebellion of students and workers in the 1970s, domestic drama—in venues from state theatres to university drama and township halls—depicted the intimate harm that apartheid inflicted on South Africans, from the inner circle, such as Senator Harmse in *Die Verminktes* through forgotten cousins of the master race such as Hester in *Hello and Goodbye*, to "step-children" (Sarah Gertrude Millin's euphemism for brown people; 1924) such as Kanna. Portraying maimed individuals in the apartheid hearth offered a critical foil to the grandiose notion of the "home for posterity" for the volk. But as this chapter will show, the drama of, in, and against the Afrikaner ascendancy focused on family feeling written in blood, sweat, and tears but never managed to keep politics out of the picture.

Melodramas of Hypocrisy

On September 3, 1961, *The Blood Knot* opened at the Rehearsal Room at Dorkay House in Johannesburg before an invited audience of blacks and whites.[7] On November 11, it reopened at the commercial and therefore all-white Intimate Theatre and went on to tour the country for a year. Directed by Fugard, who played the light-skinned Morris (Morrie) against Zakes Mokae, his collaborator from *No-Good Friday*, who played Zachariah (Zach), Morrie's dark-skinned brother, the play depicts the intimate conflict between two differently black men who act out obsessions with race on each other's bodies and minds. The conflict explodes when Morrie assumes the role of a "white gentleman" in anticipation of a visit from their white pen friend Ethel but, after she breaks off the correspondence, turns his frustration on to his brother. Infected by the trappings of whiteness as he wears the "gentleman's" suit bought for the visit, Morrie attacks Zach with racial insults, while Zach first goads and then threatens to assault his brother. The threat of violence is deflected only by Morrie's appeal to the "blood-knot" that binds them. Since Morrie and Zach are Coloured, this mark of kinship includes not only their immediate family but also the legacy of white sexual exploitation of blacks, rewritten as white fears of miscegenation.

The Blood Knot was not the first South African play to expose the contradiction between white fears of racial contamination and apartheid discrimination against black and brown people. Liberal English-speaking audience would have known Lewis Sowden's *Kimberley Train* (Library Theatre, Johannesburg, 1958) and Basil Warner's

Try for White (Cockpit Players, Cape Town, 1959), both of which portray thwarted unions between Coloured women and white men.[8] Bilingual spectators may have also read Smit's then unstaged play *Die Verminktes* [The Maimed], which juxtaposes the discrepancies between public condemnation of miscegenation and the secret practice of sexual exploitation by Afrikaners. Very few whites would have known *Ruby and Frank*, Dhlomo's play about doomed love between a Coloured woman and an African man, performed in 1939.[9] *The Kimberley Train*, *Try for White*, and *Die Verminktes* all use conflict around family in domestic settings to filter social anxieties about racial difference. They share a mode of representation that vacillates between naturalism and melodrama, between dispassionate exposure of the effects of public policy on individual psychology and a sentimental play for audience sympathy for suffering victims. Melodrama furnished the best techniques for dramatizing the consequences of apartheid's most sensational legislation, the Population Registration Act (1950), since the act not only required the social separation of "European," "Coloured," "Indian," and "Bantu" groups but also destroyed families by taking away children who apparently deviated from their parents' racial classification. Stories of brown children born to white parents or white fiancés exposed as Coloured received more publicity than Coloureds who gained official "reclassification" as African or Indian (Orkin 1991: 82–84) but these stories had the shape of melodramatic sensation scenes rather than rational analysis. Melodrama in the state and on stage replayed the contradictions of an impossible policy and unmanageable social situation in the domestic setting.

The significance of Fugard's choice to portray black characters and their points of view emerges in contrast to other plays by white authors that focused on white prejudice, even when expressed by Coloured characters. In *The Kimberley Train*, Bertha, the mother of Elaine whose marriage with John Powers is thwarted, agrees with John's father—her white employer—when she states that Coloureds are "second" as opposed to "third-class" (Sowden 1976: 27), reinforcing Nationalist propaganda discouraging Coloureds from affiliation with Africans as Black (Goldin 1987: 166–75). At the end, Elaine appears to submit to the notion that whiteness is an essential, and therefore inaccessible, birthright: "It is not enough to pretend to be white. You have to know the colour inside you and not give a damn … I wasn't able to do it" (Sowden 1976: 73), echoing a line of white writing about Coloureds that descends from Millin's *God's Step-Children* (1924).[10] Millin's later book *The People of South Africa* (1954) reflected English liberal ambivalence about Coloured aspirations; she vacillates between the idea that "whites have lost nothing by Coloureds passing for white" (265) and the insistence that Coloureds constitute a "definite, inferior and static race" whose members may "assert their whiteness" but are doomed to fail (269). But Elaine's passage into white society by way of the "Kimberley train," an underground organization supporting Coloureds "trying for white," suggests that whiteness is a product of socialization and thus that "pretending" may be enough. The Afrikaans actress Kita Redelinghuys may have persuaded white spectators of Bertha's acceptance of second-class status but casting a white person in the role suggested instead that passing was possible.[11] Although the melodrama of doomed love may make the experience of oppression feel like fate, this conclusion implies that passing is a response to policies, in this case, state enforcement of apartheid. Ironically, it is not Elaine but her white fiancé who ends up "trapped"

(Sowden 1976: 75). As Nandy wrote of the "white *sahib*," John is less a "dedicated oppressor" than a "self-destructive co-victim, … caught in the hinges of history he swears by" (1983: xv).

This contradiction between the ideology of race that allegedly determines identity from birth and the reality of conflicting responses to socialization, public policy, and personal prejudice reaches its high and low points in *Die Verminktes*. Whereas *The Kimberley Train* dwells on the suffering of victims, *Die Verminktes* indicts the powerful, the agents and ideologues of the Afrikaner Nationalist state. If the former focuses on the fate of the country's "step-children," the latter confronts the sins of its white fathers: the social bigotry, political ambitions, and bad faith of so-called Christian rulers. In Nandy's terms, these are not "co-victims" but indeed "dedicated oppressors." Smit's attack on the structural violence of apartheid policy, embodied in Professor Jan Barnard, and exposure of the contradiction between public policy and private hypocrisy, in Senator Bart Harmse, secretly the father of Frans, his Coloured housekeeper's philosopher son, made the play unperformable in Verwoerd's republic, despite Smit's earlier successes with *Moeder Hanna* (NTO 1958), an Anglo-Boer War drama, and *Don Juan onner die Boere* (NTO 1960), a comedy of country life.[12]

Despite its critique of Afrikaner hypocrisy, *Die Verminktes* is itself maimed by it. The play begins bravely, with the sound of the (recently banned) hymn, *Nkosi sikelel' iAfrika* from the African manservant's offstage room and dialogue that challenges the official line on apartheid. When Barnard vilifies Coloureds as the "hole in the dike" that should protect the "little white island" from the "black sea" (Smit 1976: 16; trans. LK), Frans retorts that the "only difference between white and Coloured is that the one was lucky enough to be born on the sunny side of the wall and the other unlucky enough to be born on the dark side" (17).[13] He debunks the "scientific" validity of the "pure race" (18), implying that desire for power has motivated Afrikaners' denial of their hybrid history. But, although the play allows Frans to expose the expediency behind Barnard's ideological crusade and the hypocrisy behind Harmse's objections to his son's marriage to his ward Elize, it apparently cannot allow the couple to escape. In the end, it abandons the logic of dramatic conflict for a retreat to racial determinism, prefigured by stereotypes like the *skollie* who blackmails Harmse while swallowing the Senator's insult "swart vuilgoed" [black trash] so long as he gets his money (24).[14] Harmse's attempt to deter Elize from marrying Frans expresses the racial panic made famous by *The Octoroon*, when he tells her that her blood and "all the generations of your people" will compel her to search Frans's body for signs of degeneration (35). Finally, Harmse's castration of his own son, while it exposes what Aimé Césaire called the "decivilization" of the colonizer (1972: 13), shifts the blame to the victim.[15] This act of mutilation provides the occasion—but not the motivation—for Frans to switch from protecting Elize to threatening her, ironically in his white father's words, with the "dark blood of Africa."(56).

At this point, the play's struggle to accommodate the competing ideologies of racial determinism and liberal individualism renders it incoherent. After Elize commits suicide, Smit has Frans suddenly switch roles from articulate hero to grotesque coon as he delivers the final speech in the language of the skollie: "Ma' die mêem hoef nie sêd te wies nie oer die castration nie–kôs why, da' wag nou 'n White Future vi' har [But the madam mustn't be sad 'bout the castration, 'cos why, now there's a White Future for her]" (57). This scene vacillates between "moral significance and an excess of thrill, sensation, and strong affective attraction" in the manner that Tom Gunning identifies with the melodrama of sensation, which forgoes the moral transparency usually associated with melodrama for the "horror of opacity" (1994: 51).[16] Juxtaposed with the crescendo of *Nkosi sikelel' iAfrika* offstage, the meaning of this mimicry is hard to decipher: is Frans fomenting revolution by throwing the "master's" racial projection back in his father's face? Or is he simply reverting to type? In the PACT premiere of 1977, seventeen years after the play's publication, Don Lamprecht played this scene in blackface caricature. Although the logic of the action thus far suggests that nurture not nature determines racial identity, the resurgence of ethnic sentiment represses that acknowledgment and the play reverts to racial typecasting, retreating into the laager.[17]

While Smit's struggle in *Die Verminktes* to represent the drama of apartheid as a national as well as personal tragedy renders the finale of his play unreadable, Fugard's focus in *The Blood Knot* on the dreams of oppressed individuals hides the structural violence that put these individuals under pressure. While Sowden and Warner remain focused on white perspectives, however, *The Blood Knot* dispenses with white characters and captures the emotional force of brown characters' absorption of white prejudice. When Zach returns home from work at the start of the play, he grapples with the impact of racial capitalism on his body as he settles into a footbath—"I do the bloody work ... It's my stinking feet that's got the hardnesses but he goes and makes my profit" (Fugard 1992: 5)—even if the agents of exploitation are unnamed: the "he" in Zach's complaint could be his boss or the man who sold the foot salts.[18] Morrie hopes that they might escape wage slavery by buying a farm in "one of those blank spaces" on the map (10) but, in a period when 100,000 Africans and several thousand Coloureds a year were displaced (Thompson 2014: 193–95), finding a farm was unlikely. These local conditions keep the story grounded in reality more concrete than "the universal human plight of Man's search for ... meaning in an alien world" (Vandenbroucke 1986: 262). Fugard's characters may resonate globally but their dramatic power comes from this vivid picture of their particular situation.

Fugard shows us in Morrie a character who has internalized apartheid prohibitions and, in Zach, one who appears at first to be "better adjusted to the humiliations and pleasures of daily life" (Vandenbroucke 1986: 65) but is ultimately as oppressed as Morrie. Morrie filters apartheid prohibitions through conflicting emotions about his own body and his brother's. Morrie's ambivalent affection for his brother is constrained by his attempts to deflect Zach's desire for sex by introducing a pen friend and by his own sense of the risk of even thinking of a white woman:

> When they get their hands on a dark-born boy playing with a white idea, you think they don't find out what he's been dreaming at night. They have ways and means, my friend ... Like confinement in a cell, ... for days without end ... All they need for evidence is a man's dreams. Not so much his hate. It's his dreams that they drag off in judgment. (58–59)

As Orkin argues, following Foucault, characters like Morrie have so internalized the state's omniscience that the actual exercise of police power is rendered unnecessary because "he who is subjected to the field of visibility and knows it, assumes responsibility for the constraints of power; he has them play spontaneously on himself; … he becomes the principle of his own subjection" (Foucault 1979: 202; Orkin 1991: 102–03). In Morrie's scenario of surveillance and punishment, the all-seeing Calvinist God whom Morrie invoked before (46) joins the police state and his internal censor to oppress him.

The pathology of this self-inflicted punishment is nowhere more striking than in the sinister game that closes the play. Morrie initially rationalizes his reluctance to wear the suit intended to woo Ethel with the notion of supposedly innate racial identity: "[t]he clothes don't maketh the white man. It is that white something inside you, that special meaning and manner of whiteness that I got to find" (Fugard 1992: 73). The final battle has each confronting the other in desperation made more poignant by Fugard's scruffy appearance in the suit (Figure 4.1). At this point, the suit is no longer the disguise that Morrie hoped might allow him to pass but he finds that "special meaning" instead in the sudden fear in Zach's eyes for this "different sort of man" (79). It is the fearful gaze of his black (br)other, not any inner drive, that makes Morrie act white and it is fear that provokes Zach in his turn to threaten violence. As the photograph suggests, Morrie draws strength

Figure 4.1 "No longer a white gentleman": Fugard as Morrie in *The Blood Knot*; Dorkay House, Johannesburg, 1962. Photograph: John Cohen.

Photograph courtesy of the National English Literary Museum, Grahamstown.

from Zach's expression of fear, but both are still trapped in the same dreary room. Although they interrupt the game before anyone is physically hurt, the characters are left with the sense that, "without a future," the "blood-knot" that binds them is all they have (96).

Many critics find this final image compelling but they appear to have missed an important but invisible figure that prompts the action. While some have read this scene as a moving, if ambiguous affirmation of brotherly love (Brown 1961), others as a depiction of resignation to oppression (Nkosi 1983: 139–41), none has acknowledged the unseen scapegoat that makes both the battle and the truce possible. When the game seems to flag, Morrie conjures up a "horribly old woman" who stands in for their mother (Fugard 1992: 91). Only once they have chased off this imaginary mother with stones and insults, blamed her for "mak[ing] life unbearable" (92), and laughed derisively at her exposed body, are they able to continue the game and reinvigorate their sense of brotherhood. By blaming his black mother rather than his unknown (and possibly white) father or the white paternalist state, Morrie blames his humiliation on a victim rather than a perpetrator of apartheid. By reducing the mother to female body parts, this play risks being consumed by its final sensation scene, rendering opaque the familial relations that both bear the brunt of apartheid brutality and constitute the crucible for resilience if not resistance. If *The Blood Knot* is an example of a "more authentic South African drama" (Orkin 1991: 90), then its claim to authenticity rests directly on its representation of black men as exemplary South Africans and implicitly on its exclusion of the black woman who gave birth to them.

The Blood Knot's exposure of the impact of white supremacist ideology and apartheid policy on black men captivated white English-speaking liberal audiences, who, in Nadine Gordimer's acerbic phrase, "sat fascinated, week after week, as if by a snake" (1964: 55). Opening in South Africa months after Verwoerd proclaimed the republic and touring during a year when state action against political resistance intensified, the play reminded audiences of the day-to-day consequences of racist legislation. It was hailed as a "milestone in South African drama" (Read 1991: 43) not merely for probing the intimate penetrations of apartheid law but also for putting a black and a white actor together on stage. By 1964, audiences in Britain, Belgium, and America had joined in praise for the play and condemnation of the society that gave birth to it (43–49). But this success marked the end rather than the beginning of the era of interracial collaboration that had begun with leftist groups in the 1930s and continued to Fugard's workshop that produced *No-Good Friday* (1958). Although it made this kind of collaboration more visible to mainstream audiences, *The Blood Knot* was not the "first multi-racial cast" (Orkin 1991: 91) but the *last* for more than a decade. After the Group Areas Amendment of 1965, casts and audiences had to be segregated. Fugard could no longer play opposite Mokae, who had to choose exile in order to continue acting and activism. The publicity around *The Blood Knot* encouraged the Anti-Apartheid Movement in Britain to intensify its efforts. In June 1963, the Anti-Apartheid Movement and 276 playwrights promised to refuse rights to "any theatre where discrimination is made among audiences on grounds of colour" (quoted: Vandenbroucke 1986: 78).

Well without Water: Sex, Race, and Poverty
in the Afrikaner Heartland

Increased isolation from metropolitan culture encouraged *verligte* as well as *verkrampte* Afrikaners to turn inward. But volkish solidarity was undermined by the unresolved discrepancy between the promise of *volksontwikkeling* [Afrikaner advancement] and the reality of poor whites left out of the Afrikaner ascendancy. It was also weakened by the state's hypocritical claim, despite its systematic brutality, to represent a Christian nation. As Fugard remarked in 1963, "this country is in the grip of its worst drought– and that drought is in the human heart" (1984: 83). Fugard's "family plays" (Fugard/ Simon 1982: 40) of this period—*People are Living There* and *Hello and Goodbye*—use encounters between family and quasi-family members in run-down domestic settings to dramatize the effects of this drought on poor whites. The "second-hand Smits of Valley Road" in *Hello and Goodbye* (1965; Fugard 1991: 115) belong to this class. To be sure, even poor whites had more than blacks: in *Hello and Goodbye*, Johnnie Smit's access to his father's disability pension from the railways enables him to keep the three-roomed house in Port Elizabeth and to enjoy beer and trips to the beach. But, as Johnnie's recollection of his father's work during the Great Depression vividly conveys, these meager privileges brought poor Afrikaners up against the fragile line that separated them from blacks: "The kaffirs sit and watch them work. The white men are hungry ... And all the time the kaffirs sit and watch the white man doing kaffir work, hungry for the work" (Fugard 1991: 121). Fugard further highlighted the comparison between the Smits of Valley Road and the brothers of Korsten by publishing these plays and *Boesman and Lena* together as *Three Port Elizabeth Plays*.

The details of place weave the local texture of *Hello and Goodbye*, but the plot focuses on two individuals who struggle with each other and the dead weight of their father. Johnnie pretends almost to the very end that their father is still alive, and his alternately violent and caressing handling of his father's crutches reinforces the old man's power and replays Morrie's obsession with an omniscient authority that is state, deity, and absent father in one. Hester, on the other hand, has something of Zach's "drive" and honest recognition of harsh facts (Fugard/Simon 1982: 44). But where *The Blood Knot* culminates in the racist game between brothers, *Hello and Goodbye* ends after Hester discovers *nothing*—no inheritance amid the bric-a-brac and no father brooding in the next room. She returns empty-handed to the uncertain life of an aging sex-worker in Johannesburg and Johnnie shifts from pretending his father is still alive to taking on his crutches.

The minimal action in both the 1965 run directed by Barney Simon with Fugard as Johnnie and Molly Seftel as Hester and in Fugard's definitive production at the Space in Cape Town (1972) with Bill Flynn and Yvonne Bryceland, who created most of Fugard's female roles until *Road to Mecca* (1984), registers the influence of Beckett, especially *Waiting for Godot*, which Fugard directed at Dorkay House, and of Albert Camus, whom Fugard was reading at the time (Fugard 1984: 62, 61). As a rebel, Hester has abandoned social constraints and faces up to her empty life but Johnnie's fatalism and bad faith represent the "point of view of the play" (1984: 44). Although Johnnie understands his fate in familial terms, he uses language that echoes Afrikaner rationalization of collective suffering to justify his own weakness. Treating both his father's loss of a leg on the job and his own failure to take his place as "God's will" (Fugard 1991: 84), Johnnie reflects the fatalistic combination of Afrikaner nationalism and Calvinist dogma, which declared, at the inauguration of the Voortrekker Monument, that "disasters, adversity, privation, reversals, and suffering are some of the best means in God's hands to form a people" (*Gedenkboek* 1940: 11). In Bryceland's performance, Hester rebels not only against her father's manipulation, his "groaning and moaning and what the Bible says" (Fugard 1991: 85–86) but also against Calvinist patriarchy: "There's no father, no brother, no sister, no Sunday, or sin ... The fairy stories is finished. They died in a hundred Jo'burg rooms ... You want a sin. Well, there's one. I *Hoer* [whore]. I've *hoered* all the brothers and fathers and sons ... into one thing ... Man" (108). While Johnnie tries to blame Hester's rebellion on impure blood—"You weren't a real Afrikaner by nature, he said. Must have been some English blood somewhere, on Mommie's side" (101)—Hester's obliteration of boundaries between kin and stranger transgresses Calvinist mores and challenges the patriarchal regime that separates women into two classes: mother and whore, guardian of national purity or scapegoat for its contamination. Hester is scandalous not merely because she challenges prejudice against sexually and economically independent women, but because she strips her mother of Afrikaner heroic endurance when she describes her— and her peers—as a small figure who "fell into her grave the way they all do–tired, *moeg*." (126). Her attack on Afrikaner symbols makes her indictment of the family an indictment of the volk as well.

At the same time, putting these words in the mouth of a whore defuses the scandal. Like the spectacle of Morrie's and Zach's bodies in intimate struggle that hypnotized white spectators, Hester's account of her life risks making the character an object of fascination rather than understanding. The premiere with Fugard and Seftel opened in the segregated Library Theatre on October 26, 1965 after a week of private performances for integrated audiences. This venue put Fugard's play in the company of English dramas such as Sowden's *Red Rand* (1937) and *Kimberley Train* (1958), and prompted distinct responses from Afrikaans and English critics. Where Simon saw Afrikaans expletives in Fugard's South African English text as "love and respect" for his mother tongue (Fugard/Simon 1982: 48), reviewers were not sure. W.E.G. Louw, brother of N.P. van Wyk Louw, described the performance in Cape Town as true to life but talky.[19] Sowden lambasted the play as a "torment" and Greyling for "exaggerating and saying nothing"; the latter—in the *Vaderland*—spoke for lower-middle-class Afrikaners perhaps too close to poor white life for comfort.[20]

Putsonderwater [Well without water], directed by Fred Engelen for PACOFS in Bloemfontein, had more potential to reach a broader Afrikaner audience but was thwarted by state interference. Although set in an unnamed town described in allegorical language, Smit's play shared features with Fugard's: both depict the sexual repression, social isolation, and economic deprivation of small-town Afrikaners and both use the figure of the whore to embody the effects of this repression and the desperate rebellion against it. But neither the abstract location nor the French source, Georges Bernanos' novella, *Sous le soleil de Satan* [under Satan's sun], made *Putsonderwater* safe for state subsidy. First performed to acclaim in Belgium, it was taken up by PACOFS in 1969 only after a student production at Rhodes University, the *English*-language institution that hosted the premiere of Fugard's *Boesman and Lena* the same year.[21] After deliberation in Parliament, the PCB granted PACOFS a short run for invited guests only.[22] Presented by Smit as an "attempt to depict the West's crisis of belief" in a "fantastic parable" (1962: i), *Putsonderwater* indicts the hypocrisy of church and society notables in a *platteland dorpie* [Afrikaans small town].[23] Following Smit's location of the action an "imaginary *dorp* in the open desert of our country" (1962: i), designer Henk Hugo (University of the Free State) used a spare set in which walls separating public and private space were only hinted at. Apart from the well, there was no naturalist clutter to interfere with the naive fancy of the central character Maria, daughter of Jan Alleman [John Everyman] (image: Kruger 1999a: 114) Nonetheless, Engelen favored naturalistic acting for the quarrels between Maria and her respectable exploiters, the doctor, the police sergeant, and the pastor or, more pointedly, *dominee*, which made the Calvinist context of *Putsonderwater* inescapable.

When the play opens, one of these men has already impregnated the girl. Although taken in by her fantasy of the City of Gold prompted by the *dominee*'s promise to take her to Johannesburg, which she associates with the apostle John (in Afrikaans: Johannes), she is nonetheless capable of twisting these self-important old men "around her little finger" by playing up to the desire of each to believe that he is "baas [boss] op Putsonderwater" (Smit 1962: 5). Each man plays a sort of Prospero, demanding obedience from Maria as Shakespeare's character did of his daughter Miranda in *The Tempest*, and encouraging her belief in their power as magicians (7): the *dominee* recites the Song of Solomon, while the doctor claims to have power over life and death. In their desire to magnify "paternal omnipotence" through displays of magic and in "neurotically touchy" reaction to perceived threats to their authority, they resemble the Prospero that Octave Mannoni endows with the petulant and arbitrary power of the colonizer (1964: 105).[24] Maria is no Miranda, however. In Rita La Grange-Steyn's performance, she resembled a younger Hester Smit (image: Kruger 1999a: 114), whose rebellion against her Calvinist father also took the form of sex, and whose vulnerability expressed itself sometimes in unpredictably aggressive behavior. Maria shoves the *dominee* down the well when he tries to rape her and the police threaten to kill her father for the crime but her attempt to confess prodded by the undead *dominee* provokes patronizing disbelief. She resembles both the fallen Magdalen and the Virgin Mary (Smit 1962: 64–65) but where Bernanos's Catholic story redeems his heroine by association with Mary, Smit's Calvinist drama leaves his closer to animal abjectness than divine grace.[25] Treated by her pursuers as a creature—from a bitch in heat (3) to a doe in the Song of Solomon (20)—she occupies a position similar to Prospero's enemy Caliban, an object of conquest and discipline. But there is no simple allegory here; Maria does not stand for the colonized masses nor does she represent all poor whites dominated by an Afrikaner elite. Nonetheless, struggling with the language of her manipulators—biblical, moral, and the lore of poor white migration to the Golden City—she speaks in part for these victims. Her incomprehension of the power struggles around her in the arid heart of Afrikaner country and her obliviousness to the indigenous people in this place make her an unwitting participant in Afrikaner hegemony.

The figure of the seer trapped by poor white conditions, manipulated by shadowy but powerful agents, plays a central role in several Afrikaans plays in the early 1970s, a brief liberal moment after the culture wars of the 1960s and before the eruption of Soweto pushed Afrikaner authorities back to the *laager*. *Siener* [seer] *in die Suburbs* (PACT 1971) by P.G. du Plessis (1934–2017) and *Die Rebellie* [rebellion] *van Lafras Verwey* (SABC Radio 1971; PACT 1975) by Chris Barnard (1939–2015) take their cue from the clash between the prosaic reality of alienated Afrikaans proles in the so-called Afrikaner Republic and their dreams of transcendence or revolt, which are ultimately shattered by the intrusion of that reality.[26]

The most famous photograph of PACT's production of *Siener in die Suburbs* shows the gangster Jakes (Marius Weyers; 1945–) on his motorbike in leather gear, with his girl Tiemie (Sandra Prinsloo; 1947–), in mini-skirt and make-up, on the pillion behind him. This image of plebeian vitality in Johannesburg's southern suburbs, which dominated the stage (Figure 4.2), was reproduced in reviews, the PACT Yearbook for 1971, and in publicity for the film version in 1973 and the rerun once the National Party lifted the prohibition on television in 1976. Its ubiquity signaled the establishment's embrace of these characters but this embrace depended on unspoken omissions. While it is unsurprising that the play excludes black characters, Du Plessis also omits

Figure 4.2 Masculine Swagger in *Siener van die Suburbs* by P.G. Du Plessis; Marius Weyers as Jake; directed by Louis van Niekerk, Performing Arts Council of the Transvaal (PACT), Pretoria 1971.

Photograph courtesy of PACT.

white characters outside the family circle, such as Tiemie's middle-class employer (and possible seducer), and neighbors that might have included the Portuguese migrants who had settled in the southern suburbs since the 1950s (Harrison et al. 2014: 269–92). Where sexual innuendo and stage violence in combination with religious or political controversy had provoked censorship of *Putsonderwater*, sex and violence purged of politics apparently made "delightful" [*heerlike*] drama.[27] Although initially discomfited by dialogue that "sound[ed] as though it had never been committed to paper" and transgressions such as simulated *dagga* [cannabis] smoking, critics warmed enough to the play to imitate its style.[28]

The press's enthusiasm did not reduce the story of Tjokkie, the plebeian seer in the southern suburbs, merely to a diverting spectacle for Afrikaner elites, however. The naturalist brick-wall-and-backyard set (Figure 4.2) made the limits of this environment clear, and the vehicles on stage do not offer escape. Jakes's bike may have seduced Tiemie but it is an unstable vehicle for her "to get out of the suburbs." Tjokkie's old Buick on blocks offers him only temporary refuge from his tormenters. By the end of the play, Tjokkie's clairvoyance and Jakes's successful attempt to get him to "see" against his will shatter this untidy but previously functional family. Tjokkie's prediction of the outcome of the races allows Giel, his mother's gambling man, to leave with the winnings; his vision of another man in Tiemie's "garden"—perhaps her boss—sprovokes Jakes to proprietary violence, smashing up Tiemie's possessions as well as her face. Weighed down by his sense of responsibility, Tjokkie retreats under the Buick, which becomes his suicide weapon, crushing him as he lowers the jack. Even if Du Plessis tried to lend his play a European pedigree by claiming affinity with "the great myths of death, exile and love" in Nietzsche and Pirandello (Polley 1973: 83–88), its dramatic force emerges from the vividly evoked locality, the yard and bungalow, and its plebeian inhabitants. Tjokkie's vision and Don Lamprecht's trance-like stumble capture in performance the weight of his world. Certainly, *Siener* depicted a narrow suburb that seems even narrower in contrast with the district that today houses black Portuguese-speaking migrants alongside the earlier white settlers, but under François Swart's direction in 1971, the performers especially Lamprecht, Weyers, and Prinsloo gave their characters gravity and vitality to depict plebeian culture marginalized by Afrikaner elite ideas of probity.

Where *Siener* portrays a man compelled to clairvoyance, *Die Rebellie van Lafras Verwey* deals with someone who, in author Chris Barnard's words, "refuses to believe his eyes, turns reason upside down and rises up against reality."[29] Lafras's refusal wells up from a reservoir of resentment against the "washed out [*bleek*] bureaucrats" who dismiss him as a "second-grade clerk" (Barnard 1971: 3). It also stems from the desire to translate his resentment into revolution, even if the man he treats as his "agent" is a drug smuggler using him as an unwitting courier. The original radio-play used musical themes, especially Prokofiev's *Kyrie Eleison,* to give Lafras a signature strong enough to encourage audience identification with him. It blurred the boundaries between the world inside his head and the outside world he refuses to see by using naturalistic sound for plausible dialogue—between Lafras and his boss, his "agent," and Petra, the hapless pregnant woman he befriends—and music for fantasy—from Lafras shouting commands to an imaginary revolutionary in the bathroom at work at the start, to his reverie of a happy life with Petra as the police break down his door at the end. In suggesting that neither society nor an alienated individual can alone determine the individual's reality, Barnard draws on R.D. Laing's *elusion*—"a relation in which one pretends oneself away from one's original self; then pretends oneself back from this pretense so as to appear to have arrived at the starting point" (Laing 1969: 30)—and on the socially constructed character of normality, "the state of total immersion in one's social fantasy system" (23). Deriving from *ludere* [Latin: play or deceive], *e-lusion* is the attempt to evade an untenable state of alienation through playing a role. The action of the play and the affect encouraged by the musical signature suggest that Lafras's usual state is the state of denial to which he returns after pretending to be a civil servant. His role-playing does not create "a world of his own" so much as a "delusionary significant place for himself in the *world of others*" (Laing 1969: 118; emphasis LK). It is an anti-social and thus also *social* rather than strictly psychological response to a society that appears to have no place for him.

The staging of *Lafras Verwey* brought spectators up against the line between invisible and visible worlds. On the one hand, the troops that Lafras summons at the start of the play are nowhere to be seen. On the other, he manages at the end to persuade the police outside his door that he has "fifty-odd" men (Barnard 1971: 49) and a machine-gun (52), until they shoot through the door and find only his body. In between, he collides with objects and people that interrupt his fantasy. Paired with Annette Engelbrecht (who played other abject women such as Fé in *Siener* and Kietie in *Kanna*) as Petra, Tobie Cronjé emphasized Lafras's clumsiness while giving his fantasy tangible weight. The minimal set and chiaroscuro lighting allowed the audience to glimpse the social dimensions of Lafras's distress, from the drab inadequacy of his kitchen to his mortifying exchange with his boss, while shrouding this world in the semi-darkness of imagination.[30] The revival at the People's Space (1979)—the successor to the Space (1971–79; Chapter 6)—pushed the confusion of inner and outer realities. By placing the spectators on revolving chairs in the center of the space, this production dropped the comforting illusion of the proscenium view and instead encouraged spectators' immersion in the drama unfolding around them.[31]

Like Billy Liar, the clerkly fibber played by Tom Courtenay in John Schlesinger's film (1963), Lafras is a fabricator: his rebellion is both substantial and illusory.[32] He subverts the orderly business of bureaucracy by wasting time and misplacing ledgers. He pretends to Petra that he can play the piano, only to be humiliated when a carnival barker and hangers-on tease him about a piano competition (Barnard 1971: 34–35). This humiliation provokes his declaration of war against "all the bigwigs [*kokkedore*], … who tread on ordinary guys and who incubate the world's money under their fat behinds" (37) but it prefigures the collapse of the boundary between his world and the "empty space in the others' world" (Laing 1969: 119) that he had failed to conquer. In depicting a misfit's attempt to occupy the "other world" of the powerful at a historical moment when Afrikaners were in power, *Lafras Verwey* brings to an end a line of alienated Afrikaners bewildered by capitalism and urban life, which began with Gert, the displaced farmer in *As die Tuig Skawe* (1926). Like Gert, Lafras rails against fat cats but where Grosskopf endorsed his hero who blames Jews for his plight, Barnard makes Lafras a victim of his own misguided rebellion. Though *volksontwikkeling* has made Lafras a clerk with a pension rather than a bankrupt farmer, he is still at the mercy of powerful agents whom he cannot identify. By making Lafras's antagonist his own volk, Barnard short-circuits the usual Afrikaner alibi of blaming the enemy. He shows Afrikaner power as corrupt as its predecessors and thus exposes the hypocrisy of appeals to a classless *volkseenheid*. Lafras is aliened as a worker as well as an individual; his role as a "cog in the machine" of the civil service (Barnard 1971: 21) and a tool in the hands of the drug syndicate deepens his alienation. This drama of a disaffected white clerk, performed at a time when black unions were on the rise after decades of repression, and white affluence had slumped in the wake of the international oil crisis in 1973, looks back on Afrikaner mythic history as well as forward to the present time, when white misfits, no longer coddled by an Afrikaner national bureaucracy, wander the streets of the Golden City.

While playwrights like Barnard and Du Plessis put street Afrikaans on stage, they remained committed to the elevation of Afrikaans into the realm of tragedy. In contrast, Afrikaans-Jewish satirist Pieter-Dirk Uys (1945–) used satire to knock down the sacred cows of Afrikaner probity. His first play in Afrikaans *Selle ou Storie* [Same old story](1973) at the Space annoyed the PCB for its allegedly foul language and queer display, as did cabaret revues that followed, especially his breakthrough show *Strike up the Banned* (1975ff) but the language and politics of these revues mixes anti-apartheid and queer performance (Lewis 2016: 101–34). In contrast, Uys's soap opera satire of the Afrikaner family saga belongs in this chapter on the drama of Afrikaans. Staged as excerpts from a radio serial, *Die Van Aardes van Grootoor*—the title translates comically as "the Earthlings of Big Ear"—was created in 1978 at the Market Theatre, which, like the Space, defied prohibitions on mixed casts and audiences. Inaugurating a venue pointedly called the Laager, this "epiese boeredrama in 780 episodes" (Uys 1979: i) covered fifty years and three generations in ninety minutes. The play begins with episode 4 in 1928—the era of farm failures staged in *As die Tuig Skawe*—and ends with episode 780 in 1978, in which the descendant of a black servant comes to buy the farm and evict the family, and narrowly escapes death as the Afrikaner matriarch blows up herself and her house rather than surrender. In contrast to her ancestor Aia, whose name means servant in demotic Malay, the language of the enslaved women that transformed Dutch into Afrikaans, Madame Daphne Quazilezi, a character who resembled in Nomsa Nene's performance a younger version of the ruthless billionaire Claire Zachanassian in Friedrich Dürrenmatt's satire of moral bankruptcy *Der Besuch der alten Dame* [The Visit of the Old Lady] (1956), speaks English to emphasize her emancipation but the mixing of languages throughout highlights the hybridity of Afrikaans to a degree unusual in the 1970s, signaling indirectly the impact of brown Afrikaans playwright Adam Small (1936–2016), whose play *Kanna, Hy Kô Hystoe* (1965) was recognized by Brink as a "high point in Afrikaans drama" (1986: 169).

African Afrikaans? *Kanna Hy Kô Hystoe* and the Languages of Home

When *Kanna Hy Kô Hystoe* [Kanna's Coming Home], whose author identified at different times as brown or black, received an all-white production at PACT's Breytenbach Theatre in Pretoria and Johannesburg's Alexander Theatre in 1974, it had already been hailed by several critics as a milestone.[33] Brink's praise of *Kanna* as an *Afrikaans* play invited readers to revise their views of the *taal* and its speakers. Written and performed in Kaaps, once the lingua franca of colonial Cape Town and later the home language of more than a million people identified as Coloured, *Kanna* reminded audiences that the volk's mother tongue was never a pure European language. Although the establishment attempted to deflect this challenge by treating Kaaps as a quaint dialect and the characters as part of an "unforgettable theatrical experience,"[34] without acknowledging the impact of apartheid or white denial of the hybrid history of Afrikaans and Afrikaners, *Kanna* nonetheless brought white spectators up against this family history.

Kanna draws on many sources from domestic drama to radio soap opera, popular even after the introduction of television in 1976. As a professor at UWC, Small was well placed to negotiate the tricky relationship between the multilingual mass culture permeating the lives of brown students and the Afrikaans high culture on the university syllabus. Where literary drama favored male protagonists, whether public heroes like President Steyn in *Die Pluimsaad waai ver* or private individuals in self-inflicted torment like Lafras, Small depicts a household held together sociologically as well as dramaturgically by a woman. Kanna, the "welfare kid" whose access to education allowed him to escape the poverty of District Six for the good life in Canada, may be the play's critical outside eye, but its center is Makiet, mother to Kanna, his brother Diekie, and his sister Kietie. In both Charlyn Wessels's performance in the Cape Flats Players neighborhood production (Figure 4.3) and Wilna Snyman's at PACT the character dominates the stage as she moves around in her wheelchair, bearing witness to the family's distress.[35] Small uses techniques that recall international dramatists as different as Brecht and Tennessee Williams—scene titles, narrative retrospection, music that alternately draws in the audience and holds them at bay—to juxtapose the play's present line of action, Kanna's brief return home for Makiet's funeral, with scenes from family history. He borrows from radio drama the use of changing voices to mark moments in time and from soap opera the fatefulness that permeates most of the characters' sense of their lot, and the heightened treatment of emotional trauma: Kietie's subjection to serial rape and Diekie's trial for murdering his sister's pimp. As Small recognized, melodrama was a risky genre since it might have encouraged the local audience to treat the story as merely a soap opera, and the white audience to reinforce stereotypes about Coloureds as resilient but irresponsible ghetto dwellers.[36]

To counter what he saw as the political liability of excess emotion, Small used a simple set of black flats for both UWC (1971) and the Cape Flats Players (1972), inscribed with graffiti from recently demolished District Six, juxtaposing political slogans—"Freedom Now"—with quips on culture—"You are now entering fairyland."[37] He also encouraged understated performances, especially by Albert Thomas as Kanna, to offset the emotional outbursts of characters like Kietie (Lynette Thomas) and Diekie (Jonathan Sam), and used music to frame emotional outbursts. Juxtaposing the play's inside chronicler, the street preacher Jakop, and the outsider commentator Kanna, the opening scene—"O, Wáar [where] is Moses?"—marks the tension between identification and critique of community attachments.[38] The guitar that accompanies Jakop's song recalls the Dixieland and *marabi* fusions of the Cape Carnival while

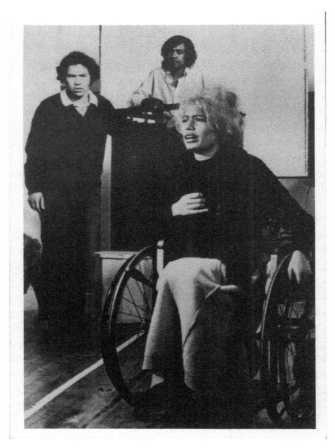

Figure 4.3 Charlyn Wessels center stage in *Kanna, Hy Kô Hystoe* by Adam Small; Athlone Cape Town, December 1972.

Source: *S' ketsh*, Photographer unknown.

sounding an ironic note in his appeal to Moses as a savior and a "murderer" (Small 1965: 7). This moment prefigures Diekie's attempt to restore his family's honor through vengeance, while also evoking the carnival's affirmation of life. Kanna's account of his progress from poverty in Cape Town to prosperity in Canada highlights, with each spot on a new character, the sacrifices made by others on his behalf, as it darkens the irony of the family's hope that Kanna has returned to save them. The succeeding scenes show Kanna's equivocal attempts to explain his family in court and by redescribing lives lived in Kaaps in "high" Afrikaans, despite resistance from the others who don't want him to tell the story because "we are not *that* bad" (32). This tension is played out between Kanna's sober narration of Kietie's first rape and Jakop's oracular testifying to her suffering and between Kanna's formal Afrikaans, and Jakop's vernacular reformulation of Dutch Reformed liturgy:

Nou vrinne [vriende]
Die Here het gebring
aan my sy wonnerwerke [wonderwerke] oek [ook]
Hy het gevra wat's in my hand
In my hand was my kitaar [gitaar]
Kô [kom] laat ons sing.
[Now friends / The Lord has brought his miracles / To me also / He asked what's
in my hand / In my hand was my guitar / Come let us sing] (33–34)

Jakob's guitar, instrument of secular entertainment, accompanies a hymn, but the dialect markers of Malay (and thus Muslim) influence on Afrikaans, challenge the Afrikaner Calvinist separation of sacred and profane. Confronted with Kietie's second rape, in this case by her pimp Poena, Jakop "oriekel van God" can take no more, however. The scene ends in cognitive and auditory dissonance as Kietie's mad laughter overlaps the hymn and the light shrinks from Jakop's dead body to the glow of Kanna's cigarette as he looks silently on.

Caught in the gulf between life lived in Kaaps and the rationalizing account of that experience in Afrikaans, the characters in this drama are trapped by the apartheid bureaucracy that makes the translation rules. Diekie's trial dramatizes the impossibility of translation in a society whose official ear is deafened by the discourse of race. The offstage judge, whose voice responds coolly to the family's attempt to explain the motivation of Diekie's fatal assault on Poena, hears only dishonesty in the plea, alongside the family's admission of dependence on income from Kietie's sex work. When Makiet attempts to translate Kietie's death into reassuringly sentimental language, "It was a nice funeral ... People were very fond of Kietie" (48), Diekie tells Kanna bluntly, "they were just inquisitive (*nieskierag [nuuskierig]*)." Diekie's moment as the voice of objectivity is brief, however; charged with murder, he "suddenly stands to attention, his voice stammering" (48) and by the end of the trial scene is condemned to hang. The family's increasingly desperate appeals for mercy prompt Kanna's attempt to use the language of the court to call for mitigation in Diekie's case and in the end, when the play finally brings him face to face with the family gathered at Makiet's funeral. His plea for mitigation is complicated by his expression of doubt: "If they allowed mitigating circumstances [*versagting*] for Diekie, they would have to do the same for thousands" (57). In the final scene, although Kanna finally speaks Kaaps on the way to Makiet's funeral in the soulless Cape Flats township where they were removed after the demolition of District Six, his remarks about Canada and their embarrassed comments on their lives fail to elicit mutual comprehension. Only the encounter with Makiet, apparently dead but vividly present in her wheelchair, pulls Kanna from his outsider role and into the family room, as he weeps for her death and his loss of family feeling. In these moments, the director and the players do not shrink from pathos but neither do they drown in it. Response to the Cape Flats production at the Nico Malan Nursing College in suburban Athlone—not to be confused with the whites-only Nico Malan Theatre in central Cape Town—included laughing and weeping with the characters, but the public display showed identification with social as well as individual conditions. Local critics also suggested that, by representing community dysfunction as the consequence of segregation, even without explicit indictment of the system, the play earned broader support from audiences than militant plays for intellectuals.[39] *Kanna*'s affinity with radio drama encouraged these audiences to identify the situation and the staging as their own without, however, blinding them with tears.

Performed by PACT's all-white cast in 1974, *Kanna* had a more ambiguous meaning—highlighted by the fact that the playwright had to apply for a permit to attend the performance.[40] Asserting the universality of a story of a "people trapped in living conditions that could affect anyone," director Louis van Niekerk did not include the fact that whites in South Africa were protected from such living conditions by privileges supported by law.[41] Van Niekerk's appeal to universality evaded the political implications of Brink's call for an integrated Afrikaans and relapsed instead into apartheid prejudice, claiming that "their language tells us that they are Coloured" and that "this language" is "different from European languages, such as Afrikaans, Italian, Spanish." Afrikaans reviewers identified the play's theme as "Coloureds' problems with communication and adaptation to the city," forgetting the similar problems that Afrikaners faced a generation before and the fact that Coloureds lived under official discrimination from which Afrikaners had benefitted.[42] In contrast, the *Rand Daily Mail* pointedly hailed the production as PACT's first by a *black* playwright, honoring Small's self-identification, and emphasized his criticism of the inadequate facilities in Coloured communities.[43] Praising the *bruinmens-egheid* [brown authenticity] of the white actors, Afrikaans critics reproduced the contradictions of blackface, whose white performers enacted their love—and theft—of black culture by claiming to re-present it more authentically than blacks themselves.[44] As Eric Lott notes of white Americans in blackface (1993), this "love and theft" articulated white working-class desire for the vitality of black culture as well as their fear of black workers; in the South African context, Afrikaners insisted on the purity of Afrikaans even while appropriating Kaaps. Struggling to exorcise the dreaded desire for kinship that had saturated the miscegenation dramas, the PACT production reproduced the logic of blackface. Although Snyman gave Makiet the emotional depth and social verisimilitude that she had given Tjokkie's Ma in *Siener*, and Lamprecht lent Kanna some of the sensitivity he had given Tjokkie, the tone was set by Annette Engelbrecht's hysterical Kietie and the chorus of smirking layabouts in the background (image: see Kruger 1999a: 125). This picture evoked the stereotype of Coloured delinquency that Small wished to escape, and encouraged white audiences to see themselves as superior to the characters on stage.

Only after the Soweto uprisings threatened white supremacy did Afrikaners become more willing to embrace Coloureds as fellow Afrikaans speakers. In 1961, the year of the Republic, Small had spoken as a "voice in the wilderness" calling for brotherhood between white and brown speakers of Afrikaans (Small 1961: 23) but met increasing skepticism from exiled intellectuals such as Vernon February who doubted that Kaaps could rise to the level of poetry (1981: 94–96), and from political activists working for Black solidarity between Coloureds and Africans (98). However willing Afrikaners were to see Kaaps as Afrikaans, even liberal Afrikaners like Jan Rabie presumed that black Afrikaans speakers would join the Afrikaner crusade against English as an "international white man's language" (Rabie 1985: 32), ignoring the longstanding association of English education and emancipation in South Africa and the intense opposition to Afrikaans education among the black majority. Writing in response to Rabie, self-described "Afrikaans-speaking *Afrikaan*" Jake Gerwel (1985: 43) reminded Rabie that Afrikaners had alienated black Afrikaans speakers with their attempt to purge the language of its black history. Nonetheless, in the late apartheid era, black Afrikaans found expression in song, carnival, and theatre and institutional support from black intellectuals such as Small and Gerwel at UWC. The Cape Flats Players in the 1970s and the Peninsula Theatre in the 1980s performed plays such as Small's *What about de Lô?* [Law] (1973) or Melvin Witbooi's *Dit Sal Die Blêrrie Dag Wies* [That'll be the Bloody Day], on the demolition of District Six (1984) (Smith 1990: 30–36). By the mid-1980s, papers like *Die Vrye Weekblad* [Free Weekly] edited by dissident Max du Preez, finally addressed the hybrid history of Afrikaans as well as its undetermined future as one of ten local official languages against global English.[45] After apartheid, Kaaps became a source of community pride and material for musicals on historical themes such as Dawid Kramer and Taliep Peterson's musical hits *District Six* (2002 [1987]) and *Ghoema* (2005). The latter combined sea shanties, carnival numbers, and spirituals from the eighteenth and nineteenth centuries with new songs about the legacy of slavery at the Cape, a legacy highlighted by the title of the 2009 revival *Afri-Kaaps*. In contrast to upbeat comic series such as Oscar Petersen and David Isaacs's *Joe Barber* (2000–), and comedians like Marc Lottering, Christo Davids's drama *Bullets over Bishop Lavis* (Davids/Abrahams 2013) revises the 1960s clash between Kanna and his family in a much harsher twenty-first-century conflict between an upwardly mobile city lawyer Ronnie, who speaks English, and his Kaaps-speaking brother in the projects who did prison time to protect Ronnie. It remains to be seen whether brown writers will continue to use Afrikaans in a twenty-first-century context where some Afrikaners identify with globally resurgent white nationalism.

The Twilight of Apartheid Idols and the Ends of Afrikanerdom

Afrikaans has been put to many uses from racist propaganda to the representation of the disenfranchised, but it is in family drama that the public and private strains on Afrikanerdom have been most intensely expressed. These strains magnify the tension between the conventions of milieu and character and the allegorical tendency of the action that threatens to burst the bounds of realism. The political challenge to Afrikaner supremacy represented by the Soweto uprising also made volkish allegory appear obsolete but it was not until the 1980s that Afrikaans literary dramatists returned to the attack on Afrikaner hypocrisy launched in the 1960s by Smit and continued mainly in cabaret by Uys and others. More than twenty years after the PCB censored *Putsonderwater, Diepe Grond* [Still Waters Run Deep], the first gothic *sprokie* [tale] of three published as *Vrystaat-Trilogie* (1991) by Reza de Wet (1952–2012), took the same stage at Rhodes that had produced *Putsonderwater* and raised a similar storm.[46] Dedicated to Smit, *Diepe Grond* recalls *Putsonderwater*'s setting—a desolate Free State parched by drought and neglect—and its central female character, Soekie, a "child-woman" whose "naive spontaneity is matched by ripe sensuality" (De Wet 1991:

12). But, where Smit situates his characters in a public village square, De Wet keeps hers inside a decaying farmhouse and, where *Putsonderwater* justifies murder as the panicked response of a child-woman, *Diepe Grond* revels in gothic travesty of Afrikaner probity. Soekie and her brother Frikkie inhabit a single squalid room, protected from the outside by their black nanny Alina, where they cajole each other in the roles of their parents in a style, played by Susan Coetzer and Dawid Minaar at the Market, that recalled the twisted siblings in Tennessee Williams's *Two Character Play* (1967). When their game is interrupted by a lawyer who has come at the bidding of relatives to find out why the pair have been selling off heirlooms for "paraffin and toilet paper" (De Wet 1991: 27), they first play "grown-up," serving tea and words of concern about the farm, only to turn to murder by *sjambok* when the lawyer proves unwilling to play along.[47] Like Smit, De Wet courts allegory but where Smit was wedded to the illumination of the Afrikaner condition, De Wet flirts with it, cunningly inviting the politically aware Market audience to look for meaning in the still water, only to trouble its surface with meta-theatrical touches in the style of Williams, just as a message seems within reach.

While De Wet twisted domestic drama to expose the myth of Afrikaner purity in the late apartheid era, Opperman confronted the public loss of Afrikaner power after apartheid in an epic drama that depicts the long-term effect of that power on the nation as well as the family. *Donkerland* (1996) dramatizes the rise and fall of Afrikaner nationalism through ten generations of De Witts. Beginning with trekboer Pieter's expropriation of Zulu land after 1838 and ending with the sale of Donkerland in anticipation of a new Land Act, the play stands on the cusp of transformation between the end of the Afrikaner ascendancy and the demotion of the chosen volk to the status of ordinary citizens. Even more than his critique of military culture in *Môre is 'n Lang Dag*, which Opperman wrote while rehearsing the South African premiere of *Somewhere on the Border* (2012 [1984]) a savage treatment of recruits in South Africa's covert war in Angola written in exile by Anthony Akerman (2012), *Donkerland* upended Afrikaner sacred history by exposing claims to divine right as an excuse for expropriation but, while it staged Afrikaner obsession with past victimization as the rationalization for oppressing the black majority, nonetheless reminded whites of the consequences of their violence toward black people. One of the last productions by PACT before funding was redistributed by the new Department of Arts and Culture (Chapter 7), it premiered at the Klein Karoo Nasionale Kunsfees in April 1996 and elicited conflicting responses in the Afrikaans press; *Die Burger* accused Opperman of "picking at old wounds" but still compared him to N.P. Van Wyk Louw, while the more urbane *Rapport* hailed the epic as a "drama-decalogue" and a political event, a "collective truth commission, catharsis for an Afrikaans audience."[48]

The fluid dramaturgy and the actors' portrayal of multiple roles, similar to *The Kentucky Cycle*, Robert Schenkkan's nine-part epic that won the Pulitzer Prize in 1992 when Opperman was at Northwestern University, burst the confines of domestic naturalism and opened up the generational conflict to critique the Afrikaner myth of suffering and of redemption through settlement of the land. Although accused of one-sidedness, Opperman used multiple dramatic conflicts over the epic's ten parts to show contesting points of view. The first act—"plant die stok" in which Pieter plants his stick to mark the boundaries of the land he claims—takes inspiration from Louw's analogy between a "klein [small] volk" "coming up between great powers" and a "little plant" reaching up between the "hoofs of big beasts" (Louw 1939: 21; Opperman 1996: 1). The analogy casts Pieter in the role of *volksplanter*—Van Riebeeck's honorific as cultivator of the nation—and appears to celebrate De Witt (white) cultivation of Donkerland (dark and by implication rich land) over nearly two centuries, but this scene ends with Pieter exercising his power to rape the Zulu woman he calls Meidjie [little maidservant], and thus exposes at the outset the racial and sexual violence at the heart of Afrikaner patriarchy. Granting only smaller parts to women, Opperman gives center stage to a male rebel from the tribal cause; the teacher Dirk, radicalized by his experience with black workers and their families, argues against his bigoted brother Ouboet that blacks "suffered more" (1996: 116) than whites during the industrialization of the early twentieth century. By casting as the rebel the same actor, André Odendaal, who played Pieter in scene one, and, near the end of the play, his descendant Arnold accused in the 1980s of raping farm worker Nomthandazo [mother of prayer], he emphasizes the *broedertwis* [fraternal conflict] of rebel and racist. The confrontation between Dirk and his racist brother in the 1930s—in the scene titled "die salf van eie gom [salve from one's own glue, or other bodily fluids]"—recalls *Die Jaar van die Vuur-os* as Ouboet here echoes the bigoted language of older brother Pieter in De Klerk's play: when Dirk predicts that blacks will "sit in parliament alongside the Boers" (Opperman 1996: 116), Ouboet retorts: "die kaffers moes nog mense word [the kaffirs would have to become people first]" 117), which recalls brother Pieter's slur: "half-people" in *Vuur-os*. In contrast, Dirk speaks for a class alliance between white and black workers, appealing to common humanity more strongly than Martin in *Vuur-os* and reminding the audience both of the school-taught literary heritage and the unacknowledged history of solidarity by class rather than race (Chapter 1).

Epigraphs before each act from canonical works by Louw and more subtle allusions to others such as the first play in Afrikaans, *Magrita Prinslo* by S.J. Du Toit (Keuris 2012), enable Opperman to represent himself as their legitimate heir but he is not content with simple emulation. By dramatizing the sexual exploitation of black dependents as the longstanding if long-denied practice that created Coloured Afrikaans speakers, he explodes the hypocritical assertion of Afrikaner purity even if he treats sexual violence more as a contest between black and white men defending "their" women than a violation of women's integrity. By depicting the humbling loss of the farm in the 1990s, he makes even unwilling members of his audience confront the possibility that, even if the "wheels of Africa" roll slowly, the Afrikaner's "klein strepie mensdom [small trace of humanity]" may disappear in the "grass of Donkerland" or, if this tenacious tribe survives, Afrikaners will not direct the future of South Africa (Opperman 1996: 157) Although the common meaning of *strepie* as "hyphen" animates a recent reading (Lewis 2016: 68–88), Opperman's citation of his predecessors suggests strongly that this phrase picks up Louw's image of the *klein volk* struggling for space between great powers (Louw 1939: 21), which Opperman quoted at the outset of his drama.

While *Donkerland* earned praise for its portrayal of monstrous aspects of Afrikaner history, *Ons vir jou* (2008–10; revived 2013) fanned the fire of white nationalist sentiment ignited by Bok Van Blerk's song *De La Rey* by including the singer and his song in this musical celebrating Boer endurance against the British, while evading the dubious impact of this nostalgia.[49] Escaping these two extremes, *Hartland*, a thirteen-episode television series on the private channel KykNET, dramatized four generations grappling with changing gender roles and racial coexistence in twenty-first-century Pretoria. The series deserves mention because Opperman came to see it as part of a trilogy begun with *Donkerland*. Further, its plot, characters, location, and casting tackle the continuities and contradictions between the old *chronotope* of the family farm—rural, patriarchal, and suspicious of outsiders—played with variations from *As die Tuig Skave* (Chapter 3) to *Donkerland*, and the new drama of the family *firm*—urban or at least suburban in outlook from the vantage point of affluent Waterkloof—open to contributions from women and blacks on condition that they are part of the family.[50] Although the firm, a cosmetics company founded by patriarch Jan Cilliers and marketing to black women as African Queen, comes closer to a case of white "love and theft" of black beauty than a viable business model, the battle for ownership after Jan's death plays out an absorbing drama between Adriaan, Jan's younger brother aggrieved by an insufficient settlement, and Elna, Jan's daughter who must fight to maintain her shares and management claims, which her male relatives dismiss despite her MBA, but who ultimately succeeds with backing by her mother and her black partner Zweli, son of a family servant. Although tensions remain unresolved between Elna and her male antagonists, uncle Adriaan and husband Bertus, who would prefer that his wife and son Neil abandon South Africa for a quiet life in Toronto, and although Elna's confidence that the company can market equally to black and white women invites skepticism, the series nonetheless acknowledges the challenges to which Afrikaners must adapt.

The drama of *Hartland* rises above the limits of the plot, however. With Wilna Snyman (1935–), whom Opperman honors as his "second mother" (2008: 3) as Ouma (Granny) Cilliers, Marius Weyers as her son Jan and Sandra Prinsloo as his wife Maria, *Hartland* invites audiences to pick up the resonance between these and previous roles from as far back as *Siener* (1971), in which these actors all appeared. If, as Roach suggests, "the actor's roles ... gather in the memory of audiences like ghosts" prompting spectators "to regard the performer as an eccentric but meticulous curator of cultural memory" (1996: 78), individual roles matter less than the sense, generated even in this non-Afrikaner spectator, that the best performances in *Hartland* spark links with the long history of Afrikaner struggle and accommodation. Snyman's portrayal of the matriarch who stubbornly cultivates the family's roots in the homeland like a plant in the earth magnifies the reverberation of the role by summoning not only Louw's roots metaphor but also a pantheon of women in her portrayal of mothers defending family from Du Plessis's plebeian *Siener* and its affluent twin *'n Seder Val* [A Cedar Falls] *in Waterkloof* (1975; published Du Plessis 1977) to *Die Teken* (1985), Opperman's homage to *Putsonderwater*. André Odendaal's Adriaan recalls the roles he played in *Donkerland* from patriarch to rebel to son spoiled rotten by privilege, giving his portrayal here of a manager and would-be entrepreneur intimidated by his ambitious wife a tragicomic as well as satirical aspect. While these characters recall the rise and fall of Afrikaner exceptionalism, *Hartland* heralds a multilingual future. Elna annoys Bertus by speaking Afrikaans to Neil but Neil and his cousins, even would-be white nationalist Vlooi, Adriaan's son, switch easily between Anglo-American slang and colloquial as well as formal Afrikaans. Zweli, in contrast to the mute retainers in the farm plays, favors English for business and Zulu as a source of family wisdom but speaks Afrikaans to the Cilliers. Afrikaans sounds alive and well, no longer an instrument of domination but rather, as avowedly contrary Afrikaner Du Preez has it, a language that accommodates democrats and dreamers (2005: 168).

*   *   *

South Africa in the twenty-first century recognizes Afrikaans as one among eleven official tongues but the language still bears the legacy of its historical role as an instrument of state power. Even before the student uprising against enforced Afrikaans-medium education in 1976, African, Coloured, and other students identifying as Black lost patience with Small and his generation's "brown Afrikaans," instead dismissing "so-called Coloured" identity as an "artifact of policy" (Simone 1994: 162). While post-apartheid attempts by Gerwel, Jonathan Jansen, and other brown Afrikaans speakers to free Afrikaans from its white supremacist taint and to bring together all Afrikaans speakers as members of the third-largest linguistic group—after Zulu and Xhosa—may be decried by white nationalists, the attempt serves as a caution against simplistic black/white oppositions. More directly, however, we should examine the impact of black consciousness on brown identifications and on the language and politics of theatre in the years before and after the Soweto uprisings. That is the subject of Chapter 5.

Dramas of Black Solidarity

Black Consciousness Movement and Beyond

In July 1972, the South African Black Theatre Union (SABTU) was launched at Orient Hall in Durban at a festival sponsored by the Theatre Council of Natal (TECON) (Ebrahim 1973). The program included South African dramas such as *The Coat* (1966) devised by the Serpent Players in collaboration with Athol Fugard, *The Lahnee's Pleasure* (1977 [1972]), by Ronnie Govender (1934–) of the Shah Theatre in Durban, as well as imported plays, such as the University of Natal production of *Encounter* (Sondhi 1968), Indian-Ugandan Kuldip Sondhi's play about the Kenyan independence struggle, and TECON's production of *Requiem for Brother X*, by African-American William Wellington Mackey. The Black Peoples Convention (BPC) and the South African Students Association (SASO) saw theatre as a means to forge political unity of Africans, Coloureds, and Indian-descendant South Africans under the banner of Black Consciousness understood as acquired solidarity rather than inherited identity. This inclusive conception of black solidarity challenged not only apartheid but also the presumption of well-meaning whites to lead the anti-apartheid struggle.

As the titles above show, theatre affiliated with the Black Consciousness Movement (BCM) drew on transnational and national sources to cultivate liberated consciousness in people identifying *as Black* against the apartheid label "non-white," using capital B to signal chosen rather than inherited affiliation. Borrowing from Brazilian educator Paolo Freire's *Pedagogy of the Oppressed* the concept of conscientization, "the process of learning to perceive social and political and economic contradictions and to take action against oppressive elements" (Freire 1972: 16), BCM hoped, as SASO's founding president Stephen Bantu Biko (1946–77) put it, to transform blacks' ability to develop values that "we set for ourselves" (1978: 51) and, as the majority, "determine the broad direction" of South Africa (24). The BCM argued that conscientization was necessary to free black people from institutionalized racism and to meet whites on equal terms. Biko argued that building black institutions did not surrender to apartheid "separate development" but rather provided the basis for the revival of black self-respect (71–72). In addition to Freire, BCM drew on Frantz Fanon's analysis of the colonized mentality and on arguments for black autonomy in the United States by Stokely Carmichael (Kwame Ture) and Malcolm X., on African leaders, especially Kwame Nkrumah (Ghana) and Amilcar Cabral (Guinea-Bissau), and the outlawed Pan-African

Congress (PAC) at home (Mangcu 2014: 119). In terms similar to Fanon's critique of Négritude (2004: 149–50), Biko argued that Black Consciousness was "not a matter of pigmentation" but rather a "mental attitude" defying white supremacy (Biko 1978: 48) and thus like Fanon critiqued racial essentialism as well as racist discrimination.

Thirty years after Biko's death by torture in 1977, the editors of *Biko Lives* stressed BCM's contribution to dialogue with African-descended people worldwide (Gibson et al. 2008: 3). Recalling that SASO's programs included health, employment, and education for adults and children, addressing black poverty and the class dimension of apartheid discrimination (see *Black Review*, 1972–79), contributors to *Biko Lives* use BCM's record of work with impoverished rural and urban communities to indict the post-apartheid government for neglect (Gibson et al. 2008: 10–13). Biko's colleague Srini Moodley highlights Biko's inclusive conception of black solidarity in the phrase "we black people" (2008: 268) and argues that the ANC had "written BCM out of the struggle" (274). Biographer Xolela Mangcu notes that Biko collaborated with Indian colleagues at the University of Natal to build SASO and, despite insisting on strategic separation from National Union of South African Students (NUSAS), maintained contact with white leftists (2008: 126–49) confirmed by NUSAS leader Glen Moss (2014: 13–19). The BCM commands attention today because its intersectional links between the multiple strands of anti-apartheid struggle challenge ANC complacency about the "black economic empowerment" of a small elite, and inspire the critical work of post-apartheid men like Mangcu and women like Pumla Madikizela. As Achille Mbembe argues (2015), this timely critique deserves more respect than the casual appropriation of Fanon's call for violence in demands for decolonization by some in #FeesMustFall and other student circles since 2015, even if the tension between the masculinist cast of BCM, in position papers and plays that habitually cast women as auxiliaries supporting men, and the active roles played by women in the movement remains unresolved.

BCM developed black solidarity through cultural practices that were both strategic and discriminating—it critiqued apartheid promotion of "Bantu" traditions and commercial entertainment produced by blacks but sometimes used popular entertainment such as comedy or melodrama. The SABTU festival of July 1972 included popular forms that had been shaped by politics, such as the poetry of lament and resistance by Mihloti [*imihloti*: tears], but student groups staged plays with dense English dialogue and abstract theory that were not easily accessible to township audiences. Nonetheless, although plays such as Sondhi's *Encounter* and Mthuli Shezi's *Shanti* spoke primarily to a student minority, their performance of defiance challenged state power and was recognized as such by black audiences and police operatives alike. TECON and Soweto counterparts such as the Peoples Educational Theatre (PET) survived only a few years before their members were tried for treason, but their "theatre of determination" (Khoapa 1973: 201) set the tone for much of the theatre that defied apartheid into the 1990s. Debates about anti-apartheid theatre in this period of intense political activism made much of a distinction between theatre of "protest," associated with the portrayal of suffering and humanist compassion exemplified by Fugard, and a more militant successor, variously called theatre of "resistance," "defiance," or "determination," but this distinction was polemical. Ian Steadman, who tracked theatre from the 1970s to the 1990s, identified resistance theatre with workshop improvisation, direct address, and political urgency (Steadman 1985, 1990, 1995), but BCM programs included melodrama alongside agitprop. Therefore, while focused on explicit "theatre of defiance," this chapter also includes plays outside BCM's direct orbit which still registered its influence, such as Govender's comedy about Indian class tension in *The Lahnee's Pleasure* (1972) or the township musical *Too Late* (1975) by the popular entrepreneur Gibson Kente, which affirmed black solidarity but used melodramatic scenarios with popular appeal.

Black Power, Beat Poets, and *The Rhythm of Violence*

SABTU members were not the first to promote a theatre of defiance but, where African National Theatre work like Radebe's *The Rude Criminal* (Chapter 3) drew on international communist agitprop, SABTU plays attempted to combine the theme of anti-colonial rebellion, the rhetoric of black consciousness, and the desire of young black intellectuals to see themselves as the vanguard of a new armed struggle. This aspiration was not itself new. Lewis Nkosi's play *The Rhythm of Violence* (1964) was written in exile and banned in South Africa, and thus not directly available to SABTU but it matters because it was the first to express the frustrations of black intellectuals drawn to political violence and because Nkosi's ironic tone offers an illuminating contrast to the single-minded militancy of *Shanti* and other plays produced by SABTU. It also holds an important place in Nkosi's career, in that it anticipates the irony pervading his later work such as "We can't all be Martin Luther King" (BBC Radio 1971; Gunner 2006) and *Mandela's Ego* (2006), a post-apartheid satirical novel. *The Rhythm of Violence* portrays a group of students planning to blow up a National Party rally at the Johannesburg City Council on the stroke of midnight. Although the first act opens several hours earlier as two policemen trade racist insults about an off-stage student demonstration and its chief speaker, the action focuses on the private behavior of that speaker, the charismatic Gama [Zulu: name], his friends and "his" women, especially on the conflict between Gama and his younger brother Tula [*thula*: quiet]. Defying his militant brother, Tula is moved to try to defuse the bomb by the plight of an Afrikaans woman Sarie Marais—her name recalls the romantic patriotism of the Boer War song title—whose father is attending the rally to tender his resignation. The interaction between Tula and Sarie in the second act provides a sentimental contrast to the ironic banter of Gama and friends but both irony and sentimentality give way in the third act to state violence. Tula dies when the bomb explodes and the police pull Sarie from his body and try to extract information from her about the others.

Anti-apartheid readings of this unperformed and in the historical context unperformable play argued that it expressed a "direct experiential link with life lived under the apartheid regime" (Orkin 1991: 109) and thus offered a "timely index" of a shift from "protest to resistance" (Steadman 1990: 217) but this reading misses Nkosi's irony. To be sure, he had anticipated a political explosion while still in South Africa, before the Sharpeville massacre in 1960 (1983: 8–9) and, after leaving on a one-way ticket to Harvard University in 1961, he followed events in South Africa, including sabotage by *umKhonto we Sizwe* [spear of the nation] and *Poqo* [pure], affiliated respectively with the ANC and PAC. *The Rhythm of Violence* draws on the rhetoric of violent resistance, but its tone expresses the recklessness and whimsy of student rebellion, closer perhaps to the African Resistance Movement than to PAC.[1] Gama's speech in the first act, from the opening slogan—"from Cape to Cairo, from Morocco to Mozambique, Africans are shouting Freedom" (Nkosi 1973: 71)—to the critique of ANC inaction, echo the PAC line and the police reaction catches the dangerous mix of arrogance and racial panic in Afrikaner discourse.[2] The second act, however, displays witty but often superficial bohemian enthusiasms; the Hillbrow club with its "avant-garde pictures [and] strong African motifs," its posters proclaiming "INTER-RACIAL SEX IS A HISTORICAL FACT" alongside "FREEDOM IN OUR LIFETIME" (79), suggests less a movement than a party where flirtation and histrionic speeches produce an inconsistent mix of political bravado, casual sexism, and self-parody.

Notwithstanding its South African setting, *The Rhythm of Violence* uses American idiom that Nkosi picked up in New York where he wrote the play. He dwells less on the militancy of Black Power than on the counter-cultural appeal of the cool Blackman. All his characters use Beat lingo, from the students who might plausibly affect it to the Afrikaans policemen who realistically would not. This American dimension does not invalidate the text's significance for South Africa but it does invite those critics who see the play as an index of post-Sharpeville activism to look closely at its urbane irony. Although moved by the civil rights drama of African-American playwrights such as Loften Mitchell, whose *Land Beyond the River* (1957) dramatized the struggle for equal education after the U.S. Supreme Court ruling on *Brown v Board of Education*, Nkosi was a keener observer of the Beat scene, with its interracial bohemia and hipster rebellion (Nkosi 1983: 65). Black Beat poet Ted Joans, whose celebration of sexual conquest Nkosi quotes with pleasure, echoes as persistently in *The Rhythm of Violence* as the voice of Potlako Leballo, volatile spokesman for the PAC in exile.[3] Joans's poems or, as he called them, "show-off stunts for Bohemian Greenwich Village, USA" (quoted: Wilentz 1960: 101), use bebop rhythm and ironic stereotypes as vehicles for sly digs at white would-be rebels. His most notorious slogan—"White America, my hand is on your thigh" (Joans 1961: 33)—quoted by Nkosi in *Home and Exile* (1983: 65), conjures up the aggressive "Negro" stereotype of Norman Mailer's essay "The White Negro" (1957) rather than the work of civil rights activists. But where Mailer sees in "the Negro" a "wise primitive in a giant jungle" (1992: 593), responding to "life on the margin" with spontaneous violence (589), Joans ironically impersonates stereotypes: "Let's play something horrible. You be Hitler ... you be Strijdom of South Africa"(Joans 1961: 9). A similar irony flavors the party banter in *The Rhythm of Violence*; Gama plays to the epithet "dark and lascivious Moor" (Nkosi 1973: 82—from Shakespeare's *Othello*) tossed to him by his white sidekick Jimmy. Jimmy is in turn mocked when his black girlfriend Kitty dismisses his praise for "mysterious and splendid African woman" as a "myth for sex-starved white men" (83). The irony in the impersonation is inconsistent, however. While Nkosi puts the racial stereotypes in quotation marks, he takes patriarchy for granted: the male characters' propensity for slapping women and the women's "melting" response suggests a casual presupposition of patriarchal power. On the other hand, the treatment of the policemen reads like a show-off stunt. Inspired perhaps by Joans's call to anarchic mimicry, Nkosi has Jan, one of the policemen who had insulted Tula moments before, act out the role of a "Native leader"(1964: 77), whom he calls *Lundula* [conceited], to the point where he is apparently "completely identified with the African cause"(79).

These ambiguous impersonations make it difficult to fix a target audience for this play. Where the banter between friends might be seen as "colonial mimicry," in Homi Bhabha's sense of a "a strategy of subversion that turns the gaze of the discriminated back upon the eye of power" (1986: 173), and thus as a way for a hypothetical performance to speak to South African activists, the policeman impersonating "Lundula" is not so easily brought in line. The incompatibility of this role-playing with a clear political message may add to the literary interest of the play, but it is hard to see how it might have mobilized political action. The value of the play lies less in representing political militancy than its dramatization of the dilemmas of intellectuals who were unevenly prepared for a potentially revolutionary situation.

Black Theatre Consciousness / White Institutional Unconscious?

Whereas *The Rhythm of Violence* registered the ambivalence of Nkosi in exile, the texts chosen by SABTU members reflected their understanding of themselves as "organic intellectuals" in Gramsci's sense as men who had emerged from the "rising subaltern classes" to act in the interests of the masses (Gramsci 1971: 6). SABTU members were mainly students from the segregated universities established under the so-called Extension of Universities Act (1959); the Durban group drew from the (Indian) University of Durban-Westville (hereafter UDW), the University of Zululand and the medical school for black students at the otherwise white University of Natal—the same institution that had produced Dlomo's *Dingana* (Chapter 3)–and sought links to the black labor movement that was reemerging in Natal. This "Durban moment," as Tony Morphet called the convergence between African and Indian-descended activists and collaboration between workers and students, was reflected in the SABTU program that included the black worker group Serpent Players.[4] SABTU regarded theatre as a "means to assist Blacks to reassert their pride, dignity, group identity and solidarity" (*PET Newsletter*, 2), in part by tapping a history of "Black civilizations" that encompassed India as well as Africa, and in part by offering "positive representations of the needs, aspirations, and goals of Black people"(Kraai 1973: 11).

Although an influential leftist critic argued that the BCM's emphasis on racism as the fundamental determinant of oppression and on solidarity among people of color as the primary means of combating this oppression ignored the impact of capitalism and of class distinctions between different groups identified as Black (Kavanagh 1985: 160), BCM writers did in fact analyze class structure in South Africa: "white workers cannot be regarded as genuine workers so long as they hide behind job reservation, discriminating wages, discriminating trade unions and the general pool of privileges open to whites in South Africa" (Khoapa 1973: 4). This analysis stressed that most South Africans experienced economic discrimination as the enforcement of white supremacy. As Fanon wrote and SASO leaders undoubtedly read: "In the colonies ...

you are rich because you are white; you are white because you are rich. This is why Marxist analysis should always be slightly stretched every time we have to do with the colonial problem" (Fanon 2004: 40). Fanon's reminder that even the meanest white person in a (neo)colonial situation enjoys white privilege echoes in Biko's retort to white leftists: "They tell us that the situation is a class struggle rather than a racial one. Let them go to Van Tonder in the Free State and tell him this" (Biko 1978: 89). Biko's critique of government favors to token blacks (1978: 89–92) drew also on Stokely Carmichael, who argued that the "integration of individual 'acceptable Negroes' did not change the structure of institutional racism" (Carmichael 1968: 125–26).[5] In addition, Black Community Programs, worked to build educational and social organizations among rural as well as urban Africans and endorsed the efforts of the Institute for Industrial Education, founded in part by NUSAS to give legal and strategic advice to black unions (Gwala 1974: 173–74).[6] For Biko, the focus on racism as the vehicle of oppression was thus a matter of strategy, a means of unifying different disenfranchised groups against the apartheid state.

The repertoire of TECON, SABTU's longest-lasting affiliate (1969–73) tracks a shift from literary to political performances, but this shift did not resolve tensions between conscientization and entertainment. This is not to deny the political impact of these performances, but rather to suggest that this impact is best understood in the context of multiple, not always compatible influences. Founded by spouses Srini and Sumboornam (Sam) Moodley and other students at UDW, TECON benefitted from the legacy of Indic (Indian origin) theatre groups such as the Shah Theatre Academy (est. 1965), and the relative stability of the Indian middle classes. Indians were denied the vote and full educational, social, and economic mobility, as were all Black South Africans, but their exemption from the pass laws that restricted Africans, their education in English, and their greater access to capital made it easier to organize and to sustain cultural institutions. The Shah Academy was founded by Krishna Shah, a director from Delhi based in New York. He brought his production of *The King of the Dark Chamber* by Rabindranath Tagore to South Africa in 1961 and returned in 1963 to conduct workshops, predominantly on Western theatre techniques (Naidoo 1997). Under the "shadow of the Shah" (Schauffer 1994), members favored realist drama rather than the Indian epics that entertained their parents, although they also produced comic revues in a format that appealed (and still appeals) to Indian audiences.

Given this exposure to Western drama, it is not surprising that TECON's first production was *Look Back in Anger*, John Osborne's 1956 portrait of a would-be rebel as angry young man in mid-century middle-class England. Their next production *In the Heart of Negritude* (1970) featured Aimé Césaire and Léopold Senghor, poets who had been formed as much by the literary scene in Paris as by their origins in Martinique and Senegal, respectively.[7] TECON's contribution to the SABTU festival, *Requiem for Brother X*, William Wellington Mackey's "dramatic dialogue about black people trapped in the ghetto"(Mackey 1986: 325), suggests an engagement with black American vernacular, and their next production, *Antigone in '71*, a South African adaptation of Jean Anouilh's modern version of Sophocles's *Antigone*, introduced the theme of militant opposition to the state, albeit under classical cover. Black interest in this theme was sharpened by the independence struggle in Mozambique, where the

Front for the Liberation of Mozambique (FRELIMO) supplanted the Portuguese in 1974. The domestic political atmosphere was also heating up as white rectors of the black universities responded to protests by detaining student leaders.[8] The festival registered the impact of these events and the desire of its participants to conscientize their audiences through dramatizing resistance. This project informed most productions such as Serpent Players' adaptation of Albert Camus' *The Just* (a.k.a. *The Terrorists*) but only Kuldip Sondhi's *Encounter*, directed by Sam Moodley for the University of Natal— Black Section, dealt directly with anti-colonial insurrection in Africa. It dramatizes conflict between British soldiers and Mau-Mau guerrillas that ends in the guerrillas' favor and by implication with Kenyan independence. Its naturalistic dramaturgy, which portrayed the protagonist's private hopes and fears, expressed through extended duologues—from the English Lt. Dewey arguing with his settler subordinate Paddy to the fatal encounter between Dewey and his Mau-Mau guerilla captor General Nyati— appealed to an audience of students. However, the direct performance style of this all-black cast worked against the naturalist portrayal of fallible men to emphasize the play's message as a "Black view of white-labeled terrorism."[9]

The SABTU program in December 1972 reprised *The Coat*, *The Lahnee's Pleasure*, and *Requiem for Brother X* from Durban but, because *Encounter* was banned, included a new play on anti-colonial struggle: *Shanti*, written by Mthuli Shezi (1947–72) and produced by PET. The South African Black Theatre Union was effectively abolished in March 1973 when its president Srini[vasa] Moodley (1946–) and director Sathasivan [Saths] Cooper (1950–), both in TECON, were banned (Gwala 1974: 94–97).[10] Before being confined to house arrest, however, Cooper attended a Black Arts event sponsored by Mihloti at Mofolo Hall, in Soweto. The proceedings included a speech written by Cooper and presented by Sipho Buthelezi: "What is Black Theatre?" calling for a "new and relevant Black theatre ... by artists who have self-love and love of all Black people"; it ended with "Before and After the Revolution," which shows a white policeman interrogated by his former prisoners.[11] This sketch shared with *Encounter* the call to revolutionary violence but, unlike *Encounter*, was delivered in terse agitprop style, using choral chants and direct audience address. The performances stressed the priority of political mobilization, favoring short, sharp presentations that could be quickly memorized, to get around the confiscation of a script or the arrest of a cast member.

This event confirmed the link between SABTU, mostly based in Durban, and MDALI [*umDali*: creator], the Music, Drama and Literature Institute, an umbrella organization for several groups including Mihloti in the Johannesburg area. While the commitment to inclusive black solidarity animated both groups, their institutional structures were shaped by the state's differential treatment of Africans and Indians. The SABTU was able to draw on Indian resources, including access to central venues like Orient Hall without immediate state interference and the Indian-oriented press in Durban reported favorably not only on the comedy *The Lahnee's Pleasure* but also on drama such as *Requiem for Brother X* and *The Just*.[12] In contrast, MDALI's African members in Soweto, Alexandra. and other townships had to endure harassment from officials ready to deport them to the Bantustans, as well as indirect pressure, such as the dearth of capital, the limited number of venues, and the everyday consequences of apartheid geography, as they lived in Soweto districts spread out 25 kilometers or more southwest of central Johannesburg.

BCM members were justly critical of white "management" of black talent in such shows as *Ipi Tombi?* [girl, where?] (1974), which used a sketchy scenario as an alibi for displaying scantily clad women dancing to *mbaqanga*, but they were also skeptical of more equitable interracial collaborations such as that between Corney Mabaso and Phoenix Players, who produced the variety show *Isuntu*, which toured Japan as *Meropa* and London as *KwaZulu* (Coplan 2008: 283, 382). Founded by Union Artists' Ian Bernhardt and director Barney Simon initially to produce Athol Fugard's *Hello and Goodbye* in 1965, Phoenix Players sponsored black-cast shows such as the Soweto Ensemble's *Shaka* directed by Mabaso in 1968, and *Phiri*, a celebrated adaptation of Ben Jonson's *Volpone*, directed by Simon in 1972. Phoenix's white members were committed to furthering the work of black producers such as Mabaso and Stanley "Fats" Dibeco, who had worked with Fugard and Simon at Dorkay House but their commitment did not alter the apartheid structures that excluded most blacks from formal education. The division of labor for *Phiri* was not so different from *King Kong*, produced thirteen years earlier.[13] As the program notes show, the mostly white production team had benefitted from formal training and informal connections in London and Johannesburg; apart from Mabaso who had studied directing in London, blacks had access only to informal training. This division of labor suggests the persistence of what might be called a *white institutional unconscious*, the assumption that whites had better capital management and organizational skills. It is this institutional unconscious, rather than the stated intentions of white facilitators, that Molefe Pheto of MDALI censured when he criticized the "concept" of "multi-racial organizations" (Khoapa 1973: 204).

In keeping with this critique, SABTU emphasized black sometimes to the exclusion of white collaborators: the Serpent Players, for example, appear in the program as actors John Kani and Winston Ntshona and director Mulligan Mbikwana without their collaborator Fugard. They had performed local adaptations of European classics such as Sophocles' *Antigone* and leftist drama such as Büchner's *Woyzeck* and Brecht's *Caucasian Chalk Circle*, before turning to improvisation on the daily lives of African participants.[14] This project produced *The Coat*, which was devised, borrowing from Brecht's demonstrative "theatre of instruction" and Grotowski's "poor theatre," as an "acting exercise" in response to the trial of key members of the group in 1966 (see Kruger 2004: 238–45). The action of *The Coat* drew on an incident at the trial: a man who had just been sentenced gave his coat to the wife of another prisoner, telling her to "give this to my wife. Tell her to use it" (Fugard 1993a: 122). Although, as editor Dennis Walder notes, it was performed initially for a white "theatre appreciation group" (1993: xxiv), the play's performance in the New Brighton township, where most company members lived, and its publication in 1967 in *The Classic*, a magazine edited and read by black intellectuals, under the name of Serpent Players secured its identification with BCM theatre and its performance at the SABTU festival in Cape Town. However, it received less critical attention than the militant plays on the SABTU program, possibly because it represented everyday social acts—from the exchange of clothing to the interaction of community members—in a matter-of-fact manner, showing the estrangement of these acts under the pressure of political trials that disrupted this community, rather than a direct call to attack the state.

Even more harshly, BCM intellectuals dismissed township shows as escapist entertainment, even when produced by blacks such as Kente and Sam Mhangwane. They were particularly critical of Mhangwane, partly because his long-running melodramas *Unfaithful Woman* (1966) and *Blame Yourself* (1970) preached Christian resignation rather than resistance, and partly because Mhangwane insisted on remaining affiliated with the white-run South African Theatre Organization, on the grounds that white professionals had much to teach black practitioners.[15] Kente was a more versatile showman and more difficult to dismiss. Like Motsieloa (Chapter 1) and Matshikiza (Chapter 3), Kente learned choral music at mission school and blended it with African and African-American variety to create the township musical. Although Kente's debt to Motsieloa and through him to African-American revues has gone largely unacknowledged, this pan-African influence played a greater role than the Western elements emphasized by the European author of an otherwise helpful study of Kente (Solberg 2011).[16] After Lovedale College, which Motsieloa had attended before him, and the Jan Hofmeyr School for Social Work in Johannesburg, Kente like Motsieloa worked as a talent scout for Gallo Records while writing music for singers such as Miriam Makeba. Like Matshikiza, he wove plots loosely around virtuoso performance numbers as in *Manana, the Jazz Prophet* (1963), or star performers, such as Kenny Majozif (Figure 5.1).[17] *Sikhalo* [lament] (1966) starring Majozi toured from Mafikeng in the northwest to Kente's home territory in the Eastern Cape including the Transkei Bantustan before reaching the Wits University Great Hall under the auspices of Union Artists. According to Aggrey Klaaste—later editor of *The Sowetan,* the newspaper that replaced the banned *World*—audiences responded with vocal enthusiasm to the music and the moral message. The show secured a place in township memory as a match for *King Kong* with its "good solid jazz and heart-rendering Xhosa hymns."[18] *Sikhalo* and *Lifa* (1967) established Kente's reputation for plots with sympathetic characters who fall victim to the pressures of township life or the wiles of tsotsis, but ended with the reconciliation of estranged family accompanied by Kente's arrangements of popular songs. The display of African talent no less than the last-minute reprieves deflected the violence of the apartheid state and its agents, white pass officers and black policemen, without confronting the state directly.

Moreover, Kente's success as a professional impresario impressed his audience. Although initially sponsored by Union Artists until Kente broke with Bernhardt (Solberg 2011: 11), *Sikhalo*'s long run was sustained by a combination of ticket sales and Kente's commission on cosmetics and other items sold at the venues. Despite apartheid restrictions on where he could perform and for whom, Kente earned enough around 1970 to pay his regular actors more than they could earn in the manufacturing sector (Kavanagh 1983: 93). Kente appealed to urban African tastes to a greater degree than did ventures like the Soweto Ensemble's productions of Anouilh's *Antigone,* or *Shaka* by Indian South African Sam Gorey.[19] As an entrepreneur supporting a retinue of actors and as a purveyor of moralistic entertainment, Kente's position resembles what Karin Barber has called the "radical conservatism" of Yoruba popular theatre. Although produced under very different political conditions, Kente's township melodrama shared with Yoruba theatre in the 1960s a conservative populist message and an entrepreneurial production structure. Although concluding on a reconciliatory note,

Figure 5.1 In the tradition of African vaudeville: Kenny Majozi in *Lifa* by Gibson Kente, Soweto, 1972.

Source: *S'ketsh*. Photographer unknown.

they "reveal in heightened and concentrated form the anxieties and preoccupations that underpin ordinary people's daily experience" (Barber 1986: 6).[20] Both respond to the precarious circumstances of entrepreneur and audience by celebrating individual virtue and satirizing status seekers and economic predators such as loan sharks.

Kente's prominence as an African entrepreneur, combined with his relatively conservative politics, provoked criticism from BCM intellectuals. Mafika Gwala, one of the editors of *Black Review*, called for a theatre whose "true representation" of the nation would be "far more serious than entertainment" (1973: 132), and quoted Mihloti's attack on township melodrama:

> Mihloti will not produce plays that tell you how unfaithful our women are. We do not present plays of our broken families, of how Black people fight and murder each other ...; this kind of theatre leaves the people broken and despaired. We tell the people to stop moaning and to start doing something about their valuable and beautiful black lives. (Gwala 1974: 113)

Mihloti criticized positive reviews in the black press of Kente's "thrilling new ventures" and black enthusiasm for *Ipi Tombi?*, which transferred to the townships after playing for a year in segregated city venues, but did not address the creative efforts of players such as Margaret Singana who wrote *Ipi Tombi?*'s hit song "Mama Tembu's wedding."[21] Black critics pushed back against this elite disdain: MDALI's Black Arts Festival at the Donaldson Orlando Cultural Club in Soweto in March 1973 provoked mixed reactions when it followed SABTU's example by offering a program of transnational writing, juxtaposing texts by James Baldwin with Mongane Serote and Jebe Masokoane— later president of PET. In *S'ketsh*, the "popular theatre and entertainment magazine," (1972–79), Sipho Sepamla endorsed the principle of black theatre but regretted that the festival chose as centerpiece Peter Weiss's *Marat/Sade*, whose subject—the French Revolution staged by the Marquis de Sade at the Charenton asylum—was remote from Soweto, and noted that Baldwin's Americanisms were hard to follow. Concluding that there was little "South African blackness in this black festival" (1973: 43), he drew attention to the unresolved tension between black intellectual interest in pan-African liberation and disdain for township taste.[22]

Manhood, Martyrdom, and Melodrama

Despite their disdain for popular entertainment, SABTU included plays whose portrayal of heightened feeling drew on the conventions of melodrama. As a genre that translates social conflict into emotional family drama using moralistic plots against the backdrop of a cruel or indifferent society, melodrama may seem an unlikely vehicle for political action, since it has tended—from its nineteenth-century heyday in the work of transnational playwrights such as Boucicault to its mid-twentieth-century manifestation as soap opera—to focus on the suffering of families rather than the political causes of their condition. Locally, Kente's *Sikhalo* (1966) shares with domestic dramas like Fugard's *Blood Knot* (Chapter 4) the depiction of families suffering in an unmanageable society against which ordinary people have no power. *Requiem for Brother X* indicts the social and economic consequences of racism more explicitly, however. Written by William Wellington Mackey in 1966 in homage to Malcolm X (assassinated in 1965) and produced by black university and community theatres in the United States, it reached SABTU via the *Black Drama Anthology* (New York, 1971), which also included *Junkies are full of SHIT* (1971) by Amiri Baraka—a.k.a. Leroi Jones. This play denounced white criminals for pushing drugs to blacks and was produced by Mihloti in February 1975. Mackey's description of his play as a "dialogue of confrontation" (1986: 327); this became the signature term for black consciousness theatre quoted by SABTU members who were inspired by Baraka and Mackey but it was the blend of melodrama and "dialogue of confrontation," sometimes mixed with the dramaturgy of trial by ordeal, which was distinctive here.

Requiem for Brother X was performed by TECON at the SABTU festivals in June and December 1972 and revived by PET in 1973. TECON's focus on the indictment of white government agents and what their program calls "dirty white politics" highlighted the play's agitprop dimension rather than its links to African-American domestic social drama, represented by Lorraine Hansberry's *A Raisin in the Sun* (1959). Nonetheless the dynamics of family interaction that Mackey borrowed from Hansberry gave more agency to women than BCM rhetoric usually did even if the ghetto conditions and the reactions of Mackey's characters were more desperate than the aspirations to upward mobility expressed by Hansberry's. In *Raisin*, Walter Lee squanders his family's savings on a fraudulent business deal; in *Requiem*, family man Matt once set his hopes on the civil rights movement led by Dr. Martin Luther King but has lost faith. His brother Nate follows Malcolm X's call to resist white supremacy but he still chases after white women, unaware that his child is about to be born to a forgotten white girlfriend who has sought refuge with his family but who never appears on stage. Despite his defense of Malcolm's principle of black self-defense, Nate's rebellion plays out a scenario in which he makes himself over into the bum that he imagines prospective employers see: "And when I go for that white man's examination, I'm gonna wear clothes that I'd have left in the alley for another week" (Mackey 1986: 344) and thus remains essentially rhetorical.

Where Nate's rebellion ends in self-parody and Matt's in resignation, the women in the family stand up. While Matt's wife Martha plays housewife to the men and midwife to the "little white girl" (328), Bonita, Nate's and Matt's sister, resembles in name and sharply critical attitude Beneatha Younger, the daughter of the house in *Raisin*, and shares with her predecessor a critique of her elders' aspirations for assimilation. She also exposes the bad faith of white social workers who see black lives in terms of the "War on Poverty" waged by the US government—"WE ARE THE DEPRIVED, THE SOCIALLY DISADVANTAGED, THE HELPLESS"—while remarking ironically that the off-stage white girl, whom the audience never sees, has stolen her role: "I'm supposed to be in there, screaming and carrying on with a baby in my belly. WE'RE SUPPOSED TO BE THE ONES WHO MAKE MISTAKES, NOT THEM!" (332). At the end Bonita and Martha deliver the baby but the last moments of the play are dominated by the complaints of the men, from father Jude's ambiguous laughter as he chants the sorrow song, "There is trouble all over this world" (345), to Matt's attack on his brother as an "ANIMAL" (346), to Nate's defiant despair—"My soul will rot in hell"—and, finally back to their father's laughter, which overlaps with the baby's cry as the lights fade. Although Bonita demonstrates capacity for action, the play as a whole is a complaint rather than an act of defiance. Jimmy Porter, would-be revolutionary and whiner protagonist of

Look Back in Anger, TECON's first production, haunts this "dialogue of confrontation," even if the self-pity that characterizes that most notorious "male complaint" does not dominate *Requiem* to the extent that it does in *Look Back in Anger*.[23] Although this complaint detracts from the critique of structural discrimination, SASO activists in key roles, such as Saths Cooper as Nate and Asha Rambally, an editor of *Black Review*, as Bonita, offset the melodramatic tenor of the complaint enough to earn the play a place as prime exhibit of a "theatre of determination, ... self-reliance and ... new awareness" (Khoapa 1973: 201).

But the value of the performance as political defiance does not mitigate the gender bias in *Requiem* or in the signature play of the BCM repertoire—*Shanti*. *Shanti's* reputation is due in part to its publication in Kavanagh's influential anthology *South African People's Plays* (1981) at a time when other BCM texts had been banned, and in part to the posthumous role of its author Mthuli Shezi as a Black Consciousness martyr. Shezi attended the SABTU festival in Durban in June 1972, after which he was expelled from the University of Natal—Black section. While on his way to the SABTU festival in Cape Town, he was pushed in front of a train by a white official whom Shezi had allegedly challenged for insulting a black woman (Khoapa 1973: 100).[24] Shezi's death in hospital, along with the banning of the SASO and TECON executive, prompted the founding of Peoples Educational Theatre (PET) in March 1973, which included Nomsisi Kraai, who played Shanti and authored "Black Theatre" in *PET Newsletter*, Jebe Masokoane as Thabo, Shanti's companion and martyr to the struggle, with Solly Ismail as director (Steadman 1985: 168). Led by Sadecque Variava, editor of the *PET Newsletter*, PET argued that Shezi's play "portray[ed] the true meaning of Black Consciousness, the evils and oppression that face the Blackman today" and called on their audience and one another to "clench our fists even higher in determination" (*PET Newsletter*, 2).[25] In this light, Masokoane as Thabo can be seen as a surrogate for Shezi, the martyred author of the play.

Shanti deals in part with the relationship between Shanti (Hindi: peace), and Thabo (Zulu: happy one), but the casting of Kraai as Shanti highlights black solidarity rather than Indian specificity as Cooper and Rambally as African-American characters had done in *Requiem*. Thabo achieves manhood by escaping the police, defecting to Mozambique, and meeting death at the hands of a guerrilla whose group he had hoped to join. Although Thabo's encounter with FRELIMO takes place only in scene eight (of eleven), it is this meeting that focuses the drama and celebrates Thabo's conversion to the armed struggle, even after Thabo is killed when the guerillas become suspicious of his attempt to contact Shanti. The rest of the action prepares the audience for this moment. The play opens with a Zulu lament, *Zixolise* [We have suffered], sung off-stage as Shanti weeps for Thabo. This song and another sung later by Thabo's fellow-prisoners, *Senzeni na sihlutshwana?* [What have we done to be punished so?], an anti-apartheid standard, recall the long tradition of African protest hymns as well as the contemporary poetry of defiance sung at the funerals of activists by groups like Mihloti. However, the dialogue spoken by Shanti, Thabo, and Koos—who represented Coloured commitment to black consciousness—is in academic English, Shezi's second language, that vacillates between sentimental expressions of love and emphatic denunciations of apartheid abuses. At its best, the terse presentation brings home the violence of apartheid power; the police who arrest Thabo and frame him for robbery is all too plausible. Likewise, the blunt exchange between Thabo and FRELIMO's General Mobu and his suspicious deputy Mangaya does not attempt to give the characters depth as individuals, but rather to harness the encounter to a lesson about sacrifice. The play endorses the armed struggle and thus publicizes a taboo topic but also shows that its agents are not uniformly heroic.

Shanti opened in Lenasia in September 1973; it played in Soweto and nearby Coronationville November 22–28 and on December 15 in Hammanskraal, north of Pretoria (Kavanagh 1985: 170). These few appearances were enough to provoke police harassment of spectators as well as performers. The play, the *PET Newsletter*, and the pamphlet praising Shezi as a black martyr, were cited as evidence in the case against Cooper, Moodley, and other SASO and BPC leaders (Mbanjwa 1975: 81–83). Charges under the 1967 Terrorism Act initially included the conspiracy to "stage, present, produce and/or participate in anti-white, racialistic, subversive and/or revolutionary plays and/or dramas."[26] Notwithstanding its academic English and its insular student milieu, *Shanti* gained legitimacy as a "means towards Black Liberation" (*PET Newsletter*, 2) or, to use the later phrase, a "cultural weapon," by virtue of its exhibition in the initial indictment (Steadman 1985: 186), even if one police operative with literary pretensions found the play's critique of apartheid to be "too ambiguous," noting in the margins of the text that it "had too little to do with the development of plot" and could not therefore "have any effect on stimulating strong terroristic action." Most of the detainees, including TECON officers Cooper and Moodley, were eventually convicted for belonging to political organizations, SASO and BPC, that were allegedly plotting the "violent overthrow of the state," not for staging plays on the subject.[27] Nonetheless, the initial charge presented before a gallery packed with black observers on March 12, and the reappearance of the text at the later trial of Variava, charged with "compiling and producing the PET newsletter and the play *Shanti*," brought the political implications of the play to the attention of a larger audience than the stage performances had been able to do. As Cooper and Nefolovhodwe later suggested (2007), public political trials gave articulate individuals in the movement one last opportunity to speak to sympathizers in the gallery before being sent away to prison.

Shanti's place in the arsenal of cultural weapons nonetheless rests on gendered ideas about who should handle those weapons, which reduce the title character to the melodramatic figure of the weeping widow. Prominent women such as Nomsisi Kraai, Sam Moodley, and others, PET, TECON, and other SABTU affiliates had to deal with the patriarchal habitus of BCM as reflected in repeated calls for women's support for black men. This habitus, more than outright misogyny, surfaces at moments in the play, such as Koos's reprimand to Shanti: "it is not good for a lady to imitate Hamlet [by thinking too much]" (Shezi 1981: 69) and drives its equation of agency and manhood, which leaves Shanti with little more to do than weep for her fallen hero. By treating suffering as a feminine foil to masculine agency and by representing that agency as martyrdom, *Shanti* replicates the melodramatic dramaturgy that PET and associates had so vigorously attacked, even more than *Requiem for Brother X*, since the latter at least has Bonita's militancy contrast with the complaints of the men around her. Bonita's persona also brings together the two apparently incompatible dramaturgical lines with which this section began—the theatre of defiance and the melodramatic complaint—as she sits in judgment of the men's failures and strives as protagonist to transcend the suffering role to which she had been assigned.

This performance of female agency was somewhat at odds with the BCM tendency to identify black identity with the "Black man" and *his* "dignity" (Khoapa 1973: 71), a tendency reinforced by women editing *Black Review*, 1974/75. Thoko Mbanjwa urged women to take part in "nutrition, childcare, basic skills such as knitting, sewing, …, cooking" (Mbanjwa 1975: 121); the following issue, also edited by a woman, argued that women were "basically responsible for the survival of their families, the socialization of the youth, and the transmission of the Black Consciousness Heritage"(Rambally 1977: 109). While many black women were responsible for their families in an apartheid economy that forced men into migrant labor, others, such as Biko's partner Mamphela Ramphele and the above editors, were politically active in their own right (Ramphele 1991), and twenty-first-century critics have recognized the work of the Black Women's Foundation (Gibson 2008: 13–15). It is therefore hard to defend BCM assertions that a "man's wife and children" were responsible for building up his self-esteem, to counter his "feeling of being emasculated under apartheid" (Manganyi 1973: 10–11). In the TECON arena, Vino Cooper and Sam Moodley, interviewed after their husbands, Saths Cooper and Srini Moodley, were banned, advocated struggle in the name of "strong black men," despite their own evident activism.[28] The association of liberation with the restoration of masculinity and the relegation of women to the role of auxiliary is not peculiar to South Africa, but it saturated twentieth-century discourses of national liberation and persists in South Africa today (Madikizela et al. 2015), despite progressive legislation supporting women's social and economic autonomy.

Beyond Black Consciousness? South African Indians and the Rainbow Nation

Although BCM theatre was a courageous response to an impossible situation, its talky format kept its content from reaching a wider black audience, even if press coverage suggests that its challenge to the police was understood by a larger public. Plays produced on the margins of the movement responded more generously to popular tastes and proved more able to move local audiences to reflection as well as to laughter and tears. Although mentioned only in passing in accounts of black theatre, possibly because they portrayed Indians and Coloureds or because they used politically ambiguous popular forms, Small's *Kanna, Hy Kô Hystoe* and Ronnie Govender's *The Lahnee's Pleasure* outlasted their appearances under the aegis of SABTU. Although more explicitly political than *Kanna*, *The Lahnee's Pleasure* shares much with Small's play. Both drew from the peculiar conditions of minority communities and the style of performance and genres favored by these audiences. While Shezi relied on English to convey abstract political ideas to a multilingual audience, Small and Govender (1934–) used the idiom of their communities, Kaaps and "Indian" English, to engage their local publics as well as black-identified intellectuals.

The Lahnee's Pleasure succeeded on several apparently incompatible fronts. It made local and national audiences laugh at the small world of Sunny the bartender, his Indian customers, and the "lahnee" [white] owner in a segregated "back-bar" in provincial Natal, yet exposed Indian class prejudice against "Indian" English (Mesthrie 2002b) and granted stage time to an advocate of black power in the person of the Stranger.[29] Provoked by Sunny's subservience to his *lahnee* boss and the *lahnee's* patronizing treatment of the customers, especially Mothie, a sugar-mill worker apparently driven to drink by his daughter's elopement, the Stranger argues that Indians should join other blacks fighting for their rights. Notwithstanding the force of this message, the Stranger's authority was compromised by the stage action. While the contradiction between his call for self-assertion against white tyranny and his endorsement of patriarchal discipline of wayward daughters—"girls are too free these days" (Govender 1977: 30)—have escaped critical attention, the comic characters stole the show. The improvisation of Mohammed Alli as Sunny and Kessie Govender and later Essop Khan as Mothie, which was incorporated into the published text (Govender 1977: ii), gave audiences an ambiguous mix of satire and ingratiation. Although the force of the satire challenging Indian class prejudice, was noted in reviews (n. 12; n. 25), the differences between the performances of Khan and Govender highlighted the ambiguity of the play. While Khan played up the absurd aspects of Mothie's plight and launched a lucrative but apolitical comic career (Naidoo 1997: 36), Kessie Govender challenged white and Indian spectators' prejudices by punctuating the comedy with Mothie's lines, such as "What you think we dirty people, what? ... We don't eat beef and pork ... We don't smell like white people" (Govender 1977: 21) and later wrote plays critical of Indian class prejudice, such as *Working Class Hero* (1979; published 2002). Kessie Govender (1942–2002) created the play at the Stable Theatre in Durban and performed it in Cape Town and Johannesburg; he drew on his experience as a bricklayer to tackle the tensions between Indian contractors and African and Indian workers.[30]

In the 1990s, writers and performers immersed in the spirit of the "rainbow nation" celebrated encounters between Indian and African cultures. Suria Govender's Surialanga dance group, one of those chosen for Mandela's presidential inauguration in 1994, celebrated the promise of national unity in its bilingual name (the Sanskrit word for "sun" paired with the Zulu) and in its fusion of Tamil and Zulu dance forms. *Looking for Muruga* (Asoka Theatre, UDW 1991; published 1995) by Kriben Pillay (1956–) portrayed a Zulu student (played by Dante Mashile) training for the classical Indian role of the god Muruga under the critical eye of his friend, an Indian bartender also called Muruga (Satchu Annamalai), who makes fun of Sherwin (Sherwin Christopher), an intellectual who wants to write about the bartender he misremembers as a comic (Figure 5.2).[31] The spirit of unity did not heal historical wounds, however; Ronnie Govender's dramatizations of his short stories in *At the Edge* (1991) and *1949* (1996) included comic impersonations by Charles Pillay of types from meddlesome aunts to self-important bartenders but recalled the still potent tension between Indians and Zulus. *1949* dealt with a Zulu worker's failed attempt to protect his Indian employer during the 1949 anti-Indian riots in Durban.[32] Prompted perhaps by *1949* or by *Coming Home*, a musical treatment (book by Pillay; music: Siva Devar; Asoka/NAPAC; Grahamstown Festival 1993) of uneasy Indian/Zulu relations, younger playwrights have dramatized

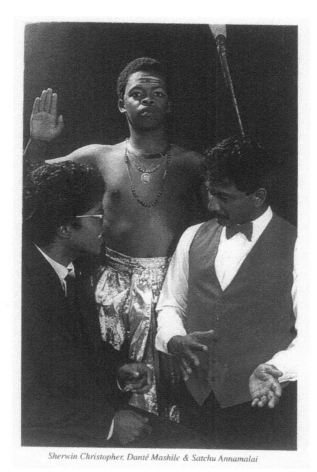

Sherwin Christopher, Danté Mashile & Satchu Annamalai

Figure 5.2 "A Zulu Indian God" (Dante Matshile) with Sherwin Christopher and Satchu Annamalai in Kriben Pillay's *Looking for Muruga*, Asoka Theatre, Durban 1991.

Photograph and permission by Kriben Pillay.

ongoing tensions. Ashwin Singh's *To House* (2003) portrays young Indians and Zulus competing for post-apartheid affirmative action; Rajesh Gopie's *Out of Bounds* (2008) depicts the 1985 attack on Indians in Inanda. Recalling an event that still lacks the recognition granted to 1949, Gopie responded in part to Indian nervousness in the wake of *Amandiya* [Indians] (2002), a provocative song by Mbongeni Ngema, which voiced Zulu grievances against Indians. In contrast, some new work addresses twenty-first-century themes: *Material* (2012), Craig Fremond and Riaad Moosa's film about a grudge nursed by one Indian draper against his brother for selling his shop to comply with apartheid eviction orders, mixes jokes from local stand-up with historical analysis of segregation to satirize consumerist behavior in the post-apartheid generation.

Populism after Politics? Gibson Kente's Legacy

The ambiguous mix of politics and entertainment in popular forms dominates the life and legacy of Gibson Kente, black capitalist, Christian, and for more than three decades (1960s–90s) the most successful purveyor of township musical melodrama, the most popular form of black entertainment. Kente's sentimental mix of tears, laughter, singing, and dancing provoked the ire of BCM intellectuals but he took up the challenge. In the mid-1970s, Kente incorporated politics into the formerly apolitical township musical but he did so not by giving his characters political speeches but by adding types such as the black policeman whose harassment of sympathetic characters would draw the audience's attention, however indirectly, to the state behind the uniform. In *How Long?* (1974) and *Too Late!* (1975), the deaths of sympathetic women (Khulu, the grandmother, in the former, and Ntanana, the crippled daughter, in the latter) are the indirect result of apartheid bureaucracy and brutality, even though the stage performance continued to rely on pathos and broad gestural acting, as the funeral scene at the end of *How Long?* suggests (image: Kruger 1999a: 150).[33] This critique, however implicit, alerted the security police who banned these plays and detained Kente, who responded to this harassment with more muted plots. In *La Duma* [Thunder] (1978), the conflict between a policeman and his activist son blamed activism for fragmenting African communities. At the height of the "emergency," Kente produced *Sekunjalo* [Now is the Time] (1985), which pitted a post-independence "African socialist" state against the entrepreneurial hero, Sechaba (nation), to protest what he saw as the anti-capitalist and anti-Christian tendencies of the ANC.[34]

Whereas Kente's plots were conservative, in the sense that the plays ended with reconciliation rather than resistance, *Too Late!* registers the impact of the BCM call for a "theatre of determination." Although the play does not portray organized rebellion, it shows characters engaged in small acts of resistance to the arbitrariness of state power, represented by the pink gloves and Afrikaans insults of a hidden bureaucrat at the pass office, or directly by the brutality of the stupid but dangerous black policeman Pelepele (hot pepper). Where BCM intellectuals favored plays such as *Shanti* that portrayed acts of resistance, Kente's audiences relished the anarchic dodging of the comic Offside, played by Ronnie Mokoena as both clown and commentator. Where *Shanti* advocated political action, *Too Late!* portrays a family drama centered on Madinto, who runs a shebeen to support her crippled daughter Ntanana and her orphaned nephew Saduva. Madinto's traffic in illegal liquor, like the petty theft of the *majitas* [township toughs], is seen as the result of restrictions on legitimate employment for Africans. Saduva's makeover from a "God-loving boy" into a *majita* when he is sent to prison for carrying an invalid pass book is likewise shown to be the result of apartheid. Even Pelepele's most brutal act, killing Ntanana as she tries to protect Saduva, is partly the effect of his job and is offset by her final act of—uncharacteristic—violence, as she kicks her assailant in the balls. As Dr. Phuza [drink] asks: "Can't something be done to curb the bitterness in both young and old, before it's TOO LATE?" (Kente 1981: 122).[35]

The style of performance in *Too Late!* follows Kente's usual mix of sentimental dialogue alongside comic gags and group mime, in which performers' bodily and facial mimicry of, say, panicked response to a pass raid, makes a more vivid impression on the audience than verbal comment lost in the noise. Kente's direction takes account of African audience's documented tendency to laugh at stage violence (Maponya 1984) as well as their fluid response to sudden shifts in mood: he invites laughter in response to Pelepele's clownish brutality *and* to Ntanana's retaliation, only to switch to sentimental mode as Ntanana's musical signature announces her death.[36] On the one hand, the musicianship and professional singing, in Klaaste's words, "make up from the flaws of articulation" (1975a: 9), due in part to Kente's insistence that his vernacular-speaking cast memorize lines in English so as to reach a broad audience. On the other, improving on the variety concert format of Motsieloa, Kente uses key songs and phrases to mark particular characters or shifts in mood. Thus, for example, the Xhosa hymn *Ngabayini lisoni sam'?* [What could it be, my sin?] first appears in a church scene, after Mfundisi has criticized the abuse of church teachings to defend unjust law and before he shames the policemen who invade the church looking for *majitas*. This moment reinforces the moral authority of the church but, when the phrase recurs, it is to ironic effect, as Saduva curtly dismisses his girlfriend's shock at his tough behavior. *Ndilahlekile* [I am lost], which is first heard as background to the scene in which Ntanana is discovered scavenging for food while Madinto is in prison for running a shebeen, returns at the end to soften Saduva's tough mask when he admits his debt to his family and thus moderates his bitterness, which might otherwise have appeared as defiance.

Despite the moralizing gloss on Saduva's bitterness, the PCB banned the play a month after it opened in February 1975, approving it for performance in Soweto after Kente agreed to modify the script but leaving performances in other townships to the whim of local authorities. While this censorship indicates the state's anxiety about the play's potential for agitation, it does not in itself prove that the performance radicalized its spectators. Kavanagh argued retrospectively for "radical elements in the audience" but concedes that Kente did not "intend his play to mobilize the revolutionary energies of the black working class" (1985: 134–35), but rather to capitalize on growing youth protest, while still satisfying audience desire for "pathos" and "bawdy hilarity" (1974–75: 8–9). While Klaaste regretted the "spurious bubble of happiness" buoyed by the music despite the protest rhetoric, Elliot Makhaya registered audience response as a combination of enthusiasm for the "pure entertainment" of Ronnie Mokoena and sympathy for the family's plight, expressed in cries of "Shame," as well as choral singing of familiar hymns.[37] *Too Late* may have lacked the militancy of *Shanti* or the critical estrangement of *The Coat* and represented a politically risky detour from Kente's usual conciliatory mode but its performance on the eve of the Soweto uprising captured the contradictory mix of anxiety and anticipation in the mid-1970s. Other plays in this period attempted to infuse melodramatic forms with Black Consciousness content. Rev. Mzwandile Maqina's *Give us this Day* (1974) aimed to dramatize the life and death of Onkgopotse Abraham Tiro, student leader at the University of the North assassinated in exile (n. 8) but, according to Klaaste, the play used "Kentesian" forms, including "exhibitionistic" acting and emphatic depiction of the "political tragedy" (1975b: 26–27). However uneven, the play was still dangerous enough to be suppressed (Steadman 1985: 469) but its publication demonstrated ongoing interest in the political deployment of the musical.

The contradictory mix of melodrama and politics strung together by musical numbers pioneered and perfected by Kente has persisted into the present, as can be seen in the Sophiatown nostalgia musicals mentioned in Chapter 3, in numerous but uneven attempts to revive Kente's plays in the twenty-first century and, to bring this trend up to date, in Aubrey Sekhabi's sentimental treatment in *Marikana—the Musical* (State Theatre 2014) of the massacre of striking miners by the ANC police in 2012. We will return to *Marikana* and the state of the post-apartheid musical in Chapter 8, but the BCM project of a "theatre of defiance," which has been analyzed in this chapter, leads directly to the anti-apartheid theatre in the 1970s and 1980s. Whether labeled "protest," "resistance," or more recently "testimonial theatre," anti-apartheid theatre grappled with the tension between popular entertainment and political aspiration, and between the township musicals pioneered by Kente and the spare concreteness of the testimonial devised in workshops by Fugard, Simon, their associates, and their many successors and, in these groups, between those determined to maintain the BCM line on creating black institutions, however precarious, and those willing to take advantage of offers from well-funded independent institutions and their predominantly white progressive managers to develop work that could then return to the townships. Bolstered by the cultural capital of liberal education and the finance capital of liberal corporations, the Space (1971–81) and the Market Theatre (1976–) allowed for relatively integrated assembly. Shielded from state violence to a greater degree than township venues by this access to capital, the Space and the Market opened their doors to Africanist groups such as the Dhlomo Theatre or the Soyikwa Institute, even if the latter, seeing themselves as inheritors of the Black Consciousness Movement, regarded the Market with ambivalence. The emergence of the Market—and the market for anti-apartheid theatre—is the subject of Chapter 6.

Spaces and Markets

Theatre as Testimony and Performance against Apartheid

In October 1972, *Sizwe Banzi is Dead* by Fugard, John Kani, and Winston Ntshona played a single Sunday night for members only at the Space in Cape Town. It went on to Johannesburg and New Brighton—Kani's and Ntshona's home-township near Port Elizabeth in the Eastern Cape—but was banned thereafter as the trio went on tour to London. In October 1981, *Woza Albert!* by Mbongeni Ngema, Percy Mtwa (1955–), and Barney Simon opened at the Market Theatre in Johannesburg for a run that would last a month, culminating in a tour and publication in London (Mtwa, Ngema, Simon 1983). The intervening nine years saw the resurgence of mass opposition to apartheid and of theatre as a witness to that struggle. This testimonial theatre dramatized individual and collective stories and provocative topics such as the pass laws, prison conditions, workers' rights, and, less often, the condition of women. It combined physical and verbal comedy, impersonation of multiple characters with minimal props, and direct audience address by performers expressing their own convictions while playing fictional roles. Its practitioners drew on different models from township musicals and variety to European experiments, such as Grotowski's poor theatre and Brecht's epic theatre, but tended to create scripts in workshops rather than commission a single author.

What distinguishes this testimonial theatre at the height of the anti-apartheid movement in the 1970s and 1980s from the political theatre that had surfaced sporadically since the 1930s was not its engagement with provocative topics or experimental form, which had occurred before, but its institutional stability. The Space and the Market had resources unavailable to their predecessors from the African National Theatre (1936–41) to the Serpent Players (1963–70s) because their white managers' access to liberal capital offset the lack of government subsidy. This capital deflected government meddling and enabled the place and occasion for social assembly as well as anti-apartheid culture, even when apartheid violence dominated global news. Their audiences were in turn visible enough at home and abroad to discourage overt state interference. After the Space closed in 1981, the Market, supported by Anglo-American and other corporations, non-profits and progressive individuals, dominated the field; it staged its own company's work and hosted black institutions, such as the Dhlomo Theatre in Johannesburg, Soyikwa in Soweto, and groups founded by writers such as Ngema's Committed Artists or the Bahumutsi Players led by Maishe Maponya (1951–) who were under surveillance by the police.

This accommodation was not always a happy one. Black Consciousness Movement activists in Soweto argued that the Market's capital enabled it to absorb the work of black groups without changing their difficult condition of production. Even if Soweto community halls such as the Donaldson Orlando Cultural Centre (DOCC) and the YMCA offered performance venues, these tended to be in better-off districts such as Orlando or Dube, and thus out of reach of poorer districts, as the township had little internal transport and the threat of violence made most reluctant to brave badly lit streets (Maponya 1984).[1] Black playwrights endorsed the BCM call for township premieres and the preference, in Zakes Mda's words, for "theatre for resistance with the overt aim of rallying and mobilizing the oppressed to fight against oppression" rather than "protest theatre," which "depicts a situation of oppression ... to the oppressor, ... appealing to his or her conscience" (1995: 40–41), but it is nonetheless difficult to draw a firm line between a theatre of resistance in the townships and a protest theatre encouraging the metropolitan audience's sympathy with the oppressed. Some theatres intent on "mobiliz[ing] the masses" were welcomed at the Market but disdained by township audiences, who preferred musicals in the Kente style. The Market straddled the line between lament and defiance, housing for instance Elsa Joubert's sentimental treatment of people displaced by apartheid in *Die Swerfjare van* [Years of wandering] *Poppie Nongena* (1979) (Joubert/Kotze 1984) and Mda's unsentimental depiction of migrants in *The Hill* (1980). Ngema's *Sarafina* (1986; published Ngema 1995), a musical loosely based on the 1976 student uprising made Ngema a celebrity but Maponya's plays from the agitprop of *The Hungry Earth* (1978) to the indictment of torture in *Gangsters* (1984) appealed more to intellectuals.

While this irony does not invalidate distinctions between protest and resistance, it highlights the flexibility of the testimonial form. This chapter tracks the factors that made testimonial theatre *the* performance form of South Africa—as the enactment of an aspirational public sphere in the name of a democratic order to come. It places key productions in the context of force fields generated by the links and friction between, in Williams's sense (1995: 35), institutions (visible structures and organizations), formations (groups of participants, whether identified as a company of artists or—as the militants have it—"cultural workers," and the forms and conventions of testimony, resistance, and restoration on stage.

Occupying Space

The Space/*Die Ruimte* opened in May 1972 with Fugard's *Statements After an Arrest under the Immorality Act* (Fugard et al. 1986). Fugard played Coloured teacher Errol Philander and Yvonne Bryceland Frieda Joubert, his white lover, and the play began by shocking the audience as a policeman's flashlight caught both in bed. But the work that led to the Space's most famous productions *Sizwe Banzi is Dead* (October 1972) and *The Island* (July 1973) began years before with *The Coat* by the Serpent Players in 1966. Although the arresting staging of *Statements*, combining physical and emotional exposure and terse report, owed much, as owner Brian Astbury (Bryceland's husband) indicated, to Peter Brook, Charles Marowitz, and other experimenters in 1960s London (Astbury 1979: n.p.), the play also harked back to the racial melodrama of the South African 1960s (Chapter 4).[2] *The Coat*, on the other hand, depicted the lives of black performers with Brechtian sobriety in the manner of his "new technique of acting" (Brecht 2014: 184–96), reporting and juxtaposing conflicting social gests so as to prompt analysis of characters' attitudes and interactions. The group had staged adaptations of European plays from Niccolo Machiavelli's *La Mandragola* (as *The Cure*) to Brecht's *Caucasian Chalk Circle* but *The Coat* drew on an actual incident at the trial of one of the players, likely Norman Ntshinga (1930s–2000) who later served time on Robben Island.[3] Fugard acted less as author than as scribe and provocateur (Fugard 1984: 124–26, 135–43). The group used the coat as the "mandate"—Fugard's term for the prompt of an improvised action—for a series of encounters, such as between the woman bearing the convict's message, and his waiting wife, played by Mabel Magada, Ntshinga's actual spouse, or between the wife and the rent board official threatening to evict her, and thus spoke directly to urban African concerns. The actors, including Kani and Nomhle Nkonyeni, both major actors in the making, introduced themselves using the names of characters they had played in earlier productions—Kani as Haemon in *Antigone* and Nkonyeni as Aniko in *Caucasian Chalk Circle*. This tactic delayed police investigation into the players' identities while directed audience attention to the social gest rather than the personalities of the actors or characters; this demonstrative focus on use value prompted activists in the 1970s to revive the play (Chapter 5).

While Brecht's coolness may seem out of sync with township melodrama, his sober style suited the Serpent Players who, unlike the "situations" that worked with Fugard in 1950s Johannesburg, were disciplined industrial workers and political activists (Fugard 1984: 96). *The Island*, performed initially (July 1973) as *Hodoshe Span*, [Blood-sucking Fly's work crew], named for a mean prison guard, distilled elements from the experience of ex-political prisoner Ntshinga, offset by a reenactment of *Antigone* derived from a performance on Robben Island with Mandela as Creon (Mandela 1995: 456).[4] The classical source and the resonance of its theme earned *The Island* international attention.[5] But *Sizwe Banzi* [the nation is strong] offers a richer synthesis of performance forms and a direct engagement with everyday experience. The story follows Sizwe who has come from the country to look for work in the city, which he can get only with a valid passbook and, with the help of Buntu [humanity], acquires the ID of a dead man, Robert Zwelinzima (hard or heavy world). It was prompted by a photograph of a man in his Sunday best, posing with a cigarette in one hand and a pipe in the other, and a broad smile on his face (image: Kruger 1999a: 158). A man with this smile, reasoned Kani and Ntshona, had to have his pass in order. The Space program, which listed the participants including Fugard by ID numbers only, highlighted the contradiction between the "dream picture" and the reality of discrimination captured in the passbook photography but it countered the bureaucratic alienation of identity with the collaborative creation of the play.[6]

The players also negotiated different modes of performance. The oscillation between Grotowskian poor theatre and exuberant impersonation, Brechtian coolness and the ingratiating sketch, played on the tension between the absurd but painful impact of apartheid bureaucracy and the energetic mockery of that absurdity. The social *gestus* of handling objects such as the passbook drew on Brecht by way of *The Coat* but the overall performance was shaped by the actors' lives, especially Kani's seven years at the local Ford factory, and by African concert form (Kani/Ntshona 1976). Kani's virtuoso performance of Styles and antagonists, from his boss to cheeky cockroaches, was not really a monologue, as often described, but a satirical variety turn. His impersonation of "Baas Bradley" and his own former self is telling:

 – Tell the boys in your language, that this is a very big day …
 – Gentlemen, the old fool says this is a hell of a big day …
 – Tell the boys that Mr. Henry Ford the Second is the big *baas*, … the *Makhulu baas* …
 – Mr. Baas Bradley says … Mr. Ford is the grandmother baas. (Fugard 1993a: 153)

Although more elaborate than Ronnie Mokoena's clowning as Offside in *Too Late!*, Kani's broad mimicry of his boss speaking to the "boys," enhanced by audience responses, shows Kente's influence.

This affinity did not please everybody. Sepamla criticized the ingratiating aspect of the impersonation that made black spectators "laugh too hard at the white man" (1973: 24) and Michael Feingold in New York compared Kani with Stephin Fetchit, even as he praised the politics of the performance, evidently unaware of earlier South African interest in this figure from the minstrel repertoire (Chapter 1).[7] In St. Stephen's Hall in New Brighton, however, audiences proved able to combine heartfelt laughter at situations they knew well with strategic intervention: "At the end of the Ford Factory story a man … entered the acting area and then, as if he was a referee at a boxing match, held up John's arm and announced that 'Kani has knocked out Henry Ford the Junior'" (Fugard 1993a: 30). Fugard calls this intervention Brechtian and, while it instantiates Brecht's active spectator, it is also thoroughly African. As Fugard noted, there was a significant difference between white spectators' response of "horror and fascination" (1984: 143) to *The Coat* and the cast's dispassionate comment on the handling of the coat and other objects, like the *umuti* [medicine] in the pocket that allegedly lightened the convict's sentence (137). The difference between passive spectators of the illusionistic Anglo-American stage and township audiences' interaction with the players may have been new to Fugard, but African preference for interaction was noted in the 1940s (Routh 1950b) and confirmed in the 1980s (Maponya 1984).

While Kani's opening act borrowed from township comedy, Kani and Ntshona developed the plot and argument through dialogue. The invisible pass in Kani's hands and Ntshona's meaningful stare conveyed the document's real power (Figure 6.1). Sizwe hesitates to give up his name for a dead man's passbook, and is persuaded only when Buntu draws him into dramatizing a series of scenarios—with a policeman and a prospective employer—to bring home the urgency of the decision. If the white audience in Cape Town was touched by the bitter comedy of this predicament and if some blacks in Johannesburg found the play too talky, those in New Brighton were moved to interrupt:[8]

Figure 6.1 Winston [Ntshona], John [Kani] and the passbook in *Sizwe Banzi is Dead*, New Brighton, 1972.

Photograph courtesy of National English Literary Museum; photographer unknown.

After watching the first few seconds of the operation [putting Sizwe's photograph into Robert's pass] in stunned silence ... a voice shouted out from the audience: 'Don't do it brother ...' Another voice responded ... 'Go ahead and try. They haven't caught me yet.' That was the cue for the most amazing and spontaneous debate I have ever heard. As I stood ... listening to it all, I realized I was watching a very special example of one of theatre's major responsibilities in an oppressive society: to break ... the conspiracy of silence. The action of our play was being matched ... by the action of the audience .... A performance on stage had provoked a political event in the auditorium. (Fugard 1982: 31–32)

What is noteworthy about this audience's participation is not exactly an expression of urgency. Fugard's stress on the "urgent and real" desire to "speak and be heard" oddly implies that this audience has never discussed the matter before. This intervention is powerful not because it "breaks the silence" but because it acknowledges the symbolic character of the action. The audience's debate, like the show it interrupts, is a *performance*; its enactment here—in the liminal space between the familiar township and the unusual character of the show—is significant precisely because theatre enables a discussion that might be dangerous outside. When Buntu and "Robert" in *Sizwe Banzi* simulate encounters with potential power brokers like the boss or the police or when prisoner John (Kani) mimes "calling home" from *The Island*, recalling the symbolic acts of Robben Island prisoners deprived of family contact, this performance reenacts ordinary acts in extraordinary circumstances. By intervening in the play, the members of the audience do not abandon the fiction; they *use* it. Their public participation performs the subjunctive action of occupying space and so entertains the possibility of a democratic future.

Engendering Environments

Sizwe Banzi is Dead set important precedents for testimonial theatre—the collective composition of scripts, the masculine vigor of the players, and the negotiation of the different knowledge bases of black and white participants—and inspired adaptations, such as Kriben Pillay's Indian *Mr. Banzi is Dead* (1997) and Eliot Moleba's post-apartheid *Sizwe Banzi is Alive* (2011). In the 1970s Space program, however, not all shows followed this pattern. Following the model of small theatres in London that avoided censorship prior to its abolition in 1966 by staging members-only club performances, Astbury registered the Space as a club to evade the PCB. The local adaptation of Jean Genet's *The Maids* featured the camp talents of Bill Curry and Vincent Ebrahim as Coloured maids, and of Pieter-Dirk Uys as the white Madam, an early incarnation of the diva that would become his alter ego Evita Bezuidenhout. Uys's own play *Selle ou Storie* (1983 [1973]), about intrigues between gay and straight urbanites, offended the censors not only by staging queer characters but perhaps more by swearing in mixed English and Afrikaans. His satirical revues from *Strike up the Banned* (1975) through *Adapt or Dye* (1981) to *Beyond the Rubicon* (1986) established him as a dissident, but, unlike his rival Robert Kirby (1936–2007), whose *How Now, Sacred Cow?* (1977) and other shows were shut down to spite his English liberal audience, Uys benefitted from Afrikaans affiliation, even earning praise from the Afrikaner politicians that he lampooned (Lewis 2016: 127).

Whereas Uys's queer satire reflected the Space's aspiration to cosmopolitan urbanity, Fatima Dike (1948–) depicted black life with unironic urgency. Born in Langa and educated in Cape Town and at the Iowa Writers' Workshop, Dike has tackled several themes; *The Sacrifice of Kreli* (Space 1976; published: Dike 1979) depicts a historic clash between the British and the Gcakela, while *The Return* (2009) portrays homecoming exiles. Dike was the first black woman published in Ravan Press's pioneering black play series but the protagonist of *The First South African* (Space 1977) is male, in keeping with the BCM equation of manhood and nationhood (Chapter 5). The hero was "a man who looked like a white man, who had the heart of a black man, and was a 'Coloured'" (Dike 1977: 46). Raised by his Xhosa mother, Ruben Zwelinzima Jama is called Rooi because of his red hair but the name also alludes to red ochre and to the historical distinction between traditionalist ("red") and Christianized Xhosa. Initially indistinguishable from the other blanketed youths at the initiation ceremony, Rooi (Joe Hartzenberg) revealed himself when his white arm reaches out from the blanket to the gifts left by the elders. In this image is distilled the unbearable tension between the brotherhood invoked by the ritual and the divisive implications of Rooi's color. The authority of male elders that might have raised Rooi is undercut by the deprivation that distorts the youths' idea of manhood into tsotsi bravado. Zwelinzima (whose name—hard world–recalls the character in *Sizwe Banzi*) abuses Xhosa custom when he sleeps with his neighbor's daughter Thandi without paternal consent and abandons his family to work as a white on the railroad. Though the dialogue in English, Xhosa, flaaitaal, and Afrikaans is mostly naturalistic, the play uses different styles to distinguish characters. After the visually striking initiation scene, Hartzenberg declaims a poem that begins with Creation and ends with the question: "Am I a man?" in the emphatic BCM manner, but Rooi's friend Max swaggers in the flamboyant manner of Kente's *majitas*, addressing spectators as marks for his stolen goods. The stick that the elders give Rooi when he comes of age taunts him at the end. Driven from his family home, he performs his self-hatred for an imaginary *baas* in skollie stereotype, "Nee, my baas. I'm quiet ... I'm listening (*He stands to attention*)," while treating the stick as symbol of paternal authority: "Leave me alone ... I'm tired of you (*He takes the stick and puts it across his shoulders and breaks it*)" (Dike 1977: 43).

Although the elders make women's subjugation part of male initiation—"with this stick, beat your mother when she forgets that she's a woman" (6)—Nomhle Nkonyeni gave Rooi's mother Freda more gravity than the suffering mother implied by the sometimes melodramatic dialog. Her first entrance, in which Freda responds to the demands of an unseen white bureaucrat to give up her child, used the sober directness from her work on *The Coat* to draw out the bureaucrat's gest of control as well as the mother's refusal. Freda's challenge to Rooi's view of manhood: "You feel that you're a man now ... Do it outside these four walls" (17) rebukes him for exploiting color privilege by seducing Thandi but refusing to pay respect to her father Hlazi. But Freda also criticizes Hlazi. When her argument with Rooi is interrupted by a loud knock on the door, Freda asks, "Ingubani yena lo unqonqoza kakubi kangaka? [Who is making such a racket?]" and, although she acknowledges Hlazi's complaint, does not allow him to silence her. To his "keep quiet; you're a woman" (18), she retorts, "he's making business with his daughter"(19) targeting not only Hlazi but all men who share his assumption of patriarchal "ownership" of women. Dike revisited African patriarchy in *The Return* (Artscape, 2009), which recalls Ghanaian writer Ama Aidoo's *Dilemma of a Ghost* (1987) in that it pits a homecoming exile and his African-American wife against his parents' view that his lack of respect for his ancestors and his dead brother is the cause of the family's misfortune, but nuances this scenario by showing the destructive power of the family's envy for the supposedly rich American and by concluding with reconciliation between matriarch and daughter-in-law (Dike 2009: 94).[9]

Other plays at the Space included women's voices, albeit sporadically. *Imfuduso* (1978) brought women from Crossroads, the informal Western Cape settlement established by women from the Transkei and Ciskei Bantustans, while Geraldine Aron's *Bar and Ger* (1978) recreated the lives of Jewish children insulated from this harsh world. Dike's *Glasshouse* (1979, the last production by Astbury's management, shows a white girl and a black girl (the child of the former's nanny) grow up in the same household but in different worlds. When Astbury and Bryceland left for London, the People's Space (*Volksruimte/Indawo Yezizwe*, 1979–81) under Rob Amato produced plays about working men in the cities such as Matsamela Manaka's *Egoli* and in rural poverty, such as Mda's *Dark Voices Ring* (1979) and *The Hill* (1980), and hosted others on similar themes, such as Kessie Govender's *Working Class Hero* from Durban (1979).[10]

With the opening of the Market Theatre and institutions such as the FUNDA (Learning) Centre in Soweto, and Federated Union of Black Artists (FUBA, est. 1978), productive energy moved to Johannesburg. The financial and cultural capital of the Market shaped theatre nationwide. After the demise of the Space, the most substantial counterweight to the Market was the Grahamstown Festival. Despite claims today that it was never subject to segregation, the festival began in 1974 as an exclusively white affair sponsored by the English 1820 Settlers Foundation with main stage performances by the Performing Arts Councils and fringe productions by student groups. By 1984, it included blacks on the fringe but was met with protests by black groups who noted that invitations without financial aid did not amount to much, and by calls from the ANC overseas to boycott the festival. Collaborating with community theatres trained by the Market Laboratory from 1989 and the Baxter Theatre in Cape Town from the 1990s to produce a more integrated program, by 1996, the National Arts Festival received funding from the post-apartheid Department of Arts and Culture, business sponsors, and non-profit foundations (Kruger: 2019).

In the 1970s, however, theatrical innovation was mostly an urban affair. Before the Market opened in June 1976, Workshop '71's *Survival*, commissioned by the Space, developed testimonial theatre similar to *The Coat*, and forged links between Cape Town and Johannesburg. Workshop '71 started as a workshop run by Robert McLaren (a.k.a. Robert Mshengu Kavanagh; 1944–), then a Wits University lecturer, but *Uhlanga* [Reed] (1975), an African *Everyman* by James Mthoba (1940s–?), established its reputation. Where *Sizwe Banzi* favored dialogue leavened with comedy, *Survival* used dialogue chiefly as a functional frame for individually presented but collectively relevant reports delivered directly to the audience; four men relate their everyday trials under apartheid to explain how they landed in prison. Using a mixture of angry address and poignant introspection, each actor delivered a report in his own name, in which he recounted, with other actors playing roles from family members to court interpreters, the events that led to his character's arrest. Edward Nkosi killed one of his mother's clients in a revolt against the conditions that pushed her into sex-work; Vusi Mabandla killed a black policeman who stopped him from driving his father to hospital without a license; Slaksa Mphahlele was jailed for striking and Leroi Williams, whose chosen American name reflects his interest in international black liberation, for disseminating Black Power pamphlets. The final scene echoes *Shanti*'s militancy but grounds this commitment in experience. As the prisoners go on hunger strike, they shout:

> Phela, phela, phela [a]malanga
> Azophela, azophela [a]malanga
> [Enough, enough, enough of these days
> There will be an end to these days](Workshop '71 1981: 167)

Despite the (mimed) beating of prisoners at the end, the actors survived to "go forward" (168).

This play may have seemed "strong and ugly" to some whites (Kavanagh 1981: 126), but the anticipation of liberation moved white as well as black audiences.[11] While the relative quiescence of 1973 had allowed the audience to play with the performance of *Sizwe Banzi is Dead*, the explosion in Soweto and beyond gave *Survival* an impact that was more direct but also short-lived. It appeared at the Space and in Cape township halls in May 1976 and in Soweto and at the Wits Box briefly after the June uprising, at which point the police banned it and threatened the cast, leading them to choose exile after their American tour.[12] While still at township venues such as the YMCA in Dube, the players faced police in the hall but incorporated them into the show, opening with a comic impersonation of an officer looking for "agitators" and encouraging audience response to the final "we go forward" to turn threats of state violence into politically enabling performance. Even after Workshop '71 disbanded, this testimony of masculine struggle set the model for plays such as Maponya's *Hungry Earth* (DOCC, Soweto, 1978), Manaka's *Egoli* (YMCA, Soweto; then Space, 1979), and many to follow. However brief its run, *Survival* participated in a "revolutionary situation" partly by conscientizing whites and partly by summoning audiences to defy laws against "riotous assembly" (Kavanagh 1981: 127). In solidarity with the student rebellion and with other dissident organizations, it showed resilience in the fact of oppression.

Survival attracted a public more diverse than BCM drama, and more vocally dissident than the audience for Western theatrical experiments. This public—or rather, overlapping publics from liberal professionals (mostly non-black) through students (black and white) to organic intellectuals and workers (mostly black)—would sustain anti-apartheid theatre into the 1990s. Kavanagh calls this formation *majority theatre*, born of collaboration between black and white participants committed to integration rather than an exclusively black project (1985: 214–15), and thus a vanguard for a future democracy governed by majority rule. The representation of a democratic majority in the theatre was no easy task but the Space had opened up a house for integrated assembly and the Market promoted integration on stage and in the house. Their example enabled the University of Cape Town to fulfill donor William Baxter's bequest for a "theatre for all" by opening the Baxter Theatre in 1977, even if it remained "more conventional and more commercial" (Tucker 1997: 349) and mostly white until *District Six* integrated the house in 1987. Despite these limitations, the Space, the Market, and township projects galvanized by Soweto and other uprisings in 1976, were sustained by the movements that grew up to establish the United Democratic Front (UDF; 1983–1993) and enabled workers, intellectuals, and aspiring theatre practitioners from different classes and ethnicities to find common ground.

Marketing Resistance / Resisting Marketing

For many South Africans, June 1976 signals not merely the rebellion of black students against apartheid education but *the* uprising that "changed South Africa forever" (Orkin 1995: 72), even if that struggle would be won only after a "long and taxing war of attrition" (Karis/Gerhart 1997: 185) that would endure until the democratic election of 1994. Although students and workers had been on the move since the founding of SASO in 1969 and the industrial action of the early 1970s, the uprising that exploded in Soweto on June 16, 1976 ignited not only township schools and beer-halls nationwide—the latter torched as symbols of state abuse—but also the popular imagination, as tens of thousands across the country marched in protest. The impact of the uprisings was slowed by the arrest and murder of leaders such as Biko, and by the suppression of anti-apartheid organizations under the Internal Security Act (1976), which allowed for indefinite detention of activists. But, despite this repression, the rebellion would redouble in the 1980s, guided by community-based groups (CBOs, locally called *civics*) that came together to create the UDF, which would lead the fight to bring down apartheid.

We will return to the dramatization of the uprising in *Sarafina*, which opened ten years later. In 1976, however, the students took most outside Soweto by surprise, including the exiled ANC (Ndlovu 2006: 219). As the police stormed the township, the Market was rehearsing *The Seagull*, Anton Chekhov's ironic portrait of the Russian gentry in decline. While this play offered no simple allegory of the dilemmas of South African whites, the local resonance of the plot was inescapable, as was the theatre's liminal position. Formerly an Indian fruit market, the building was in Newtown, on the border between the central business district and Fordsburg, a mixed neighborhood from the 1890s whose black and brown residents were expelled in the 1960s.[13] Barney Simon's vision of the theatre as a "meeting place for all South Africans ... as enriching and relevant as the market it replaced" (Graver/Kruger 1989: 273) acknowledged this dispossession but did not directly contest the acquiescence of Johannesburg's capitalist elite to the planned violence of the apartheid state. Sponsored by private corporations, the Market stood awkwardly between the historical displacement of black business and residence, and the aspiration to become "an oasis in a society of total chaos ... where people could talk together and we could put on theatre that ... said things about South Africa" (Schwartz 1988: 37).[14] By concentrating capital in the central building, the board expressed the desire for metropolitan prestige, reinforced by media comparisons with Covent Garden in London (Graver/Kruger 1989: 275). However well intentioned, this emphasis on a building in which "black people can watch theatre in a decent way," in the words of founding manager Mannie Manim (Graver/Kruger 1989: 274), betrayed a certain disdain for township theatre, and did not change the laws that made "decent theatre" in the townships precarious if not impossible.

Whereas cultural prestige of the theatre in Europe has often been marked by the physical prominence of theatre buildings, the Market instead occupied a liminal site between the legitimate city of prosperity and modernity and the illegitimate city of crime and poverty. In the "edgy city" (Kruger 2013) Johannesburg in 1976, however, the edge that had historically marked the line between the permanent white city and the supposedly impermanent black township—which prompted Fanon's analysis in 1962 of the asymmetry between "settler city" and "native location" (2004: 3–4)—was blurring. As the Market was seeking to integrate audiences, working people of color who had been expelled from the city were stealthily moving back to inner districts, contributing to the "greying of Johannesburg" (Pickard-Cambridge 1989). Although Johannesburg's centennial year 1986 saw a new Stock Exchange in nearby Diagonal Street on what had been the spine of Indian trade, and the Newtown Cultural Precinct, which included a flea market, a gallery, and some boutiques and restaurants around the Market, Black organizations such as FUBA and the Afrika Cultural Centre moved in close by, whose members boycotted the centennial celebrations even if they received funding from the same liberal patrons as the Market, such as the Urban Foundation. On the uncertain terrain between liberal progress and apartheid repression, the Market highlighted apartheid *geo-pathology*, the "problem of place and place *as problem*" (Chaudhuri 1995: 55). Chaudhuri applies the term thematically to place in realist drama, but my reading highlights the deformation of urban space by apartheid and the Market's attempt to counter with reformation on the institutional as well as artistic plane.

Despite these contradictions, the progressive impact of the Market in the decade and a half between the Soweto uprising and the release of Mandela in 1990 is clear in comparison with other institutions.[15] Apart from commercial theatres staging American or European imports, the dominant institution was the subsidized Performing Arts Council of the Transvaal (PACT). Strictly segregated by the state and largely confined by censorship and the school curriculum to a mixture of canonical drama and inoffensive comedy, PACT's well-appointed houses and professional training nonetheless gave Manim, who worked there for a decade, a model of sorts for the "decent theatre" which he hoped to extend to integrated houses. Through Manim, Simon had access to PACT's Arena studio, where he staged experimental plays such as Büchner's *Woyzeck* (1973), and welcomed seasoned actors such as Aletta Bezuidenhout, Vanessa Cooke, and Marius Weyers, who, with Paul Slabolepszy from the Space, would form the nucleus of his group, the Company. The Company performed classical adaptations, such as the perennially relevant *Antigone* (with Bezuidenhout, 1974), and local work, such as *Hey Listen!* (1974 [Simon 1986]), monologues adapted from Simon's story series *Jo'burg, Sis!*, with Weyers as a nervous queer, Slabolepszy as a handyman choked up by a young girl attacked by dogs meant for blacks, and Cooke (1948–), as a would-be Miss South Africa (Kruger 2013: 108–11). Simon's earlier encounters with experimental theatres abroad were also important. Working backstage at the Theatre Workshop in London's East End in 1959, he had observed Joan Littlewood's transformation of texts from *Macbeth* to Brendan Behan's *The Hostage* through workshops with actors and designers. His local work with Union Artists on shows such as *Phiri* (1972) reflected Littlewood's methods but also the limits of their application in a society that restricted democratic collaboration. Nonetheless, exposure to Black Arts stages during his stay in the United States (1968–70) gave him alternative institutional models to the paternalism of Union Artists, and thus ways to move the Market toward a dissident and ultimately majority public sphere.

While the Company's first season in the Market featured international drama beginning with Chekhov in the Upstairs studio, the program included significant local work. The main house opened in October 1976 with Peter Weiss's *Marat/Sade*, whose drama of sex, madness, and revolution would become the mainstay of university theatre programs, and a year later, Brecht's *Mother Courage*, but also hosted revivals of Dike's *Sacrifice of Kreli* and Fugard's *People are Living There* and *The Island*. The studio featured satirical revues by Kirby (*How Now, Sacred Cow?*) and Uys (*Strike up the Banned*), the latter's play *God's Forgotten*, on Afrikaner women under siege in a future civil war (published 1989), and an adaptation of *Waiting for Godot* developed with a Soweto cast by Benjy Francis, who had worked with TECON in Durban. The Market thus accommodated black-identified directors such as Francis and Alan Joseph as well as performers such as Mthoba and Makhene of Workshop '71. Joseph went on to run the Johannesburg Civic Theatre and PACT before the latter's demise in 1996. Francis directed Mda's *We Shall Sing for the Fatherland* at FUBA (1978), founded the Dhlomo Theatre in honor of the pioneer playwright, and set up the Afrika Cultural Centre. While the Market's accommodation of blacks did not end official discrimination, it should not be dismissed as tokenism. Their presence drew the attention of younger spectators to a submerged integrated culture that had survived in the interstices between paternalism and resistance, and thus suggested ways of harnessing that legacy to the transformation of the institution.

These institutional shifts reintroduced the 1950s generation of black actors to a wider audience and established links with a new generation whose theatre experience was shaped first by township melodrama and second by BCM performance poetry. Soweto plays in this vein, like Makhwedini Mtsaka's *Not his Pride* (1973), the first in the Ravan Press series that also included Dike, grafting political content on to township melodrama. Others such as *The Hungry Earth* (1995 [1978]) and *Egoli* (1980 [1979]), which were mediated by facilitators like Simon, Amato, and Francis, followed the example of *Survival*, using the rhythm of alternating restrained and explosive expression to create harsh and lyrical testimony to the struggle against apartheid brutality. The Market also produced European classics from Shakespeare and Brecht, modern iconoclasts such as Dario Fo and Sam Shephard, and local history plays such as *The Native Who Caused All the Trouble* (Danny Keogh, Cooke, and Nicholas Haysom 1983). Based on a 1937 incident in which a Sotho man Tselilo (played by Kani) claimed ownership of land in Cape Town, the play recalled the land dispute in *Tau* (1941; Chapter 3) and inspired a post-apartheid adaptation (see below), but in the heat of the anti-apartheid movement the combination of witnessing and spectacle in testimonial theatre would shape the Market representation of South Africa at home and abroad.

Bearing Witness / Overbearing Spectacle

Although bearing witness on stage did not lead to immediate "mobilization of the oppressed"—Mda's retrospective prescription for resistance (1995: 40)—we should not dismiss testimony as merely "protest," as he did (41). Honed by precise body techniques, voiced in whispers as well as shouts, the best testimonial plays critically re-presented local lives. Standouts such as *Egoli, Born in the RSA* (1985), and *Have You Seen Zandile?* (1986) drew on intimate as well as public acts and, especially in the latter two, featured women to a greater degree than in previous plays. *Egoli* offered an exemplary case of the power and pitfalls of testimonial theatre. It was workshopped by Manaka (1955–98) and actors John Moalusi Ledwaba (1957–2017) and Hamilton Mahonga Silwane (d. 2018) with Soyikwa Theatre—after Wole Soyinka—which benefitted from Urban Foundation support for the Soweto YMCA and the FUNDA Centre headed by Manaka from 1984 where he wrote *Pula* and *Goree* (Manaka 1997). *Egoli* [place of gold] was not the first play about miners but its influence on other plays about this industry at the literal and figurative base of the economy extends to post-apartheid drama (Chapter 8). In Maponya's *The Hungry Earth*, staged in 1978, the stories of three miners formed the basis for an epic series of scenes on migrant labor in rural as well as urban settings, which anticipated the union organization of mineworkers in the 1980s. Performed at the Wits Box after its Soweto premiere, it was well received by intellectuals locally and abroad but less so by township audiences, as noted by the editor of Maponya's plays Ian Steadman (1995: xvii).

Whereas *The Hungry Earth* portrays typical workers in abstract, often choral, speech, albeit enlivened by "spectacular action" (Steadman 1995: xvi), *Egoli* depicts the effects of apartheid by focusing on a particular miner (John) who finds solace in drink and his more sober roommate (Hamilton), and on the degrading conditions of the all-male hostel as much as the dangerous work underground. The initial performance at the YMCA relied too much, in Benjy Francis's view, on variety-style sketches of John's encounters with people on the mines and elsewhere and not enough on "economy of gesture and thought" to concentrate the actors' and the audience's attention (1979: 16). Reshaped at the People's Space, *Egoli* returned to the dramaturgy of *The Island*—two black men struggling with each other as well as their confinement. Although the action included scenes of mine work and a dream sequence in which the men imagine flight from their misery, it always returned to the hostel room, furnished only with bunks, cleaning equipment, and a precious radio. The climax comes after a narrow escape from a mine collapse, dramatized by the two men groping through a blackout lit only by their headlamps. John reacts to the news that his son was among the dead by drinking with concentrated intensity until he vomits and then collapses. Berated first by Hamilton and then by an off-stage voice reporting the death of the son John thought was at home, John is restored by his friend's "gentle, almost ceremonial cleansing of his face and torso" (Manaka 1980: 27). The play ends with the actors singing of "sweat turned into blood" in the mines and the hope of "justice, freedom and peace ... in the country of our forefathers" (28), but it is the duo's enactment of degradation and restoration rather than any anticipation of the National Union of Mineworkers (NUM; 1982–) that compels attention. By vomiting on stage, provoked by rapidly gulping water during the blackout before this scene, Ledwaba not only assailed his own body but also arrested the flow of meaning from performer to audience. His act of self-inflicted violence drew attention to the actor's testimony against violence done to his character by brutal conditions, but its excess also confounded the attempt to find a clear meaning in the enacted assault.[16] The climax (at the Market, December 1979) provoked gasps from the mostly white audience, but the black poet Oswald Mtshali argued that this scene was "deliberately honed to cut to the bone and expose the raw nerve, letting the salt of suffering run into the empty wound. It will make the smug and complacent very uncomfortable" (quoted Fuchs 2002: 151).[17]

However powerful its impact on spectators, Ledwaba's action raises an important question about the function of spectacular violence in anti-apartheid theatre and what Njabulo Ndebele decried as anti-apartheid "exhibitionism" (1994 [1986]: 49).[18] Although this question became the subject of explicit public debate only after Ndebele's essay and others such as Mda (1995), it had already emerged as a potential problem. When Fugard distinguished in the 1960s between the "horror and fascination" of white audiences and the engaged but matter-of-fact interaction of black audience with the representation of their daily lives, he acknowledged the risk of turning protest into spectacle. The display of apartheid brutality before metropolitan spectators at home and abroad whose privilege shielded them from the oppression portrayed on stage, nourished those spectators' moral outrage while allowing them to forget their implication in apartheid. This nourishment resembles what Fanon called the "catharsis" afforded the colonizer when the colonized's "scathing denunciations" and "heated words" are written primarily for the colonizer (2004: 173). Whereas audiences in Johannesburg or Cape Town were not literally colonizers, their desire for catharsis was evinced in praise for spectacular scenes of apartheid suffering and anti-apartheid defiance. Nonetheless, the question of spectacular violence might be more complex than reiterating the different tendencies of black and white audiences, even if it is true that *Egoli* prompted more interest in Johannesburg, Cape Town, and European capitals than among township audiences.[19] Even if the latter may have preferred a more episodic format, director Francis argued that the vomiting and cleansing ceremony forged an organic connection between gesture and thought that he called for emerges in the precise enactment of brutality and its redress, which in turn provided the ground for the call to solidarity at the end (1979: 16).

This tension between city and township tastes continued into the 1980s. During the "states of emergency" proclaimed at intervals in this decade, police intimidation pushed militant playwrights like Manaka and Maponya out of township venues and into the Market, whose prestige gave them some protection. In Maponya's *Umongikazi* [Nurse] black nurses confront impatient doctors and hostile administrators, who were usually white, whether in the white hospitals that grudgingly employed black nurses, or in overcrowded black hospitals. The play's concluding call for union solidarity was well received by nurses at Baragwanath Hospital in Soweto, but booed by township audiences disappointed because the show was too short and too austere.[20] Notwithstanding this reception, the police found the performance provocative enough to summon Maponya for a "friendly chat" (Maponya 1995: ix). His next project, *Gangsters* and *Dirty Work*, a diptych on the security state, opened at the Market but was restricted to "experimental" venues by the PCB (Steadman 1995: xx).

Both *Gangsters* and *Dirty Work* were shaped by transnational experimental forms as well as local politics. *Gangsters* borrowed from Samuel Beckett's *Catastrophe* (1982), which Maponya directed in 1984 (Steadman 1995: x). Beckett's spare, enigmatic scene, in which a director (D) instructs an assistant (A) to manipulate a silent, cowed protagonist (P), may have appeared remote from actual torture in South Africa but Beckett's refusal to name the catastrophe or to give the action a specific political referent informs Maponya's play. Even though *Gangsters* pours local content into *Catastrophe*'s abstract form, shown by the pointed title and the dialogue and setting in a South African prison between the prisoner Rasechaba [Tswana: father of the nation] and his antagonists Major Whitebeard and his black lackey Jonathan, it retains Beckett's resistance to the spectacle of violence. This resistance works through the refusal to indulge audience curiosity about a specific case, such as Stephen Biko, whose death from wounds inflicted by police was, like the figure on stage, covered up before the inquest. Instead Maponya plays an unknown victim.[21] *Gangsters* was performed at the Market in July 1984, with John Maythan as Whitebeard, Union Artists veteran Sol Rachilo as Jonathan, and Maponya as Rasechaba.[22] The performance opened with the silent poet covered in black and draped as if on a cross (image: Kruger 1999a: 174), with the perpetrators on either side. By starting with the death of the prisoner, the play avoids a spectacle of torture, focusing instead on the accumulation of evidence. At the same time, the retrospective confrontations between the poet and his jailers provide an occasion to include nationalist poetry that would otherwise be banned. Although the final image returns to Beckett's directions—the spot on the poet's head (Maponya 1986: 87)—it spotlights the stupidity as well as the brutality of his antagonists and grants that image the effect of silent prophecy that magnifies the power of the voice on tape. If *Gangsters* offers eloquent testimony against the torturers indicted in the title, its companion *Dirty Work* targeted white complicity. Maytham portrayed a paranoid security expert who lectures a nervous white audience but who never quite manages to cover up disturbing noises-off. More than a "humorous" prelude to *Gangsters* (Steadman 1995: xi), *Dirty Work* used satire to remind whites of their assent to the increasingly draconian "emergency" state. Like Kirby's impersonations of spineless English liberals and funny but frightening Afrikaner bureaucrats in *Separate Development* (1984), Maytham confronted this audience with a distorted but recognizable self-image. By directing a white actor in a performance whose ambiguity entertained but also discomforted white spectators, allowing them a catharsis of sorts through laughing at this paranoid "expert," Maponya confronted these spectators with their own paranoia, and thus turned the gaze of power back on its beneficiaries.

Woza Albert! [Albert, Arise!] (1981) may be the most widely performed play to originate at the Market. Its distinction lies not just in its humor, which flavors many anti-apartheid plays, but in its synthesis of variety gags and anti-apartheid testimony, and its strategy of insinuating satiric caricature of white power figures into a comic act to confront the laughing white audience with a spectacle of their kin. Although both Mtwa and Ngema acknowledged the impact of Grotowski and Brecht by way of Simon (Mtwa/Ngema/Simon 1983: i), the influence of Kente, with whom the former worked on *Mama and the Load* (1980), is clear in the variety sketches and physical comedy loosely attached to the main idea—the Second Coming of Christ to South Africa—and in the sly approach to politics.[23] The picture of Mtwa and Ngema's broad imitation of white bosses (Figure 6.2) recalls Kente stalwarts like Kenny Majozi; the ping-pong ball pink noses performed a similar function to the pink plastic gloves worn by the hidden bureaucrat in *Too Late!* but the creators of *Woza Albert!* sharpened comedy into satire, including satire of the struggle. Under cover of Christ's return as *Morena* [Sotho: Lord] and the camouflage of pink noses, police helmets, and other disguises, Mtwa and Ngema turn their bodies into distorting mirrors parodying their white spectators. In so doing, they shift the parameters of anti-apartheid testimony by unsettling rather than confirming the sympathetic spectator's presumption of solidarity.

Despite attempts to label it an authentic Soweto product during a New York tour (Ndlovu 1986: xxiii), *Woza Albert!* targeted a metropolitan audience—at the Market and overseas.[24] The impersonation of authority figures resonates with the

Figure 6.2 Pink-nose mimicry in *Woza Albert!* by Mbongeni Ngema, Percy Mtwa (pictured) and Barney Simon (director), Market Theatre Johannesburg, 1981.

Photograph and permission by Ruphin Coudyzer, FPPSA: www.ruphin.co.za.

subversive "mimicry of colonial domination" (Bhabha 1986: 173), which animated Nkosi's *Rhythm of Violence* a generation earlier (Chapter 3). Mtwa and Ngema teased audiences in Johannesburg—and New York (Kruger 1991)—by inviting them to share jokes at the impersonated "whites" only to remind them that they are themselves the butt of the joke. Mtwa impersonates a white policeman who harasses an abject Ngema while offering conspiratorial racist asides to the audience about the alleged depravity of blacks; in the second scene, both actors play prisoners to an invisible but irascible warden. The prisoners' submission to a body inspection becomes an occasion for mooning the audience: the actors' imitation of submission thus turns into an act of defiance directed at the complicity of the spectator rather than the cruelty of the invisible warden. Unlike the imitation of defiance in Ngema's *Asinamali* [We have no money] (1984), which mixed the rousing testimony of black men in prison with blunt ridicule of white bureaucrats and women in general, allowing male metropolitan spectators to have it both ways, to pity the victim and laugh at the jokes, the mimicry in *Woza Albert!* implicates metropolitan spectators, bringing them up short against their desire for a cathartic spectacle of outrage and their reluctance to confront their complicity in the spectacle. But the effectiveness of *Woza Albert!* is not limited to confronting spectators with their implication in apartheid. The opening scenes may offer "mimicry of colonial domination" designed to discomfit the privileged "eye of power" in Bhabha's phrase, but the final scene in the graveyard where Morena raises heroes from the dead addresses a majority audience. The invocation of an anti-apartheid pantheon—"Woza Albert [Luthuli]," Lilian [Ngoyi], Bram Fischer, Ruth First, and others (Mtwa/Ngema/Simon 73, 78–80)—is not simply a rousing conclusion; it makes full sense only to the mostly black South Africans who know the names and the history of resistance they represent.[25] The end of the play points beyond the spectacle of apartheid by enacting the gap between the testimonial address of the performance and the audience's as yet uncertain mastery of the critical witness role.

Whereas Maponya and other activists expressed doubt about the Market's capacity for radically transforming South African audiences, Simon produced theatre to conscientize this audience as critical witnesses of apartheid. In a series of plays from *Cincinatti* (1979 [Simon et al. 1979]; *original misspelling*) to *Black Dog/Inj'emnyana* (1984) and *Born in the RSA* (1985) (Simon et al. 1986), Simon and the casts created narratives based on research into individual lives to reflect and refract contemporary South African experiences. These experiments tacitly acknowledged others in the repertoire; they drew on the defiant black men in *Survival* and the depiction of white violence such as the thug who attacks a black man in Slabolepszy's *Saturday Night at the Palace* (1985 [1982]), the white men conscripted to fight black guerillas in such plays as *Môre is 'n Lang Dag* (1984; chapter 4), or between men and women at home in *This is for Keeps* (Cooke/Keogh/Honeyman 1983). While acknowledging the "separate development" of black, white, and those between, Market theatre makers hoped to confound simple oppositions between black struggle and white introspection by linking private emotion and public agency, testimony and action.

Born in the RSA represents personal and public responses to the extreme state violence of the 1980s that involved the arrest of children as well as the torture of adults. The title alludes to Bruce Springsteen's album *Born in the USA*, which had appeared in 1984, only in so far as it insists on the power of solidarity, but more relevant to the local scene, the play challenged the masculine bias of testimonial theatre by foregrounding women and by staging the gendered dimension of both state and domestic violence. Where *Survival* took for granted that its four male protagonists stood for the nation, *Born in the RSA* worked the gaps as well as links between nationhood and selfhood, men and women, agitation and restoration. The authors of these testimonies share a common birthplace indicated by the title but inhabit different countries. On a stage empty but for chairs, microphones and newspapers, against a backdrop of images from the day-to-day struggle, this "docudrama" (so called in the program) used the format of courtroom testimony stripped of a naturalistic set that might hem it in. From the start, the performers explored the critical and creative tension between Brechtian reporting and immersive embodiment. Mia Steinman, Afrikaner by birth, Jewish by marriage, and anti-apartheid lawyer by family inheritance and commitment, begins not with biography but with the Internal Security Act (amended 1984) that prohibited legal redress against the state or its agents and that justified the state "emergency" in July 1985, just before the play opened (Simon et al. 1986: 134).[26] By delivering this narrative in the voice of an Afrikaans woman—created by the English-speaking Fiona Ramsay— and by alluding to the Women's March thirty years earlier, the play challenged the dominance of male activists. By making this activist a snappily dressed, chain-smoking fast talker with a personal and political history, Ramsay gave this national protagonist a rounded character along with the sharp eye of a lawyer who introduces the other characters as clients and witnesses. By juxtaposing the political Mia with the apolitical Nicky (Terry Norton), a woman seeking a divorce from Glen (Neil McCarthy, 1957–), who is later exposed as a police spy, the company suggested the "endless spiral of connections" (Simon et al. 1986: 136) that entangles the spy, disguised, as many were, as a campus radical, and his targets—art teacher Susan (Vanessa Cooke, 1948–) and union organizer Thenjiwe (Thokozile Ntshinga, 1953–)—along with the unwilling witnesses, Thenjiwe's sister Sindiswa (Gcina Mhlophe, 1958–), whose son is taken by the police, and her tenant Zach, a gentle musician (Timmy Kwebulana, 1941–), who befriends the boy. Reflecting later on Sindiswa, whom she based on a woman who was searching for a child seized during a police sweep, Mhlophe highlighted the experience of inadvertently politicized people and emphasized the ethical imperative to tell this story.[27] By linking political activists with those in retreat from politics, the play plots the interplay between commitment and betrayal, agency and quietism, while at the same time stressing that the state did not allow blacks to evade politics.

The most militant character, Thenjiwe, is the only one who does not introduce herself. Preceded by Mia's words of praise for her client, as against Sindiswa's mix of awe and exasperation for her sister, Ntshinga took on her role almost casually as she began singing under Zach's account of her rapport with her young nephew (1986: 142).[28] What stuck this spectator is not just the play of voices but also the tension between embodiment and demonstration of character, the vivid recounting of known torture procedure—Thenjiwe is forced to stand for days on end—and the cool estrangement of the scene (Figure 6.3):

> **Cop (Glen)** It's not fair, the captain is at home sleeping with his wife and I have
> to sit here staring at this fucken *kaffermeid*.
> **Thenjiwe** It was a very young white cop … *ag*, shame, for a moment I pitied him.
> At least I was doing something I believed in. But what was his life locked up in
> a cell with a swaying swelling *kaffermeid* with rolling eyes? He took money out
> of his pocket and sent the black cop to buy him a cool drink. He watched me …
> He moved towards me … I wanted to tell him: "Listen man, it's no use.
> It'll take you an hour to get me to lie down …" … His gun was on the table.
> If I could just fall that way I could land on it … I saw it happen (*she mimes
> shooting poses*), kazoom, kazoom, …, like a crazy cowboy movie. [when] the
> black cop arrived with the cool drink … I think we were both disappointed
> (1986: 160–61)

There is no *enactment* of violence here or at other key moments when characters speak of violence, most vividly when the usually quiet Zach expresses his anger at police cruelty to children in a terse but terrifying fantasy of smashing up white children in a schoolyard as he walks by. In performance Ntshinga and McCarthy kept their distance from each other and from their characters. Although the words create a vivid picture of Thenjiwe's pain as well as an accurate description of documented torture techniques, Ntshinga did not mime swelling up. She remains, as Brecht had it, *sovereign* over her character's experience, presenting its aspects—suffering, tenacity, irony—for analysis

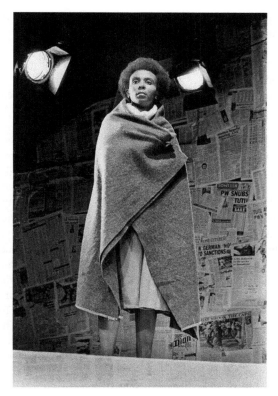

Figure 6.3 Thoko Ntshinga in *Born in the RSA* by Barney Simon and the cast; Market Theatre, 1986.

Photograph and permission by Ruphin Coudyzer, FPPSA: www.ruphin.co.za.

as well as inviting the audience to share her pleasure in imagined retribution in the popular idiom of cop and robber movies. Ntshinga reasserted her sovereignty over this material when she directed the play at the Baxter Theatre in 2015.

Singing Resistance and Restoration

This theatre of resistance also aspired to restoration. The restorative aspect came to the fore when the performers broke from their "witness boxes" to join one another in song. The first song, Thenjiwe's solo introduction *Likashona iLanga* [Sunset], a 1950s hit by *King Kong* bandleader Davashe, was also associated with the ANC and later the theme for a television documentary about the party, *Ulibambe likashona iLanga* [Hold up the Setting Sun] (1993). Most of the others came from the Soweto uprisings: *Alala amabhunu* [The Boers Sleep] sung by Mhlophe, Kwebulana, and Ntshinga, acknowledges the ongoing threat of violence after Thenjiwe has survived torture and contacted comrades outside prison:

Alala nezimbamu amabhunu ekhaya	The Boers sleep with guns at home
Adubula abantwana. ...	They shoot children ...
Ayabesaba abantwana	They are afraid of children (1986: 170; trans. modified)

These lines and the final victory song, sung by Ntshinga and the other women—*Thina sizwe esimnyama sizofela izwe* [We the Black Nation will die for our land] (176)—speak of martyrdom as well as solidarity, lament as well as struggle, and thus take their place in a lineage that stretches from Caluza's *Sixotshwa emsebenzini* (Chapter 1) via the popular hymn *Senzeni na?*, Kente's leitmotif (Chapter 5), to the mix of hymns and struggle songs replayed in the *REwind Cantata* (Chapter 7). Performed at activist funerals, songs like *Thina sizwe* highlighted the sacrifice of male martyrs. Performed by the women in the play, the song bore witness to women's contribution to resistance and restoration. *Born in the RSA* looks back to the Women's March on Pretoria on August 9, 1956 (now Women's Day), and its anthem *Wathint' Abafazi, Wathint' Imbokodo—You Strike the Women, You Strike a Rock* [lit: grinding stone], and forward to the play by that name by the Vusisizwe Players performed at various Cape Town venues and at the Market in 1986, the thirtieth anniversary of the march.[29] This play portrays three market women at Crossroads, who commiserate about their problems with their husbands—with whom they cannot legally live—as well as the police. It borrowed the testimonial form established by *Survival*, but showed women battling against African as well as apartheid patriarchy.

If the final song of *Born in the RSA* recapitulates the historical role of women in the anti-apartheid struggle, a song in the middle of the play prefigures a future beyond that struggle. At a party before they are arrested Thenjiwe, Susan, and Sindiswa serenade Mia as the Andries Susters in "I never loved a man–the way that I love you" (Simon et al. 1997: 100–01; photo: 127). The cheerful appropriation of the white American trio the Andrews Sisters by two black women and one white points to a new South African integrated urbanity. While many local appropriations of American popular culture have favored the masculine bravado of the gangster or the Blackman, these independent women recall a different lineage—from Emily Makanana, leader of the Dangerous Blues before she arranged music for her husband Griffiths Motsieloa—in the 1930s and Miriam Makeba in the 1950s to Mhlophe herself. In her autobiographical play, *Have You Seen Zandile?* (1988 [1986]), Mhlophe used the recorded voices of black singers to suggest a life beyond the rural marriage to which her mother would confine her. Her character strove instead to follow her Durban-based grandmother's example and remake herself as a storyteller. The girl's last performance at her Transkei school, praises in Xhosa for an admired teacher, preceded a scene in which Letta Mbulu's cover of Billie Holiday's "I'll never be the same" accompanied her friend's departure for Johannesburg (1988: 57). Mhlophe's focus on the aspirations of young women and on the intimate secrets of menstruation and sex shared by girls across the world, earned her criticism from the ANC-affiliated

Cultural Desk for straying from the masculine line on the Struggle but praise from audiences and an appearance opening the Women's Hearings at the Truth and Reconciliation Commission in 1997.[30]

The characters of *Born in the RSA*, as well as actors Mhlophe, Ntshinga, Cooke, and Ramsey represent mature women as national protagonists, in contrast to *Sarafina* (1986), whose teenage star represented the Soweto uprising on Broadway. Written by Ngema of *Woza Albert!* fame, this musical (published 1995) drew loosely from students at one of Soweto's exceptional institutions, Morris Phillipson High School (MHS), who were among the most visible participants but not the original instigators of the 1976 rebellion against the enforcement of Afrikaans as medium of instruction, and by extension against apartheid schools and institutions.[31] The star turn by Leleti Khumalo, later the second Mrs. Ngema, prompted claims that the play empowered women (Orkin 1991: 233) but Ngema followed his mentor Kente's example by putting a pretty girl on display rather than dramatizing her agency. As Sibongile Mkhabela—the only woman among the Soweto Eleven, the leaders sentenced under the Terrorism Act—shows in her account (2001) of her time at Naledi High School, in prison, and after, gender bias affected the student movement. While *Sarafina* gave voice to rebellious students and to a fictional version of a dedicated teacher at MHS, played in the film version (Ngema 2002) by US actor Whoopi Goldberg, her stage name "Mistress 'It's a Pity'" echoed the nicknames in Kente's repertoire. The play ended with the spectacle of youthful vitality: Sarafina borne aloft by her comrades, not as an agent of struggle but as a mascot, an object of male desire and female envy (Guldimann 1996). Principled practitioners such as Jerry Mofokeng (1996) decried Ngema's exploitation of his cast as well as the Struggle, but *Sarafina* stalked the stage like a zombie even after the 1994 election, as young women in community workshops continued to lip-synch to the musical in the hope that they too would make it to the Great White Way.[32]

The commodification of the Struggle in *Sarafina* took a scandalous turn in 1996, deep in the AIDS pandemic that gave South Africa the highest rates of HIV infection in the world. Ngema secured ZAR14 million (then ca. US$2 million) of the Health Ministry's annual budget of R90 million AIDS funding to produce *Sarafina II* as an "AIDS musical." In township melodrama style, the plot tracked a young HIV+ woman who dies after prayer and traditional medicine fail to cure her, and culminated in a spectacular funeral. It reinforced AIDS myths, especially the common incompatible assertions, that traditional herbs worked better than modern medicine and, contrariwise, that HIV led inevitably to death, blamed the victim rather than the sexual braggart who was her male partner, and dismissed safe-sex practices such as condoms. Whereas most theatre against AIDS was and is still performed for free by small touring companies or community groups, the better to reach a wide audience (Chapter 8), Ngema charged admission and played at only two locations.[33] Apart from the morality of cashing in on the AIDS crisis, what was striking at the time was the willingness of Minister of Health Nkosazana Dlamini-Zuma (then wife of Jacob Zuma, president, 2008–18) and her deputy Manto Tshabalala-Msimang—later health minister to President Mbeki who denied that HIV caused AIDS—to believe that this expensive spectacle might change the behavior of audiences. This spectacular corruption led AIDS activists to call for the intervention of the Public Protector Selby

Bacqa whose report (1997) censured both producer and minister for misuse of public funds. By recouping some of the money and reinforcing the ability of the National AIDS Consortium to check the bona fides of future applicants, the ruling confirmed the capacity of the Public Protector to challenge corruption and protect democratic institutions but, as Chapter 8 will show, also exposed their fragility.

Testifying for the Future

Sarafina may represent the commodification of the Struggle but it casts in relief the testimonial theatre that inhabited the subjunctive place and time between the act of defiance and the anticipation of a better future. Despite his emphatic distinction between protest and resistance that I cited at the outset, Zakes Mda's best plays dwell in this subjunctive space/time, while exposing the future *im*perfect of postcolonial Africa that looks all too relevant to the present. Until his return from exile in 1994, Mda (1948–) lived in Lesotho, a country completely surrounded by South Africa, which gave him a critical perspective on the region. *We Shall Sing for the Fatherland* (FUBA 1978) and *And the Girls in their Sunday Dresses* (Meso Theatre/Edinburgh Festival, 1988) cast a skeptical eye on the pretensions of African post-colonies, to use Achille Mbembe's term (1992) for dysfunctional states, where dreams of liberation run aground on postcolonial dependence, rent-seeking, and corrupt elites, and the disenfranchisement of the majority. Staged in South Africa by FUBA and the Peoples Space and abroad at the Edinburgh Festival, these plays demonstrate not only the international resonance of local theatre but also the tensions between foreign prestige and local neglect.

Mda's postcolonial plays create a bridge between anti-apartheid testimonial theatre and the emerging drama of a tentatively post-apartheid society. Those plays that tackle apartheid, *Dark Voices Ring* (1979) and *The Hill* (1980), challenge the urban bias of testimonial theatre by portraying rural people. Originating at the People's Space, directed by Amato and Nkonyeni, they focus on apparently apolitical people on the rural margins, and on the destruction of their lives by apartheid capitalism, whether on the grand scale of the mining industry or the smaller but still insidious one of hard labor on white farms. *The Hill* has received more attention partly because it takes up the themes of labor and emasculation in the mines treated in *Egoli*, and partly because it skillfully combines a realistic critique of migrant labor and a mystical sense of a life beyond.[34] Nonetheless, *Dark Voices Ring*, with its rural context, domestic space, and the blend of psychological drama and social history in dialogue, represents the more significant development of testimonial theatre and anticipates post-apartheid treatments of conflicts over land, such as Nwabisa Plaatje's 2017 adaptation in Cape Town of *The Native Who Caused All the Trouble*, which revised the 1983 original to highlight the engendering of labor on the land with Faniswa Yisa playing the male protagonist Tselilo without changing her womanly appearance or the masculinity of the character.[35]

Dark Voices Ring drew on Henry Nxumalo's 1952 article in *Drum* on prison labor and on South African Institute of Race Relations reports on the "ill-treatment of farm laborers" (Horn 1990: xx). Although the play does not directly stage white exploitation of black farm laborers, as tenants or prisoners leased by the state, this history frames the story of a nameless old couple who have been driven from the farm where the man was *baas*-boy [overseer] when prisoner-laborers rebelled and burnt down his hut and his daughter before setting fire to the white farmer's house. Mda pares the action down to the intimate encounter between the disturbed woman and her stunned husband, and a young man, buoyed by his imminent departure for guerrilla activity "in the north," whom the woman claims as her son-in-law. The woman is at the center of this drama, which pulls her between denial of her daughter's violent death and obsessive mourning for her dead child and for her lost status as the former *baas*-boy's wife. The cognitive dissonance that disables this character was in Nkonyeni's performance embodied in the tension between her tight reserve and her sudden reactions to unseen danger. Out of the contrast between the matter-of-fact account of labor before her daughter's birth—begun out in the fields and finished in the big house—which she interprets as a vindication of her family's status, and her trauma after her daughter's death, Nkonyeni's embodiment showed the consequences of the couple's destitution. The young man lectures the old for his allegedly misguided sense of duty but it is the woman's reenactment of her husband's violence and the young man's impersonation of a prisoner that shows the depth of their degradation and the difficulty of resistance: "*She flogs his back with an imaginary whip*" (Mda 1990: 62). Likewise, it is their rendering of the lament—"Senzeni na Ma-Afrika?" [What have we done, Mother Africa?] (63)— rather than the young man's militancy that gives dramatic weight to the otherwise abstract idea of "just war" (64) and anticipates the old man's sudden animation at the tenuous promise of freedom before the young man leaves.

Although written earlier, *We Shall Sing for the Fatherland* has been one of Mda's most enduring plays. First performed at FUBA in 1978 (directed by Francis) and at the Market (by Nicholas Ellenbogen) in 1979, it was revived in Lesotho in 1980, by Soyikwa in Soweto in 1988 and 1989, for student audiences at the Windybrow Theatre in inner-city Hillbrow in 1995, and updated by student performers at UCT in 2012. It deals not with the struggle against apartheid but with oppression in a postcolonial society marked by the corruption of a new African elite beholden to transnational corporate interests and by the deprivation of the majority, including veterans of the "Wars of Freedom" (Mda 1990: 30). While the published text blames "white" interests (35) for the collusion between an international Banker and local Businessman, the stage text was amended to "multinational" and the punch line added to the speech by the banker—played by a black actor on this occasion: "We must teach them that the only colour that matters is the colour of money" (Horn 1990: xvii). The veterans, Sergeant and Janabari, survive by raiding the trashcans of the new rich and by bribing the policeman Ofisiri to allow them to sleep in the city park. Recalling Beckett's tramps even if Mda claimed not to know *Waiting for Godot* (Holloway 1988: 83), the soldiers, especially Janabari played by Workshop '71 veteran James Mthoba, also resembled the Professor and others left behind by Nigerian independence in Soyinka's play *The Road* (Soyinka 1965). Like the Yoruba popular theatre on which Soyinka draws, the performers here, especially Mthoba and Eddie Nhlapo, who started out with Union Artists in the 1960s, combined buffoonery and pointed comment on a minimally decorated stage that left space for improvisation (image: Kruger 1999a: 187).

Like Soyinka's scavengers, Sergeant and Janabari seek not only food and shelter but also a measure of dignity in a society that has betrayed them. Snubbed by the businessman Mafutha (Nhlapo) and shunned by the new government that their struggle helped to create, the veterans can take pride only in national achievements that exclude them:

> **Janabari** proud to see our young men and women in positions which used to be held only by our colonial masters
> **Sergeant** Yes Janabari, proud to see Ofisiri in his neat uniform, Mr. Mafutha and his moneybags, and all the rest of them who hold the reins of power
> (Mda 1990: 39)

Even as they freeze to death in the park, they attempt to "sing for the fatherland" (44). Their "voices ... gone" (44), their corpses rifled, the ghosts of Sergeant and Janabari haunt their unmarked graves, while a local bigwig, perhaps Mr. Mafutha who might have died of a "new-fangled disease like gastric ulcers" (35), receives a grand funeral off stage. By juxtaposing death by starvation with death by "gastric ulcer"—and, by implication, conspicuous consumption—Mda invokes pan-African lore that warns against the insatiable appetites of the powerful, including those leaders, "voracious man-eaters" who "expropriate the labor and sustenance" of their own people (Coplan 1994: 37). The prisoners digging the paupers' graves in the final tableau recalled the many prisoners in anti-apartheid theatre; this discomfiting parallel led critics to comment on the play's "brave look at the darker side of independence."[36] The exact location of this postcolonial satire is left unstated; the park may bear comparison with Uhuru (Freedom) Park in Nairobi and the Businessman with the rapacious capitalists of 1970s Kenya (Horn 1990: xiii) but the dialogue alludes to South African currency and Sotho food.[37] This combination of a general state of uneven development and local details did not undermine the play's effect but instead invited audiences to ponder the specific relevance of this scenario. The relevance for South Africa was confirmed by the banning of the published text in 1981 and by its absence from stages in Lesotho, which was ruled by dictatorial cliques from the civil war of 1970 until the relatively fair election of 1993 but, as of 2018, is once again plagued by state officials more interested in raising their pay than in improving their constituents' lives. Further afield, in Zimbabwe after 2000, president Robert Mugabe, in power 1980–2017, used the pretext of giving land to veterans to seize white-owned farms as favors to cronies, while using as enforcers young men who were born after the anti-colonial struggle ended in 1980 and who were therefore not veterans at all. Less overtly, the tension today between South Africa's new black elite and growing ranks of unemployed youth suggests that the discrepancy between postcolonial rhetoric and post-colonized inequity remains potentially explosive.[38]

And the Girls in their Sunday Dresses (Meso Theatre, Lesotho 1988) deepens the exploration of the consumption of power. Whereas *We Shall Sing for the Fatherland* juxtaposed the veterans waiting in vain for the Cabinet to "take an interest in them" (Mda 1990: 37) with the objects of their envy, the policeman who bullies them and the banker, the businessman, and the pretty civil servant who pass them by, *And the*

Girls dispenses with all but two figures who are waiting to buy subsidized rice from an unnamed agency that appears to be siphoning off food and profits. The Woman has returned from South Africa, after being abandoned by her European lover, while the Lady is an aging courtesan who may or may not have had the same lover. Both have no apparent resources other than those being dispensed with the rice. The office "girls" of the title appear only fleetingly in the dialogue and not at all on stage, yet their affluent remoteness signified by "Sunday dresses" in the workplace highlights the gap between those waiting in line for food and the bureaucrats who continually postpone delivery. Whereas the personal interaction or pointed aloofness of the characters in *We Shall Sing* clearly distinguished between haves and have-nots, the absence of a character embodying power in *And the Girls* highlights the impersonal nature of that power. Further, the reduction of the Lady over the course of the play from an high-class courtesan proud of her fine clothing to one more disheveled petitioner in line suggests that distinctions between haves and have-nots in a postcolonial society dependent on outside aid are unstable and beyond the characters' control.

Setting this play in Lesotho, Mda returns to the environment of endemic poverty that shaped *The Hill*, the legacy of colonial appropriation of Basotho land reinforced by the scarcity of work that forces most able-bodied men and many women to earn their living in South Africa.[39] The earlier play depicted this experience through the eyes of male migrants waiting for the call to the mines. The few female figures—all sex-workers—function essentially as foils; they exploit the men's alienation by wooing and then robbing them—even though the oldest woman, played by Nkonyeni at the Space, offers to bribe the recruiters to take the young, naive migrant who turns out to be her nephew. *And the Girls*, on the other hand, depicts the world through the eyes of a woman who has herself crossed into South Africa, thus registering a shift in gender roles in Lesotho. After the retrenchment of migrant miners through the 1990s, the pattern of migration was reversed, with more men compelled to stay on the land, while women sought out domestic work and informal commerce in the border areas or in South Africa (Coplan 1994: 174–77). Although the Woman and the Lady appear to be dependent on the bureaucrats at the rice depot and are willing to submit to intrusive questions about sexual habits and the like before they can receive the rice, at the end they reclaim a defiant, if precarious independence. Despite its female cast and critique of sexual dependency, this play is not primarily about the "subservient role of women in the social hierarchy of Lesotho" (Marx 1994: 20). Rather than directly challenge gender hierarchies, Mda attempted to use the initial difference between the Woman's defiance and the Lady's willingness to submit to the whims of others, whether her former clients or the bureaucrats at the depot, to sharpen a distinction between aspiring African elite consumers and the mass of working people, but this allegory remains abstract in the Woman's indictments such as "We are all victims of a social order" (Mda 1993: 20). As Bhekizizwe Peterson argues in his introduction, the play shows insight "into the experience of the lower classes, of which women form a significant proportion" but only rarely highlights "the specific predicaments facing women as a gendered constituency" (1993: xxi–xxii) or delves into the complex pressures that might lead Basotho women to seek informal work on the border, including sex-work (Coplan 1994: 150–200).

And the Girls in their Sunday Dresses ends by complicating the initial opposition between a strong Woman and a compliant Lady, showing the Woman's weakness and, finally, the Lady's refusal to submit to the bureaucrat's intrusive questions: "To hell with the rice! I am going home and I know that never again will I need the food-aid rice and my chair of patience. Are you coming or not?" (Mda 1993: 37). Although the ending includes sisterly commiseration about men—"They are all children of one person" (36)—it is an invitation rather than a resolution that stages the conditions of solidarity rather than a simple enactment of empowerment. The dramatization of solidarity as well as the persistence of inequality should grant *And the Girls* a place in post-apartheid South Africa but despite its premiere at the Edinburgh Festival in 1988 and publication in Johannesburg in 1993, it was not staged professionally in South Africa until 2012, a production that was more extensively reviewed in Britain and the United States after appearing at Edinburgh than at home, although this publicity led to revivals at the Soweto Theatre (2014) and the Cape Town Fringe (2016). This revival may be belated but South African theatre makers have since 1994 experimented not only with freedom, in Anton Krueger's phrase (2010), but with the ambiguous interregnum between apartheid and liberation.

Whereas the anti-apartheid theatre that dominates this chapter and indeed most overseas views of South African theatre as such had been fired up by righteous anger and honed in the testimonial form that inspired audiences at home and abroad, the interregnum—best described as *post-anti-apartheid* (Kruger 1999: 191)—left activists and actors uncertain about both the goals and methods of theatre work. The uncertain times led one critic to dismiss the first half of the 1990s as a period of "vague hope" and "vacant postulating" (Homann 2009: 3) but, as Chapter 7 shows, post-anti-apartheid drama attempted to reformulate anti-apartheid practices for post-apartheid ends, and this dual perspective produced work that captured the historical moment and deserves attention today.

Spring Is Rebellious

Prospects and Retrospects in Post-Anti-Apartheid Theatre

Although the year 1994 ushered in the new democratic South Africa, change had been brewing for some time. The legal defeat of the Group Areas Act in the late 1980s belatedly acknowledged the return to the inner cities of brown and black people, which had been underway for a decade, leading in the 1990s to more migrants internal and external. Unions and "civics" (CBOs) created informal spaces for cultural practice while formal theatres like the Market in Johannesburg and the Baxter in Cape Town employed black theatre makers and expanded audiences. After, 1990 however, the return of the ANC, which tapped overseas funds previously supporting the UDF, pushed CBOs and cultural organizations to the margins. As the common apartheid enemy retreated, gaps between groups that had shared anti-apartheid convictions but otherwise had distinct political or ethnic affiliations opened too wide to be bridged by the arc of the "rainbow nation," leading one critic to voice a doubt shared by many: *Do South Africans Exist?* (Chipkin 2007). This ambivalence was exacerbated by battles between "third forces" armed by shadowy operatives linked to the state, and *com-tsotsis*—thugs claiming to be "comrades" or activists—and after the 1994 election, by tensions in government between the redress and reconciliation favored by Mandela, and the pursuit, led by Deputy President Thabo Mbeki, of transnational capital at the price of greater inequality,

This uncertainty may have prompted the dismissal of the period 1990–96 as one of "vacant postulating" (Homann 2009: 3) but this disparagement misses work that explored new topics such as the transformation of the inner city, and new forms such as the multi-media experiments of William Kentridge (1955–) and Adrian Kohler and Basil Jones's Handspring Puppet Company from 1993. The end of the anti-apartheid mission cleared space for theatre to address issues that had been sidelined by the singular Struggle—such as ethnic affiliation other than black or white or the impact of African and Afrikaner patriarchy on women and gender minorities. This tangle of concerns left activists in what I have called a *post-anti-apartheid* condition (1999a: 191), doubting the relevance of anti-apartheid practices and searching for new ways to dramatize global challenges from AIDS to migration, and the local abuses of the so-called party of liberation. Post-anti-apartheid indexes not only the rebellious spring after the apartheid winter but also the renegotiation of anti-apartheid forms. Ndebele called on writers as early as 1986 to redefine relevance and to "rediscover the ordinary" (1994: 41) that had been sidelined by the Struggle. Theatre practitioners responded to the challenge by jurist, later Constitutional Court Justice, Albie Sachs at an ANC meeting in exile in 1989—which appeared after his return in *Spring is Rebellious* (Sachs 1990a)—to revisit the priority of commitment over art that militants had demanded since the 1970s. In that volume, self-identified "cultural workers" in the Culture and Working Life Project argued that artistic quality mattered as much as militancy, that performance should penetrate "surface statements" to "remember better the darkness and light" of "these times" (Malange 1990: 102), and thus acknowledge failure alongside success. Their tools included testimonial plays but they also experimented with new techniques.

Post-anti-apartheid encompasses projects that play with a range of forms and scales. At the grand end of the scale, Handspring's collaborations with Kentridge used European sources and funding to illuminate local themes from migration in *Woyzeck on the Highveld* to the Truth and Reconciliation Commission (TRC) in *Ubu and the Truth Commission*. At the more modest end, practitioners schooled in anti-apartheid testimonial theatre repurposed the form to dramatize gender violence that had been eclipsed by the masculine cast of anti-apartheid activism, and drew audiences at national and community festivals. *Purdah* (1999a [Creative Arts Workshop 1993]), by Ismael Mahomed (1959–), had several runs at the Grahamstown Festival and in Johannesburg from 1993 to 1995. Working with Women Against Violence (WAVE) in the Indian district of Lenasia, actor Aasifah Omar embodied a character changing from a girl with jeans and tousled hair to a 13-year old subjected to early marriage (image: Kruger 1999a: 202), as well as her abject mother and her bossy aunts. The first to dramatize tensions among South African Muslims, *Purdah* prompted other solo pieces such as *At her Feet* (2006) by Nadia Davids (1977–), who used the Muslim *hadith* "paradise at the feet of mothers" as inspiration to play women in Cape Town and beyond reflecting on *hijab*, heritage, and women's agency.[1] Thulani Mtshali's *Weemen* (1999 [Bachaki Theatre 1996]) had two women and a man playing five roles, including a social worker and a sangoma advising husband and wife, and drew the audience's attention to economic and social pressures on gender.[2] The play invoked melodrama as the man chased his wife with a fake ax but staged realistic clashes between her attempt to earn a living and his attempt to thwart her by stealing her money and, later, as a born-again Christian, by manipulating her sense of duty. By downplaying spectacular blows in favor of subtler acts of abuse and resistance, *Weemen* preempted the laughter that African audiences often bestow on stage violence. Instead the black women in the Grahamstown audience in 1996 vocalized advice to the character and critical comparison of her situation with their acquaintances.[3]

In contrast to the above plays that used familiar forms to stage content that was newly visible rather than new per se, Theatre for Africa, led by Nicholas Ellenbogen (1948–), experimented with physical theatre, hand-crafted masks, dialogue, and body percussion to create evocative eco-parables with transnational and local resonance.[4] Created in 1989 and revived repeatedly at Grahamstown where I saw it in 1994, *Horn of Sorrow* (Ellenbogen 1999) tackles rhinoceros poaching and people who are pressured to poach by scarce alternatives—a topic that has become even more relevant today as poaching has grown with overseas demand for the horn. In *Boy Called Rubbish* (1994) by members Bheki Mkhwane and Ellis Pearson, Pearson played a shantytown boy whose life with a cruel foster-mother, a drunken foster-father, a sadistic teacher, and nosy neighbors (all played by Mkhwane) vividly conveyed the hazards of poverty as well as an eco-critical message about repurposing trash. Their comic timing and mimic skill combined juvenile idiocy (ketchup splashed on actors and audience) with analysis; in one of several false endings, Pearson dropped character to state "and so he went to bed without supper, and his life never got better, the end," only to reassure hesitantly clapping spectators that a second act might "perhaps" make things "all right."

Over and above theatre, *post-anti-apartheid* also describes key structures set up between the release of Mandela in 1990 and his inauguration in 1994—the Independent Broadcasting Authority (IBA), the Interim Constitution, the Regulation of Gatherings Act (RGA), all in 1993—that laid the foundations for post-apartheid freedom. The TRC may stand out for overseas readers but the finalized Constitution (1996) would, along with the RGA, which replaced the apartheid Riotous Assemblies Act, have a more lasting impact.[5] This legislation provided the basis for a democratic public sphere and the springboard to launch the unruly spring of cultural ferment. Whatever the metaphoric stretch between the several meanings of spring, agents such as the Public Protector and other "Chapter 9" officers mandated by the Constitution to "support constitutional democracy" (Constitution 1996: 103) by checking executive overreach have protected free expression and the rights of the vulnerable, such as HIV+ and gender minorities.[6] With the input of critical academics such as Andries Oliphant (1955–) and activists such as Mike van Graan (1959–) of the Performing Arts Network of South Africa (PANSA), the *White Paper on Arts, Culture, and Heritage* (DAC 1996) drew on anti-apartheid theatre practice, and on NGOs such as the Community Theatre for Development Trust (1992) to restructure the PACS and to use the new Dept. of Arts and Culture (DAC; 1996–) and funding arm the National Arts Council (NAC; 1997–) to redress the legacy of apartheid with more equitable disbursement of resources, as stressed by its subtitle *All Our Legacies, All Our Common Futures.* Van Graan has since argued that the NAC support was mismanaged from the start but the project of "potential employment and wealth creation" (DAC 1996: 1) to create the well-being that the Constitution presents as a human right remains a salient aspiration articulated in the more recent White Paper (DAC 2017).[7]

We will return in Chapter 8 to the Constitution as the charter of rights and responsibilities, and, in its figurative extensions, as the inspiration for staging imaginative worlds and the aspiration to well-being. In this chapter, however, we will investigate the theatre of the post-anti-apartheid moment, ambivalent, querulous, but still striving to make sense of the interregnum and to imagine a happier world beyond. The experience of dwelling in rather than moving briskly through the interregnum defines post-anti-apartheid ambivalence, which found expression in the Market, on the edge between progress and delay, and its representation of the edgy city, Johannesburg.

Theatre on the Edge: Disorder and Aspiration in the End-of-Century City

Beset by fears of crime and inconsistent management after founding director Barney Simon's untimely death in 1995, the Market Theatre nonetheless hosted new work that illuminated the gloom. These fears had a real basis in rising rates of robbery and cash-in-transit heists, to which corporations responded by fortifying enclaves in the central business district (CBD) and in the suburbs, but also reflected longstanding prejudices. The end of apartheid reignited these fears as crime that had been contained in Soweto and other townships spilled into the city as a whole.[8] Inner-city Newtown, which houses the Market and other performance venues, is far from Soweto, however: it abuts Fordsburg and Mayfair, which although declared "white" by the Group Areas Act had been reverting to their historical diversity. This "greying of Johannesburg" (Pickard-Cambridge 1989) began in the 1970s with Indians and Coloureds renting in the city through white fronts. Africans followed in the 1980s as landlords began to ignore the Act even before it was struck down in court (Morris 1999). The decay of buildings in the 1990s was precipitated by landlord neglect and exacerbated by racketeers who exploited migrants. Even after 1994, when relaxed controls made Johannesburg the destination for border crossers, most migrants came from the local hinterland (Segatti/Landau 2011).[9] While Johannesburg was not the only city caught between neglect and capital flight on the one hand and the pressures of migrants on the other, the sharp contrast between the skyscrapers, expressways, and other icons of transnational modernity and the colonization by migrants of older buildings captured the imagination of photographers, writers, film makers, and local workers who circulated tales about migrants slaughtering goats or even people in dilapidated apartments.[10] This image-repertoire reinforced Johannesburg's notoriety in the 1990s but, as I have shown in *Imagining the Edgy City* (2013), its reputation for mixing lawlessness and glamour goes back a century to the 1890s.

Even before the new city government was elected in 1996, the year Kani become artistic director (until 2004), the Market hosted playwrights from several generations: Paul Slabolepszy (1948–) through Susan Pam-Grant (1962–) to Mpumelelo Paul Grootboom (1975–) who challenged simplistic views of geo-pathology by dramatizing the transformation of the city by local and transnational forces from migration to capital flight to entrenched patterns of violence. Pam-Grant's *Curl Up and Dye* premiered at the Black Sun nightclub in 1989 but reached a larger audience at the Market and at PACT's Alexander Theatre in 1991. It anticipated the "greying of Johannesburg" report by some months; in 1988 Pam-Grant, director Gillwald, and the cast interviewed residents of Joubert Park (Pam-Grant 1993: 81), the district that houses the Johannesburg Art Gallery (est. 1910), dilapidated art deco apartments, and the park over Park Station, the gateway for migrants since 1896. In contrast to generic film plots about naive rural men in the big bad city from *Jim comes to Jo'burg* (1949) to *Jerusalema* (2008), *Curl Up and Dye*'s cast of women borrowed soap opera themes such as dysfunctional relationships or the lure of glamour to stage tensions between solidarity and suspicion among black and white women in a faded hair salon. It also offered a new perspective on the inner district shared uneasily by white pensioners and workers, and people of color. Pam-Grant's performance of manager Rolene captured white working-class anxiety but also addressed anti-apartheid progressives like herself, many living in inner districts such as Mayfair in the west or Yeoville in the east.

The dialogue charts the shifting loyalties that link Rolene to her long-suffering black assistant, Miriam (Lillian Dube), her "best friend" Charmaine, her "best customer" Mrs. Dubois (Val Donald-Bell), and her new customer Dudu Dhlamini

(Nandi Nyembe) (image: Kruger 2001: 239), a private hospital nurse and divorcee, who appears to manage her life better than the others. With fashion photos decorating the yellowing walls, the action uses hairstyles and language to stage racial conflict. The contradiction between apparently spontaneous emotion and apartheid structures of feeling plays out in English, Zulu, and Afrikaans.[11] Unlike the jokes punctuating anti-apartheid dialogue, the Zulu here is essential to the play's interpersonal dynamics. Mrs. Dubois is happy to have Miriam compare her beehive to that of Mrs. P.W. Botha (Pam-Grant 1993: 132)—wife of the hardliner replaced by the last white president F.W. de Klerk—but makes Miriam regret the compliment when she snaps: "I ask her how her child is and then I got to listen to this political nonsense. Who does she think she is ...?" (133). On the other hand, Dudu disdains Rolene's advice, asking Miriam rhetorically: "Ucabanga ukuthi ngingu lomlungu? [Who does this white (girl) think I am?]" (trans. modified; 116). In the act of translation, intimacy and publicity interpenetrate each other; the private lives of these women are social, in that they require social as well as personal solutions.[12]

As the play unfolds, Rolene is pulled between habitual loyalty to Mrs. Dubois and new admiration for Dudu but the tension snaps when Dudu and Rolene realize that they are neighbors and that this revelation threatens their uneasy interaction. Dudu deduces that Rolene is the woman whose husband threatens to shoot black passers-by and beats his wife "night after night" (135), but shares the news first with Miriam in Zulu that "this is the woman [*lo umfazi*] ... being beaten by that man [*eshaywa lanje yendoda*]" (139; trans. mod.).[13] Rolene sees that Dudu knows what she has been trying to hide, but when Dudu shifts from indirect fellow-feeling to professional and personal advice—"Rolene, you must report your husband to the police or welfare. It's enough ... I just packed my things," Mrs. Dubois demands race loyalty: "Now are you a bladdy *kafferboetie* [nigger-lover] or are you a white woman?" (139) Faced with the choice, Rolene succumbs to race pride that only heightens her abjectness; she calls Dudu a "black bitch"(140), chases Miriam out, and remains to answer an abusive call from her husband. If Rolene is still attached to an impossible comedy of a happy marriage and Miriam to the melodrama of an unhappy one, Dudu creates a new script that declares women independent in this new city.

Despite an uneven revival in 2013, *Curl Up and Dye*'s dramatization of women's solidarity has yet to be matched.[14] It offered an alternative to the casual misogyny of shows such as *Jozi, Jozi*, a series of sketches by John Ledwaba of *Egoli* fame, which appeared on stage in 1993 and on television in 1994. More thoughtful playwrights probed links between gender, violence, and urban change. After depicting dangerous rural idiots in *Smallholding* (1994 [1989]) Slabolepszy returned to the city with *Mooi Street Moves* (1994 [1992]), which pits a naive white against a streetwise black man. In collaboration with actors Martin Le Maitre and Seputla Sebogodi, Slabolepszy dramatized an encounter between Henry Stone, who is lost in Hillbrow, Johannesburg's densest high-rise district and reputedly its most dangerous, and Stix Letsebe, who lives in the flat once occupied by Henry's brother who has vanished after seeking money to buy his dream machine: a rig for extracting water from dry farmland. The play measures both characters' ability to survive the encounter in the sparsely furnished but vividly realized space (Figure 7.1) and the edgy city beyond. Although the text did

Figure 7.1 The White Naïf (Martin Le Maitre) and the Black Dude (Seputla Sebogodi) in Paul Slabolepszy's *Mooi Street Moves*, Market Theatre Johannesburg, 1992.

Photograph and permission by Ruphin Coudyzer, FPPSA: www.ruphin.co.za.

not provide much backstory for Stix, Sebogodi filled out the character by replaying his success as a salesman in the informal market on Mooi [Pretty] Street, and capturing his shock when stabbed by an offstage fixer for the racket running the building. While the fear of crime conjured by this scenario exceeded the actual risks in Hillbrow, which was inhabited by working families and local migrants in the early 1990s (Morris 1999), it anticipated the deterioration later in the decade. Stix's trade in consumer durables from the backs of trucks matches actual trade patterns tracked by urbanist AbdouMalique Simone (1998) and depicted in tele-fiction such as *The Line* (1994) (Kruger 2009). Although Stix is killed in the end, his rapport with Henry suggests the possibility of coexistence.

The quest for coexistence also animates Slabolepszy's *Fordsburg's Finest* (1998), which dramatizes an encounter between a black woman returning from New York to the city of her parents and a white used-car dealer who occupies the lot where her parents once lived. This play's treatment of women's claims on the edgy city has more depth than the "whores with hearts of gold" plots in Fugard's *Nongogo* (1959) revived by Jerry Mofokeng (1994) or in *The Good Woman of Sharkville* (1996) adapted from Brecht by Gcina Mhlophe and Janet Suzman. While these plays revive the stereotype of the female *flâneuse* as streetwalker as distinct from the male *flaneur* canonized by fans of Walter Benjamin, Thandi [beloved] in *Fordsburg's Finest* is a woman-walker who has to reinvent herself in this unfamiliar city. Her quest for the Johannesburg of memory— nurtured by parents who fled apartheid when she was a baby—has not prepared her for post-industrial squatted buildings and empty lots, still less for the encounter with "Foxy" Freddy Volschenk (Marius Weyers). As a black visitor worried about lingering apartheid habits, Thandi—played by African-American Dorcas Johnson—treats Freddy with due suspicion, while he struggles to fathom her attachment to a house that was demolished decades before. This rapprochement breaks down when she discovers that he was on the police force during the 1985 "emergency" but they reach a truce after Thandi reveals that her parents died from the pain of exile and the drink that dulled the pain, and Freddy breaks down recalling that his son, also a cop, was killed in an explosion that may have been laid by his colleagues. Although this truce is threatened by Freddy's racist brother Rocco, played by Slabolepszy in the style of the thuggish Vince in his *Saturday Night at the Palace* (1985 [1982]), Freddy and Thandi reach an understanding; she agrees to accompany him in his beloved vintage car to a local chicken shack before returning to her hotel (image: Kruger 2001: 243).

While the mimed car ride at the end suggests that transitional or indeed present-day Johannesburg may not allow the "pedestrian enunciation" that Michel de Certeau sees as essential to revising the urban environment (1988: 91), Thandi's ability to make her way to 74 Pioneer Street suggests its potential, and the staging by Lara Foot at the Market barely a mile from that location, highlighted her stubborn persistence.[15] Johnson's performance, honed by work with Slabolepszy in the USA and South Africa, deepened the script's initial sketch of the African American visitor, while Weyers drew on the dark energy that animated his Jakes in *Siener in die Suburbs* (1971) to give an edge to friendly Freddy. In addition to its complex characters, *Fordsburg's Finest* has a more precise sense of place than other urban plays of the 1990s. Pioneer Street is at the southern edge of Fordsburg close to Crown Mines, one of many post-industrial sites reclaimed by migrants. This reclamation recalls Fordsburg's liveliness before its denizens were evicted in the 1960s but also registers its uneven recovery since 1990. Slabolepszy has Thandi, motivated by the quest to find her parents' home, persuade Freddy to see in the space he took for granted as his used-car lot the memory of an integrated neighborhood that might cultivate the interaction that a local urbanist has called *sawubona* culture, the culture not only of greeting but also of acknowledging others on the street.[16]

While Paul Slabolepszy's urban drama moves from the sharp knife that ends *Mooi Street Moves* to the uneasy truce of *Fordsburg's Finest*, Mpumelelo Paul Grootboom articulates the ironic, even cynical bravado of young black urbanites apparently inured to violence by having grown up in the 1980s townships. Grootboom's ironic treatment of violence recalls 1990s television thrillers. As is common in television, Grootboom writes with collaborators: *Not with My Gun* (1998) credits his mentor at North West Arts Council in Mmabatho and later at the State Theatre in Pretoria, Aubrey Sekhabi, whose *On My Birthday* (NWAC 1996; Lincoln Center New York 1998) reproduced a popular mix of moralizing and sensation scenes that prevailed in many plays about domestic violence. European fans have dubbed Grootboom the "township Tarantino" but his spectacular sex and violence bring to mind Mark Ravenhill's *Shopping and Fucking*, directed at the Market by Yaël Farber, 1998.[17] Grootboom's first published play *Relativity* (2009a [2005], written with Presley Chweneyagae, star of Gavin Hood's film of Fugard's novel *Tsotsi*) recalls the mixture of didacticism and violence in *On My*

Birthday by having a psychologist lecture the police about the impact of "sexual abuse" and "trauma in the formative years" on serial killers (Grootboom 2009a: 7–8) but Miss Nkatho's prim lesson is out of place in a drama that topped each violent act with another more extreme and her character was cut from the State Theatre production (3). Muff Andersson discusses Miss Nkatho without noting her disappearance and observes that even at the Market revival in 2006, actors were soliciting audience input, apparently to prompt improvisation (2015: 246); these appeals were in my view driven by the challenge of animating a script that was overlong and overloaded with too many characters.

In contrast, *Foreplay* (2009b), which played in Amsterdam and Austria before South Africa, borrowed from Arthur Schnitzler's dark sex farce *Der Reigen* (1900; filmed by Max Ophuls as *La Ronde* in 1950) not only the "merry-go-round" of sex between men and women of different classes and ages but also the dramaturgical economy of brisk scenes that stripped most encounters of inessential dialogue. Grootboom disavowed serious intent, asking ironically: "what can be more fun than watching ten people having sex with each other, talk about crap, and give each other STDs?"[18] Despite this disclaimer, the mention of sexually transmitted diseases in a country with more than 20 percent of the sexually active population—young people like those in the audience—was HIV+ in 2009 recalled then-president Mbeki's notorious denial that HIV causes AIDS.[19] Shadowed by the fact of widespread sexual abuse as well as HIV, *Foreplay* nonetheless plays up the ironies of the drama. Mimicking Dr. Schnitzler's clinical portrayal of lust that levels class and age distinctions to leave individuals at the mercy of their reflexes, each scene shows a tryst between a lustful and an unwilling partner, beginning with resistance, moving through thrusting and yielding, and ending in consummation signified by blowing and popping bubble-gum balloons.

Some characters resembled Schnitzler's bourgeois, such as the plump, nervous preacher's wife visiting a student or "spoilt young man" (Mandla Gaduka, who played sidekick Mhlanga in Neil Blomkamp's film *District 9*), who speak formal English. But most scenes mixed English with Grootboom's North Sotho and enhanced the trysts with local elements. The sex-worker (Excellentia Mokoena) in scene one propositioned a man who was not a real soldier but a robber who had stolen the soldier's uniform. The preacher (Sello Zikalala, also playing the fake soldier) quoted Rev. Jimmy Swaggart on forgiveness while seducing a schoolgirl but his forceful exaggeration also recalled a long line of hypocritical preachers on township stages and drew sharp responses from black spectators critical of corrupt authority figures. The girl with the preacher resembled other students exchanging sex for school fees and sundry favors, as imagined in Trevor Makhoba's painting *Summer Friday Night with the Taxi Driver* (1996) and documented by research (Sellkow/Mbulaheni 2013). Koketso Mojela may have seemed slight and innocent at first but she effectively combined naiveté and worldliness here (Figure.7.2) and in her television roles such as the cynical secretary in the caustic satirical series on Parliament, *90 Plein Street*.

The final scene confronted the audience with a new and disturbing figure: a politician who threatened the sex-worker with retribution if she did not return compromising photographs. The politician—embodied with menacing bulk by Boitumelo Shisana—followed his threat with targeted blows that recalled the torture techniques revealed in

Figure 7.2 The Schoolgirl (Koketso Mojela) and the Sugar Pastor (Sello Zikalala) in Mpumelelo Paul Grootboom's *Foreplay*, Market Theatre Johannesburg, 2009.

Photograph and permission by Ruphin Coudyzer, FPPSA: www.ruphin.co.za.

the TRC hearings, and ended by stripping and raping his antagonist but this scene did not allow critical distance. Mokoena's character's descent from bravado to panic left those spectators who had been discomfited by her naked solicitation in the first scene too stunned even for nervous laughter. In the final image Mokoena staggered to her feet clad only in a mini-skirt and clutching a big red beach ball. Leaving the audience wondering whether the ball signified bloodletting or an orgasm proportionately more powerful than the usual bubble, Grootboom risked making a spectacle of rape but female characters like the schoolgirl hooked up with a sugar daddy complicate the picture of victimization. Indeed, a black female critic argued that the most disturbing scene was the one depicting psychological rather than physical violence (Tiisetso Tlelima; quoted: Andersson 2015: 249).[20] Gaduka, playing a playwright teaching an acting class, tormented Mojela's schoolgirl by telling her that acting required revealing painful memories—such as her father's suicide in the face of creditors' threats—and then forbidding her school mates to comfort her when he reduced her to tears (Grootboom 2009b: 52). This focus on verbal manipulation, in combination with the brief but striking allusion to the consuming problem of debt in South Africa (Makhulu 2012), indicates a critical horizon beyond the exhibition of sex and violence.

Apart from this scene, the exhibition of violence in *Foreplay* replayed the scenario of crime and disorder that dominated 1990s television. In contrast, the last play in this series on urban transition, *Love, Crime and Johannesburg* (Purkey/Steinberg 2000 [Market 1999]) attempted to move beyond the street thriller to capture the structural transformation of the post-apartheid city and the alliance between government corruption and capital speculation that in 1999 anticipated the systemic capture of the state by crony capitalists by 2016.[21] Urbanist Edward Soja's term (1997) "post-metropolis" captures the polycentric sprawl of expanding conurbations in Africa, as well as his base Los Angeles. *Love, Crime, and Johannesburg* encompassed not only personal dramas but also the social impact of city mismanagement. The play was inspired by Brecht's *Threepenny Opera*, especially Macheath's indictment of big capital: "What's the burgling of a bank to the founding of a bank?" (Brecht 1964: 62) but locally prompted by the conviction for bank robbery of Mzwakhe Mbuli, the "people's poet" at Mandela's inauguration. Arthur Molepo played Lewis Matome, a glamorous criminal who becomes chairman of the bank, as "dashing, dangerous and business-like" (Purkey/ Steinberg 2000: 7) but goes beyond criminal glamour to satirize the collusion between government and dubious speculators—image and analysis in Kruger (2004: 271–80).

While Molepo recalled the sinister charm of his gangster Mingus in JATC's *Sophiatown* (1986), *Love, Crime and Johannesburg's* robber-banker plays for bigger stakes. Disdaining petty criminals "squabbling for territory" (9), he moves on a "whole new world" of opportunity in "the most cosmopolitan and fastest moving metropole in the Southern hemisphere" (35). Personified by the anti-apartheid guerrilla turned post-apartheid tycoon, Johannesburg may fit the image of unrestrained capitalism described in *The Communist Manifesto* as the "uninterrupted disturbance of social conditions, everlasting uncertainty, and agitation" (Marx/Engels 1971 [1848]: 476). But, even though "all fixed fast-frozen relations … are swept away" (476) and the powerful in the play act as though there is "no other nexus between people [*Menschen*] than naked self-interest" (475; trans. modified), this turbulence is unlikely to produce revolution. While JATC's satire may not dig deep enough to expose the long history of collusion between politics and speculation, as Florian Becker regrets (2010: 172), the play's depiction of rampant self-interest and private appropriation of public funds eerily prefigured the conspicuous consumption of the twenty-first-century *post-colony,* which Mbembe characterizes as a state run by people feeding off public assets according to the logic of "subordination" and "patronage" (1992: 2) rather than democratic accountability. We will examine theatrical responses to this logic, which South Africans call "state capture" (Madonsela 2016), in Chapter 8.

Leaping across Borders: Handspring, Kentridge, and Transnational Animation

In the 1990s, the instability of the Market led some key productions, such as Brett Bailey's *Zombie*, discussed in the introduction, to bypass the house altogether.[22] Other innovative projects, such as the series of collaborations between Handspring and Kentridge, passed through briefly on the way elsewhere. These breathtaking fusions of puppetry, moving images, and human actors, *Woyzeck on the Highveld* (1993ff; revived 2011ff), *Faustus in Africa* (1995ff), and *Ubu and the Truth Commission* (1997ff; revived 2014; 2016), was enabled by sponsors such as the Goethe Institut to tour more widely in Europe than in South Africa.[23] They are transnational animations because they convey vivid moving images based on Kentridge's charcoal drawings of South African scenes for audiences mostly overseas, and because they combine these South African scenes with European sources. Nonetheless, overseas success should not be allowed to eclipse the lesser-known fact that both Handspring and Kentridge began their work in anti-apartheid theatre nor obscure the degree to which this work reflects the dual perspective on past and future that I have identified as post-anti-apartheid. Kentridge was an actor and designer with JATC in the 1970s (Kruger 2004: 256–61) before a scholarship to Paris jump-started his career in drawing and animation. Kohler and Jones met at Michaelis Art School in Cape Town after which Kohler worked in Britain and Jones for Laedza Banani, a theatre for development in Botswana. In South Africa, they founded Handspring in the 1980s and worked with JATC on *Tooth and Nail* (1991), in which interaction between human actors and wooden puppets animated by the puppeteers' breath opened up a vista beyond apocalyptic visions of the transition. Their collaborations with Kentridge combined European drama, African themes—urban migration and exploitation in *Woyzeck*, the legacy of colonization and racialized capitalism in *Faustus*, and the tension staged by the TRC between giving voice to victims of human rights violations and a platform to the perpetrators of that violence in *Ubu*—and experimentation with puppetry, animation, and performance to explore the current resonances of these stories.

Although *Woyzeck*'s moving pictures of urban desolation and the highveld sky dwarfing the puppet protagonist, his peers, and their exploiters had perhaps greater visual impact, especially in the digitally enhanced revival circulating since 2011, *Faustus in Africa* deserves more attention than it has received. Animating world literature's most powerful and ambiguous legend of modernization and the will to power, it provides a sharper angle on J.W. Goethe's *Faust* than Guy Butler's *Dam* (Chapter 3). While Butler's 1952 drama of white hubris and black exploitation alludes indirectly to Faustian overreach in white claims to African land even as it hints at cracks in the structures that support these claims, the 1995 *Faustus* combined versions of the story by Goethe, Christopher Marlowe, and local dub-poet Lesego Rampholokeng (1965–) with an image-repertoire that juxtaposed the iconography of advertising with the dark secrets of imperial plunder. Rampholokeng rapped on the *Knittelvers* [doggerel] spoken by Goethe's master manipulator Mephisto, framed by projections of text in gothic script (see Kruger 1999a: 197). On the screen, the animated Faust flying over Victoria Falls recalls the megalomaniac attempt to tame the sea in the climax of Goethe's *Faust II* and suggests, in an old postcard of the Zambezi River, the former colonial regimes of Southern and Northern Rhodesia (now Zimbabwe and Zambia). While the images emphasized the history of imperialism, the soundtrack traced the syncretic African modernity that challenged colonial gentility: Motsieloa's jazz-*marabi* mixed with Congolese and Tanzanian tunes trace the history of modern African music or, as Todd Matshikiza had it (Chapter 3), "music for moderns."

Fans of Goethe's magnum opus might wish for more than the image of the Falls to dramatize Faust's exploitation of thousands in the attempt to master the sea (Goethe 1981: 3:339; l.11273), but the animation and puppetry offered compelling visual analogues of the abstract forces of capitalism, imperialism, and racism penetrating the bodies of Africans. Although the found images allude to the colonial era, Kentridge introduced animations here that he amplified in *Ubu*: when a clip shows Faust supping with the devil with the proverbial long spoon, the spoon turns into a drill penetrating a mine, disturbing the remains of Africans buried en masse underground. The set, which resembled a Victorian customs house, was cluttered with commodities—including a well-known advertising poster of a black cherub washed by Pear's soap that indexed transnational capitalism's art of "soft-soaping Empire" (McClintock 1995: 207)—and magic lantern images showed Faust on safari, leaping across borders, shooting at animals framed for his hunting pleasure. In front of this apparatus, puppet Faust and his sidekick Mr. Johnson—after Joyce Carey's sad exemplar of colonized consciousness—performed with white and black puppeteers (Kohler and Louis Sebeko) whose presence created in flesh and breath a human response to the shape-shifting bodies on screen. As Mephisto, Leslie Fong was the only performer not paired with a puppet, which emphasized his power as master of ceremonies and master manipulator but he was stalked by a hyena—a nocturnal predator that incarnates cunning in African tales—animated by Jones (Figure 7.3). This supple-jointed creature seduced Johnson with promises of glory, turning him into a puppet ruler whose leopard-skin hat copied the trademark of Mobutu, former dictator of Congo-Zaire backed by Western capital and the apartheid regime. The stealthy hyena also anticipated the dogs of war that stalk the stage in *Ubu*.

Due to the international coverage of the TRC, the published adaptation of Alfred Jarry's *Ubu Roi* (Taylor/Kentridge et al. 1998), Dawid Minaar's vivid portrayal of a

Figure 7.3 The Hyena and his Masters; Puppet makers: Adrian Kohler and Basil Jones, *Faustus in Africa*, William Kentridge and Handspring Puppet Theatre, Market Theatre Johannesburg, 1995.

Photograph and permission by Ruphin Coudyzer, FPPSA: www.ruphin.co.za.

shifty Ubu, and Kentridge's animation of instruments of torture as horrible as those discussed at the hearings, *Ubu and the Truth Commission* has garnered more attention (see Kruger 2004: 361–4; Krueger 2010: 101–06; Hutchison 2013: 57–61) than other Handspring/Kentridge collaborations. While *Faustus in Africa* anticipated twenty-first-century explorations of African modernity, *Ubu* is a transitional work facing past and future Janus-like. Prompted by Kentridge's prior interest in Jarry's king of mayhem (Taylor/Kentridge et al. 1998: x), it premiered in 1997, when the TRC hearings (1996–2000) were underway but their outcome far from certain, and offered a vivid but provisional response to unfinished business. Minaar's charismatic evildoer and his puppet accomplices—the three-headed dog of war and the Groot [big] Krokodil, a monster shredder of incriminating evidence (Taylor/Kentridge et al. 1998: viii) and stand-in for former president P.W. Botha who acquired the nickname from the anti-apartheid press—threatened to overshadow the more modest puppet witnesses, even if their lined, expressive faces animated by the puppeteers' breath made them compelling petitioners for justice.[24] This imbalance also diminished the play's answer to Kentridge's question: "What is our responsibility to the people whose stories we are using?" (xi). Kentridge saw the ethical answer in deploying puppets to avoid the "contradiction" between actor and "actual witnesses"(xi), but the tension between acting and witnessing and between survivors and impersonators in the triangle linking theatre, testimony, and therapy makes it difficult to resolve.

Truth and *Trauerspiel*: The Play of Mourning and Resolution in TRC Theatre

Twenty thousand survivors of brutality perpetrated directly by apartheid police, indirectly by apartheid laws, and sometimes by ANC and other guerrillas, applied to the TRC's Human Rights Violations (HRV) Committee, but only two thousand were chosen to testify at the hearings. The trauma relived by many who spoke challenged respondents—Archbishop Desmond Tutu who chaired the TRC, clergy, therapists, and theatres working with survivors—to review the assumption that underlies anti-apartheid testimonial theatre: that testimony empowers witnesses, enlightens audiences, and enables both to work through trauma and mourning to act as whole persons.[25] The limits of enlightenment reflect the "play of mourning" [*Trauerspiel*], at once a rich dramatic genre and a mode of staging restoration after suffering,-which takes TRC representation deeper than the spectacular drama of the perpetrators, whether at their TRC hearings or in staged drama. That drama, from *Ubu* through John Kani's *Nothing but the Truth* (Kani 2002) to Farber's adaptation of the *Oresteia* and related Greek tragedies in *Molora* (2008 [2004])—has been discussed exhaustively elsewhere.[26] Public performance risks retraumatizing survivors with the uncontrolled eruption of the "intrusive past" (Van der Kolk/Van der Hart 1995: 160) but it also raises questions of artistic integrity. If third parties create testimonial theatre that revises and re-presents a witness's remembered testimony rather than the witness's verbatim speech, who owns this speech and how is its aesthetic and ethical value to be judged? Julie Salverson, a therapist working with survivors of torture stresses that there is a risk of "eroticizing injury" (2001: 119) in spectacles of suffering for a theatre audience unconnected to the persons so represented.

Those making theatre out of testimony have had to tackle the ethical problem, the phenomenological difficulty, and the artistic challenge raised by these questions: does the witness perform her own testimony or, if not, how do the writer, director, and actors justify their intervention while honoring the witnesses? The ethical problem is clear in the risk of exposing the survivor to retraumatization or exploitation. The phenomenological difficulty arises in the "unshareable" character of pain and its "resistance to language" (Scarry 1985: 4) and the question as to whether the experience that cannot be directly shared might be communicated by gestural as well as verbal resources of performance. The artistic challenge lies in the tension between the writer or director's desire for authentic expression by real survivors and the recognition that these subjects are not always good interpreters of their experience because the "intrusive past" may confound attempts to reinterpret trauma in the present. The moral, phenomenological, and artistic challenges of representing truth, trauma, and perhaps reconciliation emerged forcefully when anti-apartheid practitioners attempted to create theatre for survivors to share experiences of violation and to use truth to reach reconciliation, with themselves and those close to them, if not with those who harmed them. Performances that articulate these challenges are compelling in their own right but also track the movement in TRC theatre from emphatic testimony by actual witnesses facilitated by a veteran anti-apartheid player in *The Story I Am About To Tell* (1998), to the scripted mediation of a witness recalling his experience alongside an actor's impersonation of his younger self in *He Left Quietly* (2002), to the combination, in the *REwind Cantata* (2006), of choral and solo song in Xhosa, Zulu, English, and Afrikaans with recorded testimony from the TRC hearings and new music by Philip Miller, who has collaborated with Kentridge since 1993. While all of these moved audiences, only the last, by blending the Western cantata with the two-century-old tradition of vernacular hymns, summoned South Africa's many languages and repertoires to move decisively away from the post-anti-apartheid moment to create in sound and images a truly post-apartheid work.

To track this evolution, we should start with the reminder that anti-apartheid theatre practitioners in the 1970s and 1980s drew from Brecht, as I showed in *Post-Imperial Brecht* (2004: 337–44), the conviction that the truth in testimonial theatre would set actors and audience free to become agents rather than victims. Attempting to fill anti-apartheid forms with TRC testimony, however, brought theatre practitioners up against the gap between the hope that truth would liberate those who speak and hear it, and the powerful but under-acknowledged force of unresolved trauma that resisted reconciliation.[27] Chairman Tutu's call for national reconciliation rested on the idea that truth would produce catharsis but provoked skepticism about the relevance of catharsis in dealing with the legacy of apartheid violence; the Commission acknowledged this difficulty in its retrospective distinction between the unrealistic appeal to reconciliation and the more modest repair of resolution.[28] Both hopeful appeal and skeptical response resonate in the tension between translations of reconciliation. In Afrikaans, *versoening*, like *Versöhnung* in Hegel's theory of tragedy, invokes transcendence. Xhosa and Zulu, by contrast, draw on *uxolo* [peace] to create the concept of *uxolelwano*, coming to peace, which highlights the process of resolution in the spirit of *ubuntu* [common humanity], a more modest but more productive goal than cathartic reconciliation.

This goal of "coming to peace" shaped survivor organizations such as *Khulumani!* [Speak out!] at the Centre for Violence and Reconciliation (CSVR) but could not easily dissolve the tensions between truth and resolution or between testimonial theatre and retraumatization, tensions that could be fatal, as the life and death of Duma Khumalo suggests.[29] Khumalo survived police torture and the death sentence pronounced on him as one of the Sharpeville Six in 1985 for the mob killing of a city councilor in his hometown. Even though he had left the scene before the killing took place, he was convicted of "murder by common purpose," an apartheid application of a colonial law that the state used to convict those allegedly present at a murder as co-perpetrators (Parker 1996). Khumalo spent three years on death row, endured preparations for death including measurements for his coffin, and a sudden reprieve along with the other accused in 1988.[30] Released due to international pressure in 1991, he worked with Khulumani from 1995 and in the group's performance of survivor testimony in *The Story I Am About To Tell* from 1998 to 2001. This performance inspired Farber to write *He Left Quietly* (Farber/Kumalo 2008]) in which Khumalo spoke lines in English that Farber culled from interviews with him, interspersed with prayerful songs in Zulu. Having spent a decade and a half since his release trying to clear his name by writing to the outgoing minister of justice (Matshoba 2002: 137), testifying to the TRC, and speaking on stage for himself and those who died, hoping to give the dead a voice when he "open[ed] his mouth" (Farber/Kumalo 2008: 189), Khumalo committed suicide at the age of 48 in 2006. While the impact of his experiences on death row, his failed quest for a retrial, and the repeated public display of these experiences is hard to measure, his "ordeal," as Mtutulezi Matshoba put it in his interview-based report (2002: 131), bears witness to the risks, expressed also in the idea of living "on borrowed time" (Farber/Kumalo 2008: 189), to survivors caught between testimony and trauma or in an unstable triangulation of testimony, theatre, and trauma.

To trace this unstable triangle in TRC theatre, we should return to the tension between therapy and theatre, between private exchanges between survivors and therapists that encourage survivors to "be witness to the trauma witness and thus witnesses to their own trauma" as psychiatrist Dori Laub has it (1995: 58) and the public re-presentation of this act of witnessing in which the witnesses impersonate themselves. In collaboration with Ramolao Makhene, anti-apartheid veteran of JATC and the Market (Kruger 2004: 259–74), *The Story I Am About To Tell* incorporated the testimony of three witnesses. In addition to Khumalo, Catherine Mlangeni, whose son was killed by a cassette-player-bomb wired by the police, and Thandi Shezi, an activist tortured and raped in prison, testified at the TRC in mid-1997.[31] They traveled with this play to places such as Sharpeville, the site of Khumalo's arrest and previously of the massacre of protesters in 1960 that served as the starting date for the human rights violations investigated by the TRC. Their testimony recalled statements each had made to the TRC but was reframed by a fictional taxi ride and Makhene's roles as driver and facilitator, accompanied by actors playing other passengers. This device worked largely because Makhene's affability in his double role as a fictional driver and actual workshop animator engaged audiences and drew out witnesses while providing a stable foil against which their unevenly mediated trauma stood out sharply: Khumalo wrung his hands as though still chafed by the chains he wore in prison, while Shezi covered her face as she spoke of her experience of rape. Even if the title invoked the conventional disclaimer of TV docudrama "The story I am about to tell is true; only names have been changed to protect ..." this play instead shared the names of surviving witnesses, and its leisurely pace opened up more generous pauses than *docu-dramatic* plotting would allow, so as to give the witnesses moments of quiet to recollect themselves. The lines of dialogue varied in shape and in language in response to local audiences from Sharpeville to Grahamstown and the art in the performance emerged in the interplay of Makhene's low-key prompts and the witnesses' testimony recollected in intense gesture as well as voice. This intense expression did not easily transmute the symptoms of trauma into the gests of understanding and demonstration that Brecht and his anti-apartheid students expect of the actor but instead indexed the gaps between trauma and performance, acting and acting out, therapy and theatre. While self-presentation by the witnesses could bridge these gaps and move audiences with testimony both authentic and artistically absorbing, the pauses and gestures also highlighted its fragility.

Unlike Khulumani's collective work to which witnesses contributed in their own words, *He Left Quietly* presented Farber's adaptation of Khumalo's testimony and appeared in print under her name in 2008.[32] The dramaturgy evolved in rehearsal at the primary sponsoring institution, the Haus der Kulturen der Welt in Berlin in 2002; it foregrounded the play's aspiration to art, enhanced by Philip Miller's music. Seated center stage and speaking in a quiet baritone at the State Theatre, the second sponsor of the work, Khumalo began by asking the question, "Is it possible that I stayed here among you—the living—long after my soul left my body behind?" answering with a telling reflection on performance and death: "In my time I have died many times. But here I am again and again—alive" (Farber/Kumalo 2008: 188) His dignified demeanor contrasted with the enacted anguish of Lebohang Elephant playing Khumalo as a young prisoner (Figure 7.4). A white female interlocutor, Farber's stage manager whose role was added ten days before the premiere in 2002 (Farber/Kumalo 2008: 182), asked questions based on Farber's interviews and summarized points of South African history from a chair in the house, and then stepped on stage to help Khumalo confine Elephant in a portable wire cage signifying Khumalo's cell (Figure 7.4).

The performance in Pretoria owed its power, as Farber notes, to Khumalo's quiet way of "sharing his story that extends far beyond himself" (182), as well as, in my view, to the affective force of the accompanying music, which included Zulu hymns in traditional settings as well as Miller's modern variations, and the apt transmutation of a classic struggle song *Siyaya ePitoli* [We are marching to Pretoria] into a melody more like a dirge for those who died in the wake of struggle.[33] Even as Khumalo recounted his story, using objects imprinted with his experience—the uniform he wore on death row and the cardboard case that he made in jail and used thereafter to carry letters he wrote in vain to clear his name (188)—his performance was punctuated by Farber's surrogate, whom Farber pushed to intervene beyond her useful role as narrator of information unfamiliar to non-South Africans; at one point, she lay "on top of" Elephant, enacting a "feverish" embrace, as Khumalo recalled dreaming about women

Figure 7.4 "I have died many times": Duma Khumalo and Lebohang Elephant in *He Left Quietly* by Khumalo and Yaël Farber, State Theatre, Pretoria, 2002.

Photograph and permission by John Hogg; https://johnhoggphotography.co.za.

in prison (216), detracting from Khumalo's sober testimony. Further, while Khumalo's gravity ensured the power of his testimony to remind South African audiences of their complicity in his fate, however indirect, the English text appeared addressed to spectators abroad, in Dublin, Amsterdam, and Berlin. After Khumalo's death, the play may become a malleable script that allows producers and audiences outside South Africa to appropriate those aestheticized elements of testimonial theatre, such as the abandoned personal objects that have come to substitute for victims of state violence in theatre and museum displays, and to "eroticize" injury in the name of theatre art.[34]

By contrast, *REwind: Cantata for Voice, Tape and Testimony* draws its power from deep wells of South African cultural expression, particularly the two-century tradition of hymns composed first in Xhosa and later in other African languages by clergy trained partly in British colonial institutions and, in some cases, in Britain and the United States, from the nineteenth century.[35] Rather than creating dramatic fiction, Miller's musical composition and found-sound assemblage, and librettist Mduduzi Mofokeng's textual sampling followed the arc of the TRC hearings from solemn dedication to provisional peace but interspersed musical, visual, and textual quotations from the informal struggle repertoire—for instance, bass singer Kaiser Nkosi leading the chorus in a rousing version of *Siyaya ePitoli* as they danced the *toyi-toyi*—blending forms and voices from several sources. The power of the choir and the four soloists was modulated by video and audio extracts of TRC testimony, using wordless cries and microphone feedback as well as voice, threaded together by traditional and modern music and footage from the hearings playing behind the performers. The same Xhosa hymn that Dhlomo inserted into *The Girl Who Killed to Save* seventy years before (Chapter 2), Bokwe's setting of *Lizalis' idinga lakho, Thixo Nkosi yenyaniso* [Fulfill your promise, Lord God of Truth] introduced the TRC hearings from the first session in the largely Xhosa-speaking Eastern Cape, and provided the leitmotif for the cantata. It was sung in John Knox Bokwe's familiar setting (1915) near the start and returned in Miller's dissonant echo behind the taped testimony of Fr. Michael Lapsey who was maimed by a state parcel bomb. The cantata's premiere on December 16, 2006 paid homage on the Day of Reconciliation to the slaughter mostly of Africans since the Battle of Blood River in 1838 and, in its location in St. George's Cathedral in Cape Town where Tutu once presided, to the church's historic role as sanctuary. The cantata took on its full form, with video projection and animation design by Gerhard and Maja Marx, at the Brooklyn Festival (NY) in 2007, revived at the Market Theatre in 2008 and, after the Royal Festival Hall in London (2010), again in Cape Town, this time at the Baxter Theatre (2011).[36]

The cantata's title quotes Eunice Tshepiso Miya who testified in 1996 about the death of her son Jabulani (celebrate!), who was killed by police in Gugulethu [*igugu lethu*—our pride], near Cape Town, in 1986. Mrs. Miya recalled how she saw her son's body on the television news and expressed the anguished wish at the hearing that she might "rewind the picture."[37] In the cantata, her testimony appeared on screen near the beginning, after Nkosi, dressed in black, had sung a Zulu version of the oath "I solemnly swear to tell the truth, the whole truth …" but mezzo soprano Sibongile Khumalo, in a concert gown with Zulu headdress and beaded collar, did not attempt to impersonate Miya, any more than Nkosi's later rendering in Afrikaans of former president P.W. Botha's belligerent defiance of the TRC pretended to impersonate the Groot Krokodil. Khumalo began by quoting—following Miller's staccato phrasing—Miya's gasp and intake of break that preceded her testimony, and continued with the witness's wish, with Xhosa inflection, to "rewayinda i-picture," as the chorus modulated and repeated the phrase. In the third part, the cantata returns to the poignant elevation of profound grief in soprano Kimmy Skota's rendering of the scream uttered by Nomonde Calata upon hearing of her husband Fort Calata's death in Cradock, accompanied by excerpts from her defiant response to the policeman Roelf Venter who had invaded her home—in Venter's Afrikaans and then in her own Xhosa, echoed this time by Khumalo's deeper mezzo, to "get off her bed."[38] While not strictly theatrical, this counterpoint of conflicting personas highlights moments of dramatic conflict and the challenge of embodying testimony. The cantata concluded with a lullaby—*Thula, Sizwe* (Quiet, Nation)—that lent national scale to an intimate song-form as it recalled a familiar phrase, "Thula thul', thula baba," that even white children who know no Xhosa or Zulu have absorbed from their nannies. The transmission of affect through familiar song along with less familiar transformations through precisely modulated gasps and cries resonates in the pride expressed by those whose voices inspired its music—as in Miya's thought that the cantata would give her "good memories" of her son (quoted Cole 2010: 154) whose name means "[you all] rejoice!" This mode of transmission, partly explicit but partly subliminal, lends the cantata potentially more power to reach South Africans who would not seek out TRC theatre and more capacity to "bring home" its legacies in words and music.[39]

REwind's effective and affective fusion of European, American, and African traditions, popular and classical forms, global English and local languages from Afrikaans to Zulu, cannot alone restore South Africa to itself or heal the ambivalence reverberating in the question—do South Africans exist?—that I quoted that the top of this chapter. Nonetheless, although *REwind* recalls the violence and suffering of the late apartheid 1980s and the difficult search for truth and resolution in the post-anti-apartheid 1990s, it inhabits and illuminates a post-apartheid present. Its affective fusion of disparate sources enlivens the hope for national structures of feeling that might instantiate the preamble to the Constitution of 1996, which begins by recalling the Freedom Charter of 1955:

> We the people of South Africa / Recognize the injustices of the past / Honour those who suffered for justice and freedom in our land / Respect those who have worked to build our country and / Believe that South Africa belongs to all who live in it, united in our diversity. (Constitution 1996: 1)

This Constitution has been hailed worldwide for its innovative provision for, among others, the rights of gender minorities but cases decided by the Constitutional Court affirming the right to housing, health care and other "social rights" in addition to classical provisions for freedom of speech, assembly, movement, and worship, demonstrate that the struggle to realize this promise continues. Prompted by the breadth and ambition of the Constitution, the final chapter will begin with theatre that aspires not merely to disseminate health and other educational messages but also to change the deep structure of gender violence that plagues the country, and to draw attention to the harm done to the nation and its citizens by entrenched inequality. It will go on to explore links and gaps between the pragmatics of applied theatre and the aesthetics of theatre art and will also test the hypothesis implied by *REwind*'s points of origin and return at the Cape of Good Hope, and by Mark Fleishman in *Performing Migrancy and Mobility in Africa*, that Cape Town is the "gateway" to the country and the African continent, an "important node in the network of flows, ... and exchanges" (Fleischman 2015: 3), and a key, perhaps primary, site for new and compelling performances.[40]

The Constitution of South African Theatre at the Present Time

South Africa's Constitution is distinguished by its social rights, including housing, health care, and environmental protection—and thus its defense of well-being—alongside individual rights to equality before the law regardless of ethnicity, gender, or sexual orientation. It is also noteworthy for agencies charged with "supporting constitutional democracy," enumerated in Chapter 9—in particular the Public Protector, the Human Rights Commission, and the Commission for the Promotion and Protection of Cultural, Religious and Linguistic Communities (Constitution 1996: 103ff). This last-mentioned commission is obviously relevant to verbal expression, as shown by debates about the alleged rise of Zulu or decline of Afrikaans, but endemic gender violence, the growing wealth gap, and the misuse of state revenue prompted other officers to take an interest in theatre, as early as the Public Protector's investigation of *Sarafina II* in 1997 (Chapter 6). Twenty years on, the young black women who challenged then-president Zuma three days before National Women's Day 2016 with #RememberKhwezi invoked the right to equality and freedom from violence mandated by the Constitution while also, in describing their action as a "beautiful theatre piece," highlighting the productive friction between performance and politics under the critical conditions of the present time.[1] While the constitution is in the first instance the document that lays out the rights and duties of South African citizens and government to pursue the well-being of the nation and people within it, we should entertain the figurative meaning of constitution as the ensemble of structures and norms that enable acts of imagination and social action—or what I have called subjunctive and indicative practices—along with the institutions to support these practices. In democratic South Africa, the constitution of the expanded field of play extends beyond professional theatre art to encompass performance practices that develop citizens' skills to tackle social problems of national and international magnitude, from the AIDS pandemic to the inequity exacerbated by local mismanagement and global resource extraction.

Theatre and performance in twenty-first-century South Africa are not determined at every step—from institutional support to dramatic form or content—by the Constitution but widespread awareness of the constitutional right to well-being and of the Public Protector and other "Chapter 9" agencies protecting those rights has heightened activism in the courts, the streets, and on stage. This awareness, enabled by input into drafting the document in town meetings and written submissions (Skjelten

2006) and reinforced by media and protest statements, has prompted citizens to see the public sphere as a key site of creative and political agency. At the same time, however, the sharp lines of the anti-apartheid struggle have given way to shifting allegiances and sometimes to self-indulgence. Some high-profile shows such as *Exhibit B* (2010), which earned Bailey notoriety for displaying people in cabinets reminiscent of colonial expositions (Sieg 2015) or *Protest* (2014), Grootboom's send-up of citizen outrage at corrupt officials (Kruger 2015a) may sacrifice critique to self-regarding irony. More modestly, solo township players use direct address and vivid mimicry to dramatize multiple characters engaged in quotidian but no less vital battles. Without enumerating rights to "improved conditions of life" (Constitution 1996: 1), these performers offer keen insights into the gulf between the promised fruits of liberation and the daily struggle for livelihood. Plays such as *Itsoseng* (2008) by Omphile Molusi or *Fruit* (2015) by Paul Noko illuminate communities in North West Province and Soweto respectively. Finally, institutions occupying space between global fame and local engagement, such as Magnet Theatre and the Baxter create work that delights audiences at home and abroad, while honing practitioners' skills in managing as well as making performance. Whereas the Market has produced important work such as Van Graan's *Green Man Flashing* (2004; revived most recently in 2018), which challenges abuses of power in the post-apartheid state, this chapter will test Fleishman's hypothesis that the Western Cape—from the colonial "Mother City" around Table Mountain to the township of Khayelitsha [new home] 30 km to the east—is an "important node in the network of flows and exchanges" (2015: 3).[2]

While acknowledging differences of scale and emphasis, assembling aesthetic and pragmatic acts in the expanded field of performance highlights their intersections, as indicated for instance in contrasting treatments of issues such as patriarchal power and women's response. The performance in a school hall by adolescents enacting competing scenarios that reinforce or challenge their presumption of masculine privilege, as documented in Patricia Watson's *Heart to Heart* performance and graphic narrative project in the rural Mhala Mhala district near the Kruger National Park, may look and sound very different from the treatment of rape and resistance in the lyrical writing and subtle staging of Lara Foot's *Karoo Moose* at the Baxter Theatre in Cape Town, but both merit attention not only for the urgency of their shared subject but also for their play with the forms and functions of social and theatrical action. As Lynn Dalrymple founder of DramAide, the oldest HIV/AIDS theatre organization (est. 1992) argues, "applied art is still art" (2013: 229) insofar as it inspires practitioners as well as directing them to apply art to a specific goal such as HIV awareness. Conversely, the creators of captivating drama with minimal elements—such as the two actors, a carpet made of refugee agency rice sacks, and a metal frame conjuring in sequence a house, a boat, and a camp in *Every Year Every Day I Am Walking* (Magnet Theatre 2007; published: Reznek et al. 2012; Figure.8.1)—meets the highest standards of artistic innovation and also enables the training of actual migrants.

The *Revised White Paper on Arts Culture and Heritage* (DAC 2017) may tip this delicate balance between aesthetics and pragmatics, between the idea of inherent artistic value and the shifting range of claims for more measurable social impact. Whereas the writers of the 1996 White Paper (see Chapter 7) were conscious of the

Figure 8.1 Violence distilled in a pair of shoes. Jenny Reznek and Faniswa Yisa in Magnet Theatre's *Every Year, Every Day, I Am Walking*, 2007.

Photograph by Hennie Coetzee.

caesura marked by the Constitution and thus of their contribution to South Africa's transformation, and cited the Bill of Rights to proclaim "access to, participation in, and enjoyment of the arts" as "basic human rights," and to stake the broadest political claim to link the right to art with the right to freedom of expression as a "fundamental prerequisite for democracy" and the deepest psychological claim for the power of art to foster the "full potential" of "human beings" (DAC 1996: 7), the 2017 revision links the Bill of Rights to international norms, expressed in UNESCO declarations on intangible cultural heritage (2003), cultural diversity (2005), and culture industries (2015), and to the National Development Plan 2030 (DAC 2017: 6) to develop the "African, European, and Asian" strands of South African theatre (19). As to "core values," this White Paper moves briskly from the aesthetic value of innovation to the pragmatic—in the sense of goal-directed—social and economic value of artistic production and potential to "generate wealth" and "sustainable employment" (2017: 10). A skeptic might retort that DAC officials think innovation involves "problem-solving" but not the capacity to challenge social norms or to play without determined ends; nonetheless, innovative and resourceful practitioners have sustained this balance.

In the expanded field of play, this chapter on the constitution of South African theatre and performance recalls the transnational provocation of Armand Gatti, Brecht student and French son of Italian migrants, who wrote that "in order to create theatre, it is necessary to leave it behind" (1982: 71). This call to question if not quite "liquidate" aesthetics (Brecht 2014: 36), alongside Sepamla's query about the African vocabulary of theatre with which I began this book, stimulates productive friction between art and activism, the inspiration of wonder and the call to commitment that has animated performance here for a century. The institutions in the culminating sections—Baxter and Magnet Theatres—tap this energy to bring the practices of theatre art, education, and community development into alignment. Before we can appreciate the aesthetic and pragmatic value of their projects, however, we should begin with formations that respond directly to the constitutional directive to "improve lives" by cultivating the terrain of "theatre for development" or more broadly "theatre for social change."

Politics and Poetics of Participatory Dramaturgy in the Age of AIDS

Although the term "applied theatre" signals to potential funders the applicants' intention to produce outcomes—better health, better education, better life skills—the more elastic term "theatre for social change" includes the aspiration to inspiration as well as pragmatics, and hence, as Dalrymple insists, to the "art of the application" (2013: 229) alongside more—but never entirely—measurable goals of developing skills, sustaining employment, and helping people to change risky behaviors that have fueled the multiple crises that we summarize under AIDS. In South Africa, where 19 percent of people in the sexually active age range (15–49) defined by the United Nations are HIV+, a majority of them women, AIDS is much more than a health problem. As Emma Durden writes, it is a "multi-faceted issue that permeates all levels of society" in which "political, social and biological factors" shape sexual conduct to "feed the epidemic" (2011: 1), even if the rate had dropped to 19 percent by 2017.[3] Organizations such as Acting on HIV have joined prominent stakeholders such as the Treatment Action Campaign to demand resources from the ministries of health, education, and arts. These projects strive to enhance the capacity of social actors to tackle—understand, imagine, and change—the complex of challenges from scarce employment and life skills to the scapegoating of women, minorities, and migrants, challenges that exacerbate the immediate problems of unwillingness to undergo medical tests or access treatment thereafter.

While the National AIDS Consortium enabled the coordination of public and private funding with health workers and theatre makers whose activities have gained more visibility since 2009, when Zuma's health department set aside Mbeki's denial (Chapter 7) in favor of biomedical diagnosis and treatment of HIV, practice has not quite matched policy. Current practitioners acknowledge that dispensing information about infection, testing, or safe-sex practices has not eradicated the fear of community shaming that keeps people silent and unwilling to test, nor has it led decisively to changes in behavior sufficient to radically reduce transmission (Doubt 2015). As visiting Africanist Louise Bourgault noted (2003: 40–43) and Durden confirms (2011: 1–3), masculine entitlement—to sex and other privileges— fuels HIV contagion and harms women, children—and men. More broadly, Dennis Francis acknowledges, as did English theatre activist John McGrath thirty years ago, that "theatre cannot *cause* a social change," (McGrath 1981: vii). Francis suggests instead that "acting on HIV" means "using drama to create *possibilities* for change"

(2011: 1; emphasis LK), and colleagues Dalrymple, Durden, and Hazel Barnes at the University of KwaZulu-Natal (UKZN) emphasize the value of process—via participatory dramaturgy—to "enhance the capacity of theatre practitioners and their communities to take responsibility for the quality of their lives" not only for HIV but also "peace building, transformation and diversity management" (Barnes 2013: xiii), resonating with McGrath's assertion that theatre "can articulate the pressures" toward change by providing means whereby "people can find their voice, their solidarity and their collective determination" (1981: vii).

With these complexities in view, this section's topic is not "AIDS theatre" but rather dramaturgy for social change in the age of AIDS. Outcomes in health provision or longevity are best assessed by those evaluating policy; my goal as performance historian is to contextualize this work within the record of theatre for social change and thus assess its claims for innovation. The application of theatre to social action from strikes to HIV activism has a longer history than practitioners acknowledge and offers archival and repertoire resources for present attempts to embed the dramatization of a particular crisis—in this case, AIDS—in the social networks that impact behavior and beliefs. Noting the links between anti-apartheid and applied theatre reminds us that testimonial theatre in the 1970s anticipated participatory dramaturgy in the 1990s. The oft-cited source for participatory dramaturgy—Augusto Boal's *Theatre of the Oppressed* (1974)—draws evidently on Freire's "problem-*posing* education" in *Pedagogy of the Oppressed* (1972: 45) and less obviously on Brecht's *Lehrstücke*–learning experiments that dispensed with audiences in favor of participation and analysis by all (Kruger 2004: 25–28). Boal's gloss on Brecht's processes, "dissecting, disassembling and reassembling" character and action (1979: 99)—which Brecht called *Versuche* [essays or experiments] and Boal calls forum theatre—also fits South African work. Serpent Players' *The Coat* (1966) and the Brecht-inspired collaboration between JATC and industrial unions in the 1980s (Chapters 5 and 6) used participatory dramaturgy to test scenarios before strike action or to articulate conflicts in vernacular speech before translating into English for litigation (Von Kotze 1989; Malange 1990; Kruger 2004: 261–66).

Without citing Boal, Barney Simon's work with black nurses, who tend even today to treat patients rather haughtily, used role-play to encourage them to experience the medical encounter from patients' point of view. This work was funded 1972–75 by the US Ford Foundation—which later supported DramAide and similar organizations—and anticipated applications of forum theatre in the 1980s and 1990s.[4] These applications include health education theatre by the Progressive Primary Health Care Network extending from Johannesburg to the Wits Rural Facility in Acornhoek, Mpumalanga, and from global English to regional Tsonga via Zulu as a lingua franca (Evian 1992; Kruger 1999a, 1999b), and also theatre-in-education work that grew into DramAide in KZN, the province with the highest HIV rates. DramAide encourages community stakeholders to stage their own understanding of the interaction of HIV risks with rape and other forms of violence, badly distributed resources, and the overall poverty that hampers individual ability to make life-saving choices (Parker et al. 2000: 3) but its current mission as an "independently funded" non-profit affiliated with UKZN emphasizes "HIV prevention messaging" and thus the functional application of theatre-in-education.[5] Drama for Life, directed at Wits by Warren Nebe, draws on DramAide's example but "rejects functional approaches to applied theatre" in favor of practice-based research that aims to create "critically reflective pedagogies, spaces and aesthetic forms that give rise to different ways of being in the world."[6] This program brings applied theatre into productive friction with artistic experiment, offering HIV- and school-based theatre-in-education alongside professional training. The Drama for Life volume *Applied Drama and Theatre in an Interdisciplinary Field* (Barnes 2013) includes contributions from HIV educators from Zambia to Uganda, highlighting transnational networks of knowledge production while also analyzing local projects.

Claiming to "enhance the capacity of communities to take responsibility for the quality of their lives," this volume and others like it do not always acknowledge earlier work that might illuminate their attempts to "integrate activism, education, and therapy" (Barnes 2013: xiii) to tackle gender violence as well as HIV. As former Justice Sachs noted, patriarchy is one of South Africa's most enduring "non-racial institutions" (1990b: 53) in that it spans apartheid and post-apartheid eras and affects people of all backgrounds. Whereas the HIV scenarios developed by Evian and the Progressive Primary Health Care Network in the 1980s and the Johannesburg Health Dept. in the 1990s treated theatre as a tool to dispense advice without directly addressing entrenched patriarchal entitlement or the nuances of performance, they nonetheless pointed the way forward in scenarios that favored the agency of women. The basic plot depicted the conflict between a young woman and a male partner who violently refuses to discuss condoms, and resolved the conflict by having them discuss the matter with friends at a party, who persuade them to use condoms—and tact (Evian 1992: 35–37). While male workers I observed watching a Zulu version in a single-sex hostel in 1994 made disparaging comments about women performers and called AIDS a white disease—still a potent belief—students at Orlando High School in their teens and twenties mixed jokes in English, Zulu, and other vernaculars about the party action with arguments about sexual rights and obligations, followed by questions about performance process and access to training, implying that the value of the event lay for them in the prospect of social agency through employment. Likewise, *Heart to Heart*, the performance and graphic narrative facilitated by Watson and the Storyteller Group (Watson 1998; Kruger/Watson 2001) prompted heated debates between male and female students about the former's expectation of sexual favors, which generated the fantasy scenario of masculine potency and a spectacular wedding in the graphic fiction *Dream Love*, even though young men in poor rural areas could not hope to offer much of value in exchange for sex. Whereas the revised *True Love* hammered out in workshops gave women characters and to an extent women performers more agency, this representation remained aspirational rather than fully realized.

These 1990s projects anticipated Durden's key question—"just how participatory is participatory practice?" (2011: 8)—a question that shows the gap between participation and agency and prompts another query that she hints in the assertion that "understandings and beliefs about HIV" require local solutions (9). While this directive alerts critics to respect participants' priorities, such as stock theft, water rights, and conflicts over resources and ecological survival, rather than HIV, it may discourage facilitators from addressing global problems that shape local knowledge.

In contrast, *Heart to Heart* assembled Tsonga-speaking rural students, who hoped that English fluency would lead to work in one of the nearby game parks, or in the alluring world of TV soap opera that inspired the dubious *Dream Love* scenario. Watson also analyzed the structural inequity that made these hopes unlikely and the male students' frustration potentially dangerous. Two decades on, however, Alexandra Sutherland's "Dramatic Spaces in Patriarchal Contexts" (2013) charts the difficulty of promoting safe sex and critically analyzing distressing situations—e.g. a schoolgirl abused by her stepfather—ending with Sutherland's "disillusionment" (184) at being unable to help the girl. While Sutherland may not have accessed 1990s work by Watson and others on forum theatre dramatizing social and sexual behavior, her base in KZN could have led her to projects such as the "rough aunties" in Durban (Longinotto 2009) who have created safer spaces for young girls to talk about abuse by projecting their experience in play and might have exposed her and others of her generation to a greater range of practices and to the temporal, spatial, and ideological limits of her attempts to change behavior.

Recognizing the limits of applying theatre to trauma, whether of TRC witnesses or AIDS survivors, Kennedy Chinyowa (2013) critiques the instrumentalization of participation and the fetishization of the local. Drawing on experience with HIV/AIDS theatre in Zimbabwe, and in Gauteng and KZN in South Africa, he argues that "participation" risks being "dis-embedded from its socio-cultural contexts" and thus treated as a "thing" or a commodity packaged to appeal to donors (2013: 209). He cautions that deference to local knowledge cannot simply replace outside expertise when risky behavior keeps HIV prevalence stubbornly high. Rather, practitioners should confront the blind spots of local actors and outside facilitators, acknowledge tensions between "localization and globalization in HIV/AIDs interventions" (203), and explore the potential of open-ended play or "poetics" as a way out of the instrumentalization of pragmatic applications. This poetics should deploy political "tension" along with artistic "creativity" (204) or, in other words, treat the friction between contradictory ideologies and practices in, for example, the fraught field of gender relations, as potentially productive, just as the friction between inherited and imported forms produce ongoing invention. Chinyowa's poetics of contradiction critiques the conundrum of applied theatre but he also invites us to investigate the productive friction among form, function, and structures of support and patronage in theatre—established or aspirational—that dramatizes conflict in the state of capture.

Staging State Capture: From *Green Man Flashing* to *The Man in the Green Jacket*

As many argued in the Zuma era (2008–18), South Africa's democracy was "suspended" (Habib 2013), even "stolen" (Bhorat et al. 2017) not only by corrupt individuals but through "state capture" (Madonsela 2016) by rent-seeking clients of state-owned enterprises and their allies defrauding tax-payers and "short-changing" the nation (Bundy 2014).[7] The *State of Capture* investigation by Thuli Madonsela (Public Prosecutor 2009–16) targeted the influence of the Gupta family on the Zuma administration but her report exposed a larger and more tangled patronage network that has ensnared law enforcement, and undermined revenue collection and basic services such as water and electricity to enrich a favored few. Cultural institutions, especially in Gauteng, the richest province and seat of executive power, have not been immune to capture, even if corruption in theatre institutions has not led to outright asset looting—as in the SABC (Matisonn 2015)—but rather taken the more subtle form of pleasing the powerful by pleasing rather than provoking the audience. But, before we examine the state of theatre—and the State Theatre—we should look at a usually provoking play at the Market, the historically preeminent house of resistance theatre, which shows that theatre can challenge the state of capture.

Mike van Graan's *Green Man Flashing* (2004; published 2010) initially addressed politicking before the election that made Mbeki president in 1999 but its resonance grew louder under Zuma and it is still relevant today.[8] The drama highlights tensions between accountability and corruption, the rule of law and party loyalty, and between bonding among powerful men and persistent violence against women. Eerily anticipating Zuma's 2006 rape trial—although *his* accuser was black—this play dramatizes the fictional case of Gabby, a fortysomething white divorcee, who spent the 1980s in exile so she and her black husband Aaron could join the anti-apartheid struggle and live together, which was forbidden by apartheid. The conflict erupts when Gabby reports rape by her boss Khumalo, kingpin of the ANC faction in the contested province of KZN. Van Graan worked initially with Cape-based actor Jennifer Steyn who played Gabby at the Grahamstown try-out in 2004 and returned when the full-length play moved from the Market to the Baxter in 2005, but at the Market Gabby was played by Michelle Douglas, who seemed too young for the role.[9] The male cast nonetheless gave the Market staging a sharp political edge. Aaron, played by James Ngcobo as a skillful politician, is sent by the party to persuade his now ex-wife to keep quiet in the name of "national unity" (Van Graan 2010: 73). Entering her house without permission, Aaron offers her a consular job overseas but insinuates through the "green man flashing" analogy that should she go to trial, she might be hit by vehicles running "red lights" (75), and leaves his bodyguard Luthando, embodied by TV heavy Sechaba Morojele, to repeat the threat. Although Luthando is killed under dubious circumstances, the investigating detective appears persuaded that Gabby pulled the trigger in self-defense, and the play ends with Gabby starting her video testimony in the presence of her lawyer. The Market production left the substance of this statement open but provoked fierce audience debate about the high rape rate and the abuse of power. The play's exposure of attacks on the rule of law in favor of narrow party interests remains as relevant as it was when Ndebele observed that the play "lays bare the difficult paradoxes South Africans have to confront in achieving the promise of our inspiring constitution" (quoted: Van Graan 2010: 16), its relevance confirmed by revivals at Cape Town's Artscape (2012), Sandton's Theatre on the Square (2018), and at the Hexagon Theatre (2017) in Zuma's home province of KZN.

Green Man Flashing's five characters, black, white, and brown, probe the intimate and social harm of patriarchal privilege and state capture. *The Man in the Green Jacket* (Grahamstown 2014) by Eliot Moleba is by contrast an intimate dialogue between a father and son. Its title alludes to Mgcineni "Mambush" Noki, dubbed the "man in the green blanket," who led the strike at the Lonmin platinum mine at Marikana in North West, where thirty-four miners including Noki were killed and over seventy wounded by the national police on August 16, 2012. In order to evaluate Moleba's play, we must clarify this event, the most shocking case of police violence since apartheid officers killed sixty unarmed protesters at Sharpeville in 1960. When falling platinum prices after 2008 exposed the weakness of the industry, especially the over-leveraged Lonmin, which was apparently unable to meet required social investments in the local community including three thousand houses of which it built three, 10,000 miners across the industry protested work conditions and poor representation by the ANC-aligned National Union of Mineworkers (NUM) (Alexander, Lekgowa et al. 2013: 15); despite defending miners' rights in the apartheid1980s, NUM has drawn its salaries from the Chamber of Mines and by degrees become more an enforcer for the boss than advocate for the worker (Marinovich 2018: 69–72) and thus part of the patronage network criticized in *Betrayal of the Promise* (Bhorat et al. 2017).[10] At the center of the strikes were rock drill operators who tend to be migrants from the Eastern Cape or Lesotho doing dangerous work for low pay and little recognition from NUM (Harford 2013: 159–63) but who had won wage increases at Impala Platinum (Implats) and had informal negotiations with managers at another Lonmin mine, Karee in 2011.

In anticipation of similar treatment at Marikana, 3,000 rock drill operators went out in August 2012 in a strike that, while unauthorized by NUM, was legal under the Constitution. After a peaceful march to Lonmin observed by local police (Marinovich 2018: 60) ended when two miners were shot, apparently from the NUM office, the botched response by Major General William Mpembe who spoke Zulu rather than the miners' Xhosa or Sotho left police exposed to retaliation from strikers who killed a security guard and two officers (109–116). The strikers gathered on Wonderkop [Wonder Hill], a rocky outcrop that the miners call Thaba [mountain] and invest with restorative powers similar to Thaba Bosiu (Chapter 2), hoping in vain to dialog with Lonmin. In response to demands from Lonmin human capital director Barnard Mokoena and Cyril Ramaphosa, at the time Lonmin director for Black Economic Empowerment and also deputy state president, to treat the entire strike as a criminal rather than a labor action (docs. cited Marinovich 2018: 136–44), national top brass summoned extra rounds of lethal ammunition, and mortuary vehicles as if anticipating bloodshed (149), and special talk forces who arrived in Casspirs, army vehicles used in the assault on Soweto 1976, and in helicopters that recalled the air force deployed against miners in 1922 (Alexander et al. 2013: 148). On August 16, heavily armed units used barbed wire to trap and shoot seventeen men who were leaving Wonderkop in view of reporters including Reuters cameraman John Mkhize (Marinovich 160–61), and then killed another seventeen that tried to shelter on a second hill.

In statements to the media and the Marikana Commission, Police Minister Nathi Mthethwa, who moved to Arts and Culture in 2014, and National Police Commissioner Ms. Riah Phiyega, who was suspended in 2015 with full pay until the end of her contract in 2017, claimed not to recall meetings at which the police assault was planned and blamed strikers for allegedly threatening police. Nonetheless, miners' testimony (Alexander et al. 2013: 75–138), Mkhize's footage, Rehad Desai's film *Miners Shot Down* (2014) and independent coroners (Marinovich 195–200) showed that many were shot in the back or at close range. The Commission chaired by retired judge Ian Farlam took testimony initially from Lonmin and the police until the Social and Economic Rights Institute (SERI), whose name highlights the social rights in the Constitution, and the Center for Applied Legal Studies (Wits) compelled the Commission to hear survivors and family members before filing the report in 2015. Despite recorded and forensic evidence of culpability, the police generals responsible for ordering the assault were not prosecuted but 270 strikers were arrested and their leaders charged under the "murder by common purpose" statute for being in a group allegedly responsible for killing two policemen: these charges were later dropped.[11]

Several performative points emerge from this material, particularly the ruses used by the powerful to blame others for their failings and the contrasting roles of men and women in official and unofficial spaces. Phiyega and the more experienced General Miriam Mbongo, commander for North West, claimed not to recall planning meetings that led to the police actions; Mpembe, who viewed the field from a helicopter asserted against evidence not to have heard any fire, and commanders on the ground likewise gave contradictory statements to the commission (Marinovich 2018: 175–86), which sound uncomfortably like the exercises in deception that were the rule in apartheid commissions after crimes such as the police killing of Biko and others. Photojournalists Leon Sadiki and Felix Dlangamandla captured scenes at Wonderkop that included Sadiki's shot of Noki addressing the crowd (Jika et al. 2013: 58L), dancers stomping to strike songs, carrying sticks like those at anti-apartheid marches, as well as machetes, but not the guns that the police—armed with automatic weapons—claimed were turned on them. The men in blankets on the cold hillside remain far from the men in suits directed by Ramaphosa, a BCM student in the 1970s, lawyer, and leader of the NUM in the 1980s, ANC representative at the negotiations of 1993, and in 2018 state president, who acknowledged that he called for national police intervention after ten people including the two local policemen and a security guard as well as seven strikers were killed before August 16, but not that he tried to end the strike by force. Miners' widows and other women, even after they were allowed to testify at the Commission, received little compensation but have organized under the name *Sikhala Sonke* [We all complain] and sent one of their own to join the opposition EFF in Parliament.[12]

The most lavishly staged response to the massacre *Marikana—the Musical* (Grahamstown 2014) by Aubrey Sekhabi deployed the resources of the State Theatre to create striking images of the massed men sitting on a wire-mesh facsimile of Wonderkop (Figure 8.2) and performing the gumboot dances historically associated with miners and later with masculine ensembles in anti-apartheid plays such as Ngema's *Asinamali* [We have no money, 1985). According to an unsigned program note, the musical was based on the book *We Are Going To Kill Each Other Today*, which includes Dlangamandla's and Sadiki's photographs, and compelling reporting by Thanduxolo Jika and Lucas Ledwaba (2013), but the performance did not shed light on the power structure or the men in suits who hold it up. Rather its dramaturgy favored the visual clash between workers' overalls and police uniforms, culminating in the clash between miners and special force police in riot gear on a darkened stage lit by searchlights. The musical concluded with dueling laments—one widow of the

Figure 8.2 "Wonderkop." *Marikana—the Musical*; written and directed by Aubrey Sekhabi, National Arts Festival Grahamstown, 2014.

Photograph by Alexa Sedgwick; courtesy of the National Arts Foundation.

dozens who lost their miner husbands against the widow of one of the two policeman killed—that recalled the tear-jerking songs of Kente's musicals and implied that all mourners were equal. This sentimental treatment left scarce stage time for managers who had little to say about their role in the showdown between miners and police. The searchlights glittering on barbed wire on stage vividly recalled the tools of apartheid but neither plot nor program attempted to represent the more complicated struggle between post-apartheid elites and workers, including miners who each support ten or more dependents (Harford 2013: 160), while 30 percent of adults survive on small income grants.[13]

The female relatives of dead or maimed miners and their testimony at SERI workshops and eventually at the Farlam Commission drew on the repertoire of Khulumani and other CBOs at the TRC (Chapter 7), in that they tempered their grief with assertions of their right to redress by the state and Lonmin, including work in the mines which some received, but it was apparently the keening widows of *Marikana— the Musical* that encouraged some to link Marikana to the TRC. *MARI+KANA*, created by Mandisi Sindo and Theatre4Change for the 2015 Infecting the City festival in Cape Town, drew on lament but to critical purpose. The performance took place on the lawn between Parliament and the South African Museum, once the vegetable garden planted by the Dutch in the 1650s and thus colonial ground zero, on this occasion marked with white crosses recalling Dlangamandla's photograph on Wonderkop (Jika et al. 2013: 123). Mature women in black or dark blue dresses in nineteenth-century Xhosa style danced with younger men in scarlet overalls. While identified by visitors as a "requiem" (De Smet et al. 2015), the duets suggested mothers and sons in conflict as well as shared sorrow, and the men's red overalls resembled those worn by the EFF parliamentary delegation that claims to represent miners and other workers better than the ANC. While women sang in the chorus, a solo male voice recounted the events of August 2012 in Xhosa, punctuating his account with the question why black police [*amaphoyisa amnyama*] were felling black men [*amadoda amnyama*]—to cheers from the audience. The song *Vuka Mntomnyama* [*vuka umntu omnyama*: wake up, black person] accompanied by young men whose white clay make-up recalled male Xhosa initiation, implied defiance as much as reconciliation.[14] In this light, *Sikhala Sonke* should be translated "we all complain" rather than "we cry together," given the vocal challenge of its members to the captured state, as heard also in the documentary *Strike the Rock* (Saragas 2017).

Although there is a world of difference between the lavish *Marikana—the Musical* and the austere *MARI+KANA*, the visual appeal of both allowed audiences who know no Xhosa—or much about the conflicts over rights to work and well-being that came to a head in the strike—to enjoy the spectacle. In contrast, Moleba eschewed visual novelty in *The Man in the Green Jacket*, focusing like Van Graan on dialogue, and setting the scene in a realistic shack interior like those typical for Marikana workers (photos: Marinovich 106–7). In contrast to the display of masculine muscle in the musical, it showed the intimate imprint of the exploitation shaping lives off stage. Through dialog in English and Tswana, the play portrays the relationship between father John Ledwaba and adult son Oupa, both miners at Marikana (Tau Maserumule and Pusetso Thibedi, Grahamstown 2014), and the latter's unseen but vividly described young son whom his father hopes to see one day in a better job than dangerous mine work. The drama of the strike emerged slowly, while the dialogue and the sparsely furnished room, lit apparently by a kerosene lamp, registered Lonmin's stingy provision for employees' needs, but the scenario gained historical depth in John's recollection of apartheid-era conditions and Oupa's account of his son's enthusiasm for soccer mixed with regret that he could not afford to buy proper boots. The soccer theme highlights Moleba's avoidance of spectacular heroics; whereas the charismatic Noki was known as a soccer star, the man in this play speaks of the aspirations of his young son whom we never see. The dialogue in the Grahamstown premiere remained matter-of-fact, but the accompaniment—a ballad reinvention of *maskanda,* migrant guitar music made famous by the band Savuka at Mandela's inauguration–composed and played here by Yogin Sullaphen—offered a poignant counterpoint.[15]

Beyond the immediate impact of the massacre, the play references the legacy of miners' exploitation and its stage representation, using the character John's reflections on anti-apartheid strikes, his age (60s) and name Ledwaba to honor the actor who created the role of the miner in Manaka's *Egoli* (1979; Chapter 6). Whereas the actor Ledwaba had expressed his character's grief at his son's death by drinking until he literally vomited on stage during *Egoli*, Moleba avoided any violent expression of emotion. Instead of the "exhibitionist" writing criticized by Ndebele, the performance concluded as John sat alone responding to news by telephone that his son had been shot by police, and then held up the green jacket that Oupa left behind (Figure 8.3) while saying in sober Brechtian fashion "On 16 August, they came for my son but I was not here to speak for him ... Tomorrow they will come for you and me," lines that echo anti-Nazi pastor Martin Niemöller's poem warning of the risks of quiescence as well as of protest.[16] Even after being injured by police fire, many strikers were arrested and tortured (Marinovich 219–26). The name Ledwaba also recalls reporter Lucas Ledwaba, whose book *Broke and Broken* (2016) indicts the exploitation of workers and the abandonment of miners who contracted phthisis and other diseases.

The Man in the Green Jacket brings to mind another play from North West, where wealth generated by corporations, whether dealing in minerals or in conspicuous consumption, as in the casino resort Sun City, has not trickled down to the majority. Molusi's *Itsoseng* (published 2009) dramatizes the narrator's account of the destruction of the Itsoseng shopping center—in his account by protesters without a clear sense of purpose in 1994, the year of liberation—and its abandonment by corrupt officials who pocketed the reconstruction funds. The play in performance, honed by runs across South Africa and abroad in Stratford, London and Chicago, compelled attention thanks to Molusi's ability to repurpose trash to bring to life a vivid cast of characters and their favorite objects, from the narrator's blue funeral suit, to the sunglasses that recall a childhood sweetheart dead from AIDS, to a blanket that he folded one way to portray his old mother and another to show a cynical city journalist reporting the looting, ending with the narrator's resignation in the face of inequity, as he drops the props in apparent despair. Like many solo plays, *Itsoseng* is a series of sketches rather than a singular drama. In contrast, *The Man in the Green Jacket* captured the father's

Figure 8.3 "They came for my son." Tau Maserumule in *The Man in the Green Jacket* by Eliot Moleba, National Arts Festival Grahamstown, 2014.

Photograph by Alexa Sedgwick; courtesy of the National Arts Foundation.

grief in Maserumule's deft handling of the green jacket but also framed this family tragedy with the conditions—enrichment for a few and misery for the many—that define the state of capture. While the green blanket worn by Noki on Wonderkop may have been an accident of history, the green jacket of Moleba's invention harks back to that versatile *Coat* imagined by the Serpent Players as a means of survival in bleak times (Chapter 6). Also hinting at the ANC flag—green land, black people, and gold wealth—the *Green Jacket* implicitly indicts the party behind the flag for abandoning the goal of national well-being.

Standing Firm and Cultivating Hope: Baxter Theatre and Zabalaza Intsika

In contrast to its contemporaries the Space and the Market, the Baxter (1977–) did not have a distinctive vision in its early decades but in the twenty-first century it has supplemented work by seasoned playwrights in the house with new writers and performers in Zabalaza Intsika [Xhosa: stand firm pillar], established in 2011 by Lara Foot, Bongile Mantsai, Mdu Kweyama, and others.[17] The enduring inequality between rich and beautiful Cape Town, wrapped around the peninsula's mountain spine and the districts alongside it such as Rondebosch and the University of Cape Town which houses the Baxter, as against the windswept Cape Flats that extend out to Khayelitsha 30 kilometers away, from which the mountain is barely visible, has deep consequences for social and ecological well-being and for activities including performance that might foster skills and structures needed to overcome this persistent apartheid. Projects from Khayelitsha include Sindo's Theatre4Change and Mandla Mbothwe's redirection of Magnet Theatre's migration drama to the well-traveled but under-dramatized national highway N2 between the impoverished Eastern Cape and the affluent Western Cape, but many have been supported directly or indirectly by the Baxter and Zabalaza. The Baxter has moved beyond staging occasional festivals for aspiring practitioners to developing work to command attention in the central house. Junkets Press's publication of Zabalaza Festival winners along with established playwrights such as Van Graan has given Zabalaza a national profile and narrowed the gap between "town" and "township" theatre.

The integration of art and social agency, schooled audiences in the city and the "active pursuit of audiencing" in the townships (Morris 2017: 146) has been Foot's mission as Baxter artistic director and CEO since 2010. Before joining the Baxter as resident director in 2000, Foot worked at the Market from 1996. There she directed among other plays Slabolepszy's *Fordsburg's Finest* (1998; Chapter 7) before adapting and directing Zakes Mda's novel *Ways of Dying* (1991) in 1999. This adaptation spotlighted women's agency; the role of narrator that Foot created for Nomsa Nene offset the masculine swagger of Mda's hero Toloki, the professional mourner. Nene had appeared several times at the Market since her debut in *Die Van Aardes van Grootoor* (1978; Chapter 4) but her deeper voice and greater bulk twenty years on gave her narrator power to challenge Toloki. Foot's original plays, especially *Tshepang* (2003), *Karoo Moose* (2007) and "Fishers of Hope" (2014), have dramatized the lives of women and raised the profile of female collaborators such as Zoleka Helesi on the Zabalaza team, but her example has not as yet changed the overwhelmingly male cast of new playwrights fostered by Zabalaza, even if some have written strong parts for women and attempted to address endemic violence against women and girls.

Comparing plays on this topic highlights the challenge of transcending the habit of spectacular violence inherited from the post-anti-apartheid repertoire—as in Sekhabi's *On My Birthday* (1996)—underpinned by the gendered violence that saturates the society at large. Foot's first published play, *Tshepang—The Third Testament*, although a modest two-hander in which one actor remains silent, offers a nuanced treatment of the child named Tshepang [Tswana: hope] by the nurses who treated the nine-month old whose rape in 2001 by her mother's partner provoked national headlines about this and twenty-thousand other reputed cases of "baby rape" (Foot 2003: v).[18] Developed in 2002–3 as Foot's Wits University MA project, and assisted by Bheki Vilakazi's on site research in Northern Cape Louisvale (Foot 2005: vii), Foot's script and Gerhard Marx's design avoided direct representation of violence but had the silent Ruth (Nonceba Didi) carry on her back a small bed in lieu of a baby, a miniature replica of the full-sized rusty bed in front of which the narrator Simon—Mncedisi Shabangu, who had played coffin-maker Nefolovhodwe in *Ways of Dying*—began to tell the story.[19] A third, even smaller bed is later uncovered beneath one of the miniature houses signifying the village; this tiny bed is carried to the clinic as if it were a child. *Third Testament* highlights the fragile hope borne by the violated child that Simon imagines as Jesus's sister (22) in the rough-hewn nativity scenes that he tries to sell to those who descend on the village, but also signals the limits of trusting a savior that might "take away the sins of the world"(23) and the community.

Simon sketches the inhabitants who have been battered by drought, poverty, and thirst quenched by *vaalwyn*—wine made from rotten grapes that farmers historically gave to workers in lieu of wages (February 1990: 100)—and by unprotected sex with multiple partners. Simon introduces the perpetrator whom he calls Alfred Sorrows as an object of pity as well as revulsion, one of many "surplus people" abandoned by the new South Africa and unable to support themselves from increasingly arid terrain. Although this phrase was once used by activists to denounce the apartheid state for hounding black people from their homes, it now applies to those left behind by the new elite who have presided over a wealth gap that is worse than under apartheid. Simon recounts formative moments in his adolescence, including sex with schoolmate Sarah pimped by her brother who forced Simon, Alfred, and other boys to finish "inside a half-loaf of white bread" (26). He also recalls Alfred's abuse at the hands of his stepmother, whose beatings with a broom Shabangu reenacted until the broom breaks to signify Albert's broken bones (29). While Shabangu talked, Didi focused on the labor of curing animal skins and appeared to pay little mind to his stories. When he brought out the nativity figures, Didi looked briefly at the wooden Mary but did not react to Simon, even when Shabangu said to the audience "She doesn't talk, not any more" (17). Instead, she stared out into the distance, as if waiting for someone to bring back her child. This story is bleak but after Simon recounts one sensational headline after another culminating in the reputed national rates of child rape (44), Ruth allows him to rest his head on her shoulder and, breaking three years of silence, spoke the last word "Tshepang" (45). While very far from reconciliation, personal or public, Simon's narrative and Ruth's final word escape the passivity to which one critic consigns them (Graham 2008: 113). Instead, as clinical psychologist Tony Hamburger argues in his introduction, the ending grants a fragment of dignity to damaged people in a damaged land and offers audiences "hope, not solutions" (in Foot 2005: 16), while setting the stage for future dramas of hidden lives.

Using domestic objects, the loaf of bread, the beds, and the broom, Foot and Shabangu made an unsettling connection visible between abused children and violent adults without resorting to staged violence on human bodies. Further by keeping the script economical, Foot allows outbursts such as Simon's rant indicting the media for "pointing ugly painted fingers" (40) at the village to stand out without overwhelming the story. But more recent Zabalaza plays have not always escaped the "exhibitionism" that Ndebele hoped would end with apartheid. In Khayalethu Anthony's *The Champion* (2014; published 2015), Anthony acted not only the young narrator-protagonist Thulani but also his girlfriend Amanda, his mother Bongeka, and her partner Bra Mike. Thulani admires Mike even though he beats Bongeka and, when he finds Mike's hanging body he blames his mother, who dies when their shack goes up in flames. The climax comes when Thulani kills a man who is with Amanda, blaming her and the community for their apathy and indicting the audience as well. Although Anthony acted the lead in Foot's play *Solomon and Marion* (2013) and won a Fleur du Cap award for his multiple roles in *The Champion* (Morris 2017: 158), the protagonist's misogyny taints the women characters and the play piles up incidents to a degree that seems excessive in contrast with more effective solo plays on gender violence such as *Fruit* (2015; published 2016), by Paul Noko.

Fruit won the Zabalaza Festival prize after a try-out at the Market Laboratory where Noko trained (Noko 2016: 9), and performances at the Windybrow and Wits Theatres in Johannesburg. A single woman on stage (Matshikido Mokoteli in 2015) played 14-year old Matlakala and, with the help of a white doll called Lucy and a series of stones, introduced other characters: her foster-mother Vuyeka [Zulu: rejoice], who named her Matlakala [Sotho: rubbish] after finding her near the open sewer that the locals call the "periodic river" (30), step-brother Jabulani, the latter's friends, and her mother's neighbors. Like *Champion*, *Fruit* turns on a climactic fire, but like *Tshepang* it avoids sensationalism as Mokoteli uses the stones and recycled objects such as milk cartons to recreate the township environment in miniature and to show the protagonist's journey from her throw-away status as Matlakala to her renaming as Mpho [gift] by the neighbor Granny who rescues her from the fire. In addition to the stones that she played with like a child on the ground at doll's eye level, Mokoteli used avocados to track Matlakala's progress. She began the play by trying to place an avocado back in its tree but the meaning of this gesture emerged only after she showed without naming the gang rape by Jabulani and friends by smearing avocado between her thighs and trying to sew the avocado skin back together, before setting fire—staged with steel wool and baking soda—to the shack and the men inside it. *Fruit*'s expression of hope does not downplay the wretchedness of its characters' lives but the delicate use of these objects and of the imported avocado, whose cultivation supports local communities, keeps the drama free of poverty porn. At the end, Mokoteli retrieved one last avocado from a miniature house but this time gestured as Mpho to the tree that "will stand firm" (36), signaling not only the character's growth but also the fostering organization Zabalaza.

Between *Tshepang* and the "fruit" cultivated in its shade stand Foot's *Karoo Moose* (2009 [2007]) and "Fishers of Hope" (2014). "Fishers" featured Lesedi Job as Ruth, the wife of a disabled fisherman, and Shabangu again as narrator and also Ruth's previous suitor Njawu who, unlike her husband, supports her endeavors to earn a living even if over-fishing by multi-nationals in the unnamed central African lake has decimated the harvest. The evocative staging between nets that hung like dhows shimmering as they reflected water on the boards (design: Patrick Curtis) transported audiences and also added a transnational dimension to the story of women struggling with scarce resources and recalcitrant or dangerous partners. As I have discussed the Grahamstown premiere of "Fishers" (Kruger 2015a), I will focus here on *Karoo Moose*, whose revival in the Grahamstown Festival's 2016 commemoration of the Women's March of 1956 invites a reassessment. The play is set in an impoverished village in the Karoo and depicts women, children, and the men who prey on them in a world "where children don't stay children for very long and where adults cannot really afford to be adults" (Foot 2009: 9–10).[20] While the cast led by Thami Mbongo shared the responsibility of narration in 2007 and 2016, the center of the drama was Chuma Sopotela who played Thozama, a 14-year-old girl. Foot borrowed the name from collaborator Thozama Jacob to whom, along with her children and Jacob's, she dedicated the play. In the absence of her mother who was run over by a white farmer, Thozama is burdened with a drunken father Jonas whom another narrator (Mdu Kweyama) describes as a "man without" (12), and has to stay home to help her grandmother Grace while her younger siblings go to school. Staying at home does not protect her from Khola, a thug to whom Jonas owes money. Khola rapes Thozama claiming payment for Jonas's debts and, after the birth of the child, briefly kidnaps the infant by buying off Thozama's younger sister with sweets.

The rape of Thozama echoes *Tshepang* but *Karoo Moose* weaves the assault into a more complex scenario. With Bongile Mantsai providing lyrics and musical direction for songs in Xhosa, Foot drew on forms familiar to South African audiences. Xhosa *iintsomi* traditionally feature an elder, often a grandmother, telling a story that blends supernatural and everyday elements, aided by responses from listeners, often children. The players blended *iintsomi* elements with experimental forms used since the 1970s: poor theatre techniques of Grotowski, mime from Le Coq and other schools, and the techniques of estrangement, quotation, and musical punctuation in Brecht's epic theatre, that is *narrative* theatre that tells stories of common people with social-critical intent, all of which demonstrates the capacity of body and voice aided by a few portable props to represent both the specific reality of a Karoo village and a tale of universal dimensions. Even before introducing the villagers, the performance began with a scene that consecrated the space. The six performers entered "ritualistically," each carrying a prop identified with one of the several characters that each will play, except for Sopotela who played only Thozana and whose entrance, carrying a cabbage "proudly" on her head (7), highlighted the charm and vulnerability of the adolescent. Thami brought the beer bottle and belt associated with Khola, who used them and a fishing net to catch and subdue Thozama, but banged on the bottle to prepare the ritual, calling forth a response from Mdu who shook the curved giant reeds that represented the moose's antlers (cover image) until he "leaps into the air and becomes a frightened animal" (7). The unlikely presence of an American animal in the Karoo is initially explained by junior police officer Brian van Wyk as an "accident on the freeway" that freed the moose supposedly intended for a "zoo or a game park" (11) but this account by a white character—played like his mother by a black actor—gave way to the black characters' perception of the moose as an embodiment of evil, until Thozama kills the creature and turns it into food.

The script makes the Van Wyks better-off than others in that they have a house rather than a shack and enough food but they are also troubled by bad memories: Brian's sister committed suicide because her father raped her. However, while her ghost haunts Brian and his mother in their heads, Thozama, her family, and fellow villagers see the moose in the village, and several members of the ensemble come together to animate this enormous beast. In the opening ritual in 2016, however, Mdu showed a creature as more terrified than terrifying, and Thozama assured her sister that the moose "doesn't eat children" (14). It is Thozama who delivers the death blow when a group of children and dogs surrounded the moose, despite the "terrible scream" that may be either the moose or Thozama (32), and it is she who cooks the meat. This act provoked the police sergeant Malokwe to arrest her despite his partner Brian's hesitation and despite Grace's attempt to explain that this is the first meat that her family has eaten since Khola came to consume Jonas's chicken and violate his daughter.

This contrast between supernatural threats and everyday ordeals like hunger, embedded in the overall tension between aspiration and exhaustion, pervaded the performance in 2016. When Sopotela had Thozama give birth in a vehicle identified as a police car, possibly the same one in which she was taken to prison for killing and cooking the moose, the narrators juxtaposed the magical image of the "moon hang[ing] like a cradle in the sky" with Thozama's "exhausted and desperate" struggle to give birth after two days of labor (46). Mdu beat a cowhide drum to announce the birth and then places it on the ground where it framed Sopotela's "infant-like" re-emergence as Thozama's baby through this narrow opening (46). After Thozama named the child Liqhawe (hero), Thami interjected: "Here our story insists on taking a new turn ... Should birth not bring hope? Desperate for new beginnings [the play] plots a new story for Brian and Thozama" (47). This interjection highlighted the dangers of "superficial optimism" and the artificiality of fictional solutions to real social problems, as Brecht warned (2014: 268). In this case, the entangled problems of poverty, misogyny, AIDS, and government incompetence may appear overwhelming, but rather than presuming to offer global solutions, the play more modestly suggests the potential power of individual and collective agency. While Brecht may have been skeptical of attempts to represent the real effects of supernatural beliefs, *Karoo Moose* allows the possibility of grasping the improbable. When Thozama "takes on the power of the beast" to attack Khola (61), the vivid image of the girl carrying the moose antlers (see cover image) before being lifted into the air rests literally on the shoulders of the ensemble. Thozama's rescue in turn depends on Jonas, who emerges from the shadows to kill Khola and thus return to the family, more than the "man we expected him to be" (61). The final image, a truck that might carry Brian, Thozama, and the children to "somewhere better," may seem to outsiders superficially optimistic but to local audiences it represents commitment against difficult odds to changing their world step by step. As Thami said in conclusion, "we do not know where somewhere better is or even if it exists" (63). This image, as the adult ensemble mimed the movement of the truck and, by holding up small brightly colored clothes, highlighted without mimicking children the power of the imagination to conjure hope, as Ernst Bloch defined it, –"not confidence" in the future or naive optimism but instead both a historically informed "consciousness of danger" and the resistance to failure (1988: 17).

From the Oceans to the Hinterland: Tracing History across Territory

While much theatre today is preoccupied with current tumult, some playwrights have turned to history, whether to seek origins of the present crisis or to imagine scenarios whose counterfactual plots conjure alternate futures. The contested province of KZN has inspired absorbing historical as well as current political scenarios. Rajesh Gopie's *The Coolie Odyssey* (Grahamstown 2011) tracks Indians since the voyages of indentured sugar workers (the "coolies" of the title) across the Indian Ocean or *kala pani* [Hindi: dark water] to colonial Natal, recalling Ronnie Govender's *At the Edge* (1994; published 1996), a story prompted by the anti-Indian riot in Durban in 1949 that deals also with Indian settlement since 1860. *Abnormal Loads* (Durban Playhouse 2012), written, directed, and designed by Neil Coppen, is a family saga that rivals *Donkerland* (1996; Chapter 4), even if Opperman's play began earlier with the Boer encroachment on Zulu territory before the British arrived. Coppen weaves a tapestry that binds the English colonial Bashfords—whose cottage is represented on stage—to the Zulu Ngobese clan who have worked for them for six generations, and the Afrikaans Jouberts, their neighbors and antagonists, who clash in a fictional town named Bashford for William, who earned a Victoria Cross for valor in the Anglo-Zulu War (1879), and on Heliograph Hill, whose stylized facsimile dominated the stage behind the cottage (Coppen 2012: 12). This imagined town and the hill behind it recall the real town of Dundee, where Coppen has also designed historical *tableaux vivants*, and which is close to Anglo-Zulu and Anglo-Boer battle sites.

Abnormal Loads uses rival Anglo and Afrikaner reenactments to frame historical conflicts but the opening scene sets up a new scenario. Vincent Bashford Liverage (played by Mothusi Magano), the Bashford heir who is supposed to play his forefather William, is black. In the reenactment we see, however, white Clinton Small plays William in the British defeat at Isandlwana (1879) in a mock-heroic style that recalls Cy Enfield's film *Zulu* (1964). This scene and others like it are summoned to the backdrop by Vincent's grandmother Moira (Allison Cassels) former mayor and perennial chair of the tourist board. Despite Vincent's color, Moira pesters him to reenact ancestral fictions rather than answering questions about his real parentage. Vincent is tormented by headaches that Prudence Ngobese (Fortunate Dhlomo), who inherited her mother's position as household servant because she could not pay university fees, interprets as his ancestors trying to talk to him. The truth eventually emerges: after his white activist mother was killed in a dubious crash with an "abnormal load" truck, his black father Sizwe left him with Moira. Vincent dreams that he hears his father knocking on the security gate, and leaves at the end to look for him. In between, the characters play out present-day dramas and represent their ancestors in scenes that contradict Moira's scripts. Moira wants Vincent to play a scene in which William is shot in an Anglo-Boer War battle by Dawie Joubert, enacted by his descendant Leon Joubert who resents the Bashfords for supplanting Boer settlement in the region, but Leon's sister Katrien (Jenna Dunster) spins another tale that has Dawie kill William not in battle but because he was in love with Dawie's wife Anna (also played by Dunster). Katrien would like to reenact this romantic tale of love and escape with Vincent, without her ancestor's suicide finale, so she persuades him to send her secret messages from the antique heliograph. Although Katrien's version is vindicated when she discovers William's Victoria Cross in a box that he gave Anna, which glowed with spectral light in Dhlomo's hands when Prudence returned it, Vincent will not fulfill that romantic role, as he leaves to look for his father and thus hopefully to shed the abnormal load that his ancestors have placed on him, as on other South Africans haunted by ghosts.[21]

While *Abnormal Loads* created fictional characters out of performance remains that might well be found on the former battlefields traversed by the descendants of those who fought there, Duncan Buwalda's *Hinterland* (2014) presents a counterfactual but absorbing encounter between two historically significant men who never met. Solomon Plaatje (1878–1932), the black intellectual best known for his denunciation of the 1913 Land Act in the landmark book *Native Life in South Africa* (1914), an admirer of Shakespeare and a founding member of the ANC, was reporting from Mafeking during the Boer siege of the town in 1899, while Cecil John Rhodes (1853–1902) was in Kimberley, the center of the diamond industry which he controlled and also Plaatje's home town. The fictional scenario, framed by Rhodes's documented feud with Lt. Cl. Kekewich, commander of British forces at Kimberley, over the competing powers of military strategy and mining capital, has Plaatje take a position as Rhodes's secretary on Kekewich's recommendation. It imagines a conflict between the aging imperialist and the African Renaissance man who, while still young, carried the black intellectual's burden to represent African aspirations at the same time as deflecting white caprice. Although this chamber play makes Plaatje carry the burden alone, history puts him in the company of other critics of Rhodes's imperial highhandedness, such as the writer Olive Schreiner (1855–1920), who did meet Rhodes but came to despise him.[22]

Although the #Rhodesmustfall protests that erupted in March 2015 against Rhodes statues and his legacy on university campuses prompted *Hinterland*'s revival in April that year, the play's evolution predates the protest, even if the title is taken from the inscription on the statue pointing north from the colonial heart of Cape Town—"Your hinterland is there" (Buwalda 2014: 3). In Buwalda's words and Nhlakanipho Manqele's effectively guarded embodiment, Plaatje's critique begins subtly; alone in Rhodes's study in the opening scene, he expresses exasperation with the plethora of works by arch-imperialist Rudyard Kipling. When Rhodes enters, Plaatje conceals his dismay with the white lie—"Kipling is one of my favorites" (36)—but continues with a laconic critique of Rhodes's scheme to bribe the guards at the military roadblocks: "Bribery. Roman in origin," in other words, "very European" (41). Dukas played Rhodes as a man who expected obedience but whose physical decline made him irascible rather than imposing, as when he demanded—in keeping with the historical Rhodes's contempt for military authority—that the British army protect his interests: "Patience? Your time may not be valuable, Colonel ... Queen Victoria's time and the PM's time may not be valuable but Cecil John Rhodes' time is *extremely* valuable," but ended the speech after slamming his hand on the desk, wheezing as he claims that "Africa is waiting" for him (49). The stage directions have Rhodes forget that Plaatje is still in the room during the outburst but the contrast on stage between the quiet young man and the blustering older one did not favor the latter. After Kekewich confirms that Rhodes's friend Lt. Henry Scott-Turner was killed in action, Rhodes attempts to seduce Plaatje but manages only to insult him. After this showdown, the play shifts from the chamber drama to a series of telegraphic confrontations that span the duration of the war. The actors presented Plaatje's letters to the editor of the *Kimberley Diamond Advertiser* berating Rhodes for reserving siege supplies for whites, staged an imagined dialog that covered topics from Plaatje's defense of the universal franchise against Boer and British racism, through his judgment of Rhodes's sexuality in the language of the day as "degenerate" (85), to Rhodes's parting compliment, quoting Kipling's phrase "you'll be a man, my son" (89), and concluded with Rhodes's reputed final words "so little done" and Buwalda's invented rejoinder for Plaatje "so little done right" (91). While critics might argue that the bulkier Dukas dominated the stage to the last, Manqele's steadfast stance and final words resonate with the present time.

Migrating, Unearthing, and Rebuilding: Magnet Theatre and the Cape of Flows

Buried in the heart of *Hinterland* is Mzilikazi of the Ndebele, whom Rhodes praised even while plotting to usurp the king's resting place in the Matopos Hills outside Bulawayo (place of slaughter). Mzilikazi played a major historical role as leader of the breakaway Nguni clan that fled north a thousand miles from Shaka's kingdom in the turbulent nineteenth-century migration known as the *mfecane* (Chapter 2), and as father of Lobengula (Chapter 1), who was forced to negotiate with Rhodes. In postcolonial Zimbabwe, formerly Rhodesia, the Ndebele minority is on the move again. In the wake of land seizures and economic disruption promoted by former president Robert Mugabe (Mlambo 2014: 239–53), Ndebele and many in the Shona majority migrated in the opposite direction—to Johannesburg, where, despite nativist attacks, their resilient "tactical cosmopolitanism" (Landau/Freemantle 2010) has earned respect. Although these migrants and others from farther away have inspired more film and fiction than plays, some have performed their own journeys while others have written roles for Zimbabweans in South Africa. Among the latter, James Whyle created in *Rejoice Burning* (BBC 2003; published 2006) a man named Rejoice who works like many Zimbabweans as a gardener in Johannesburg but whose quiet negotiation of his failing health from AIDS inspires the living. In the former category, Jonathan Nkala charts in *The Crossing* (2006; published Nkala 2014) his journey from Zimbabwe across the Limpopo River to Johannesburg and on to Cape Town. Nkala's vivid recreation of this trek prompted its posthumous publication and celebration by the Cape-based company that has found inspiration in migration routes and burial grounds: Magnet Theatre.[23]

Since Magnet's work has been covered in a comprehensive collection of textual and visual essays (Lewis/Krueger 2016) and featured also in *Performing Migrancy* (Fleishman 2015), this section will spotlight key works and their broader resonance rather than try to summarize these books. Fleishman and Jennie Reznek founded Magnet in 1991, combining her skills in embodiment drawn in part from the Le Coq School in Paris and his work with anti-apartheid drama at the Market Theatre. Magnet's breakthrough adaptation with JazzArt Dance Theatre of Euripides' *Medea* (1994–6) tapped the turbulence of 1994, mixing Kaaps and Xhosa with English, fragments of Latin, and Tamil—but no Greek—and movement vocabularies, from Le Coq and modern dance, to gumboot stomping, to Indian kathakali. Although movement did not strictly correspond to sources—kathakali comes from Malayalam-speaking Kerala not Tamil Nadu—this mix foregrounded Medea's alienation as a foreigner among the Greeks. In common with André Serban's Romanian mixed with Greek, the untranslated words encouraged the audience to concentrate on the corporeal expression of conflict, even if this *Medea* appeared on a proscenium stage in Grahamstown without the immersive sight, sound, and smell of Serban's surround staging (e.g. at La Mama in New York in 1990). Miki Flockemann argues (2016: 91) that Bo Petersen's artfully shaved hair showed Medea's affiliation, despite the actor's whiteness, with her brown nurse-confidante but Dawn Langdown gave this Colchian nurse more than local color; she dominated the scene berating her mistress in native Kaaps. Langdown's bearing (photos: Lewis/Krueger 2016: c2; c4) in this role—and in a solo piece *So Loep Ons ... Nou Nog* [This is how we walk ... still] (1996–7)—recalled the resilience of indigenous Khoe and enslaved South Asian women whose domestic work and childrearing in the VOC era created Afrikaans and whose stage presence here celebrated brown South Africans in the era of post-anti-apartheid uncertainty.

While these pieces launched the company as a magnet attracting disparate elements from multiple places and practices, Magnet's twenty-first-century projects go beyond syncretic assembly to forging new tools and training new theatre makers to embody and investigate the imprint of histories and present crises on impulses, experiences, and understanding, at once visceral, psychological, and sociological. Fleishman stresses the "knowledge work" (2016: 55) that entails "research for" and "research by means of" theatre (55), beginning with impulse or intuition and moving through "micro-level" improvisation and analysis to "macro-level" events and institution-formation (57) and back again, so that the networks and nerve tissue connecting macro and micro levels may nourish, renew, and revise all elements. These quests to experience, to know and to act coincide in two sets of works: the migration plays that explore the movement of people, their possessions, and dispossessions, and archeological performances that reanimate remains—material or imagined—from particularly resonant sites in and around Cape Town. In *Every Year, Every Day I Am Walking (EYED)*, Reznek and Faniswa Yisa perform acts of flight and refuge, conveying the intense family feeling of a mother and daughter escaping violence in central Africa and their fear provoked by predators in the refugee camps and immigration bureaucrats in South Africa, using pairs of shoes distinguishing victims and attackers (Figure 8.1). *EYED* is Magnet's most portable play in that its stage effects fit into a suitcase and in the sense that it has traveled the world to tell the story of migrants moving within Africa—who number many more than those trying to get to Europe (Segatti/Landau 12)—and to speak of broader experiences of loss and displacement, but Magnet's reanimation of remains arrest and animate the "flows" around the Cape and perform neglected histories that shaped this country and its region, with ripple effects well beyond. While Fleishman and colleagues play with the figurative extensions of excavation in Schneider's *Performance Remains*, they also explore the productive friction between excavation—digging down—and migration— moving on or moving in—to investigate traces of embodied practices around sites of memory (in Pierre Nora's sense of places that concentrate and contest remembrance [1989: 14]), conjuring scenarios that are no less grounded for being imagined.

Magnet's reanimation of performance remains and archival finds led to several works combining performance with exhibitions in historic sites: *53 Degrees* (2002–3) explored the history of Robben Island long before Mandela served time there (1964– 82) and the cold Atlantic Ocean around it that claimed Xhosa king Nxele Makana who died trying to escape in 1819 and inspired Florrie Berndt who tried to swim the distance in 1926 (Fleishman 2016: 64–68). *Onnest'bo* [Topsy-turvy] (2002–6) used the District 6 Museum, a former church in the district that marked the eastern edge of the British colonial city, and the occasion in 2002 of the government's belated return of property deeds to the mostly brown residents uprooted in the 1960s, to illuminate this contested ground. While not site specific, *Cargo* (2007), Magnet's final work with JazzArt, used the excavation of a paupers' burial ground by developers at Prestwich Place in 2003, in the former District 1 on the western edge of the colonial city, marketed since then as De Waterkant [Waterfront], as a stimulus to investigate Cape slavery (1652–1838).[24] Prompted by pottery shards that Reznek found on a beach nearby, *Cargo* does not attempt to reconstruct an orderly record of slavery. Instead, it tries to find "appropriate images in the present" (Fleishman 2011: 12) for a past in fragments.

Conjuring with fragments may not produce analytic history—of, for instance, slavery at *Cargo*'s commissioning venue, the Spier Wine Estate (est. 1692), since 1993 also a "holistic" art center with a restaurant in the old slave quarters (Mountain 2004: 181). As did all wine farms of this vintage, Spier profited from enslaved labor until 1838 and from "free" workers bound by restrictive law and alcohol dependency abetted by employers dispensing *vaalwyn* in lieu of wages thereafter (February 1990: 100), but although performers read from court records of punishments, they did not address the longer legacy of brown people at the Cape. While it borrowed music from the historical repertoire reanimated by *Ghoema* (2005; Chapter 4), *Cargo* left open the gaps between this distinctly Cape repertoire and JazzArt's mostly brown dancers on the one hand, and the history of white and black South Africans on the other. The latter were vocally represented by Reznek and Yisa, whose critical distance from the legacy of enslavement and creative reassembly of historical acts and narratives were marked not only by English speech but also by costume—modern slacks as against the slave smocks and skirts of the female dancers. The cast of ten men and ten women was also at odds with the record: less than 30 percent of those sold into slavery were women (Shell 1994: 46–48).[25] Nonetheless, this casting reanimated the historical role of enslaved women who not only raised their owners' children but also, in the absence of more than basic education in a colony run for VOC profit rather than Dutch cultural hegemony, made over their Malay-Portuguese-Dutch creole into the "kitchen Dutch" spoken by women and children of all colors (Shell: 60–64), long before it was proclaimed the supposedly "pure" Afrikaans of white men (Chapter 4).

Staged also in Grahamstown and at the Baxter, *Cargo* began with a closed cargo chest more than twice human height framed by blue-lit sail-ships held aloft by hidden performers.[26] Heralded by composer Neo Muyanga playing harmonium—which he associates with the South Asian origins of many enslaved people (2016: 79)—the vessels, some resembling European tall ships and others Chinese junks, alluded to the route from the Netherlands via the Cape to the richest VOC "possession," Batavia, now Indonesia. The chest opened to reveal a Cape Dutch house façade and stoop, with the cast dressed in britches or skirts in the style of rough slave muslin. Still wearing shoes as they recited the inventory of arriving ships whose names were also ports of call—e.g. Molucca, Walvis—they removed the shoes as each sale was announced to enact the VOC rule that enslaved people had to go barefoot (Shell: 226). Apart from occasional scenes with male dancers—such as a torchlit vignette evoking one of many nighttime raids on farms by runaways—the piece focused on women's work. Van Riebeeck's 1652 letter to the VOC requesting male slaves for the "heaviest and dirtiest work" was read in English by Reznek, the sole white performer, but the inventory presented in the first scene—linens, "negro cotton," and the enslaved themselves—was unpacked by female dancers. Other quotations from the archive spotlighted the fate of women, in scenes that sometimes called for direct embodiment and at others for estrangement. The most vivid examples of the first were Levern de Villiers's performance of an enslaved woman who drowned three enslaved children but was caught before drowning a fourth, in a scene that began with the title "two buckets of water" and ended with De Villiers covered in mud as if hauled from the sea, and Ilse Carroll's immersion in the character of Katie Jacobs, whose life was recorded before she died a free woman in 1910 (Shell: 129). Carroll recounted the story in Afrikaans of the young girl whose mother was sold away from her and who went on to bear thirteen children while serving as a wet-nurse for her owner's infants—the Afrikaans *borsmoeder* [breast mother] poignantly rendered the expropriation of her nourishment. Carroll danced this story holding a rocking chair as if it were a child to be soothed, and then straddling the chair and arching as if in labor. In contrast to this immersion in a visible role, Yisa spoke in sober English in semi-darkness of cruel and astonishing punishments—most shockingly by a mistress who "crammed hot bread" down an enslaved woman's throat "til she had choked her," quoting the 1806 report of English slave-owner Samuel Hudson (Shell: 316). Although the lights came up on this report to show Reznek astride Yisa's neck, this and comparable accounts were critically estranged as Yisa repeated before and after each violent act: "this was not *my* story; this did not happen to *me*." This refrain marked at once a critical distance from the staged violence and a way for audiences to acknowledge a history that included these unspeakable acts, even if such acts were not part of their own ancestry.

Prestwich Place likewise made an indirect impression that implied the fragility of activists' desire to claim it for their ancestors. In the scene "*13 Grawe*/13 Spades" introduced by Reznek sitting on the stoop reading an article about the burial ground and Capetonians who braved bad weather "to carry the remains from City Hall," dancer Jackie Manyaapelo, whose grandfather lived in the area before being evicted by the apartheid state in the 1960s, emerged from a steamer trunk full of paper, accompanied by construction noise.[27] As Reznek read the Slavery Abolition Act of 1833 in which it was deemed "just and expedient" that persons in "diverse British colonies" held in slavery "should be manumitted and set free" but also stipulated that manumission meant not liberation but hard labor in unpaid "apprenticeship" from 1834 to 1838, and exploitative conditions after that, Manyaapelo rapped her knuckles on hard parts of her body, especially bones and teeth, as though testing her own fitness for work on an auction block and, when Reznek came to the Act's provision of the extended servitude deemed "just recompense" for slaveowners, fell back into the trunk.[28] Although helped out by two male dancers, whose livery and shoes marked their roles as servants rather than chattel slaves, Manyaapelo hinted at the imperfect resurrection of the dead and the unfinished business of the living. Looking beyond this work and those who might claim manumission as their legacy, the living majority of South Africans whose families endured servitude short of slavery still claim the right to well-being that could not be resolved by a single act of emancipation.

While *Cargo* and *EYED* trace global routes that pulled the Cape into networks of forced migration as well as culturally enriching "flows," Magnet's more recent projects have returned to national routes and the paths of the uprooted searching for well-being. Mbothwe's migration plays follow Xhosa-speakers along the N2 linking the poorer Eastern and richer Western Cape (see introduction), and his ongoing work in Khayelitsha generates drama and social agency out of experiences of displacement and settlement in this not-so-"new home" (Mbothwe 2016; Morris 2016). Other chapters in the *Magnet Theatre* volume (Lewis/Krueger) tracing routes out of Cape Town highlight flows other than the global currents around the colonial "tavern of the seas" to trace lines of migration that may yet nourish the hinterland. Magnet's Clanwilliam Arts Project (2007 ff) and from 2012 the Community Networking Creative Arts has animated the Cederberg district along the N7 in the dry northern end of the Western Cape—but like the projects in Khayelitsha build skills as well as create art with a community which has seen uneven benefits from tourism and a little more from the cultivation and global sale of *rooibos* [red bush tea] which grows nowhere else on the planet. Lavona de Bruyn, who developed the project with Mbothwe and input from Fleishman and Morris, describes a Coloured community historically marked by encounters between Boer and British colonists and indigenous herders and hunter-gatherers including !Kung, Nama, and others described by the portmanteau word KhoeSan.[29] Among the Cederberg projects, she notes one that highlights the transformation of place names through migration. *Vastrap van Jan Dissel tot Tra Tra* (Cederberg Arts Festival 2011) translates not only as "stand firm" (De Bruyn 2016: 261) but also as "quickstep" from Clanwilliam to Wuppertal, suggesting a dance along the gravel road over the pass between town and village past ancient cave paintings: the town on the Jan Dissel River was renamed Clanwilliam by the British in 1814 and the mission station on the Tra Tra was named by Moravian evangelists who settled there in 1829.

As indicated by debates over the human remains in the South African Museum in Cape Town (Deacon 1996) and those found at Prestwich Place, claims for KhoeSan inheritance have been vigorous but the lives and languages of people far from the so-called Mother City have received less attention. The /Xam were the subject of investigation a century ago by Wilhelm Bleek and Lucy Lloyd who accommodated /Xam speakers in their Cape home while translating their stories both ancient—myths of origin—and modern—accounts of dispossession and imprisonment (Bleek/Lloyd 1924) in, for example, the Breakwater Prison that now houses UCT's Business School on the Waterfront. Although /Xam is no longer spoken and KhoeSan descendants are a minority today, this ancient language has found its way into present performance. Magnet's projects in the Cederberg have favored student performances of the ancient stories in English and Afrikaans translation but /Xam has since 2000 furnished the motto that graces the national coat of arms and every South African passport: *!ke e: ǀxarra ǁke*—diverse peoples unite! This motto in a dormant language celebrates unity in diversity and the nation's first people, while avoiding political disputes that might have arisen had the motto issued from one of the eleven official languages. This motto has prompted recitations in public places and on mediated platforms, performances that spotlight the Cape of Storms that is also the Cape of Good Hope, the home of Africa's ancient people and the destination of travelers from around the world as well as across this continent. This Cape, which bore witness to imperial looting and launched the colonization of the hinterland, is today the site of a democratic if sometimes disorderly parliament as well as the incubator of performance practices that strive to link play with well-being, imagination with social work in the largest sense. The spectacular contradictions of this still breathtaking location began this book and it offers a fitting place to conclude this chapter on the constitution of South African theatre at the present time.

Coda

Since the last chapter left off in 2018 with work in progress and a new political dispensation under President Ramaphosa that may or may not enhance art, life, and well-being in South Africa, it would be foolhardy to attempt to write a tidy wrap-up of a century and more of theatre and performance. I end therefore with a coda rather than a conclusion. This book has woven together apparently disparate threads from different times, places, and cultural practices that belong in the expanded field of play, and I hope that my observations will resonate with ongoing research in South Africa and in other locations in the world where researchers and practitioners aspire in these turbulent times to forge links in performance between subjunctive and indicative acts, imaginative and social practices, public spheres and intimate moments to illuminate the struggles of citizens, migrants, and other people that inhabit nations or animate spaces between them. To highlight impulses and investigations that recur across history, I draw attention to the following nodes of inquiry in this *Century of South African Theatre*:

1. *Genres of performance*: this book has demonstrated the importance of tracing historical connections across the last hundred years, to track the persistence of older forms such as *ingoma, intsomi*, the pageant, and the sketch, as well as syncretic genres such as the variety concert and the workshop, as well as musical and testimonial forms of drama, which have responded to political and cultural clashes from colonization to apartheid to present-day battles for justice and well-being. The investigation of archives and repertoires across history in South Africa and transnational spaces beyond its borders has reanimated nineteenth-century figures that have appeared on twentieth- and twenty-first-century stages, from African kings cetshwayo, Moshoeshoe, and their antagonists such as Theophilus Shepstone, to mid-century political actors who deserve a hearing, such as anti-apartheid communist advocate Bram Fischer or the African farmer who appeared in court and on stage as Tau, and make visible the ties forged by local adaptations of transnational writers from Shakespeare to Goethe to Brecht, Harriet Beecher Stowe, W.E.B Dubois, and Lorraine Hansberry.
2. *Languages and legacies*: in addition to reviewing internationally known playwrights writing in English, this book recalls to the stage South African writers of the past, such as Herbert Dhlomo or Lewis Sowden, and of the present, such as Paul Slabolepszy or Gcina Mhlophe, who are known to some but eclipsed

for many by famous names such as Fugard or rising stars such as Lara Foot or Paul Grootboom, and urges the mostly English-language readers of this book to pay attention also to writing in other languages by, for instance, Bartho Smit or Deon Opperman in Afrikaans, or Mandla Mbothwe in Xhosa, as well as to the majority of South African theatre makers who work in multiple languages. It spotlights multilingual actors from Sokobe playing his father Moshoeshoe in 1910 to the Mthethwa Brothers in the 1930s, to women as different as Wilna Snyman, Yvonne Bryceland, Nomhle Nkonyeni, and Thembi Mtshali, and men from Marius Weyers and John Kani to John Ledwaba and Mncedisi Shabangu, whose careers run from the 1960s and 1970s into the twenty-first century.

3. *Words and music*: alongside texts and photographs, this book notes the contribution to the stage of musical composition and performance from John Knox Bokwe to Reuben Caluza and Todd Matshikiza to Gibson Kente, and today Philip Miller and Neo Muyanga, and reminds theatre audiences and readers worldwide of the longer and more widespread impact on practitioners and audiences of sacred and secular music in South Africa, as shown by the resonance across the century of the hymn *Lizalis' idinga lakho, Thixo Nkosi yenyaniso* in Bokwe's 1915 setting of Rev. Tiyo Soga's text, from the Emancipation Centenary in 1934 to the TRC hearings in 1996, and the diverse linguistic and political variations of marching songs, such as *We Are Marching to Pretoria*

4. *Audiences and advocates as active publics*: recent research on "participatory dramaturgy" has highlighted the active role of audiences making theatre and performance live in their community but the century shows audiences, publics, and patrons actively shaping performance and civic agency since the Union in 1910: from Africans rising to the occasion to sing of emancipation and Afrikaners trekking across the country in the Voortrekker centenary in 1938, to the anti-apartheid audiences debating Sizwe Banzi's name and passbook in 1973 or raising Albert Luthuli from the dead in 1981. Practices such as testimonial theatre or participatory dramaturgy, which may appear to be new to practitioners who came of age after apartheid, grew out of roots planted by anti-apartheid theatre or even earlier, and have responded in different ways to the challenges, posed by unjust and unequal social and economic structures and relations, to the aspirations of the present time. In addition to animating practices, this book excavates structures of support and of constraint, on the scale of the apartheid state and its democratic successor, and on the level of cultural institutions, from the well-known anti-apartheid Space and Market Theatre to lesser-known historical precedents such as the Bantu Peoples Theatre or the Johannesburg Repertory, to the current town and township collaborations of Baxter and Magnet Theatres, who have combined inherited forms with new ways of acting, participating, and "audiencing" to generate energy and innovation in the representation of South African life, longing, and the pursuit of justice.

As the final chapter reminds readers, the 1996 Constitution of South Africa mandates the right to well-being and to "improvements of life." While the realization of these rights may be thwarted by local mismanagement as well as global battles prompted by climate change and scarce resources exacerbated locally by endemic drought, the constitution has inspired citizens to demand accountability from government, even as the ruling party has retreated from its democratic obligations. Moreover, the other inspiring document of 1996, the White Paper on Arts and Culture, called for theatre and other genres of performance to enhance as well as to represent the good life and declared access to the arts a "fundamental prerequisite for democracy." The revised White Paper of 2017 may have a more modest focus on "skills development" but it recognized the democratic diversity of cultural origins and practices in African, Asian, and European traditions and inventions, even if it missed the contributions of Americans and African Americans that have been with us for more than a hundred years. *A Century of South African Theatre* hearkens to the call of the Constitution to hold government accountable and to stimulate community striving for the "improvement of life" and to the potential for theatre, performance, and the preservation, revival, and innovations of other creative arts and industries to inspire all to foster their full potential so as to enhance the social, cultural, and economic well-being of citizens and guests across the country and beyond, from the Cradle of Humankind near the northern border of South Africa to the cosmopolitan Cape at the confluence of two oceans in the south.

On these terrains, national, transnational, and regional currents meet and mix to create multiplying practices too complex to be treated as simply an instance of a generalized "global south." This book has traced flows from many sources in the world that have fertilized South African culture and nourished exemplary performances on stage, street, and other platforms for more than a century and points to developments in theatrical and (trans)national representation and contestation that invite further investigation in the century to come.

Chicago/Johannesburg/Cape Town, 2018

Notes

Introduction

1   Although he wrote poetry and prose, Sepamla had an abiding interest in performance. In the 1960s he worked for the white-run Union Artists, and in the 1980s directed the black-run Federated Union of Black Artists (Kruger 2013: 104–36). The *Rand Daily Mail* was the most outspoken daily paper until the state closed it in 1985 (Matisonn 2015: 212). Despite censorship, some of its journalists regrouped to found the *Weekly Mail*, which today plays a critical role as the *Mail and Guardian* (hereafter *M&G*).

2   For postcolonial "hybridity," see Bhabha (1986, 1991); for the syncretic character of postcolonial performance, Balme (1999); for South African discomfort with "hybridity," see Mngadi (1997), and for critical analysis of apartheid racial "science," Dubow (1987).

3   While church schools taught Shakespeare (Johnson 1996), Dhlomo was influenced more by early twentieth-century "new dramatists" Galsworthy and John Drinkwater (Chapter 3).

4   Habermas cautions against the corruption of *Öffentlichkeit* by "public relations," which has rendered the word "publicity" "unusable" (1989: 3). For the theatrical public sphere, see Kruger (1992) and Balme (2014). While the above studies focus on Europe, I highlight here how theatre in formations opposing apartheid or the post-apartheid state constitutes critical public spheres.

5   For the history of *Nkosi sikelel' iAfrika*, see Chapter 1; for *Siyaya ePitoli*, Chapter 7.

6   This section uses coverage by the South African Broadcasting Corporation, and press reports both enthusiastic, as in the *M&G* (May 13–19, 1994), and cautious, as in the Afrikaner flagship *Die Burger*, May 10, 1994. I cite Mandela's official speech from the *Sunday Nation Inauguration Special*, May 15, 1994; the Mandela Foundation website includes the speech (Mandela 1994) but no mention of Mandela's informal comments in Afrikaans, which were broadcast on television.

7   *Izimbongi* have historically used their skills to "mix veneration and criticism" (Vail/White 1991: 43). By praising ongoing struggle, Mkhive used the anti-apartheid repertoire to revise the *imbongi*'s customary deference to the leader, affiliating himself instead with international revolution.

8   As Hobsbawm and Ranger note, *invented tradition* is "a set of practices ... of a ritual or symbolic nature, which seek to inculcate certain values and norms of behavior by repetition" and "attempt to establish continuity with ... a suitable historical past" (1982: 1). Rewriting history for present purposes, the invention of tradition is thus a thoroughly modern practice. For the "white Zulu" see Chapter 2 and Sanders (2016).

9   Turner's characterization of liminoid phenomena as "ludic offerings placed for sale on the 'free market'" (1982: 54) is apt, but his conclusion–that such phenomena are "personal-psychological"—falls short of explaining the mass production of objects such as T-shirts with Mandela's face or clan name Madiba, and other commodities marketing the "rainbow nation."

10   The first third of Zuma's 2016 address was devoted to praising dignitaries and celebrating anniversaries such as the 1956 Women's March on Pretoria, now National Women's Day; questions and interruptions were deflected by the Speaker. For the text, see Zuma (2016); the speech and the opposition's interruptions aired on SABC Digital News, but the video, accessed February 22, 2016, is no longer available.

11   Maluleke (2016: 23). I have modified Maluleke's translation of *fundelwa* [passive of *ukufundela*—to educate]; his abstract noun "education" is more elegant but "being educated" picks up the emphasis in the Zulu on the process of schooling.

12   While deputy president in 2006, Zuma was acquitted of rape in a trial that violated South African law by exposing the victim's intimate history (Motsei 2007; Gqola 2015). He was also indicted but not tried for corruption, and in 2016 ordered by the Constitutional Court to reimburse the state for Nkandla. The EFF chant articulated the widespread view that Zuma was beholden to the Gupta family, who enjoyed privileged access to him; see the Public Protector's *State of Capture Report* (Madonsela 2016).

13   Simamkele Dlakuvu and colleagues dubbed their action #RememberKhwezi to honor the woman who brought the rape charges, the late Fezekile Kuzwayo, whom the court called Khwezi to shield her from Zuma supporters' death threats (G. Nicolson, "#Remember Khwezi," *Daily Maverick*, August 8, 2016; http://www.dailymaverick. co.za/article/2016-08-08-rememberkhwezi-it-worked-like-a-beautiful-theatre-piece/#.V6mjezYrLAx; June 29, 2018. Zuma spoke on August 6 to announce local election results, but this date, three days before National Women's Day, prompted the activists to recall the tenth anniversary of Zuma's trial and the high rate of assaults against women (allegedly one woman in three). Despite this act of feminist solidarity, they were ejected by security working for the ANC Women's League.

14   For English in South Africa, see Mesthrie (2002a), and for ESL, see Posel and Zeller (2015).

15   Arguments about democratizing English have taken different directions, such as celebrating local "englishes" (Njabulo Ndebele 1994), or promoting English as a vehicle of pan-African unity (Es'kia Mphahlele 2002). Post-apartheid policy has, however, vacillated between promoting endoglossic languages and defending the practical value of English (Hunter 2015).

16   Purkey made this remark in *Theater Heute* in 2006 but later said that he meant it ironically (2008: 18). Fleishman and Pather (2015) criticize the asymmetry between aspiring practitioners and paying audiences but Morris, who coined the word *audiencing* (2017: 146), argues that township spectators are active audiences as participants in community events even if they are not paying customers.

17   Revised as *Ipi Zombi?* (Bailey 1999, 2002), the play acquired the campy citational style that became Bailey's signature, with an urban actor playing a drag queen playing a rural girl and a title that ironically quoted *Ipi Tombi?* (1974), which was a frivolous but controversial revue that paired men in workers' overalls and gumboots with topless women in grass skirts (Chapter 5).

18   The editors defend the published title, claiming that it shows "the way language changes in different contexts" (Reznek et al. 2012: 55) but, mindful of two centuries of Xhosa literacy, I would point out that *Ingcwaba lendoda lisecalen' kwendlela* is not only "grammatically correct" as the editors admit (55) but also articulates meaning more elegantly, and thus better reflects Mbothwe's commitment to treat Xhosa as literature not just as a medium for "making people laugh" (2016: 132), while still allowing for stage variation.

19   In 1910, the colonies at the Cape (British since 1806) and Natal (since 1845) joined the former Boer polities, the Orange Free State and the South African (Transvaal)

Republic, which were ruled by Britain after the Anglo-Boer War in 1902, to form
a self-governing Union. In today's language, the Union was neocolonial in its
dependence on British imports and its restriction of the rights of the black majority.

20   *The Archive and the Repertoire* (Taylor 2003) highlights the force of transmission
through repertoire and reenactment as against the power of the state and other
authorities vested in material archives; this book stresses the value of both archive
and repertoire as forms of historical transmission while also insisting on the labor of
investigation required to correct lapses in individual recall.

21   Sarah Roberts's reliance on "recollection" leads her to grant "pioneer" status to
1980s work performed at the Market (2015: 36), where she worked as designer, but
director Simon deployed methods there that he had been developing in various
venues at home and abroad since the 1960s. As indicated by my critique above of
Mda's ahistorical claim about Fugard, Roberts is not the only one to conflate the arc
of a career with longer histories of intersecting institutions but, rather than listing
culprits, this book will correct errors in context and highlight historical material that
deserves more attention from researchers.

Chapter 1

1   The Emancipation Centenary program is in the South African Institute for Race
Relations (SAIRR) collection, Witwatersrand University Library Historical Papers
(hereafter WUL): AD843/B47.

2   "Africans Celebrate Emancipation Centenary," *Bantu World* (*BW*), June 9, 1934, 4;
"The Emancipation Centenary Celebration," *Umteteli wa Bantu* (UwB), June 9, 1934,
2. Couzens (1985: 99) suggests that Dhlomo was influenced by John Drinkwater's
play *Abraham Lincoln* but newspaper accounts suggest the pathos of Stowe's novel
rather than Drinkwater's heroic protagonists.

3   [R.V. Selope Thema], "Honour the Great Emancipators," *BW* June 2, 1934, 1.

4   "This Day of Freedom," *UwB*, August 5, 1933, 2.

5   For Du Bois and Washington's influence in South Africa, see Couzens (1985: 86–98).
Souls of Black Folk and *Up From Slavery* were in the Carnegie Non-European Library
at the BMSC.

6   Ali Mazrui and Maurice Tidy (1984: 282) coin this term for tactical appeals to
tradition made by modern African leaders; Mudimbe (1988: 169) notes the irony of
invoking tradition in the service of modernization.

7   Separate development appealed to chiefs defending their ebbing authority but the
state's intentions were entirely modern: to create a reserve labor force. Zulu Cultural
Society's ties to the Dept. of Native Affairs were forged by "intense ideological labour
by black intelligentsia and white ideologues" (Marks 1989: 217).

8   Thema, "Before the Advent of the White Man, the Dead Ruled the Living with a Rod
of Iron in Bantu Society," *BW*, May 12, 1934, 8–9.

9   Music critic Mark Radebe used Marcus Garvey's phrase "Africans in America"
to describe "the enormous influence of Bantu rhythms on the world's music";
Musicus, "The All-African Music Festival," *UwB*, October 29, 1932, 2; "The
Coming of Paul Robeson," *UwB*, June 1, 1933, 2. *Marabi* combined American
swing with African rhythms. Usually played on piano for dancing couples, it
was modern and "pan-ethnic," appealing to Africans regardless of ethnic origin
(Coplan 2008: 441).

10   Apart from MacAdoo, who toured in the 1890s (Erlmann 1991: 21–53) and the impact of sheet music and recordings, study abroad—by Motsieloa in London in the 1920s and Caluza in Virginia and New York in the 1930s—made black South Africans aware of African-American shows, including those marketed by white impresarios—such as Ziegfeld's production of Lubrie Hill's *Darktown Follies* in 1913, described by African-American composer James Weldon Johnson (1991: 174).

11   The Mthethwa claim to Zuluness was offset by historical irony. Although Shaka's benefactor, the Mthethwa chief Dingiswayo later broke with him and was praised for bringing the Mthethwa under European influence by Theophilus Shepstone, Native Affairs Secretary (Hamilton 1985: 104).

12   This was a popular part of the centenary celebration of the American Board Mission, Adams College, KC70, MS 62a/11.2; Killie Campbell African Library (hereafter KCAL) University of KwaZulu-Natal.

13   *BW* April 11, 1936, 17, and May 30, 1936, 17.

14   Following Johannes Fabian's point that "primitive" is a "category, not an object, of Western thought" (1983: 18), I use *primitivist* to denote the attribution of naiveté to Africans by whites who considered themselves more advanced.

15   "Africa's Wonder City," *Rand Daily Mail* (*RDM*): *Jubilee Supplement*, September 23 1936, n.p.; Empire Exhibition collection, WUL (A1092, boxes 37–43, 93–97, 114).

16   "South Africa's Empire Exhibition," *South African Mining and Engineering Journal*, May 18, 1935, 72.

17   Bellasis (1935: 228) complained that the "modernistic" structures showed "too much Chicago" but this complaint was ignored by local architects; see Kruger (2013: 29–34).

18   Despite Bellasis' reassurances that there would be "no restrictions on Native visitors" (Letter to J.D. Rheinallt Jones, SAIRR secretary, June 27, 1936; SAIRR: AD843/B66.3), *Bantu World* registered repeated complaints to the contrary: "The Empire Exhibition," *BW*, August 24, 1936, 17 and November 14, 1936, 17. For the display of iron-smelting, see Kruger (2007: 36–37).

19   Ballenden, "The City's Army of Native Workers," *Johannesburg Star: Jubilee Supplement*, September 22, 1936.

20   "Mr. Van Gyseghem, Pageant Master," *Star,* March 5, 1936, focuses on debutantes, while the *Uganda Herald* (February 26, 1936), discusses his time in the Soviet Union and the United States, where he worked on the Federal Theatre's Living Newspapers.

21   "The Pageant," *Pretoria News* May 8, 1936. Preller's work, such as *Piet Retief* (1906), which treated the Boer invaders as victims of King Dingane's wrath, set the tone for apartheid textbooks (Hofmeyr 1988).

22   For Neethling-Pohl's report on Nuremburg, see State Archives (SA 450/33); Louw confirmed the "regrettable" popularity of "Blut und Boden" talk among Afrikaners (1939: 10). *Die Bou van 'n Nasie* was praised by Afrikaners but provoked Anglophile protests in Johannesburg (Davis 1996: 148).

23   "Brilliant Pageant of South African History," *RDM*, December 17, 1936, 12; "The South African Pageant," *Star*, December 17, 1936, 26.

24   "The Empire Exhibition," *BW*, August 24; September 17 and 26, 1936, 20; "The City Thanks Africans," *BW*, November 7, 1936, 20.

25   "A Day at the Empire Exhibition," *BW*, November 21, 1936, 11.

26   *BW*, April 16, 1932, 8; E. Ntombela, "On Indlamu," *Native Teachers Journal* 28, 2 (1949), 97.

27   Ntombela 98; Marks (1989: 230).

28 *BW*, May 7, 1932, 17; September 28, 1935, 4; March 14, 1936, 4.
29 W. Mbali, "Darktown Strutters and Merry Blackbirds play in Queenstown," *BW*, April 24, 1937, 17.
30 Critic at Large [Walter Nhlapo], "Pitch Black Follies at the BMSC," *BW*, February 12, 1938, 18; SAIRR records, AD843/Kb28.2.2.
31 Matheus wrote "The 'Cruter" (1975 [1926]) after close to a million rural African Americans had come to northern US cities. The play portrays an encounter between sharecroppers and a white recruiter, distinguished by formal wear—hat and gloves—as well as formal speech, as against the sharecroppers' dialect.
32 "African Theatrical Syndicate Show," *BW*, February 24, 1940, 20.
33 Dhlomo, "The Nu-Zonk Revue," *Ilanga lase Natal*, May 18,1946, 8.
34 [Nhlapo] "Drama vs. Jazz," *BW*, February 24, 1940, 20.

Chapter 2

1   Johannesburg Public Library: Strange Theatre Collection (hereafter JPL/STC).
2   Stephen Black, Editorial, *The Sjambok*, November 14, 1930, 18.
3   For performative commemoration of the Rand Revolt, see Kruger (2013: 46–49); for comparison between 1922 and the Marikana massacre in 2012, Chapter 8 of this volume.
4   *The Bram Fischer Waltz* appeared in Afrikaans in Fischer's birthplace Bloemfontein in 2012 (Kalmer 2016: 12) and in English in Grahamstown in 2013 and 2014, performed by David Butler. Fischer was considered so dangerous that, although he was released to die of cancer in his brother's home, the state confiscated his ashes (Clingman 1998: 457). His party's reputation is still so controversial among Afrikaners that even a sympathetic critic asserts that "communists appropriated" the tune of *The Red Flag* from "O, Tannenbaum" (Keuris 2015: 122), missing the song and songwriter's long association with the British Labour Party, hardly a communist organization, as well as its appearance at the Rand Revolt.
5   *Red Rand* won the Repertory Reading Group's play competition in 1936. Citations quote act and page numbers (e.g. I, 3), which begin anew for each act in the script (WUL: A406).
6   "Red Rand at the Library Theatre," *Johannesburg Star*, December 3, 1936, 26. Sowden's stage directions (Sowden 1937: I, 1) call for actors planted in the house but the review's phrase "new device' reflects the impact of avant-gardists Van Gyseghem and Kurt Baum, who founded the Johannesburg Art Theatre after working with Erwin Piscator in Berlin.
7   The Australian stage was also dominated by British tours; see Love (1984). In Canada, the "first self-declared National Theatre" (1915) stressed the British aspirations of "English" Canadians (Filewod 1990: 5).
8   "On Some South African Novelists" (Campbell 1949: 171). Campbell left South Africa in 1927.
9   Twala attended the Johannesburg Rep's dress rehearsal at His Majesty's (Hoffman 1980: 39).
10 "The Africans Invade the Stage," *BW*, April 15, 1933, 1; "Unique Gathering at the BMSC," *BW* May 6, 1933, 1; "The Bantu Dramatic Society Stage their First Show," *UwB*, April 15, 1933, 4.
11 Rheinallt Jones: letter to C. Bullock, November 20, 1935 (SAIRR: WUL: AD843/RJ/Kb28.2.2).

12 "African Art Forcing its Way to Realisation," *BW*, March 2, 1935, 1. Thorndike and her husband Lewis Casson were performing Shaw, not Goldsmith, and took an interest in the Johannesburg Rep. and the BDS.

13 In a front-page article "The Growth of African Literature," *BW*, March 4, 1933, Dhlomo insisted that Africans were not to be forced to write in African languages, citing Sol Plaatje, who wrote *Native Life in South Africa* (1914). Rheinallt Jones' attribution of the weak *uNongqause* to a Xhosa rather than its actual English author reflects the belief that "Europeans" had a better command of "dramatic knowledge" (AD843/ RJ/Kb28.2.2).

14 To avoid too many variants I follow the spelling of *Nongqause* used by Dhlomo and contemporaries, rather than the present-day *Nongqawuse*, although the latter may be easier to pronounce.

15 For the reference to *Masses and Man* [*Masse-Mensch*], see *Johannesburg Sunday Times*, November 8, 1936. Drinkwater and Galsworthy were taught in mission schools and available in the BMSC library.

16 See Dhlomo's typescript "Nongqause–or, The Girl Who Killed to Save" and songs in tonic-solfa; Rhodes University Cory Library Lovedale Collection: 16/309; thanks to Johann Buis for transcription into staff notation. The preface stresses Dhlomo's intent to make the play available free for educational performances.

17 The venue was changed apparently to comply with a 1936 by-law that forbad African men from performing where white women were present (BMSC Annual Report 1937; SAIRR, AD843/B.73.1) but, since the Wits audience included women, the law was used to discriminate against the black-run BMSC.

18 Bantu Peoples Theatre, Draft Constitution, SAIRR: AD843 /RJ/Kb.14. BPT letter to J. Rheinallt Jones, July 31, 1937; SAIRR: AD843/RJ/Kb28.2.2.

19 [Selope Thema,] Editorial, *BW*, January 18, 1936, 4.

20 *Izibongelo* is derived from the verb -*bongela* [praise for someone] and suggests performance for an audience who is also the object of praise. The target here would be the nation as a whole.

21 Dhlomo annotated his copies of Rider Haggard's and other colonial accounts— Colenso's *History of the Anglo-Zulu War* and Sullivan's *The Native Policy of Theophilus Shepstone* (1928)—(Couzens 1985: 138).

22 While Dhlomo's Dunn is an opportunist playing British against Zulu, Dunn's descendants received respect from the African press in the 1930s. Even in 1994, photographs in the Zulu Historical Museum at Fort Nongqai showed Dunn as a powerful landowner who married twenty wives from prominent Zulu clans.

23 The mistranslation of *Verfremdung* as "alienation" persists, confusing Marx's *Entfremdung* [alienation or dispossession] with Brecht's estrangement or critical disillusion; for analysis, see Kruger (2004: 39–48).

24 Writing to Shepherd on April 16, 1938, Dhlomo listed groups keen to stage his work, including one led by Motsieloa and sponsored by Sowden. Shepherd dismissed the plays for "weak verse" (May 19, 1938) but his rejection of Dhlomo's novella "An Experiment in Colour" for "strident tone" and alleged hostility to whites (March 3, 1939) suggests bias against African aspirations; Rhodes University Lovedale Collection (16/309(h) and Midgley (1993: 110–50).

25 Coplan (1994: 34–35) notes that the consultative role of the *pitso* persisted even after the destabilization wrought by the *mfecane* pushed Moshoeshoe to rule more autocratically than before.

26 Celebrated in Basutoland on March 12 to honor the 1862 treaty with Britain, Moshoeshoe Day had varied dates in South Africa. On the opening day of the play, the king was praised as an "embodiment of democracy in undemocratic South Africa": "Moshoeshoe Day Celebrations," *UwB*, May 6, 1939, 7).

27 "*Moshoeshoe* Produced by Africans," *BW*, May 6, 1939, 20.

28 "Moshoeshoe," *UwB*, May 6, 1939, 4. Khutlang was BMSC Physical Director, organizing sports and dancing. Salome Masoleng was the wife of Johannes Masoleng, choreographer for the Darktown Strutters.

29 Dhlomo continued in the 1950s to argue that English was the language that transcended tribalism. "Reflections on a Literary Competition," *Ilanga lase Natal*, October 31, 1953, 3, criticized the 1953 Bantu Education Act for mandating primary education in African languages on "tribal lines."

30 Couzens (1985: 161–62) highlights the link at the end of the play between Mt. Thaba Bosiu in Lesotho and its local namesake, the much smaller hill in Pimville.

31 "The meaning of our name" plays on the double meaning of *izibongo*—either clan names or praises, by implication of the clan and its leaders (Dhlomo n.d.).

Chapter 3

1 The 1946 census (Thompson 2014: 178) put 24 percent of Africans in the cities, as against 76 percent of whites, 70 percent Indians, and 62 percent Coloureds. The significance of the African figure is best gauged by comparison with 1936 (17 percent). 1946 was also the first census in which Africans outnumbered whites in the urban areas.

2 Links between the ANC and dispossessed workers, such as the 90,000 squatters near what is now Soweto, were as yet tenuous; in 1948, the ANC had only about 6,000 members nationwide (Lodge 1985: 16).

3 Bantu Peoples Theatre, Drama Festival (July 25–27, 1940), 10; (Johannesburg Public Library, Strange Theatre Collection (hereafter: JPL/STC).

4 *The Dreamy Kid* (1919) was praised by African American James Weldon Johnson (1991: 183). Routh worked for the Garment Workers Union but was also active in experimental theatre influenced by Soviet director Meyerhold (Routh 1950a: 26).

5 "The African National Theatre," *Inkululeko*, June 1941, 5, 7.

6 "Three Good Plays," *Inkululeko*, September 1941, 5. Charles van Onselen identifies Tau a.k.a. Kas Maine as a farmer fined in 1931 for refusing to pay for a dog license (1996: 3) but does not mention the play.

7 Dhlomo, "Tshaka—a Reevaluation," *UwB*, June 18, 1932, 4.

8 City Hall program (August 16 and 17, 1954), Dhlomo papers: Campbell Library: KCAL, 8282.

9 The 1937 *Dingane* (Dhlomo 1985: 69–113) includes songs and characters peripheral to the action. The stage version, *Dingana* (1954) is shorter but framed by material inserted by Branford (Couzens 1985: 344).

10 Under apartheid, "Afrikaner" (lit: African) applied only to whites, who labeled Africans *naturelle* [natives] and later *Bantu* and thus used language as well as law to deny Africans the right to Africa.

11 Plays about Boer sacrifice include *Die Pad van Suid-Afrika* (The Road of South Africa, 1913) on the Anglo-Boer War by C.J. Langenhoven, who wrote the anthem

Die Stem van Suid-Afrika, and Uys Krige's *Magdalena Retief* (1939), whose husband Piet's death at the hands of the Zulus spurred Boer revenge. Neethling-Pohl directed both at the Pretoria Volksteater (Naudé 1950: 9), supported by the University of Pretoria.

12 Sagan, "Aims and Objects of a National Theatre," Sagan collection: Wits University Library Historical Papers (WUL): A855/D. Sagan is known chiefly for her film *Mädchen in Uniform* (Germany 1932); for her theatre work and long life in South Africa, see her autobiography (1996).

13 Although the opening sentence could be rendered colloquially as "you know that the first Van Niekerks came to clean things up around here," the General's assertion of divine right calls for a more elevated—or bombastic—turn of phrase.

14 This mix of blood and reason recalls Edmund Husserl, who, although a Jewish refugee from Germany, celebrated the *geistige Gestalt* [spiritual form] of Europe in terms that recalled the white supremacist ideology that exiled him, extolling civilization through conquest while delegitimizing "non-Europeans" (1970: 273–74) including those "races" that appear to wander over [*herumvagabundieren*] rather than belong to the land.

15 The 2nd edition of 1989, the year that F.W. de Klerk (no relation) became the last Afrikaner president, replaces early apartheid crudities such as "Native [*Naturelle*] Trust" with late apartheid euphemisms—"Homeland [*Tuisland*] Trust"—but does not acknowledge the 1988 United Nations accord that led Namibia to independence in 1990.

16 Commentary on Sophiatown varies from systematic study to retro-tourism. After Modisane, Nkosi, and Matshikiza were banned, little appeared until the 1980s, when these writers were republished, along with photo-essays (Schadeberg 1987), memoirs (Mattera 1987), interviews (Stein/Jacobson 1986), and a DVD of Rogosin's film *Come Back Africa* (2010 [1960]). Drawing on these sources and on Visser (1976), Chapman (1989), Gready (1990), Coplan (2008) and others, my discussion also includes the post-apartheid legacy.

17 Sophiatown was not the only integrated enclave to suffer this fate. District Six, the mixed neighborhood in Cape Town demolished in the 1960s, received nostalgic treatment in *District Six–the Musical* (music: Dawid Kramer; book: Taliep Pieterson, 1987), and analysis in the District Six Museum.

18 Modisane notes that, though Africans could not buy tickets to see *Look Back in Anger* at His Majesty's, "Alan Dobie, the British actor invited to play Jimmy Porter ... negotiated an arrangement for me to watch the play through a hole in the back of the auditorium" (1986: 172).

19 Union Artists was chaired by advertising executive Ian Bernhardt. Although Coplan claims that Routh initially held the chair (2008: 213), he had left for London by 1950 (Routh 1950a).

20 Nkosi and Nakasa, who wrote for *Drum*, were familiar with their colleague Henry Nxumalo's exposé of apartheid labor relations on white farms.

21 Bloom claimed that *King Kong* was proposed because Union Artists was unable to secure rights for *The Threepenny Opera*; see program for *King Kong* (February 1959), JPL/ STC. Schadeberg (1987: 177) mentions *West Side Story*, as did Irene Menell, interviewed September 7, 1994.

22 "Negro Shows Sweep the World," *Drum*, August 1953, 7. For Langston Hughes, whose writing was available in the BMSC library, *Porgy and Bess* was "not a Negro opera but Gershwin's idea of what a Negro opera should look like" (1976: 699).

23   Despite Bloom's name on the book, Menell (n. 21) remembers collaborative creation, as does Schadeberg (1987: 177). After Bloom and Matshikiza sketched a series of numbers on the boxer's life, Bloom moved to Cape Town, leaving the rest of the team to write a plot, which he revised on a later visit. Bloom claimed to know *tsotsitaal* (Glasser 1960: 18) but Menell credited Matshikiza, whose own "Matshikese" flavored his *Drum* columns.

24   Kwanele Sosibo, "King Kong confined to history," *M&G*, October 4, 2017; https://mg.co.za/article/2017-10-05-00-king-kong-confined-to-history.

25   Unlike *King Kong*, which ran for over a year, *Mkhumbane* closed shortly after opening in Durban (March 1960) because of police harassment. See "Mkhumbane," *Drum*, July 1960, 72.

26   Coplan (2008: 268) claims that Union Artists refused to support Masinga but the program (JPL/STC) is headed "Union Artists Presents ..."

27   For the evolution of JATC, see Orkin (1995) and Kruger (2004).

28   The film and vinyl versions of *Oh! What a Lovely War* reached South Africa shortly after their London releases. Simon, who assisted Littlewood's team in 1959, directed *Mother Courage* at the Market in 1976, and JATC members were familiar with Brecht's theatrical and theoretical writings.

29   Themba's blend of cynicism and feeling is captured in *The Will to Die*, which includes the stories "Crepuscule" and "The Suit." As a graduate of Fort Hare University (1916–), whose alumni include Mandela, Themba had more formal education than most of his colleagues; see Nkosi's introduction, *The Will to Die* (1972: vii–xi) and Kruger (2013: 71–78).

30   This productive tension is undone in Peter Brook's uncharacteristically sentimental adaptation *Le Costume* (on tour 2002), which had Sophiatown songs interpreted by African-American singer Princess Erika as Tilly mimicking Makeba rather than recreating the corrosive sharpness of the original story.

31   *Crepuscule's* first professional production was in Cape Town in 2012, directed by Gumede with Jennifer Steyn (Gumede 2014: 7). It was remounted with another cast at the Market in 2015. The revival touted at the 2016 Grahamstown Festival as a commemoration of the Market's fortieth anniversary had the same cast as 2015 except for Nat Ramabulana as Can. Comments based on the 2014 text and the 2015 production.

32   For Sassen's review, see: https://robynsassenmyview.wordpress.com/2015/07/17/impeccable-crepuscule/.

33   Triomf once signaled apartheid's triumph but, as captured in the first post-apartheid Afrikaans novel *Triomf* (van Niekerk 1994), now recalls the hubris of the regime that built it. Retreat is a suburb on the Cape Town train line where Coloureds were exiled by the Group Areas Act, but prompted Richard Rive's ironic anticipation of apartheid's demise in his short story collection *Advance, Retreat* (1989).

Chapter 4

1   Fugard denied PACT rights to *People* in 1967, expressing "distaste for Government sponsored theatre" (1984: 149), but gave the play to CAPAB in 1969 because Yvonne Bryceland was engaged there. The deal with CAPAB led black intellectuals to accuse Fugard of adding to the "erosion of human decency" (Fugard 1984: 128–29) but he still endured police harassment.

2   By 1976, the SABC employed 250 Afrikaans actors for 2,000 roles in radio drama as opposed to 143 English-language actors for 934 roles. The PACs produced seven Afrikaans for every five English-language plays, with similar employment patterns to the SABC: see Commission of Inquiry (1977: Appendix G).

3   My translations analyze rather than replicate the ideology of the Afrikaner ascendancy. While *volkseie* might have meant "the people's identity" and *volksontwikkeling* "people's development" for the beneficiaries of these programs, the outcome was the advancement of the Afrikaner minority at the expense of the majority.

4   The PCB targeted political texts like Fanon's *Wretched of the Earth* and African autobiographies but also banned *Black Beauty*, a children's book about a horse (Cope 1983: 74). It was not until 1973 that an Afrikaans novel was banned, Brink's *Kennis van die Aand* [*Looking on Darkness*], the same year that PACT staged his play *Die Verhoor* (Brink 1970), about *trekboers* rebelling against British colonial authorities in the Eastern Cape.

5   The play ran for a few weeks in Pretoria, an Afrikaner stronghold (Breytenbach papers; State Archive (hereafter: SA): 261/1099).

6   Jakobus Hercules de la Rey was one of the generals who represented the Boers at the Vereeniging conference that ended the war in 1902 but he rebelled again in 1914 when the Union followed Britain into the First World War. Before he could join other rebels, however, he was shot by Johannesburg police while fleeing a roadblock set up to catch William Foster's robber gang (Du Preez 2008: 111–28).

7   September 3, rather than October 22 (Orkin 1991: 91); see Read (1991: 41).

8   For *Try for White* and director Leonard Schach, who concluded his career at the Cameri Theatre in Tel Aviv, see Schach (1996). For *The Kimberley Train*, see Orkin (1991: 86–89).

9   *Ruby and Frank*, directed by Dhlomo with music by Salome Masoleng who also composed for *Moshoeshoe*, played at the BMSC and on tour in 1939. Although not published in Dhlomo's *Collected Works*, it deserves note for juxtaposing a melodrama of love and prejudice between Africans and Coloureds with the political conflict between the ANC and the Non-European Unity Movement.

10 Millin repeats the common contradictory notion that Coloureds were superior to Africans because of white blood and European socialization but degenerate because their mixed blood allegedly diluted the "pure" European or African. For local versions of "degeneration" ideology, see Dubow.

11 Redelinghuys was married to Smit, whose *Verminktes* draws on *The Kimberley Train*. Bernard Sachs criticized the play's verbosity, but praised Redelinghuys's Bertha, in "A South African Play That Impresses," *South African Jewish Times*, September 19, 1958, and Library Theatre program (SA 459/115).

12 See Smit, "Toneelkrisis is Volkskrisis," *Dagbreek en Sontagnuus*, July 30, 1961, 32.

13 Barnard's speech echoes the propaganda in *Tuiste vir die Nageslag*: "the more consistent the policy of apartheid …, the greater the security for the purity of our blood, [and] … European racial survival" (Cronjé 1945: 79). Once Frans's challenge to his father moves from politics to claiming the Senator's ward as his wife, Harmse reverts to the ideology of superior blood (Smit 1976: 35).

14 Possible sources for *skollie* include Dutch *schoelje* [rogue] or Yiddish *schuol* [jackal]; see *Dictionary of South African English on Historical Principles*, s.v. *skolly*.

15 Rewritten in the 1977 production as the Zulu servant's idea, the castration becomes a barbaric threat shunned by the "civilized" Senator but his racist invective effectively maims his son without this violation.

16 Gunning contests Peter Brooks's argument that melodrama is driven by the "moral occult" (Brooks 1976: 5), the hidden power of virtue, the revelation of which restores the heroine to her rightful place. The difference between the melodrama of sensation and the melodrama of virtue should be clear in the difference between the sensation scene that ends *Die Verminktes* and the conclusion of Black's *Helena's Hope Ltd.* (1910), where the impoverished heroine receives her inheritance.

17 Even though Smit noted that under apartheid conditions Frans "had to" play white (1985: 225), his formulation suggests that he blames individual deception rather than a corrupt society.

18 Citations refer to *The Blood Knot* (Fugard 1992; premiere 1962) rather than *Blood Knot* (Fugard 1991), the shorter version directed by Lloyd Richards in New Haven, CT for the play's twenty-fifth anniversary.

19 W.E.G. Louw, "Ervaring wat kan skud," *Die Burger*, November 23, 1965; "Spelers roep met hul gepraat 'n hele lewe op," *Die Beeld*, November 25, 1965. For reviews in English, see Read (1991: 60–61).

20 Sowden, "A Torment of Poor Whites in the Library Theatre's *Hello and Goodbye*," *Rand Daily Mail* (*RDM*) October 20, 1965; L. Greyling, "*Hello* oordryf en nikssegend," *Die Vaderland*, October 22, 1965.

21 *Putsonderwater* premiered at Volksteater Vertical in Ghent in 1968 and toured Belgium for a year. At Rhodes, Abraham de Vries directed, calling on the state to explain why the play was denied a professional production; see Smit files (SA 459/48). *Boesman and Lena* was directed by Fugard first at Rhodes in July 1969. He played Boesman, Bryceland played Lena and Glynn Day, also white, the unnamed African.

22 "*Putsonderwater* Maar—Onderdiekombers," *Die Burger*, July 20, 1969. Terry Herbst, "Why was Bartho Smit's *Putsonderwater* axed at the last minute?" *Cape Times*, August 10, 1970. It was revived only in 1981.

23 Engelen, Program note for *Putsonderwater* (PACOFS 1969), Smit files, (SA 459/43). *Platteland dorpie* might be translated as "country village" but that phrase is too close to the English image of a "green and pleasant land" to capture the arid plateau that covers most of the South African hinterland.

24 Shakespeare's Prospero did not rape his daughter but his testy response to Miranda's defense of Ferdinand—"one word more / Shall make me chide thee, if not hate thee" (*Tempest*, I, 2, ll.478–79)—makes him sound jealous.

25 Calvinist doctrine allows for the virgin birth of Jesus but not for the immaculate conception of the Catholic Mary free from sin that animates *Sous le soleil de Satan*. The Calvinist underpinning of *Putsonderwater* makes this Mary a fallen woman. Opperman returned to this theme in *Die Teken*, produced two decades later in the same theatre, to portray a father so scandalized by his unmarried daughter's belief that she bears the messiah that he murders the child as the antichrist.

26 *Christine* (PACT 1974) is Smit's most ambitious play and the only one published in English translation (Smit 1974). Like *Putsonderwater*, it deals with bad faith; sculptor Paul Harmse abandons his Jewish lover to the Nazis and is haunted by his betrayal but this version of Brecht's *Jewish Wife* replaced Brecht's poignant portrayal of the woman with the man's self-pity; for analysis of the male complaint, see Chapter 5.

27 See Barnard's review, *Rapport*, August 20, 1971 (quoted: Du Plessis 1971: 58).

28 "Sien dan 'n slag, toe ou Tjokkie, jong: wie gaan vanjaar die Herzogprys kry ? [Have a quick see, come on, Tjokkie: who's going to win the Herzog Prize this year?]"; R. van Reenen, "Herzogprys lê vanjaar tussen *Siener* and *Christine*," *Rapport*, April 23, 1972).

29 Barnard, Program note for *Die Rebellie van Lafras Verwey* (PACT 1975), n.p.

30 P. Breytenbach, "Doemprofete verkeerd met Lafras," *Die Transvaler*, April 17, 1975, 4, suggested that PACT's staging gave Lafras's "petit-bourgeois" character more definition.

31 See "New Plays at the People's Space," *Cape Times*, November 15, 1979.

32 Brink faults *Lafras* for borrowing from *Billy Liar* (1986: 145) while praising Barnard's earlier play, *Pa, maak vir my 'n vlieër, Pa* (CAPAB 1964). But the latter is merely a variation on Pinter's *Birthday Party*, whereas the former offers a more complex portrait of delusion than Keith Waterhouse's fibber.

33 The review in *S'ketsh* (1972: 26) of the Cape Flats Players' production cites Brink's verdict as "the best play in Afrikaans." My version of the play's title restores the idiomatic rhythm lost in the published Kanna: He *is coming home* (Small 1990). Quotations cite Kaaps first, then formal Afrikaans and English translation.

34 W.E.G. Louw, "Kanna, 'n onvergeetlike toneel-ervaring," *Die Burger*, November 20, 1974.

35 Canadian legislation in the 1960s facilitated the migration of brown South Africans especially those with skills; the return of many after 1990 prompted Mandela's thanks to the Canadian government in 1994.

36 Small notes, "there is a very real danger of a play like this becoming melodramatic" (Thomas 1972a: 34) but argues that the audience's emotion signals a quest for "self-understanding."

37 Coloureds in Cape Town have for various reasons—cosmopolitan contact in the port and disaffection with African and Afrikaner patriarchy—tended to be more tolerant of LGBTQI + people (Gevisser 1994b: 28).

38 The dialogue for both Cape Flats and PACT productions mostly matched the 1965 text though only PACT could afford to reproduce the stage directions for a naturalistic portrayal of District Six.

39 See Thomas (1972b: 26), who played Kanna; and (anon) "Cape Town's passionate response," *City Post*, February 25, 1972, 4.

40 Small confirmed this during a visit to Kingsmead College (high school attended by LK), when the PACT production toured Johannesburg in 1974.

41 Van Niekerk's program note, *Kanna Hy Kô Hystoe* (PACT 1974).

42 P. Breytenbach, "Kanna ist ontroerend en aangrypend," *Die Transvaler*, June 28, 1974.

43 Raeford Daniel, "A Terrible Affinity," *RDM*, May 31, 1974.

44 "Díe Kanna is beslis Louis se Triomf," *Pretoria Oggendblad*, July 5, 1974.

45 See essays under the rubric "Elke Tong het sy Afrikaans" *Die Vrye Weekblad*, September 29, 1993: 13–21, and the report on the second Black Afrikaans Writers Symposium, *Die Suid-Afrikaan* 55 (1995/96): 25–27.

46 "Still waters run deep" hints at the devil in the proverb—*stille water/diepe ground/ onder draai die duiwel rond*—more effectively than either the literal translation of the titular shorthand—deep ground—or the market-driven title "African Gothic" (De Wet 2005). The original was directed at Rhodes by Denys Webb and at the Market by Lucille Gillward, and published with De Wet's other Free State plays: *Op Dees Aarde* [On this Earth], about a blithe spirit who died giving birth to a "bastard" but returns to visit her "ugly" sisters, and *Nag Generaal* [Goodnight General], which tackles Anglo-Boer War myths from the perspective of women left to patch up the wounded (De Wet 1991). I cite the Afrikaans text (1991) and the Market production; for De Wet's career, see Anton Krueger (2015).

47 The arid farm with stunted inhabitants functions as an allegory for national decline also in Paul Slabolepszy's *Smallholding* (1989), in which a demented "Boere-Rambo"

and his crazy son J.J. torment Christiaan, a "god-fearing" postal worker (Slabolepszy 1994: 163).

48 J. Botha, for *Die Burger*, and Opperman's response are both in *Vuka SA*, 1, 6 (1996): 60–62; Barry Hough's review in *Rapport*, cited on the play's back cover (Opperman 1996: 162), praised the "honest" treatment of Afrikaner "inhumanity" to "fellow human beings." English-language critics hailed its "powerful depiction of Afrikaner history" (e.g. Adrienne Sichel, *The Star Tonight*) (Opperman 1996: 162), and an overseas writer hailed Opperman's transformation of "the history of his people from a heroic tale of righteous battles" to "conflicts with … black compatriots whose humanity they refuse to recognize" (Graver 1997: 56). I draw on the Grahamstown performance, the published play, and analysis by Keuris (2012) and Lewis (2016).

49 Lewis (2016: 57–69) illuminates the song, the musical—written by Opperman with Pepler's producer Sean Else—and the legend of De La Rey but does not mention the general's ambiguous death (n. 6 above).

50 *Hartland* (2011) drew from his play *Kaburu* (Boer; Opperman 2008) and cast some of the same actors, notably Snyman. The series had more subplots such as Vlooi's foiled plan to blow up the Union Buildings, and his cousin Gerhard's search for his birth father which stirred up the dirty secrets of the latter's acts of torture and his adoptive father's collusion as army chaplain, both during the invasion of Angola in the 1970s.

Chapter 5

1 The African Resistance Movement was founded after the ANC and PAC were outlawed, and consisted mostly of students whose rebellion was undermined when leaders were arrested or manipulated to betray the movement (Dlamini 2014).

2 The Africanist Manifesto of April 1959, which heralded the PAC's breakaway from the ANC, reads: "The African people of South Africa … recognize themselves as part of one African nation from Cape to Cairo, Madagascar to Morocco" (Karis/ Carter 1977: 517). The manifesto also drew on Nkrumah's speech at the Pan-African Convention in Accra, December 1958.

3 After PAC leader Robert Sobukwe was sent to Robben Island, Leballo moved PAC to Lesotho but his boasts about Poqo sabotage endangered others at home (Karis/ Gerhart 1997: 19–62).

4 Morphet coined this phrase in a 1990 lecture in honor of Richard Turner, who taught politics at the University of Natal until assassinated by police in 1978; quoted: Mangcu (2014: 113).

5 Carmichael's critique of institutional racism influenced SASO's arguments for separatism, even if the minority status of African Americans differed from the black majority in South Africa.

6 Texts in *Black Review* were often anonymous to avoid prosecution; quotes refer to the editors.

7 Mudimbe (1988: 85) criticizes negritude's application of "anthropology, existentialism and French poetics" to create an African mystique.

8 The incident that ignited unrest was Onkgopotse Abraham Tiro's graduation address, which denounced apartheid education at the University of the North at Turfloop (Khoapa 1973: 21–24). Despite opposition from the white rector, several Turfloop students contributed to black education and politics, which encouraged Professor

Es'kia Mphahlele to teach there on his return from exile (1974) before moving to Wits University in 1978.

9   See SABTU Program, Black Peoples Convention (BPC); Wits University Library Historical Papers (WUL): A2177: 6.1.2).

10 The 1962 Criminal Law Amendment authorized detention without trial in prison or under "banning" or house arrest, prohibiting visits by more than one person, or quotations in the press.

11 "What is Black Theatre?" delivered at Mofolo Hall, Sunday January 21, 1973 (BPC: A2177: 6.1.4) was submitted as state evidence in the terrorism trial in 1975.

12 D. Moodley, "All-Race Theatre Ahead," *Durban Post*, July 2, 1972, 17.

13 The program for *Phiri* (JPL/STC) lists a black technical director and Mackey Davashe (of the *King Kong* band) as bandleader, but the director (Barney Simon) was white.

14 Fugard (1984: 81) remembers Serpent Players emerging when Norman Ntshinga asked Fugard for help setting up a theatre group in 1963 with Mbikwana and others. Kani admits that he and Ntshona joined with the production of *Antigone* in 1965 but asserts that the group predated Fugard (Kani/Ntshona 1976: 15–17). For Mbikwana, see Kruger (2004: 241–45).

15 Mhangwane qutd. Elliot Makhaya, "Sam Mhangwane says: Black Theatre Must Wake Up," *Johannesburg World*, April 4, 1975: "the white man is experienced in theatre and will guide you on how to do it … within your own culture."

16 Solberg interviewed Kente and associates but appears not to know the variety tradition that shaped Kente's format: morally uplifting plots loosely attached to musical and dance numbers leavened with comic sketches. This tradition reached Kente through fellow Lovedale alumnus Motsieloa and evidently influenced his work more than Stanislavski and other Western sources floated in the white press.

17 Interview with Mandla Tshabangu, *S'ketsh* (1972): 8–11. The comparison with Motsieloa is mine.

18 Klaaste, "Gibson Kente has a thrilling new venture for the stage. It's very much like *King Kong*," *World*, February 3, 1966.

19 See *Shaka* program (JPL/STC).

20 Black businessmen under apartheid faced restrictions far more systematic than the pressures on Nigerians. Nonetheless, their melodramatic and comic plays and their audience's tastes were similar, as was the glamour of successful entrepreneurs in an otherwise struggling community.

21 See Makhaya's reviews in *World*, November 25, 11, and November 30, 1975, 9. For Singana, see Makhaya, "Mama Tembu," *World*, February 4, 1975, 5. Despite the critique, Thembi Mtshali (-Jones) credited *Ipi Tombi?* for launching her career in anti-apartheid theatre (Farber/Mtshali-Jones 2008: 3). For the afterlives of *Ipi Tombi?*, see Kruger (1995) and Sanders (2016: 80–94).

22 In his preface to the facsimile reprint of *S'ketsh*, Kavanagh distinguishes among "township theatre," mostly musicals by Kente and others, "town theatre," including integrated companies such as Workshop '71, and "Black consciousness theatre" by SABTU and PET (2016: xiii) but does not discuss the disagreements about these categories expressed by the writers in the magazine.

23 Like Jimmy Porter, the male complainer is a misogynist masquerading as a rebel. Whatever their differences, Nate and Jimmy both seek refuge from their failure to impact society—expressed in Jimmy's phrase "there are no good causes left"—in misogyny at home. If the female complaint "manages the social contradictions that arise from women's sexual and affective allegiance to a phallocentric ideology that

has ... denied women power, privilege, and presence" (Berlant 1988: 243), the male complaint manages the contradiction between patriarchy and the subordination of lower-class men by blaming this subordination on women's supposed domination of the domestic sphere.

24   Shezi's father Ambroise Shezi spoke to his son in hospital before Mthuli died and recounted this final meeting at the TRC hearing in Alexandra, October 1996; http://www.justice.gov.za/trc/hrvtrans/alex/shezi.htm.

25   The *PET Newsletter* appeared once in September 1973 before being banned. Kraai's article reproduced parts of Cooper's January speech, thus evading censorship of his banned text.

26   Citations in this paragraph from the Special Branch (political police) Charge Sheet, March 12, 1975, 5 (WUL: National Indian Council: AL2421: N5). Cooper and Moodley were sentenced to Robben Island. Kraai and Pheto were detained and later exiled.

27   The initial charge in March for "staging ... revolutionary plays and/or dramas" was dropped in the charge sheet for August 18, 1975; "The Trial of SASO/BPC Detainees"; Northwestern University Library: Africana collection.

28   "SASO Leaders Banned," *Durban Post*, March 11, 1972, 3, expressed conventional sympathy for the women facing "the prospect of being the breadwinner" while their husbands were banned.

29   "Back bars" were segregated Indian bars behind white establishments. The *lahnee* here is the white boss, but it also denotes a pretentious person of any ethnicity. Performed in one act at the SABTU festivals, the play ran in two acts directed by Govender at the Shah Academy in 1977 and directed by Benjy Francis at the Market Theatre in 1978, and in Durban again in 1979.

30   For clips from performances and Kessie Govender's commentary, see his 1997 television profile directed by Liza Aziz, produced by Junaid Ahmed for SABC; uploaded to YouTube October 17, 2018 by Kriben Pillay.

31   For clips from performances and Pillay's commentary, see his television profile by the same producers; uploaded to YouTube October 17, 2018. After the merger of UDW with UKZN in 2004, the Asoka Theatre and the press formerly associated with UDW Drama were closed.

32   The 1949 riots erupted after an Indian merchant allegedly punished an African child for theft. Zulus set fire to Indian homes and businesses but the ammunition was reputedly supplied by whites who resented Indian competition. This event left Indian South Africans with an enduring sense of their precarious position between black and white.

33   *How Long?* Program (JPL/STC) and Solberg (2011: 23–26).

34   Attempts to revive Kente's plays were hampered by the loss of his archive in a 1989 fire allegedly set by youth angered by his critique of violence (Solberg 2011: 96). Jerry Mofokeng's revival of *Lifa* (1997) relied on Kente's memory; after Kente's death, his legend prompted the Market to commemorate the fifty-fifth anniversary of *Manana* (1963) with a concert in April 2018.

35   The script published in *S'ketsh* (Kente 1975) ends with Saduva's fate in the balance. The 1981 text ends instead with his reconciliation with Pelepele supervised by Mfundisi. He treats Saduva as a victim of politics—"politics was forced on him" (Kente 1981: 123)—whose problems can be resolved by community support of his essentially good character.

36   Sagan observed that her students at the Hofmeyr School for Social Work, which Kente attended in the late 1940s, found Polonius more interesting than Hamlet,

apparently responding more to the "social" than to the "emotional" drama (1996: 211). More recently Purkey (2008) and Morris (2017) have made similar observations.

37 Makhaya, "New Life and Lustre in Kente's *Too Late!*," *World*, June 2, 1975, 8–9.

Chapter 6

1 In an interview with me (April 1995), Maponya supplemented his earlier statement by noting that the rise in violence in the late 1980s exacerbated the difficulties of developing audiences.

2 Like Marowitz's Open Space, the Space dropped "theatre" from its name to proclaim its experimental aspirations. Brook's theatre of cruelty influenced *Orestes*, generated by Fugard and cast from the *Oresteia* and the "image of a man with a suitcase … in the Johannesburg Station concourse" (Fugard 1978: 84). The man was John Harris, whose bomb killed a child and maimed an old woman in 1964 (see Kruger 2012c).

3 For Ntshinga's role and the history of Brecht in South Africa, see Kruger (2004: 215–80).

4 *Antigone*'s dramatization of resistance to tyranny has inspired many performances from TECON's version of Anouilh's in *Antigone '71* to Simon's adaptation of Sophocles' in 1974. Peter Se-Puma's 1988 adaptation *Igazi Lam* [my blood] placed the tragedy in a hypothetical post-civil war country.

5 *The Island* was paired with *Sizwe Banzi* in London, New York, Australia, and West Germany but revived alone in Paris, Dublin, East Berlin, Washington, and other US cities (Read 1991: 91–117). Although the play was printed as *Sizwe Bansi*, Xhosa and Zulu dictionaries have only *banzi* [broad; by extension strong].

6 This program (Fugard Collection, National English Literary Museum) vacates Kani's claim that the play was "devised by Serpent Players, assisted by Athol Fugard" (Vandenbroucke 1986: 158).

7 Feingold, "Son of Stephin Fetchit and a Vigorous Bolshevik," *New York Village Voice*, May 5, 1975, 98.

8 For the first reaction, see Jean Marquard, "Sizwe Bansi is Alive and Well," *To the Point*, December 23, 1972; for the second, Sepamla (1973: 24).

9 As of 2018, Dike was director of the Siyasanga company, affiliated with Artscape, Cape Town, which produced *The Return* and partly sponsored its tour to the Black Theatre Festival in Winston-Salem NC.

10 Amato directed Imita Players in East London in adaptations of *Oedipus* (1971) and Molière's *Miser* (1975), among other plays. At the People's Space, he produced South African premieres of Sam Shephard's *Cowboy Mouth* and David Hare's *Fanshen* as well Barnard's *Lafras Verwey* (Chapter 4).

11 Roy Christie's positive "note of anticipation" in the *Johannesburg Star* (August 12, 1976) vacates Kavanagh's generalization about a uniformly hostile white press.

12 Jerry Mofokeng revived the play in New York in 1990 with the same actors Fana Kekana, Dan Selaelo Maredi, Themba Ntinga, and Seth Sibanda, who had been living in US exile. Although not capitalized in *Survival*, by 1990 the "Struggle" had become something of a commodity especially but not only for overseas audiences (Kruger 1991), hence the use of capital S at relevant moments in this chapter.

13 Comments on productions are based on personal observation since 1976 and cited sources; for the Market's history, see Schwartz (1988), Fuchs (2002), and: http://markettheatre.co.za/publications/.

14 Anglo-American and other corporate sponsors profited from the exploitation of black workers but funded non-profits such as the Urban Foundation; individuals also donated money and labor to free the Market from government pressure. The inclusion of blacks such as Kani on the Management Committee from 1986 (Schwartz 1988: 278) was ambiguous: on the one hand, it expressed a liberal desire to open doors; on the other, it confirmed the structural discrimination that marginalized blacks until the 1990s.

15 Comments drawn from interviews with Simon in September and November 1994.

16 The heroic depiction of miners in post-apartheid museums cannot hide the fact that mining claims hundreds of lives a year, especially if one includes deaths due to lung disease that many suffer without compensation; see Lucas Ledwaba (2016).

17 Critics at the Space (*Cape Times*, August 7, 1979) and the Market (*Star*, December 27, 1979 and *Rand Daily Mail*, December 28, 1979) praised its intensity. Ledwaba went on to contribute to the workshopped play *Black Dog* (Market 1987) and create his own *Township Boy* (1987) (Kros/Cooke 2018).

18 "The Rediscovery of the Ordinary" (1986) is cited here from Ndebele's essay collection (1994).

19 Selaneng Kgomongwe (1979) voiced the preferences of many black spectators for song rather than the body techniques used by Ledwaba to portray John's collapse. Ledwaba complained that "these audiences do not know what theatre is about" because they wanted to see "girls' thighs," qutd: Makhaya, *City Post*, May 19, 1980.

20 Maponya suggested that "the oppressed prefer entertainment to redirection" due to "false consciousness" (*Star*, July 19, 1985, 14); in interview with me (April 1995), he recalled that some patrons demanded another performance on the spot to bring the evening to the expected two hours.

21 Duma Ndlovu, organizer of the tour to Lincoln Center, New York, claimed that Maponya had Biko in view (1986: 59), but Maponya said in interview (April 1995) that the black hood was intended instead to acknowledge unsung activists. For Biko's life and death, see Mangcu (2014).

22 The double bill was praised by black and white critics; see Kaizer Ngwenya, "Maponya's Sparkler," *Sowetan*, July 17, 1984, and Beatrice Hollyer, "Two Plays to Savour," *Star* July 12, 1984.

23 *Woza Albert!* opened in October 1981 and was published in 1983 for the London tour. *Mama and the Load* was the first play by Kente to receive attention from the non-black press.

24 Makhaya noted the influence of Kente and the use of comedy to "present explosive political material in a compassionate and humorous way," *Sowetan*, March 3, 1981.

25 The two white activists were added in the overseas tour (Benson 1997: 120). The first was killed by a South African letter bomb while working for the ANC in exile. For Fischer, see Chapter 2, n. 4.

26 I cite the post-production script (Simon et al. 1986), except where the performance corresponds to the posthumous edition by Schwartz (1997). Although rougher, the earlier text provides more translations of Afrikaans, Zulu, and local English idiom in the dialogue.

27 Mhlophe's responses to my questions on cassette, January 1995. Tom Leshoai, "Born in the RSA–United by Boerehaat," *Sowetan*, September 30, 1985, was skeptical of white contributions, even though progressive whites in the UDF had been harassed by the police, but he acknowledged the play's critique of state violence and its effects on peaceable individuals.

28 Ntshinga's work at the Space exposed her to plays of different genres, from Dike's history play *The Sacrifice of Kreli* to the revival of Fugard's 1959 melodrama *Nongogo*.

29 The literal translation "grinding stone" highlights women's work and captures their power to crush foes; the cast—Thobeka Maqutyana, Nomvula Qosha, and Poppy Tsira—created the play with Phyllis Klotz at the Community Arts Project, Cape Town; published in *More Market Plays* (Vusisizwe Players 1996).

30 Mhlophe, who played Zandile, director Maralin Vanrenen and co-star Thembi Mtshali (-Jones) were co-authors. In 1991 Mhlophe founded Zanendaba [Tell me a story], noting on tape (January 1995) that political pressure on playwrights was partly responsible for her shift to storytelling. From 2001, she was also involved in rural literacy. For Mhlophe's praises of women at the TRC, see Kruger (2004: 372–74).

31 Despite the legend of MHS (Glaser 2015), the rebellion began with junior high students who were directly affected by the imposition of Afrikaans, rather than high school students, who were provisionally exempt; see former activist, now historian Sifiso Ndlovu (2006).

32 I saw one such lip-synching show at the Market Lab in November 1994. At Mohlakeng High School, 40 km west of Johannesburg, which I visited a week later with Lab facilitators Mncedi Dayi and Phumudzo Nephawe, teachers and students expressed the hope that visiting Americans would launch them in "another *Sarafina*," and seemed unaware of the abuse charges that dogged Ngema on tour. For this problem, see Erika Munk, "Cultural Difference and the Double Standard," *Village Voice*, June 21, 1988.

33 AIDS theatre expert Emma Durden estimates that *Sarafina II* was seen by five thousand (2011: 16) rather than the eight million touted by Ngema but she repeats his claim that it toured widely. Bacqa's report mentions only Durban Playhouse, which Ngema controlled, and the Eyethu Cinema in Soweto (1997: 11).

34 *The Hill* appeared at the Peoples' Space, the Market, and township venues in 1980. It was revived at the Windybrow (1995) and by James Ngcobo (now Market artistic director) with a student cast at Wits in 2007.

35 Faniswa Yisa is a principal member of Magnet Theatre in Cape Town (see Chapter 8).

36 On the Soyikwa revival, see "Brave Look at the Darker Side of Independence," *New Nation,* April 5–11, 1979, and Victor Metsoamere, "Soyikwa Students Excel," *Sowetan,* April 5, 1979. For the Space, "Mda's latest offering fills up the Space," *The Voice* 1, 44 (October 28, 1979).

37 *We Shall Sing for the Fatherland and other Plays* was banned in South Africa in 1981 and available only when the expanded edition appeared (Mda 1990).

38 On Mugabe's manipulation of veteran politics, see Mlambo (2014). On the ANC's shift from reconstruction and development to accommodating elites and enforcing austerity on the majority, see Bundy's aptly titled *Short-Changed?* (2014).

39 Coplan (1994) noted that most Basotho men worked in South Africa at some point, many leaving their families to survive on NGO support or on informal labor from crafts to sex-work.

Chapter 7

1 *Hijab* refers not only to a headscarf but also to the prescription that women and girls should shield themselves from the male gaze (Göle 1997: 62). *Purdah* was inspired by the case of Amina Begun, a 13-year-old Indian girl sold as a bride to a 56-year-

old Saudi, sponsored by the Islamic Students Association, and premiered at Wits University Orientation (1993). Mahomed wrote other vivid solo pieces about women caught between black and white e.g. *Cheaper than Roses* (1999b), and as director of the Grahamstown Festival (2008–16) curated clusters of productions on the agency of women (2016) and on the diversity of Muslim life in South Africa (2014) (Kruger 2015a).

2 Mtshali worked with Bachaki ("visitors") Theatre (1988–98) from its first play *Top Down* (1988) (Bachaki Theatre 1989), which exposed the corruption of principals and teachers in the Bantu Education system.

3 Kerr (1995: 137) reads African audiences' laughter at violence as self-protective rather than derisive. The active response to *Weemen* did not reflect naiveté; the same women who offered advice to the protagonist had critically discussed other plays before the show. Their reactions expressed praise for the actors' skill and a keen appreciation of the social conflicts on stage and off.

4 Critics of physical theatre favor the Buckland family who dominate the scene from their base in Grahamstown. Robyn Sassen mentions Theatre for Africa only twice (2015: 81, 91), despite his popular shows such as the *Raiders of the Lost Aardvark* series on the festival circuit, the publication of *Horn of Sorrow* (1999), international tours, and his lifetime achievement award in 2014. Ellenbogen hails from Bulawayo, Zimbabwe not Durban; he studied at UCT and began working with Durban-based actors such as Mkhwane while directing at NAPAC in the 1980s.

5 The diversity mandated by the IBA has diminished since 2000 (Matisonn 2015) but the Constitution and the RGA support freedom of expression against state overreach, if unevenly acknowledged (Duncan 2016).

6 Chapter 9 describes "State Institutions Supporting Constitutional Democracy" (Constitution 1996: 103). I cite the paginated print copy but the Constitution can be found at: http://www.gov.za/DOCUMENTS/CONSTITUTION/constitution-republic-south-africa-1996-1.

7 For the 1990s, see Van Graan's editorials in the PANSA organ *The Cultural Worker*; for current comment: https://mikevangraan.wordpress.com/.

8 White complaints underestimated the impact of apartheid—social exclusion, economic discrimination, and stunted schooling—on the culture of crime (Altbeker 2007), while blacks, who had been victimized by local tsotsis for decades, often blamed supposedly blacker foreigners, a disturbing trend toward "negrophobia," as Pumla Gqola (2008) calls black South African hostility to African migrants.

9 Despite research—Pickard-Cambridge (1989), Morris (1999), Segatti/Landau (2011), and the African Centre for Migration and Society, http://www.migration.org.za/ — many South Africans seem unaware that people of color began to return to the inner city in the 1970s, barely two decades after the Group Areas Act.

10 Black South Africans shared these anecdotes at inner-city bus stops in the 1990s in English with me and in more colorful Zulu with others in the queue. Although debunked by Morris (1999), similar anecdotes have reappeared in film, television, and prose fiction (see Kruger 2009, 2013).

11 The structure of feeling "is as firm and definite as 'structure' implies, yet operates in the most delicate parts of our activity" (Williams 1979: 106). The term highlights the intimate operation of norms that enforce gender as well as racial hierarchies; as Sachs has noted, "one of the few non-racial institutions in South Africa is patriarchy" (1990b: 53).

12   As Nancy Fraser notes, "the theoretical separation of intimate and public spheres
      is predicated on the conventional assumption of their separation in fact" (1989:
      114). This assumption rests on a mystification of the intimate sphere as a pre-social
      "life-world," which obscures the ways in which institutional or habitual boundaries
      around intimacy retard women's attempts to change their public roles.

13   The text renders *eshaywa y lanje yendoda* as "beaten by that dog of a husband"
      (139). Whereas "dog" may be apt for Rolene's husband, it may over-translate "lanje
      yendoda" [that man, or possibly "that jerk of a man" in the double demonstrative
      "lanje ye-"] by reading "lanje" [that kind of] as "le inja" or "that dog."

14   Pam-Grant directed the revival at the Theatre on the Square in Sandton, the suburb
      that owes its affluence to capital flight from the Johannesburg CBD. She attempted to
      update the play by casting brown Quanita Adams as Rolene, amusing suburbanites
      with Robert Colman's drag version of Mrs. Dubois, and targeting younger black
      women with Lesedi Job-Smith's singing Dudu, but this version—like the neo-Tuscan
      pastiche of the surrounding mall—had lost its link to the urban fabric.

15   Charl Blignault dismissed *Fordsburg* alongside Fugard's sentimental *Playland* as
      "reconciliation theatre" *M&G* February 13, 1998; http://mg.co.za/article/1998-02-13-
      the-drinking-mans-hero. But, whereas *Playland* ends as the black nightwatchman and
      the white army officer "walk off together" (Fugard 1993b: 47), *Fordsburg* ends with a
      realistic truce honed by Foot's direction of Johnson's challenge to Weyers; seasoned
      critic Robert Greig noted this nuance in "Slabolepszy makes a bold move," *Johannesburg
      Sunday Independent,* February 15, 1998. For Slabolepszy's career, see Sichel (2015).

16   Lucille Davie introduced the phrase "*sawubona* culture" in "Making Hillbrow a
      neighbourhood," Johannesburg Development Agency; www.jda.org.za/2008/10mar_
      hlb.stm; site is no longer active. For the fusion of greeting and acknowledgment in
      sawubona—hello in Zulu but literally "still seeing you"—see Kruger (2013: 194–236),
      and for urban renewal by planners, activists, and artists, Harrison et al. (2014).

17   Andersson (2015: 253) attributes "township Tarantino" to Jos Shuring, who reviewed
      the premiere of *Foreplay* in Amsterdam. Rolf Hemke (2010: 166) repeats Grootboom's
      claim that his generation is inured to violence but asserts that Grootboom "likes
      Tarantino too much to be compared to him" (167).

18   Grootboom's program note: *Foreplay* (Market Theatre, 2009), 2. I focus on the Market
      production, which was crisper than the published play (Grootboom 2009b) but quote
      that text where relevant.

19   Mbeki ignored Mandela's appeal for biomedical treatment of HIV, even after Mandela
      disclosed that his own son Makgatho died of AIDS, and exacerbated the pandemic
      when he refused to release available funds and drugs to prevent mother-to-child
      transmission until compelled by the Constitutional Court in 2002; see: http://www.
      tac.org.za/ and Hoad (2007: 90–112).

20   Other black women–Pamela Bambalele, "Grootboom back with a brave new play,"
      Sowetan, February 10, 2009, and Kgomotso Moncho, "A daring reflection of our
      sexual selves," *Pretoria News* March 24—also praised Grootboom for portraying
      sexual conduct without moralizing.

21   Purkey and Carol Steinberg were the principal writers (2000: v) but all of JATC's
      work was created in workshops with actors and others.

22   Only Bailey's *Big Dada: The Rise and Fall of Idi Amin* (2001) landed at the Market, in
      2005 after two runs in Cape Town and tours to Brussels, Vienna and Berlin; see Purkey
      (2013) and Third World Bunfight's archive: http://thirdworldbunfight.co.za/big-dada/.

23   Ff. indicates the starting dates of tours lasting for several years. For Handspring's
     collaborations with Kentridge and with other partners, such as the National Theatre
     in London on *War Horse*, and their training of South Africans in puppetry and other
     skills, see: http://www.handspringpuppet.co.za/.
24   On animating puppets through the puppeteer's breath, see Jones (2009).
25   The TRC began hearings in 1996 and concluded deliberations in 2001 after an
     extension for those applying for amnesty. HRV hearings were led by seventeen
     commissioners from diverse ethnic groups, political positions, and professions,
     including clergy, therapists, and lawyers, in that order. Commentary on the TRC's
     successes, documenting human rights violations and giving survivors a public
     forum for relating their experiences and confronting their tormenters, and on its
     controversial outcomes—the abandonment of reparations, the uneven response to
     trauma, and the question of amnesty—is too vast to cite here. For bibliography, see
     Kruger (2004, 2011), Cole (2010), and Hutchison (2013).
26   For the performance of perpetrators at the TRC, see Kruger (2004: 334–64), for *Molora*,
     Kruger (2012c), and for TRC plays by Kani and others, Hutchison (2013: 54–90).
27   For instance, Bongani Linda's company, with the militantly anti-apartheid name of
     Victory-Sonqoba Theatre, proved unable—in the absence of therapy—to support
     retraumatized survivors (Marlin-Curiel 2002: 282–5); for Linda's Brechtian training,
     see Kruger (2004: 342–3).
28   *TRC Final Report*, vol. 1, chapter 5; http://www.justice.gov.za/Trc/report/index.htm.
29   The CSVR was by the mid-1990s researching a range of areas from police brutality to
     the escalating rape rate, as well as providing therapy for TRC witnesses and others;
     see: http://www.csvr.org.za/.
30   I follow the spelling of Khumalo's name from his TRC testimony–http://www.justice.
     gov.za/trc/hrvtrans/sebokeng/seb861.htm–rather than Farber's posthumous Kumalo.
     The latter spelling has become more common but it drops the helpful distinction
     between plosive "kh" and implosive "k": the plosive is correct for Khumalo.
31   Comments draw on *The Story I Am About To Tell*, Grahamstown, July 1999,
     the report by Khulumani founder and torture survivor Shirley Gunn on Radio
     Netherlands, rebroadcast on WBEZ-Chicago, 91.5FM, April 29, 2001, and Marlin-
     Curiel (2002). For Shezi's testimony at the special hearings for women, see Kruger
     (2004: 372–75) and http://www.justice.gov.za/trc/special/women/shezi.htm.
32   *Theatre of Witness* also includes *Women in Waiting*, based on the life of Thembi Mtshali-
     Jones whose performance career began in the 1970s (Chapters 5 and 6). The cover states
     that the plays were "created with and based on the lives of the casts" but, while cast
     members are named, the copyright warning has Farber only; Khumalo died two years
     before publication (Farber 2008: 2). As for funding, Farber mentions a commission from
     Haus der Kultur [*sic*] and a "season at the State Theatre" (182) but not the latter's—and
     her play's–sponsor Spoornet (South African Rail); see Adrienne Sichel's interview on the
     Khulumani site, August 26, 2002, accessed August 17, 2018, http://www.khulumani.net/
     khulumani/in-the-news/item/150-hes-out-of-prison-but-dumas-still-not-free.html.
33   The song in its Nguni forms—as distinct from Anglo-Boer versions in Afrikaans
     and English—dates to the Women's March on Pretoria in 1956 but anti-apartheid
     marchers popularized it in the 1970s. Post-apartheid versions include an upbeat
     disco number by Innocent Modiba for Justin Chadwick's biopic *Mandela* (2013) and
     a more militant one by Peter Keetse and the EFF celebrating election success in 2016.
34   Leora Morris's revival of the play with a local cast at Toronto Summer Fest (2014)
     prompted writer Daniel Karasik to argue that, absent Khumalo and his South African

interlocutors, audience participation—e.g. sorting shoes piled up on stage—recycled a "generalized liberal gesture" of concern for "global atrocity" without penetrating the distinct histories behind these objects. Karasik removed his post to "repair" his connection to colleagues in Toronto (email to LK; June 29, 2018), but his concerns resonate with Salverson's critique of the "erotics of injury."

35 Cole's account of the cantata (2010: 135–62) is the best to date albeit marred by some historical errors. She identifies the Day of Reconciliation as a "new holiday" (154), missing the post-apartheid reclamation of December 16, the date that used to commemorate the Afrikaner victory over the Zulus, copies a common mistranslation of *Lizalis' idinga lakho*, and mistakenly attributes the *19th century* origin of hymns by African Christians, educated in part by British and American missionaries in the British Cape Colony (1806–1910), to the eighteenth century Dutch VOC outpost (152), which had no secondary schools—not even for whites.

36 Comments based on the Market staging (2008) and Key's film (2009), which includes interviews with Miller and TRC witnesses, clips from the hearings and the cantata, and archival footage of related events.

37 For Miya's testimony at Pollsmoor, the mainland prison that housed Mandela after he was moved from Robben Island in 1982, see: http://www.justice.gov.za/trc/hrvtrans/polls/ct00818.htm.

38 For Calata's testimony, see: http://www.justice.gov.za/trc/hrvtrans/hrvel1/calata.htm.

39 "REturning REwind is a REvelation," *Cape Argus*, April 26, 2011; http://www.iol.co.za/tonight/music/returning-rewind-is-a-revelation-1061322.

40 In an interview with Kwanele Sosibo, *M&G* May 12, 2017, Neo Muyanga, composer for Magnet Theatre, affirmed the central role of song in drama as well as in sacred and secular music, and thus the many transnational and local currents shaping South African performing arts; see https://mg.co.za/article/2017-05-12-00-muyanga-settles-old-scores-on-a-visible-stage.

Chapter 8

1 For #RememberKhwezi, see introduction. My echo of "The Function of Criticism at the Present Time" (1867) by critic and avowed imperialist Matthew Arnold (Arnold 1880) may prompt uproar but Prof. Es'kia Mphahlele (1919–2008), in his lecture at historically black Fort Hare University on the "function of South African literature at the present time" (2002 [1996]: 407), argued that the times required us to grapple with the whole history of South African writing, not just texts that fit current politics.

2 Although misidentified as the area's "newest" township (Lewis/Krueger 2016: 9), Khayelitsha's formal core of brick houses dates from 1983 in the apartheid era but has since accrued informal settlements housing half a million people. In Johannesburg, outgoing Market director Purkey praised "new and challenging work" that appeared there over his nine-year tenure (2013). This included plays by Van Graan and Craig Higginson, adaptations of anti-apartheid prose by James Ngcobo, and *Itsoseng* whose author Molusi trained at the Market Lab—although his play premiered in Mmabatho, North West in 2008. Most shows were classics by Fugard and others, visitors from Cape Town (Foot and Bailey), Pretoria (Grootboom), or Durban (Neil Coppen). Under Ngcobo's direction (2014–), the main stage hosts mostly music and dance while the small spaces have housed some new work among local classics such

as *Woza Albert!* and revivals of African-American plays such as Hansberry's *A Raisin in the Sun* and George C. Wolfe's *The Colored Museum.*

3   See http://www.unaids.org/en/regionscountries/countries/southafrica/ and, for the history of epidemics in South Africa, Phillips (2012). South Africa has the largest treatment program in the world but infection remains high, especially in KwaZulu-Natal (KZN). More than 50 percent of the newly infected countrywide are women, who are more vulnerable than men, due in part to sexual violence but more broadly to norms that reinforce masculine entitlement. Prevalence rates are therefore derived from records of women seeking prenatal care rather than the smaller group seeking HIV tests.

4   Hospital staff comments in *Health Education Tour* 1974–75 (Simon collection, NELM). In interviews with me, Dr. Evian (September 1994); Dr. Helen Schneider and R.N. Shirley Ngwenya (Wits Rural Facility November 1994)—noted that black nurses schooled in biomedicine were suspicious of African traditional remedies and often disdainful of patients. Health policy consultant Jane Doherty confirmed (March 2016) that this behavior is still endemic. See Graver (1999: 8).

5   https://www.devex.com/organizations/dramaide-10549.

6   https://www.dramaforlife.co.za/academic-1.

7   Expanding the Public Protector's *State of Capture Report* (Madonsela 2016), *Betrayal of the Promise* distinguished between corrupt individuals dispensing favors to patrons and the systematic "repurpos[ing of] state institutions to suit a constellation of rent-seeking networks," creating a "symbiotic relationship between the constitutional and the shadow state" (Bhorat et al. 2017: 2). As of 2018, President Ramaphosa had not undone the networks that permit rent-seeking nor repaired the damage to government, even if he has dismissed some cabinet ministers and reshuffled others.

8   Directed by Clare Stopford, the full two-act version (2005) was the first production under Purkey's tenure at the Market (Van Graan 2010: 11).

9   As Ellen in Van Graan's *Rainbow Scars* (Market 2013), Steyn played the adoptive mother of Lindiwe, daughter of her late domestic worker, who struggles to raise teenager Lindi and confront the demands of Lindi's brother Sicelo whose township life has been far harsher than his sister's suburban one. The title alludes to the once bright but now faded "rainbow nation."

10 In addition to Marinovich, whose book *Murder at Small Koppie* provides the best account of Lonmin's history of reckless investments and indifference to labor, my sources include interviews with miners' families in the Eastern Cape and Lesotho by Jika, Ledwaba et al. (2013), and in North West Province by Peter Alexander, Thapela Lekgowa et al. (2013); the film by Desai, who has been documenting miners since the 1980s; the Farlam Commission transcripts, accessed March 3, 2016, at http://www.marikanacomm.org.za/documents.html but no longer online; the Farlam report, available at: https://www.sahrc.org.za/home/21/files/marikana-report-1.pdf and SERI's representation of survivors trying to correct the facts and to compel Lonmin to meet social housing and compensation obligations– http://www.marikana-conference.com/–.

11 The full toll of forty-four included ten killed days before Lonmin called in the troops: a security guard, two policemen, and strikers apparently shot from the local NUM office, as well as the thirty-four killed by special forces on August 16. For state abuse of "murder by common purpose," see Parker (1996) and the *Khumalo* case (Chapter 7). For the militarization of the "people's police," and constraints on protest despite the constitutional right, see Jane Duncan (2014, 2016).

12   Ramaphosa's evasion of the conflict of interest between the role of ANC deputy
      president and that of Lonmin director provoked outrage after he gave the Moses
      Kotane lecture (after the late unionist) at Rustenburg near Marikana; Vuyolwethu Toli,
      Daily Maverick, June 13, 2017; https://www.dailymaverick.co.za/opinionista/2017-
      06-13-marikana-unmasking-ramaphosas-rhetoric-narrow-apology-and-lies/. For
      critical background to Ramaphosa, see Marinovich (2018: 133–49), and for EFF MP
      Nokulunga Primrose Sonti (235–42); for Sikhala Sonke and women's pursuit of jobs at
      Marikana, see Toli and the documentary film *Strike a Rock* (Saragas 2017).

13   Official unemployment in mid-2018 stood at 27 percent; see *Statistics South Africa
      Quarterly Labour Force Survey*, http://www.statssa.gov.za/publications/P0211/
      P02112ndQuarter2018.pdf. The State Theatre as a "national cultural institution" is
      expected to generate a minimum of 40 percent of production costs "through box
      office, sponsorship and other income generating activities" (DAC 2017: 15), implying
      that it enjoys a 60 percent outright subsidy inherited from the defunct PACT, despite
      the misuse of funds that forced the DAC to close the theatre in 2000–01 (Van Graan/
      Ballantyne 2003: 19, 27). Sekhabi acknowledged that his house received more state
      funds than the Market (2015: 341) but neither he nor interviewer Greg Homann
      mentioned the scandal.

14   Sindo worked with Shack Theatre in Khayelitsha from 2007 and with Zabalaza
      from 2012 (Morris 2017: 153), but De Smet and colleagues appeared too intent on
      finding affinities between African performance and European post-dramatic theatre,
      "destabilizing" supposedly "dominant" text-based theatre (2015: 231) to seek a proper
      translation of this question or of *Vuka Mntomnyama*, which they render as "wake up
      black man" (230) despite the gender-neutral *umntu* [Xhosa: person]. Sindo's YouTube
      video of *MARI+KANA* had Xhosa narration and songs but no subtitles; https://www.
      youtube.com/watch?v=VjrgAIYqu-Q; accessed September 20, 2017.

15   Comments based on the 2014 performance and the script supplied by Moleba. The
      play has not been published but Moleba's Wits MA thesis on Marikana youth focuses
      like the play on "ordinary narratives" in an "extraordinary place" (2016: iii).

16   This 1946 poem begins, in the usual free translation: "First they came for the
      communists but I did not speak out for I was not a communist" and ends: "And
      then they came for me but there was no-one left to speak for me." For the German
      original, see: http://martin-niemoeller-stiftung.de/martin-niemoeller/als-sie-die-
      kommunisten-holten.

17   Unlike Artscape, which inherited CAPAB's national subsidy for 70 percent of its
      income and its mixed program of comedy, ballet and ice spectacles with occasional
      new work by Van Graan and others, the Baxter receives no NAC funding and
      generates 77 percent of its income with supplementary support from UCT. In
      keeping with the national DAC's view of art as a means of generating "sustainable
      employment," the Western Cape Dept. of Culture and Sport partly funds Zabalaza's
      skills-building projects but not the theatre art of the main house, which relies on
      box office and revenue from overseas tours of work by Foot, Farber, and others; for
      budget data, see Morris (2017: 148–51).

18   Lucy Graham faults Foot for replicating allegorical thinking treating "baby rape"
      as emblematic of violence defiling the new nation, and the children's treatment
      as "sacrificial victims and vehicles for audience catharsis" (112) but concedes that
      Tshepang was more restrained than media reports. For the child behind the *Tshepang*
      case, the life of her mother, who was also a rape survivor, and of similar women and
      children, see Gqola (2015: 65–72).

19   Citations of the Wits UP edition include author's and designer's notes.
20   Comments refer to the published play (2009) and the Baxter revival in 2016 with the original cast. For other plays by Foot not discussed here, see Kruger (2015b).
21   Comments refer to the published play and the Playhouse production on tour at the Market (2012). Coppen is not the first to explore the drama of ancestors enmeshing the living in conflicts between modern and inherited custom. *Born through the Nose* (2005) by Greig Coetzee and Bheki Mkhwane portrays a black businessman whose son refuses to be born until his father makes time to consult the ancestors; it featured Mkhwane in a more restrained performance than his manic comedy in *Boy Called Rubbish* (1994; Chapter 7), enacting a more sober script than Coetzee's famous anti-draft satire *White Men with Weapons* (Coetzee 2009 [1994] and Kruger 2006, 2012b).
22   Comments refer to the published play and the 2014 Grahamstown revival. For Rhodes's sexual conduct, see Buwalda's comments and sources (2014: 11–12).
23   Nkala whose middle name Khumbulani means "remember!" is said to have died of cancer (Nkala 2014: 5) but his age at death—34—raises questions. Fleishman dedicates *Performing Migrancy* to his memory (2015: x) and the article on Nkala (Ravengai 2015) in this volume illuminates his work.
24   Rev. Michael Weeder, who lived in the district until evicted with his parents by the state in the 1960s, notes (2004) that the archeologists' report showed that paupers of European, Asian, and African descent were interred at Prestwich Place well after emancipation. Despite the report, a "hastily formed Hands off Prestwich Place Committee" (Fleishman 2011: 9) claiming to speak for the descendants of the enslaved resisted any excavation.
25   The literature on slavery at the Cape is too vast to cover here. Research by Shell, Mountain, and February is most relevant to *Cargo,* but Worden and Crais (1994) usefully compare Cape slavery under the VOC (to 1795) and the British (1806–38), with the United States. Whereas the Cape had 40,000 enslaved people at its peak around 1770 as against four million in the USA around 1850, the Cape number represented more than half the total population against 14 percent of the USA. Even if larger Cape wine farms had less than 100 enslaved workers each, a fraction of the large plantations in South Carolina, the fact that most Cape households had at least one enslaved person helped to create a society psychologically as well as economically dependent on slavery (Shell: 1–39).
26   Unattributed quotations are from *Cargo* (DVD recorded at the Baxter Theatre, August 2007).
27   Both Dutch and Afrikaans use the verb *grawe* [dig] and in Afrikaans *graaf* [spade] resembles *graf* [grave]. This similarity between spade and grave may have inspired this scene as Reznek suggests on the DVD but has no etymological basis; the Dutch word for "spade" used in the slavery era and still today is *schop*; Instituut voor de Nederlandse Taal: http://gtb.inl.nl/search/#.
28   It is perhaps ironic that the Slavery Abolition Act is easier to access from the Irish Statute Book than the British– http://www.irishstatutebook.ie/eli/1833/act/73/enacted/en/html, here p.1.
29   The anthropological term KhoeSan (or KhoiSan) covers both Khoe herders who were the first people to encounter Europeans at the Cape in the seventeenth century and the hunter-gatherer-cave-painters that the Khoe called San, whom Dutch colonists called Bushmen. Since San allegedly means "tramp" in Khoe languages, Bushman is still used by people who speak !Kung or Nama or those who identify as descendants even if they speak only Afrikaans or English.

Abbreviations, Glossary, and Linguistic Conventions

In keeping with standard sociolinguistics (Mesthrie 2002a), this book refers to other languages (e.g., Zulu) without importing prefixes (e.g., isiZulu) into English except when the distinction between language (isiZulu) and people (amaZulu) requires explanation. It lists Nguni words in standard dictionary format with the root followed by prefix, thus: Zulu (Nguni: isi) but alerts readers to discrepancies between dictionary form and common usage. The glossary also includes English words that have taken on meanings peculiar to South Africa. For the meanings of African names, see Kalumba (2012).

AAC: All-African Convention: internationalist but short-lived rival of the ANC in the 1930s

Africans: Historically, speakers of Bantu languages; more recently claimed by other South Africans

Afrikaans: derived from Dutch with elements of Malay-Portuguese, the lingua franca of enslaved people brought to the Cape from the Indies, and local *Khoe* languages (Roberge 2002). Currently native language of about 15 percent of South Africans and second language for more

Afrikaners: Historically denoted white speakers of Dutch and later Afrikaans but, since Afrikaner means "African," Afrikaner ideology effectively deprived blacks of African identity; see also *Boer*

Afrikaner National Party (a.k.a. NP or Nats): ruling 1948–94; by 2000, remnants split between Democratic Alliance (DA), and white separatist factions such as the Freedom Front

ANC: African National Congress (1912–) suppressed 1960–90; ruling since 1994

Anglo-Boer War: 1899–1902; a.k.a. the South African War, as brown and black people served as auxiliaries, on both sides. For Afrikaners, the second such war, which they lost, as opposed to the first (1880–81), which they won, compelling the British to recognize the South African [Transvaal] Republic

ANT: African National Theatre (1936–41)

Apartheid: (apart-ness): Afrikaner Nationalist policy 1948–90. Distinguished from earlier segregation by systematic deportation of black and brown people from desirable land, racial classification of the entire population, and racial discrimination in education, housing, and public services of all kinds

ATKV: *Afrikaner Taal- en Kultuurvereniging* (Afrikaans Language and Cultural Union; Cape Town 1930–)

baas (Afrikaans): boss (favored by Afrikaner employers under apartheid)

banning order: apartheid directive confining dissidents to a single magisterial district or house arrest and restricting their right to work, public appearances, writing or quotation by others, and sometimes also talking to more than one person at a time

Bantu (Nguni:-*aba-ntu*) people: used by apartheid state for segregated institutions such as Bantu Education

Bantustans: ethnically marked "independent" enclaves created by apartheid state (1970s–1980s)

BCM: Black Consciousness Movement, most active 1969–90; today linked to Stephen Biko's legacy

BDS: Bantu Dramatic Society, informal theatre company in Johannesburg in 1930s, staging mostly English drawing room comedy, only rarely local plays

BEE: Black Economic Empowerment (1999–). ANC program requiring companies to sell 25 percent of their shares to black shareholders, in theory to workers and/ or community representatives but in practice enriching a small number of well-placed black executives

BPT: Bantu Peoples Theatre (1936–41), more experimental group, staging American and local political plays

Black: Lowercase *black* usually refers to Africans. Capitalized, *Black* was claimed by BCM to represent all people demeaned by the official labels "non-white" or "non-European," including those South Africans classified *Coloured* or *Indian*

BMSC: Bantu Men's Social Centre: performance venue in central Johannesburg (1924–1960)

Boer: (Afrikaans) farmer, by extension whites descended from Dutch, German, French settlers; see *Afrikaner*

bongelo (Nguni pl.: *izi-*) H.I.E. Dhlomo's neologism: performances for audiences, i.e. theatre

bongi (Nguni: *im-*); plural *izimbongi*: praise poet(s)

bongo (Nguni: *isi-*) clan name; plural: *izibongo*: praises or praise songs

Bophuthatswana: Bantustan (1977–94) whose "independence" was belied by multiple territorial fragments and the South African-owned casino complex Sun City; after 1994 absorbed into North West province

BPC: Black Peoples Convention (1969–77); convention of black community organizations supported in part by SASO and SPRO-CAS until these organizations were shut down by the apartheid government; see also SASO and SPRO-CAS

Bushmen: contested term for hunter-gatherers who were Southern Africa's first peoples; see *KhoeSan*

BW: Bantu World (later *World*): Johannesburg newspaper targeting black readers

Bywoners (Afrikaans): land tenants; "poor whites"

CAPAB: Cape Performing Arts Board (1962–96)

Cape: 1652–1795: *Cabo de Goede Hoop*: VOC-run settlement of Dutch, German, and French burghers and slaves from Asia, Africa, and islands between; 1806–1910: British Cape Colony; 1910–94: one of four provinces in the Union and Republic; 1994: divided after the democratic elections into Western, Eastern, and Northern Cape

cathamiya (Zulu: *isi-*): soft-shoe dance; performed by Zulu migrants in formal suits

CBOs: Community-based organizations, locally called "civics" (as against NGOs, non-governmental organizations funded and often managed by overseas entities)

Coloured: apartheid classification for brown as distinct from black people and thus not equal to US Colored

concert: 1920s ff., variety show including not only instrumental, choral and dance music but also dramatic sketches and comic gags; term still in use in black communities

coolie: derogatory British colonial label for indentured Indian workers and by extension Indians broadly

COSATU: Congress of South African Trade Unions (1985–); ANC-aligned

COSAW: Congress of South African Writers (1980–)

CPSA: Communist Party of South Africa (1919–50). After the CPSA was banned under the Suppression of Communism Act, the South African Communist Party (SACP) reconvened in exile; it returned under this name to local politics in 1990

CSVR: Centre for the Study of Violence and Reconciliation, independent NGO founded in 1989 to promote state accountability and collaboration with communities affected by violence

DA: Democratic Alliance, 1994. Absorbed liberal capitalist Progressive Party and United Party, former official opposition under apartheid; in 1996 it became the official opposition to the ANC

DAC: Department of Arts and Culture (1996—); subject to repeated reorganization, this department has been a sinecure for ministers sent down from "harder" departments

dagga (Khoe): cannabis

DOCC: Donaldson Orlando Community Centre: performance and community venue in Soweto

dominee (Afrikaans): pastor

EFF: Economic Freedom Front: populist breakaway party led by former ANC Youth leader Julius Malema; not to be confused with the white nationalist Freedom Front

Egoli (Nguni: *eGoli*): Place of Gold; Johannesburg

Eisteddfod: Welsh (later British) music festival

European: official designation from seventeenth to late twentieth centuries for whites in South Africa. Opposed to "non- Europeans" or "non-whites"

FAK: *Federasie vir Afrikaanse Kultuur*: Federation for Afrikaans Culture (Bloemfontein, 1929–)

fecane (Zulu-*um*-)/(Sotho: *di*): scattering or dispersal of clans by Zulu expansionism in the mid-nineteenth century including those now in present-day Zimbabwe and even Kenya. Often spelled *mfecane*

flaaitaal (a.k.a. *tsotsitaal*): possibly Cockney "fly" + Afrikaans "language"; Makhudu 2002: preferred name for the Africanized Afrikaans-based slang spoken by outlaws, *tsotsis*, and others in the townships

Fort Hare (1916–): Historically black university educating international as well as local Africans

FRELIMO: Front for the Liberation of Mozambique; 1960s–74: guerrilla movement against Portuguese colonialism; 1975 to the present: ruling party of Mozambique

FUBA: Federated Union of Black Artists (1970s–2000s)

ganekwane (Zulu: *izin-*): folktales

Gauteng (Sotho): place of gold; South Africa's richest province; includes Johannesburg and Pretoria

ghoema (Kaaps): barrel-shaped drum played during Cape Carnival

goma (Nguni: *in-*): music or dance; *izingoma* (pl.) drums

goma ebusuku (Nguni: *in-*): night (i.e. urban, commercial) music

Great Trek: 1835–38 migration of *Voortrekkers* to protest the emancipation of slaves and British colonial rule generally; centenary commemorated in 1938

HRV: Human Rights Violations Committee convened by the Truth and Reconciliation Commission to evaluate survivors' testimony

IBA: Independent Broadcasting Authority (1993–99); independent adjudicator of broadcasting in South Africa; replaced in 2003 by the Independent Communications Authority of South Africa (ICASA) run by the Ministry of Communication

Indians: in South Africa, "Indian" denotes South Asian descendants of those brought by the British between 1860 and 1899 as indentured sugarcane workers, usually Tamil or Telugu speakers, or of self-funded traders, usually Gujarati; this usage excludes the descendants of South Asians enslaved by the Dutch in the seventeenth and eighteenth centuries, who were classified under apartheid as Malay

Inkatha: founded in 1924 as a Zulu organization but dormant after 1940 until revived in 1975 by Mangosuthu Buthelezi to run the KwaZulu Bantustan. After 1994, as the Inkatha Freedom Party (IFP), briefly in the government of national unity

JATC: Junction Avenue Theatre Company (1976–99)

jikela (Nguni: *uku-*): to swing; urban dance music 1940s–1960s, by the Merry Blackbirds, Jazz Epistles, etc.

Jozi: nickname for Johannesburg; see *Egoli*

Kaaps: Cape dialect of Afrikaans, spoken mostly by brown people

kaffir (Arabic): *kafir*: infidel originally denoted all non-Muslims and therefore most whites, but used by white colonists to refer to blacks and remains an insulting term to the present

kappiekommando (Afrikaans): bonnet commando; women in Voortrekker costume at cultural events

KhoeSan: Khoekhoe (Khoi), herders, and San, hunter-gatherer-cave-painters; South Africa's first peoples

kwaya (Nguni: *ama-*): Anglo/American choir melodies adapted to the African Christian repertoire

Kwela: 1950s urban music often played on a penny-whistle

Kwerekwere: (Nguni: *ama-*): those who speak funny, used by black South Africans to denigrate black migrants

KZN: KwaZulu-Natal, today one of nine South African provinces created after the merger of Natal and the Bantustan of KwaZulu — formerly part of Natal province — in 1994

laager (Afrikaans): historically, the circle of wagons turned against hostile intruders; applied metaphorically to the isolationist mentality of Afrikaner Nationalists

Land Act (1913): Union parliamentary act that confined the black majority to only 13 percent of the land

Lenasia: Indian township established on the former Lenz army base beyond Soweto

Liberal: closer to British than to US usage. South African liberals such as Alan Paton describe themselves as defenders of individual liberty and the rule of law; leftists and African Nationalists criticize liberals as capitalist, individualist, or elitist rather than broad-minded, socially inclusive, or progressive

linganiso (Zulu: *um-*): living imitation, Credo Mutwa's neologism to translate theatre

lobola (Zulu: *i-*): bride-payment due from groom's to bride's male relatives

M&G: Mail &Guardian: Johannesburg weekly paper founded by journalists who published the anti-apartheid *Weekly Mail* after the *Rand Daily Mail* (*RDM*) was banned in the 1980s

marabi: urban dance music, 1920s–1950s; first recorded by Griffiths Motsieloa

mbaqanga: applied to different dance music styles from 1950s to 1970s, including disco variants

MDALI: (Nguni-*u-*): creator; Music, Drama and Language Institute (1970s–1980s)

mfecane: see *fecane*

MK: *umKhonto we Sizwe* (Nguni): spear of the nation; guerilla arm of the ANC (1961–93)

Moshoeshoe I (1786–1870): Basotho king famous for securing Lesotho independence by negotiating with the British against the Boers and for offering shelter to Nguni and others displaced by the *mfecane*

NAC: National Arts Council (1997—) funding arm of DAC; replaced the provincial Performing Arts Councils of the apartheid era

NAPAC: Natal Performing Arts Council (1962–96)

Native: under British colonial (1806–1910) and Union (1910–48) rule applied to institutions controlling Africans—e.g. Native Administration—as against all people born in a specific location. See *Bantu*

Nguni (*isi-*): Bantu language group including Ndebele and Swati (aka Swazi) as well as Xhosa and Zulu

NTO: National Theatre Organization (1946–62) bilingual and relatively liberal performing company

NUM: National Union of Mineworkers (1982–)

NUSAS: National Union of South African Students (1924–)

Orange Free State: former Boer Republic (1854–1902), and later province (1910–); now Free State (1994–)

PAC: Pan-African Congress (1961–); the ANC's main rival in the exile years; now a small party

PACOFS: Performing Arts Council of the Orange Free State (1962–96)

PACT: Performing Arts Council of the Transvaal (1962–96)

Pass: official "reference book" or ID; apartheid document regulating work and residence of black South Africans (but not those classified Coloured or Indian); unofficially: *dompas*: (Afrik. stupid pass)

PCB: Publication and Entertainment Control Board (1963–1993): official censor of sex, politics, and subversive language in literature, drama, film, and—from

1976—television; although the PCB was abolished in 1993, censorious tendencies have returned as some in government seek, despite constitutional protections, to repress speech by women, LGBTQI+, and political critics generally

PET: Peoples Educational Theatre (1973)

pitso (Sotho): assembly

Reef: historically, the gold seam (largely depleted) running parallel to the Witwatersrand; refers by extension to the settlements alongside the deposits, as in Main Reef Road

RGA: Regulation of Assembly Act (1993); legislation governing free speech and democratic assembly; replaced the apartheid-era Riotous Assemblies Act, which restricted and often banned free assembly

Rhodes University (1904–): founded in honor of mining magnate Cecil John Rhodes (1856–1902); since 1970s host of the Grahamstown (later National Arts) Festival

RSA: Republic of South Africa (est. 1961 when South Africa left the British Commonwealth)

SABC: South African Broadcasting Corporation (1920s–); state-run national broadcaster; see IBA

SABTU: South African Black Theatre Union (1971–73)

sangoma (Nguni: *i-*): diviner or healer

SACP: see CPSA

SASO: South African Students Organization (1969–77); Black breakaway from NUSAS

SERI: Social and Economic Rights Institute; independent NGO founded in 2009 to defend the social and economic as well as civil rights guaranteed to South Africans under the 1996 Constitution

Shaka (1781–1828): Zulu ruler of a substantial empire in South-Eastern Africa; blamed for the *mfecane*, murdered by his half-brother Dingane

Shebeen: under apartheid, an unlicensed township bar serving a range of drinks from traditional sorghum beer to cocktails made from dangerous solvents. In the post-apartheid era more often a licensed establishment trading on nostalgia for the old illicit gathering places

Situation: township nickname used to mock black intellectuals applying for white-collar "situations" published in newspapers rather than manual labor arranged at the pass office. See *pass*

skollie (Afrikaans): street-smart, devious, but obsequious scoundrel

Sotho (*Ba-*): dominant clan in the central Highveld and in Lesotho (Basutoland); *(Se)Sotho:* language

Soweto: South West Townships (1964–); absorbed older townships Orlando, Pimville, and Meadowlands

SPRO-CAS: Special Projects of Christian Action in Society; anti-apartheid CBO supported in part by the South African Council of Churches until its banning in 1977

suburb: in South Africa as in Britain, a subsection or district *in* a city, as opposed to US usage designating separate municipalities *outside* a major city *suiwer* (Afrikaans): pure; ideological cover masking Afrikaans origins in Dutch-Malay-Portuguese creoles

taal (Afrikaans): language

TECON: Theatre Council of Natal (1969–77)

thoko (Sotho: *li*): chronicle songs

township: apartheid-era black districts (e.g. Soweto); a.k.a. "location"; planned as distinct from informal settlements, although the latter often have settled cores and the former usually include shanty areas

Transkei: "independent" Bantustan (1976–94); after 1994, absorbed along with Ciskei into Eastern Cape

Transvaal: former province (1910–94), previously (Boer) South African Republic (1880–1902)

TRC: Truth and Reconciliation Commission (1996–2002); post-apartheid government commission mandated to investigate human rights violations during the apartheid era and to adjudicate applications for full or partial amnesty by perpetrators of violence on all sides

Triomf (Afrikaans) triumph: the white suburb that displaced Sophiatown (1959–94); now Sophiatown

tsomi (Xhosa-*iin*-): tales

Tsonga(*xi*): Bantu language spoken in northeastern South Africa and Mozambique; a.k.a. Shangaan

Tsotsis: gangsters or township tough guys; for language, see *flaaitaal*

Tswana (*Ba*-): dominant clan in Northwest South Africa and in neighboring Botswana, formerly Bechuanaland (British) protectorate; *(Se)Tswana*: language spoken

tuis (Afrikaans): at home; by extension: homeland

UCT: University of Cape Town (1829–) historically liberal institution but mostly white under apartheid

UDF: (1983–93) United Democratic Front; anti-apartheid umbrella organization

UDW: University of Durban-Westville (1970–2004): founded under apartheid for Indian South Africans

UFS: University of the Free State, a.k.a. Vrystaat (1904–): first Afrikaans-medium university; historically pro-apartheid but now contested

UKZN: University of KwaZulu-Natal; post-apartheid integrated university formed after the merger of the historically white University of Natal and the historically Indian UDW

Union of South Africa (1910–60): (white) self-governing British Commonwealth dominion; see RSA

UP: University of Pretoria (1908–): historically Afrikaans and whites-only; now contested

UWC: University of the Western Cape (1960–); founded under apartheid for Coloured students but now integrated

Venda (*tshi*-): Bantu language spoken in northern South Africa. Related to Shona, the most populous language in Zimbabwe

VOC: *Vereenigde Oost-indische Companie* (Dutch United East India Company); corporation chartered by the United Dutch Provinces to run the Cape and "possessions" in Asia, 1602–1799

volkseeinheid (Afrikaans): Afrikaner unity

volkseie (Afrikaans): Afrikaner identity, or distinctiveness

volkskapitalisme (Afrikaans): Afrikaner capitalism

volksontwikkeling (Afrikaans): Afrikaner development

Voortrekkers: (Afrikaans) pioneers: *Boers* who left the Cape colony in thousands in the 1830s, vs. *trekboers*, smaller groups of farmers appropriating African land beyond the colony's borders in the eighteenth century

Witwatersrand: white limestone ridges on which Johannesburg was built and the watershed between rivers flowing north and east to the Indian Ocean, and those flowing south and west to the Gariep (a.k.a. Orange) River and the Atlantic. Poetically but inaccurately "ridge of white waters"

Wits: University of the Witwatersrand, Johannesburg (1922–) historically liberal institution but mostly white under apartheid

Xhosa (*isi-*): South Africa's second most populous language and the first local African language in print

Zulu (*isi-*): South Africa's most populous language; in addition to first-language speakers, speakers of other African languages use Zulu as a lingua franca

Zululand (1824–1978): British colonial and local English name for KwaZulu [Zulu territory]; 1978–94: KwaZulu Bantustan; 1994: merged with Natal to become KwaZulu-Natal (KZN); see *Inkatha*

Note: the above list glosses words and abbreviations used in this book. It does not offer complete coverage of languages, groups, institutions, or other entities in South Africa.

References

Archival sources, interviews, and newspaper reviews appear in the relevant chapter notes. Internet links were live at the time of submission but cannot be guaranteed.

Scripts and Recordings

Unpublished scripts include date and place of performance or archival source. University Press abbreviated as UP.

Aidoo, A.A. (1987) *The Dilemma of a Ghost*, London: Longman.
Akerman, A. (2012 [1977]) *Somewhere on the Border*, Johannesburg: Wits (Witwatersrand) UP.
Anthony, K. (2015) *The Champion*, Cape Town: Junkets.
Bachaki Theatre (1989) "Top Down." Synopsis: D. Graver, L. Kruger, *Maske und Kothurn* 35 (1): 81–85.
Bailey, B. (1999) "Ipi Zombi," D. Graver (ed.) *Plays for a New South Africa*, Bloomington: Indiana UP.
Bailey, B. (2002) *Plays of Miracle and Wonder*, Cape Town: Second Storey Press.
Barnard, C. (1971) *Die Rebellie van Lafras Verwey*, Cape Town: Tafelberg.
Beukes, G. (1952) "Langs die Steiltjies," Official Program of the Van Riebeeck Tercentenary, Western Cape Archives Jeffrey Collection: A1637/ 322.
Black, S. (1984) *Three Plays*, S. Gray (ed.), Johannesburg: Ad Donker.
Bleek, W.H., L.C. Lloyd (1924), *The Mantis and His Friends*, Oxford: Blackwell.
Bloom, H., P. Williams et al. (1961) *King Kong—An African Jazz Opera*, London: Collins.
Bokwe, J.K. (1915) *Amaculo ase Lovedale—Lovedale Music*, Lovedale Mission Press.
Brecht, B. (1964 [1929]) *The Threepenny Opera*, adapted by D. Vesey, New York: Grove.
Brink, A.P. (1970) *Die Verhoor*, Cape Town: Human Rousseau.
Butler, G. (1953) *The Dam*, Cape Town: Balkema.
Buwalda, D. (2014) *Hinterland*, Cape Town: Junkets.
Coetzee, G. (2009) *Johnny Boskak is Feeling Funny and Other Plays*, Pietermaritzburg: University of KwaZulu-Natal Press; hereafter UKZNP.
Coetzee, G., B. Mkhwane (2006) "Born through the Nose" (Market Theatre 2005).
Cooke, V., D. Keogh (1983) "This is for Keeps," in S. Gray (ed.) (1986), *Market Plays*, Johannesburg: Ad Donker.
Coppen, N. (2012) *Abnormal Loads*, Cape Town: Junkets.
Davids, C., J.D. Abrahams (2013) *Bullets over Bishop Lavis*, Cape Town: Junkets.
Davids, N. (2006) *At Her Feet*, Cape Town: Oshun.
De Klerk, W.A. (1947) *Drie Dramas*, Cape Town: Nasionale Pers.
De Klerk, W.A. (1952) *Die Jaar van die Vuur-os*, Cape Town: Tafelberg.
De Klerk, W.A. (1989) *Die Jaar van die Vuur-os*, 2nd ed., Cape Town: Tafelberg.
De Wet, R. (1991) "Diepe Grond," *Vrystaat-Trilogie*, Pretoria: HAUM.

De Wet, R. (2005) "African Gothic," *Plays Two*, London: Oberon.

Dhlomo, H.I.E. (1939) "Ruby and Frank," UKZN: K. Campbell Africana Library (KCM): KCM 8267.

Dhlomo, H.I.E. (1954) *Dingana*, Durban: University of Natal Press.

Dhlomo, H.I.E. (1985) *Collected Works*, T. Couzens, N. Visser (eds.), Johannesburg: Ravan.

Dhlomo, H.I.E., R.R. Dhlomo, G. Motsieloa (1934) Dramatic Display for the Emancipation Centenary Celebration (Wits University Library, hereafter WUL): SAIRR Collection).

Dike, F. (1977) *The First South African*, Johannesburg: Ravan.

Dike, F. (1979) "The Sacrifice of Kreli," in S. Gray (ed.) *Theatre One*, Johannesburg: Ad Donker.

Dike, F. (2009) *The Return*, Cape Town: Junkets.

Drinkwater, J. (1925) *Collected Plays*, London: Sidgwick & Jackson.

Du Plessis, P.G. (1971) *Siener in die Suburbs*, Cape Town: Tafelberg.

Du Plessis, P.G. (1977) *'n Seder Val in Waterkloof*, Cape Town: Tafelberg.

Ellenbogen, N. (1999) "Horn of Sorrow," in D. Graver (ed.) *Plays for a New South Africa*, Bloomington: Indiana UP.

Farber, Y. (2008) *Molora*, London: Oberon.

Farber, Y., D. Kumalo (2008) "He Left Quietly," in Farber, *Theatre as Witness*, London: Oberon.

Farber, Y., T. Mtshali-Jones (2008), "Woman in Waiting," in Farber, *Theatre as Witness*.

Fleishman, M., A. Hinkel (2008) *Cargo* (DVD), Cape Town: Magnet Theatre, JazzArt Dance Theatre.

Foot, L. (2005) *Tshepang*, Johannesburg: Wits UP.

Foot, L. (2009) *Karoo Moose*, London: Oberon.

Foot, L. (2014) "Fishers of Hope," Cape Town: Baxter Theatre.

Fugard, A. (1978) "Orestes," in S. Gray (ed.) (1979) *Theatre One*, Johannesburg: Ad Donker.

Fugard, A. (1991) "Hello and Goodbye," in Fugard, *Blood Knot and Other Plays*, New York: Theatre Communication Group: hereafter TCG.

Fugard, A. (1992 [1964]) *The Blood Knot*, Oxford UP.

Fugard, A. (1993a) *Township Plays*, Oxford UP.

Fugard, A. (1993b) *Playland: A Place with the Pigs*, New York: TCG.

Fugard, A., J. Kani, W. Ntshona (1986) *Statements: Three Plays*, New York: TCG.

Goethe, J.W. von (1959) *Faust II*, P. Wade (trans.), Harmondsworth: Penguin.

Goethe, J.W. von (1981) *Faust II, Werke*, Munich: C.H. Beck.

Gopie, R. (2008) *Out of Bounds*, Cape Town: Junkets.

Gopie, R. (2011) "The Coolie Odyssey" (Grahamstown Festival).

Goudvis, B. (1925) *Where the Money Goes and Other Plays*, Johannesburg: Sterling.

Govender, K. (1979) "Working Class Hero," in N. Bose (ed.) (2009) *Beyond Bollywood and Broadway: Plays from the South Asian Diaspora*, Bloomington: Indiana UP.

Govender, R. (1977) *The Lahnee's Pleasure*, Johannesburg: Ravan; reprinted: Bose, *Beyond Bollywood*.

Govender, R. (1996) *At the Edge and Other Cato Manor Stories*, Pretoria: Marx.

Grootboom, M.P. (2009a) "Relativity: Township Stories," in D. Peimer (ed.) *Armed Response: Plays from South Africa*, Calcutta: Seagull.

Grootboom, M.P. (2009b) *Foreplay*, London: Oberon.

Grosskopf, J.F.W. (1940) *As Die Tuig Skawe*, Johannesburg: Afrikaanse Pers.

Gumede, K.D (2014) *Crepuscule*, Cape Town: Junkets.

Hansberry, L. (1987) *A Raisin in the Sun*, 25th anniversary ed., New York: New American Library.

Joubert, E., S. Kotze (1984) *Die Swerfjare van Poppie Nongena*, Cape Town: Tafelberg.

JATC: Junction Avenue Theatre Company (1995) *At the Junction: Four Plays*, M. Orkin (ed.), Johannesburg: Wits UP.

Kalmer, H. (2016) *The Bram Fischer Waltz*, Johannesburg: Wits UP.

Kani, J. (2002), *Nothing but the Truth*, Johannesburg: Wits UP.

Kente, G. (1975), "Too Late!" *S'ketsh* (Winter): 17–28.

Kente, G. (1981) "Too Late!" in R. Kavanagh (ed.), *South African People's Plays*, London: Heinemann.

Keogh, D., V. Cooke, N. Haysom (1983) "The Native That Caused All the Trouble," in J. Kani (comp.) (1996) *More Market Plays*, Johannesburg: Ad Donker.

Kramer, D., T. Peterson (2002 [1987]) *District Six—the Musical* (DVD), Cape Town: Blik Music.

Kramer, D.T. (2007) *Ghoema*, Cape Town: Blik Music.

Krige, U. (1939) *Magdalena Retief*, Cape Town: Nasionale Pers.

Louw, N.P. van Wyk (1938) *Die Dieper Reg*, Cape Town: Nasionale Pers.

Louw, N.P. van Wyk (1972) *Die Pluimsaad waai ver*, Cape Town: Human Rousseau.

Mackey, W.W. (1986 [1971]) "Requiem for Brother X," in W. King (ed.) *Black Drama Anthology*, 2nd ed., New York: New American Library.

Mahomed, I. (1999a) "Purdah," in D. Graver (ed.) *Plays for a New South Africa*, Bloomington: Indiana UP.

Mahomed, I. (1999b) "Cheaper than Roses," in K. Perkins (ed.) *Black South African Women Plays*, London: Routledge.

Manaka, M. (1980) *Egoli: City of Gold*, Johannesburg: Ravan.

Manaka, M. (1997) *Beyond the Echoes of Soweto: Five Plays*, G. Davis (ed.), Amsterdam: Harwood.

Maponya, M. (1984) "Problems and Possibilities: The Making of Alternative Theatre in South Africa," *English Academy Review* 2: 19–32.

Maponya, M. (1986) "Gangsters," in D. Ndlovu (ed.), *Woza Afrika!* 55–88, New York: Braziller.

Maponya, M. (1995) *Doing Plays for a Change: Five Works*, I. Steadman (ed.), Johannesburg: Wits UP.

Maqina, M. (1975) *Give us this Day*, Johannesburg: Ravan.

Matheus, J. (1975 [1926]) "Cruter," in J. Hatch, T. Shine (ed.) *Black Theater USA: 1847-1974*, New York: Macmillan.

Matshikiza, T., P. Williams (n.d.) *King Kong—Original Cast Recording*, Paris: Celluloid.

Mbothwe, M. and cast (2012), "Ingcwaba lendoda lise cankwe ndlela," in Reznek et al. (ed.) *The Magnet Theatre "Migration" Plays*, Cape Town: Junkets.

Mda, Z. (1990) *The Plays of Zakes Mda*, Johannesburg: Ravan.

Mda, Z. (1993) *And the Girls in Their Sunday Dresses, and Other Plays*, Johannesburg: Wits UP.

Mhlophe, G., M. van Renen, T. Mtshali-[Jones] (1988) *Have You Seen Zandile?* London: Methuen.

Mkhwane, B., E. Pearson (1994) "Boy Called Rubbish" (Grahamstown Festival).

Moleba, E. (2013-14) "The Man with the Green Jacket" (Grahamstown Festival).

Moleba, E. (2014) "The Immigrant" (Royal Court New South African Season).

Molusi, O. (2009) *Itsoseng*, Cape Town: Oxford UP.

Mtsaka, M.J. (1978) *Not his Pride*, Johannesburg: Ravan.

Mtshali, T. (1999) "Weemen," in Perkins (ed.) *Black South African Women Plays*.

Mtwa, P., M. Ngema, B. Simon (1983) *Woza Albert!* London: Methuen.

Ngema, M. (1995) *The Best of Mbongeni Ngema*, Johannesburg: Skotaville.

Ngema, M., D. Roodt et al. (2002) *Sarafina* (DVD), Burbank, CA: Buena Vista Entertainment.

Nkala, J.K. (2014) *Cockroach: A Trilogy of Plays*, Cape Town: Junkets.

Nkosi, L. (1973) "The Rhythm of Violence," in G. Wellwarth (ed.) *Themes in Drama*, New York: Crowell.

Noko, P. (2016) *Fruit*, Cape Town: Junkets.

Opperman, D. (1986) *Môre is 'n Lang Dag; Die Teken*, Cape Town: Tafelberg.

Opperman, D. (1996) *Donkerland*, Cape Town: Tafelberg.

Opperman, D. (2008) *Kaburu*. Pretoria: Protea Books.

Opperman, D. (2011) *Hartland* (DVD), Johannesburg: KykNET Productions.

Pam-Grant, S. (1993) "Curl Up and Dye," in S. Gray (ed.) *South Africa: Plays*, London: Nick Hern.

Pillay, K. (1995) *Looking for Muruga*, Durban: Asoka; reprinted Bose, *Beyond Bollywood*.

Purkey, M., C. Steinberg (2000) *Love, Crime and Johannesburg*, Johannesburg: Wits UP.

Reznek, J., M. Fleishman, F. Yisa (eds.) (2012) *The Magnet Theatre "Migratio'" Plays*, Cape Town: Junkets.

Serpent Players (1967) "The Coat," *The Classic* 2 (3): 50–68.

Shezi, M. (1981) "Shanti," Kavanagh (ed.) *South African People's Plays*.

Simon, B. (1986) "Hey Listen," in S. Gray (ed.) *Market Plays*, Johannesburg: Ad Donker.

Simon, B., Market Theatre cast (1979), "Cincinatti," in T. Hauptfleisch I. Steadman (ed.) (1984) *South African Theatre: Four Plays*, Pretoria: HAUM.

Simon, B., Market Theatre cast (1986) "Born in the RSA," in Ndlovu (ed.), *Woza Afrika!*, New York: Braziller.

Simon, B., Market Theatre cast (1997) *Born in the RSA: Four Workshop Plays*, Johannesburg: Wits UP.

Singh, A. (2003) "To House," in C. Fourie (ed.) (2006) *New South African Plays*, London Aurora.

Slabolepszy, P. (1985) *Saturday Night at the Palace*, Johannesburg: Ad Donker.

Slabolepszy, P. (1994) *Mooi Street and Other Moves*, Johannesburg: Wits UP.

Slabolepszy, P. (1998) "Fordsburg's Finest" (Market Theatre).

Small, A. (1965) *Kanna Hy Kô Hystoe*, Cape Town: Tafelberg.

Small, A. (1990) *Kanna—He is Coming Home*, C. Lasker A. Small (trans.), New York: Garland.

Smit, B. (1962) *Putsonderwater*, Cape Town: Tafelberg.

Smit, B. (1974) "Christine," T. Hauptfleisch I. Steadman (eds.) (1984) *South African Theatre: Four Plays*.

Smit, B. (1976 [1960]) *Die Verminktes*, 2nd ed., Johannesburg: Perskor.

Sondhi, K. (1968) "Encounter," C. Pietersen (ed.) *Ten One-Act Plays*, London: Heinemann.

Sowden, L. (1937) "Red Rand," (WUL: A406).

Sowden, L. (1976) *The Kimberley Train*, Cape Town: Timmins.

Soyinka, W. (1965) *The Road*, Oxford UP.

Taylor, J., W. Kentridge et al. (1998) *Ubu and the Truth Commission*, University of Cape Town Press.

Themba, C. (1972) *The Will to Die*, London: Heinemann.

Themba, C. (1993) "The Suit," adapt. M. Mutloatse, B. Simon, and Market Theatre cast (Market Theatre).

Uys, P.D. (1979) *Die Van Aardes van Grootoor*, Johannesburg: Taurus.

Uys, P.D. (1983) *Selle ou Storie*, Johannesburg: Ad Donker.

Van Graan, M. (2010) *Green Man Flashing*, Cape Town: Junkets.

Van Graan, M. (2013) *Rainbow Scars*, Cape Town: Junkets.

Vusisizwe Players. (1996) "You Strike a Woman, You Strike a Rock," in J. Kani (comp.), *More Market Plays*, Johannesburg: Ad Donker.

Whyle, J. (2003) "Rejoice Burning," in Fourie (ed.) *New South African Plays*, London: Aurora.

Workshop '71 (1981) "Survival," in Kavanagh (ed.) *South African People's Plays*.

Xaba, M. (2013) *Running and other Stories*, Johannesburg: Modjaji.

History, Theory, Criticism

Alexander, P., T. Lekgowa, et al. (2013) *Marikana: Voices from South Africa's Mining Massacre*, Athens: Ohio UP.

Altbeker, A. (2007) *A Country at War with Itself: South Africa's Crisis of Crime*, Johannesburg: Jonathan Ball.

Anderson, B. (1983) *Imagined Communities: Reflections on the Origins and Spread of Nationalism*, London: Verso.

Andersson, M. (2015) "Mpumelelo Paul Grootboom," in M. Middeke et al. (eds.) *The Methuen Guide to Contemporary South African Theatre*, 241–57, London: Bloomsbury; hereafter: *Methuen Guide*.

Arnold, M. (1880) "The Function of Criticism at the Present Time," in *Essays in Criticism*, London: Macmillan; available online via Hathi Trust.

Ashcroft, B. et al. (1989) *The Empire Writes Back: Theory and Practice in Postcolonial Literature*, London: Routledge.

Astbury, B. (1979) *The Space/Die Ruimte/Indawo*, Cape Town: Space Theatre.

Bacqa, S. (1997) *Investigation of the Play "Sarafina II,"* Pretoria: Office of the Public Protector.

Bakhtin, M. (1987) *The Dialogic Imagination*, M. Holquist (ed., trans.), Austin: University of Texas Press.

Ballantine, C. (2012) *Marabi Nights: Early South African Jazz and Vaudeville*, 2nd ed., Durban: UKZNP.

Balme, C.B. (1999) *Decolonizing the Stage: Theatrical Syncretism and Post-Colonial Drama*, Oxford UP.

Balme, C.B. (2014) *The Theatrical Public Sphere*, Cambridge UP.

Barber, K. (1986) "Radical Conservatism in Yoruba Popular Plays," *Bayreuth African Studies* 7: 5–32.

Barker, H.G. (1922) *The Exemplary Theatre*, London: Sidgwick & Jackson.

Barnes, H. (2013) (ed.; intro.) *Applied Drama and Theatre as an Interdisciplinary Field in the Context of HIV/AIDS in South Africa*, Leiden: Brill.

Bauman, R. (1989) "Performance," *International Encyclopedia of Communications*, 3: 262–66, New York: Oxford UP.

Bellasis, B.M. (1935) "Johannesburg's Jubilee: Exclusive Interview," *African World* 2 (March): 227–29.

Benjamin, W. (1980) "Über den Begriff der Geschichte," *Gesammelte Schriften*, I, pt. 2: 691–704.

Benjamin, W. (2006) "On the Concept of History," H. Zohn (trans.), in H. Eiland (ed.) *Selected Writings by Walter Benjamin*, 389–400, Cambridge, MA: Harvard UP.

Benson, M. (1997) *Athol Fugard and Barney Simon*, Johannesburg: Ravan.

Berlant, L. (1988) "The Female Complaint," *Social Text* 19–20: 237–59.

Berman, M. (1988) *All that's Solid Melts into Air: The Experience of Modernity*, New York: Penguin.

Bhabha, H.K. (1986) "Signs Taken for Wonders: Reflections on Questions of Ambivalence and Authority," in H.L. Gates (ed.) *"Race," Writing, and Difference*, University of Chicago Press.

Bhabha, H.K. (1991) " 'Race,' Time and the Revision of Modernity," *Oxford Literary Review* 13: 193–219.

Bhorat, H., M. Buthelezi, et al. (2017) *Betrayal of the Promise: How South Africa is Being Stolen*, Johannesburg: PARI; http://pari.org.za/wp-content/uploads/2017/05/Betrayal-of-the-Promise-25052017.pdf.

Biko, S.B. (1978) *I Write What I Like*, New York: Harper.

Bloch, E. (1977), "Non-synchronism and the Obligation to Dialectics," *New German Critique* 11: 22–38.

Bloch, E. (1988 [1975]) "Something is Missing," in *The Utopian Function of Art and Literature*, J. Zipes (trans.), Cambridge, MA: MIT Press.

Boal, A. (1979) *Theater of the Oppressed*, C.A. McBride, M.O.L. McBride, and E. Fryer (trans.), London: Pluto Press.

Bosman, F.C.H. (1969) *Drama en Toneel in Suid-Afrika: 1800–1962*, Pretoria: Van Schaik.

Bourdieu, P. (1993) *The Field of Cultural Production*, R. Nice (trans.), New York: Columbia UP.

Bourgault, L. (2003) *Playing for Life: Performance in Africa in the Age of AIDS*, Durham, NC: Carolina Academic P.

Branford, W., J. Claughton (2002) "Mutual Lexical Borrowings among Some Languages of Southern Africa," in R. Meshrie (ed.) *Language in South Africa*, 199–215, Cambridge UP.

Brecht, B. (1998) *Werke: Berliner und Frankfurter Ausgabe* (BFA), Frankfurt: Suhrkamp.

Brecht, B. (2014) *Brecht on Theatre*, 3rd ed.; M. Silberman et al. (ed., trans.), London: Bloomsbury.

Brink, A.P. (1986) *Aspekte van die Nuwe Drama*, Cape Town: Human Rousseau.

Brooks, P. (1976) *The Melodramatic Imagination*, New Haven: Yale UP.

Brown, J.A. (1982 [1961]) "Review: *The Blood Knot*," in S. Gray (ed.) *Athol Fugard*, 25–26, Johannesburg: McGraw Hill.

Bundy, C. (2014) *Short-Changed? South Africa since Apartheid*, Athens: Ohio UP.

Buthelezi, Q. (1995) "South African Black English," in R. Meshtrie (ed.) *Language and Social History*, 242–50, Cape Town: David Phillip.

Caluza, R. (1992) *Caluza's Double Quartet*, V. Erlmann (ed.), Bexhill, Sussex: Interstate Music.

Campbell, R. (1949) *Collected Poems*, London: Brun.

Carmichael, S. [K. Ture] (1968) "Towards Black Liberation," in L. Jones, L. Neal (eds.) *Black Fire*, New York: William Morrow.

Césaire, A. (1972) *Discourse on Colonialism*, J. Pinkham (trans.), New York: Monthly Review.

Chakrabarty, D. (1992) "Postcoloniality and the Artifice of History," *Representations* 37: 1–26.

Chapman, M. (1989) "More than a Story. *Drum* and its Significance in Black South African Writing," in Chapman (ed.) *The Drum Decade: Stories from the 1950s*, Pietermaritzburg: UKZNP.

Chaudhuri, U. (1995) *Staging Place: The Geography of Modern Drama*, Ann Arbor: University of Michigan Press.

Chinyowa, K. (2013) "Poetics of Contradiction: HIV/AIDS Intervention at the Crossroads of Localization and Globalization," Barnes (ed.) *Applied Drama and Theatre as Interdisciplinary Field*, 203–17.

Chipkin, C. (1993) *Johannesburg Style: Architecture and Society, 1880s–1960s*, Cape Town: David Phillip.

Chipkin, I. (2007) *Do South Africans Exist?: Nationalism, Democracy and the Identity of the People*, Johannesburg: Wits UP.

Clingman, S. (1998) *Bram Fischer: Afrikaner Revolutionary*, Amherst: University of Massachusetts Press.

Coetzee, J.M. (1988) *White Writing: On the Culture of Letters in South Africa*, New Haven, CT: Yale UP.

Cole, C.M. (2010) *Performing South Africa's Truth Commission: Stages of Transition*, Bloomington: Indiana UP.

Colenso, F. (1881) *A History of the Zulu War*, London: Chapman & Hall.

Comaroff, J. and J.L. Comaroff (eds., intro) (1993) *Modernity and its Malcontents: Ritual and Power in Postcolonial Africa*, University of Chicago Press.

Commission of Inquiry (1977) *Commission of Inquiry into the Performing Arts in South Africa*, Pretoria: Govt. Publications.

Constitution (1996), *Constitution of the Republic of South Africa*, Pretoria: Govt. Publications; http://www.justice.gov.za/legislation/constitution/SAConstitution-web-eng.pdf

Cooper, S., P. Nefolovhodwe (2007) "Steve Biko and the SASO/BPC Trial," in C. van Wyk (ed.) *We Write What We Like; Celebrating Steve Biko*, Johannesburg: Wits UP.

Cope, J. (1983) *The Adversary from Within: Dissident Writing in Afrikaans*, Cape Town: David Philip.

Coplan, D. (1994) *In the Time of Cannibals: The Word Music of South Africa's Basotho Migrants*, University of Chicago Press.

Coplan, D. (2008) *In Township Tonight: South Africa's Black City Music and Theatre*, 2nd ed., University of Chicago Press.

Couzens, T. (1985) *The New African: Life and Work of H. I. E. Dhlomo*, Johannesburg: Ravan.

Cronjé, G. (1945) *'n Tuiste vir die Nageslag*, Cape Town: Afrikaanse Pers.

Curtis, N. (1920) *Songs and Tales from the Dark Continent*, New York: Schirmer.

DAC (Dept of Arts and Culture; 1996) *White Paper on Arts, Culture, and Heritage*, Pretoria: Govt. Publications; http://www.dac.gov.za/white-papers.

DAC (2017) *Revised White Paper on Arts, Culture, and Heritage* (4th draft), Pretoria: Govt. Publications; http://www.dac.gov.za/white-papers.

Dalrymple, L. (1992) *Drama to the People: The Challenges of the 1990s*, Ngoye: University of Zululand Press.

Dalrymple, L. (2013) "Applied Art Is Still Art," in H. Barnes (ed.) *Arts Activism, Education, and Therapies*, 229–42, Amsterdam: Rodopi.

Davis, P. (1996) *In Darkest Hollywood: Exploring the Jungle of Cinema's South Africa*, Athens: Ohio UP.

Deacon, J. (ed.) (1996) *Voices from the Past: /Xam and the Bleek-Lloyd Collection*, Johannesburg: Wits UP.

De Bruyn, L. (2016) "Magnet's Clanwilliam Community Intervention Project," in M. Lewis, A. Krueger (eds.) *Magnet Theatre: Three Decades of Making Space*, 253–69, Bristol: Intellect: hereafter: *Magnet Theatre*.

De Certeau, M. (1988) "Walking in the City," in *The Practice of Everyday Life*, S. Randall (trans.), 91–110, Berkeley: University of California Press.

De Klerk, W.A. (1975) *The Puritans in Africa: A Story of Afrikanerdom*, Harmondsworth: Penguin.

Dept of Information (1966) *Performing Arts in South Africa: Cultural Aspirations of a Young Nation*, Pretoria: Govt. Publications.

Desai, R. (2014) *Miners Shot Down* (DVD), Johannesburg: Uhuru Productions.

De Smet, S. et al. (2015) "When the Past Strikes the Present: Performing Requiems for the Marikana Massacre," *South African Theatre Journal* 28 (3): 222–41.

Dhlomo, H.I.E. (1933) "The Importance of African Drama," *Bantu World*, October 21: 17.

Dhlomo, H.I.E. (1977a [1936]) "Drama and the African," in N. Visser (ed.) *Literary Criticism and Theory of H. I. E. Dhlomo*, special issue: *English in Africa* 4 (2): 3–11.

Dhlomo, H.I.E. (1977b [1939]) "African Drama and Poetry," *Literary Criticism and Theory* 4 (2): 13–18.

Dhlomo, H.I.E. (1977c [1939]) "African Drama and Research," *Literary Criticism and Theory* 4 (2): 19–22.

Dhlomo, H.I.E. (1977d [1939]) "Nature and Variety of Tribal Drama," *Literary Criticism and Theory* 4(2): 23–36.

Dhlomo, H.I.E. (1977e [1939]) "Why Study Tribal Dramatic Forms?" *Literary Criticism and Theory* 4 (2): 37–42.

Dhlomo, H.I.E. (1977f [1943]) "Masses and the Artist," *Literary Criticism and Theory* 4 (2): 61–62.

Dhlomo, H.I.E. (n.d.) "The Evolution of Bantu Entertainments," UKZN: KCM 8290/2.

Dlamini, J. (2009) *Native Nostalgia*, Johannesburg: Jacana.

Dlamini, J. (2014), *Askari: Collaboration and Betrayal in the Anti-Apartheid Struggle*, Johannesburg: Jacana.

Dominy, G. (1991) "Thomas Baines: The McGonagall of Shepstone's Zulu Expedition?" *Natalia* 21: 73–79.

Doubt, J. (2015) "HIV/AIDS and Silence in South Africa," *Journal of Southern African Studies* 41: 1349–58.

Douglass, F. (1999 [1893]) *The Reason why the Colored American is not in the Columbian Exposition*, Douglass, I.B. Wells, R. Rydell (eds.), Urbana: University of Illinois Press.

Drake, St. C., H. Cayton (1993 [1945]) *Black Metropolis*, University Chicago Press.

Du Bois, W.E.B. (1989 [1903]) *Souls of Black Folk*, New York: Bantam.

Dubow, S. (1987) "Race, Civilization and Culture: Segregationist Discourse in the Interwar Years," in S. Marks, S. Trapido (eds.) *The Politics of Race, Class, and Nationalism in Twentieth Century South Africa*, 71–94, London: Longman.

Duncan, J. (2014) *The Rise of the Securocrats: The Case of South Africa*, Johannesburg: Jacana.

Duncan, J. (2016) *Protest Nation: The Right to Protest in South Africa*, Pietermaritzburg: UKZNP.

Du Preez, M. (2005) *Oranje, Blanje, Blues: Vrye Weekblad 1988–94*, Cape Town: Zebra.

Du Preez, M. (2008) *Of Tricksters, Tyrants and Turncoats*, Cape Town: Zebra.

Durden, E. (2011) "Participatory HIV/AIDS Theatre in South Africa," in D. Francis (ed.) *Acting on HIV: Using Drama to Create Possibilities for Change*, Rotterdam: Sense.

Ebrahim, C. (1973), "*Review of the First SABTU Festival*," S'ketsh (Summer), 44.

Empire Exhibition (1936) *Official Guide Celebrating the Golden Jubilee of Johannesburg*, Johannesburg: Empire Exhibition (WUL).

Erlmann, V. (1991) *African Stars: Studies in Black South African Performance*, University of Chicago Press.

Evian. C. (1992) "Community Theatre and AIDS Education," *Progress* (Summer): 34–37.

Fabian, J. (1983) *Time and the Other: How Anthropology Constructs its Object*, New York: Columbia UP.

Fanon, F. (2004 [1962]) *The Wretched of the Earth*, R. Philcox (trans.), New York: Grove.

February, V. (1981) *Mind Your Colour*, London: Routledge.

February, V. (1990) *The Afrikaners of South Africa*, London: Routledge.

Filewod, A. (1990) "National Theatre, National Obsession," *Canadian Theatre Review* 62: 5–10.

Fleishman, M. (2011) "*Cargo*: Staging Slavery at the Cape," *Contemporary Theatre Review* 21 (1): 8–19.

Fleishman, M. (ed., intro) (2015) *Performing Migrancy and Mobility in Africa*, New York: Palgrave.

Fleishman, M. (2016) "Making Space for Ideas: The Knowledge Work of Magnet Theatre," in Lewis, Krueger (eds.) *Magnet Theatre*, 53–75.

Fleishman, M., J. Pather (2015) "Don't Start Him on the Funding Question," in M. Maufort, G. Homann (eds.) *New Territories: Reconfiguring Theatre, Drama and Performance in Post-Apartheid South Africa*, 383–93, Brussels: Lang.

Flockemann, M. (2016) "Being There: The Evolution of Performance Aesthetics from *Medea* to the *Magnet Theatre Migration Plays*," in Lewis, Krueger (eds.) *Magnet Theatre*, 83–103.

Foucault, M. (1979) *Discipline and Punish*, A. Sheridan (trans.), New York: Random House.

Francis, B. (1979) "*Egoli*—a Wealth of Talent," *S'ketsh* (Winter): 16.

Francis, D. (ed., intro) (2011) *Acting on HIV: Using Drama to Create Possibilities for Change*, Rotterdam: Sense.

Fraser, N. (1989) *Unruly Practices: Power, Discourse, and Gender in Contemporary Social Theory*, Minneapolis: University of Minnesota Press.

Freire, P. (1972) *Pedagogy of the Oppressed*, M.B. Ramos (trans.), Harmondsworth: Penguin.

Fuchs, A. (2002) *Playing the Market: The Market Theatre, Johannesburg*, 2nd ed., Amsterdam: Rodopi.

Fugard, A. (1982) "Sizwe Banzi is Dead [essay]," in R. Harwood (ed.) *A Night at the Theatre*, 21–33, London: Methuen.

Fugard, A. (1984) *Notebooks: 1960–77*, New York: TCG.

Fugard, A., B. Simon (1982) "The Family Plays of the Sixties," in S. Gray (ed.) *Athol Fugard*, 40–52, Johannesburg: McGraw Hill.

Gatti, A. (1982) "Time, Space, and Theatre Event," N. Oakes (trans.), *Modern Drama* 25 (1): 69–81.

Gedenkboek (1938) *Gedenkboek van die Voortrekker-Eeufees*, Johannesburg: Sentrale Volksfeeskomitee.

Gedenkboek (1940) *Gedenkboek van die Ossewaens op die Pad van Suid-Afrika*, Cape Town: Nasionale Pers.

Gerwel, G.J. (1985) "Afrikaner, Afrikaans, Afrika," *Skrywer en Gemeenskap*, Pretoria: HAUM.

Gevisser, M. (1994a) "SA's reconciliation in motion," *Johannesburg Weekly Mail* (May 13–19): 9.

Gevisser, M. (1994b) "A Different Fight for Freedom: History of Gay and Lesbian Lives in South Africa," in Gevisser, E. Cameron (eds.) *Defiant Desire*, Johannesburg: Ravan.

Gibson, N.C., A. Mngxitama (eds.) (2008) *Biko Lives: Contesting the Legacies of Steve Biko*, New York: Palgrave.

Gilbert, H., J. Tompkins (1996) *Post-colonial Drama*, London: Routledge.

Glaser, C. (2015) "Soweto's Islands of Learning: Morris Isaacson and Orlando High Schools and Bantu Education, 1958–76," *Journal of Southern African Studies* 41: 159–71.

Glasser, M. (1960) *King Kong—A Venture in the Theatre*, Cape Town: Howell.

Goldin, I. (1987) "The Reconstitution of Coloured Identity in the Western Cape," S. Marks, S. Trapido (eds.) *The Politics of Race, Class and Nationalism*, 156–81.

Göle, N. (1997) "The Gendered Nature of the Public Sphere," *Public Culture* 10 (1): 61–81.

Gordimer, N. (1964) "Plays and Piracy," *Contrast* 3 (4): 50–59.

Gqola, P.D. (2008) "Brutal Inheritances: Echoes, Negrophobia and Masculine Violence," in S. Hassim et al. (eds.) *Go Home or Die Here: Violence, Xenophobia and the Reinvention of Difference in South Africa*, 209–22, Johannesburg: Wits UP.

Gqola, P.D. (2015) *Rape: A South African Nightmare*, Johannesburg: Jacana.

Graham, L. (2008) "Save us all! 'Baby Rape' and Post-apartheid Narrative," *Scrutiny2* 13 (1): 105–19.

Gramsci, A. (1971) *Selections from the Prison Notebooks*, G.N. Smith, Q. Hoare (eds.), New York: International Publishers.

Graver, D. (1997) "Review: National Arts Festival, Grahamstown," *Theatre Journal* 49: 56–59.

Graver, D. (1999) (ed., intro.) *Drama for a New South Africa: Seven Plays*, Bloomington: Indiana UP.

Graver, D., L. Kruger (1989) "South Africa's National Theatre: The Market or the Street?" *New Theatre Quarterly* 19: 272–81.

Gray, S. (1984) (ed., intro) *Three Plays*, by S. Black, Johannesburg: Ad Donker.

Gready, P. (1990) "The Sophiatown Writers of the 1950s: The Unreal Reality of their World," *Journal of Southern African Studies* 10 (1): 139–64.

Grundlingh, A., H. Sapire (1989) "From Feverish Festival to Repetitive Ritual? Changing Fortunes of Great Trek Mythology in Industrializing South Africa," *South African Historical Journal* 21: 19–37.

Guldimann, C. (1996) "The (Black) Male Gaze: Mbongeni Ngema's *Sarafina*," *South African Theatre Journal* 10 (2): 85–99.

Gunner, E. (2007) "BBC Radio and the Black Artist: Lewis Nkosi's 'The Trial' and 'We can't all be Martin Luther King," in L. Stiebel, L. Gunner (eds.) *Still Beating the Drum: Critical Perspectives on Lewis Nkosi*, Johannesburg: Wits UP.

Gunning, T. (1994) "The Horror of Opacity: The Melodrama of Sensation in the Plays of André de Lorde," in J. Bratton et al. (eds.) *Melodrama: Stage, Picture, Screen*, London: BFI.

Gwala, M.P. (1973) "Towards a National Theatre," *South African Outlook* (August): 131–33.

Gwala, M.P. (ed.) (1974) *Black Review 1973*, Durban: Black Community Programs.

Habermas, J. (1989 [1962]) *Structural Transformation of the Public Sphere*, T. Burger (trans.), Cambridge, MA: MIT Press.

Habib, A. (2013) *South Africa's Suspended Revolution*, Athens: Ohio UP.

Haggard, H.R. (1882) *Cetywayo and His White Neighbours*, London: Trübner.

Hamilton, C. (1985) "Ideology, Oral Traditions and the Struggle for Power in the Early Zulu Kingdom" M.A. thesis, Wits University.

Hamilton, C. (1998) *Terrific Majesty: The Powers of Shaka Zulu and the Limits of Historical Invention*, Cambridge, MA: Harvard UP.

Harrison P. et al. (eds.) (2014) *Changing Space, Changing City: Johannesburg after Apartheid*, Johannesburg: Wits UP.

Harford, A. (2013) "The Mining Industry: Strikes, Causes and Solutions," in T. Jika et al. (eds.),"We Are Going to Kill Each Other Today": The Marikana Story, 159–63, Cape Town: Tafelberg.

Hegel, G.W.F. (1956) *The Philosophy of History*, J. Sibree (trans.), New York: Dove.

Hegel, G.W.F. (1974) *Aesthetics: Lectures on Fine Art*, T.M. Knox (trans.), Oxford UP.

Hemke, R. (ed.) (2010) *Theater in Africa South of the Sahara*, Berlin: Theater der Zeit.

Historical Sketch (1910) *Historical Sketch & Description of the Pageant at Cape Town on the Opening of the First Parliament of the Union of South Africa*, Cape Town: Pageant Comm.

Hoad, N. (2007) *African Intimacies: Race, Homosexuality, and Globalization*, Minneapolis: University Minnesota Press.

Hobsbawm, E., T. Ranger (eds.) (1982) *The Invention of Tradition*, Cambridge UP.

Hoernlé, A. (1934) "The Bantu Dramatic Society," *Africa* 7: 223–27.

Hoffman, A. (1980) *They Built a Theatre: The Story of the Johannesburg Repertory*, Johannesburg: Ad Donker.

Hofmeyr, I. (1987) "Building a Nation from Words: Afrikaans Language Literature and Ethnic Identity, 1902–1924," in S. Marks, S. Trapido (eds.) *The Politics of Race, Class and Nationalism*, 95–123, London: Longman.

Hofmeyr, I. (1988) "Popularizing History: The Case of Gustav Preller," *Journal of African History* 29: 521–35.

Holloway, M. (1988) "An Interview with Zakes Mda," *South African Theatre Journal* 2 (2): 88–92.

Homann, G. (2009) "Preamble," in Homann (ed.) *At this Stage: Plays from Post-apartheid South Africa*, 1–16, Johannesburg: Wits UP.

Horn, A. (1990) (intro.) *The Plays of Zakes Mda*, Johannesburg: Ravan.

Hughes, L. (1976 [1966]) "Black Influences in the American Theater, Part 1," in M. Smythe (ed.) *The Black American Reference Book*, Englewood, NJ: Prentice Hall.

Huguenet, A. (1950) *Applous*, Cape Town: HAUM.

Hunter, M. (2015) "Schooling Choice in South Africa: The Limits of Qualifications and the Politics of Race, Class, and Symbolic Power," *International Journal of Educational Development*, 43: 41–45.

Husserl, E. (1970 [1936]) "Philosophy and the Crisis of European Humanity," D. Carr (trans.), in *The Crisis of European Sciences and Transcendental Philosophy*, Evanston, IL: Northwestern UP.

Hutchison, Y. (2013) *South African Performance and Archives of Memory*, Manchester UP.

Jabavu, D.D.T. (1935) *The Findings of the All Africa Convention*, Lovedale Mission Press.

Jaji, T.E. (2014) *Africa in Stereo: Modernism, Music, and Pan-African Solidarity*, New York: Oxford UP.

Jeyifo, B. (1990) "The Nature of Things: Arrested Decolonization and Critical Theory," *Research in African Literatures* 20 (1): 33–48.

Jeyifo, B. (1990) (1996) "The Reinvention of Theatrical Tradition: Critical Discourses on Interculturalism in the African Theatre," in P. Pavis (ed.) *The Intercultural Performance Reader*, London: Routledge.

Jika, T., L. Ledwaba et al. (2013) *We Are Going To Kill Each Other Today: The Marikana Story*, Cape Town: Tafelberg.

Joans, T. (1961) *All of Ted Joans and No More*, New York: Excelsior.

Johannesburg City Council (1936) *Official Guide to the Empire Exhibition*, Johannesburg: Jubilee Comm.

Johnson, D. (1996) *Shakespeare in South Africa*, Oxford UP.

Johnson, J.W. (1991 [1930]) *Black Manhattan*, New York: Da Capo.

Jones, B. (2009), "Puppetry and Authorship," in J. Taylor et al. (eds.) *Handspring Puppet Company*, 252–69, New York: David Krut Publishing.

Kabane, M.L. (1936) "The All-African Convention," *South African Outlook* (August): 185–89.

Kalumba, P.S. (2012) *Jabulani Means Rejoice: A Dictionary of South African Names*, Athlone (Cape): Modjaji.

Kani, J., W. Ntshona (1976) "Art is Life and Life is Art: An Interview with John Kani and Winston Ntshona," *UFAHAMU: Journal of the African Activist Association* 6 (2): 5–26.

Kannemeyer, J.C. (1983) *Geskiedenis van die Afrikaanse Literatuur*, Pretoria: Academica.

Kannemeyer, J.C. (1988) *Die Afrikaanse Literatuur, 1652-1987*. Pretoria: Human & Rousseau.

Karis, T., G.N. Carter (eds.) (1977) *From Protest to Challenge: A Documentary History of African Politics in South Africa*, vol. 3: *Challenge and Violence, 1953–64*, Stanford, CA: Hoover.

Karis, T., G. Gerhart (eds.) (1997) *From Protest to Challenge*, vol. 5: *Nadir and Resurgence, 1964–79*, Bloomington: Indiana UP.

Kavanagh, R.M. (1974–75) "Gibson Kente '74," *S'ketsh*: 24–25.

Kavanagh, R.M. (ed. and intro) (1981) *South African People's Plays*, London: Heinemann.

Kavanagh, R.M. (1983) "The Theatre of Gibson Kente," *African Communist* 95 (3): 91–103.

Kavanagh, R.M. (1985) *Theatre and Cultural Struggle in South Africa*, London: Zed.

Kavanagh, R.M. (2016) Introduction, *The Complete S'ketsh: Facsimile Edition*, ix–xiv, Johannesburg: Themba.

Kelly, M. (1934) *Conference on African Drama: 1934*, London: British Drama League.

Kelly, M. (1938) *Conference on African Drama: 1938*, London: British Drama League.

Kerr, D. (1995) *African Popular Theatre*, Portsmouth: Heinemann.

Keuris, M. (2012) "Theatre as Memory Machine: *Magrita Prinslo* (1896) and *Donkerland* (1996)," *Journal of Literary Study* 28 (3): 77–92.

Keuris, M. (2015) "Portrait of an Afrikaner Revolutionary: Harry Kalmer's," *Bram Fischer Waltz, South African Theatre Journal* 28 (2): 117–28.

Key, L. (2009) *Rewind, a Documentary* (DVD of *REwind: A Cantata for Voice, Tape and Testimony*, music by P. Miller, Cape Town: Key Productions.

Kgomongwe, S. (1979), "Egoli at the YMCA," *S'ketsh*: 15.

Khoapa, B.A. (ed.) (1973) *Black Review 1972*, Durban: Black Community Programs.

Klaaste, A. (1975a) "*Too Late*—Gibson Kente," *S'ketsh* (Winter): 8–9.

Klaaste, A. (1975b) "*Give Us this Day*—Mzwandile Maqina," *S'ketsh* (Summer): 26–27.

Koch, E. (1983) "'Without visible means of subsistence': Slumyard Culture in Johannesburg, 1920-1940," in B. Bozzoli (ed.), *Town and Countryside in the Transvaal*, 151–75, Johannesburg: Ravan

Kraai, N. (1973) "Black Theatre," *PET Newsletter* 1: 11–12.

Krikler, J. (2005) *White Rising: The 1922 Insurrection and Racial Killing in South Africa*, Manchester UP.

Kros, C., V. Cooke (2018) "Listening to the Market Theatre Archive," *Critical Arts*, 32 (3): 31–47.

Krueger, A. (2010) *Experiments in Freedom: Explorations of Identity in New South African Drama*, Newcastle on Tyne: Cambridge Scholars.

Krueger, A. (2015) "Reza de Wet," in Middeke et al. (eds.) *Methuen Guide*, 145–62.

Kruger, L. (1991) "Apartheid on Display: South Africa Performs for New York," *Diaspora* 1 (2): 191–208.

Kruger, L. (1992) *The National Stage: Theatre and Cultural Legitimation in England, France, and America*, University of Chicago Press.

Kruger, L. (1993) "Placing the Occasion: Raymond Williams and Performing Culture," in D. Dworkin (ed.) *Views Beyond the Border Country: Essays on Raymond Williams*, 55–71, London: Routledge.

Kruger, L. (1995) "So What's New? Women and Theater in the New South Africa," *Theater* 25 (3): 46–54.

Kruger, L. (1999a) *The Drama of South Africa: Plays, Pageants and Publics since 1910*, London: Routledge.

Kruger, L. (1999b) "Theatre for Development and TV Nation: Educational Soap Opera in South Africa," *Research in African Literatures* 30 (4): 105–26.

Kruger, L. (2001) "Theatre, Crime, and the Edgy City," *Theatre Journal* 53: 223–52.

Kruger, L. (2004) *Post-Imperial Brecht: Politics and Performance, East and South*, Cambridge UP.

Kruger, L. (2006) "Letter from South Africa," *Theater* 36 (1): 166–73.

Kruger, L. (2007) " 'White Cities,' 'Diamond Zulus' and the 'African Contribution to Human Advancement'," *The Drama Review* 51 (3): 19–45.

Kruger, L. (2009) "*Africa Thina*: Cosmopolitan and Xenophobic Agency in Johannesburg's Film and Television Drama," *Journal of Southern African Studies* 35: 237–52.

Kruger, L. (2011) "Beyond the TRC: Truth, Power, and Representation in South Africa After Transition," *Research in African Literatures* 42 (2): 184–96.

Kruger, L. (2012a) "Theatre: Regulation, Resistance and Recovery," in D. Attwell et al. (eds.) *Cambridge History of South African Literature*, 564–86, Cambridge UP.

Kruger, L. (2012b) "South African Theatre in the Age of Globalization," *Theatre Journal* 64: 119–27.

Kruger, L. (2012c) "On the Tragedy of the Commoner: Elektra, Orestes and others in South Africa," *Comparative Drama* 46 (3): 355–77.

Kruger, L. (2013) *Imagining the Edgy City: Writing, Performing and Building Johannesburg*, Oxford UP.

Kruger, L. (2015a) "Letter from Grahamstown: The National Arts Festival at Forty," *Theater* 45 (2): 159–78.

Kruger, L. (2015b) "Lara Foot," in Middeke et al. (eds.) *Methuen Guide*, 195–208.

Kruger, L. (forthcoming) "The National Arts Festival in Grahamstown," in R. Knowles (ed.) *Cambridge Companion to International Festivals*.

Kruger, L., P. Watson [Shariff] (2001) " 'Shoo, this Book Makes Me To Think': Education, Entertainment, and Life-Skills Comics in South Africa," *Poetics Today* 22: 475–513.

Laing, R.D. (1969) *Self and Others*, New York: Pantheon.

Landau, L., I. Freemantle (2010) "Tactical Cosmopolitanism and Idioms of Belonging," *Journal of Ethnic and Migration Studies* 36 (3): 375–90.

Laub, D. (1995) "Bearing Witness," in D. Laub, S. Felman (eds.) *Testimony: Crises of Witnessing in Literature, Psychoanalysis, and History*, 57–74, New York: Routledge.

Ledwaba, L. (2016) *Broke and Broken: The Shameful Legacy of Gold Mining in South Africa*, Johannesburg: Blackbird Books.

Lewis, M. (2016) *Performing Whitely in the Postcolony: Afrikaners in Theatrical and Public Life*, University of Iowa Press.

Lewis, M., A. Krueger (2016) "Plotting the Magnetic Field," *Magnet Theatre*, 1–50.

Linscott, A.P. (1936) "R.U.R.," *South African Opinion* (November 14): 15.

Linscott, A.P. (1937a) "Mr. van Gyseghem and the Bantu Players," *South African Opinion* (January 23): 15.

Linscott, A.P. (1937b) "Mr. van Gyseghem and the Pageant," *South African Opinion* (January 23): 15–16.

Lloyd, T.C. (1935) "The Bantu Tread the Footlights," *South African Opinion* (March 6): 3–5.

Locke, A. (ed.) (1992 [1925]) *The New Negro*, New York: Macmillan.

Lodge, T. (1985) *Black Politics in South Africa since 1945*, London: Longman.

Longinotto, K. (2009) *Rough Aunties* (DVD), New York: Women Make Movies.

Lott, E. (1993) *Love and Theft: Blackface Minstrelsy and the American Working Class*, Oxford UP.

Louw, N.P. van Wyk (1939) *Berigte te Velde*, Pretoria: Van Schaik.

Love, H. (1984) (ed.) *The Australian Stage: A Documentary History*, Sydney: UP of New South Wales.

Madikizela, P.G., S. van Schalkwyk (eds.) (2015) *Exploring New Frontiers of Gender Research in South Africa*, Newcastle on Tyne: Cambridge Scholars.

Madonsela, T. (2016) *State of Capture*, Pretoria: Office of the Public Protector http://www.pprotect.org/library/investigation_report/2016-17/State_Capture_14October2016.pdf.

Mailer, N. (1992 [1957]) "The White Negro," A. Charters (ed.) *The Portable Beat Reader*, New York: Viking.

Makhudu, K.D.P. (2002) "Introduction to Flaaitaal (or Tsotsitaal)," in R. Mesthrie (ed.) *Language in South Africa*, 398–406, Cambridge UP.

Makhulu, A.-M. (2012) "Conditions for After-Work: Financialization and Informalization in Post-transition South Africa," *Publications of the Modern Language* Association 127: 782–99.

Malange, N. and the Culture and Working Life Project (1990) "Albie Sachs Must Not Worry," in I. de Kok, K. Press (eds.), *Spring is Rebellious*, 99–106, Cape Town: Buchu Books.

Maluleke, T.S. (2016) "Imbongi's Drift not Lost on the Unschooled," *Johannesburg Mail & Guardian* (February 19): 23.

Mandela, N.R. (1994) Statement of Nelson R. Mandela on his Inauguration as President of the Republic of South Africa, *Nelson Mandela Foundation*; http://db.nelsonmandela.org/speeches.

Mandela, N.R. (1995) *Long Walk to Freedom*, Boston, MA: Little, Brown.

Manganyi, N.C. (1973) *Being-Black-in-the-World*, Johannesburg: Ravan.

Mangcu, X. (2014) *Biko—A Life*, New York: Palgrave.

Mannoni, O. (1964) *Prospero and Caliban: The Psychology of Colonialism*, P. Powersland (trans.), New York: Praeger.

Marcuse, H. (1968 [1935]) "The Affirmative Character of Culture," *Negations*, J. Shapiro (trans.), 88–133, Boston, MA: Beacon.

Marinovich, G. (2018) *Murder at Small Koppie: The Real Story of South Africa's Marikana Massacre*, East Lansing: Michigan State UP.

Marks, S. (1986) *The Ambiguities of Dependence*, Johannesburg: Ravan.

Marks, S. (1989) "Patriotism, Patriarchy, and Purity: Natal and the Politics of Zulu Ethnic Consciousness," in L. Vail (ed.) *The Creation of Tribalism in Southern Africa*, 215–40, Berkeley: University of California Press.

Marlin-Curiel, S. (2002) "A Long Road to Healing: From the TRC to TfD," *Theatre Research International*, 27 (3): 275–88.

Marx, K., F. Engels (1971) *The Marx-Engels Reader*, R. Tucker (ed.), New York: Norton.

Marx, L. (1994) Review: *And the Girls in Their Sunday Dresses, Southern African Review of Books* 6 (2): 20–21.

Masilela, N. (2007) *The Cultural Modernity of H.I.E. Dhlomo*, Trenton, NJ: Africa World Press.

Matisonn, J. (2015) *God, Spies and Lies: Finding South Africa's Future Through Its Past*, Vlaeberg, South Africa: Missing Ink.

Matshikiza, T. (1953) "How Musicians Die," *Drum* (October): 38.

Matshikiza, T. (1956) "Masterpiece in Bronze: Emily Motsieloa," *Drum* (May): 22–23.

Matshikiza, T. (1957) "Jazz Comes to Jo'burg," *Drum* (July): 38–39, 41.

Matshoba, M. (2002) "Nothing but the Truth: The Ordeal of Duma Khumalo," in D. Posel, G. Simpson (eds.) *Commissioning the Past: Understanding South Africa's Truth and Reconciliation Commission*, 131–44, Johannesburg: Wits UP.

Mattera, D. (1987) *Memory is a Weapon*, Johannesburg: Ravan.

Mazrui, A., M.Tidy (1984) *Nationalism and New States in Africa*, London: Heinemann.

Mbanjwa, T. (ed.) (1975) *Black Review 1974/75*, Durban: Black Community Programs.

Mbembe, A. (1992) "The Banality of Power and the Aesthetics of Vulgarity in the Postcolony," J. Roitman (trans.), *Public Culture* 4 (2): 1–30.

Mbembe, A. (2015) "Decolonizing Knowledge and the Question of the Archive": https://wiser.wits.ac.za/system/files/Achille%20Mbembe%20-%20Decolonizing%20 Knowledge%20and%20the%20Question%20of%20the%20Archive.pdf

Mbothwe, M. (2016) "A Conversation with Mandla Mbothwe [A. Krueger]," in Lewis, Krueger (eds.) *Magnet Theatre*, 127–32.

McClintock, A. (1992) "The Angel of Progress: Pitfalls of 'Postcolonialism'," *Social Text* 31: 79–92.

McClintock, A. (1995) *Imperial Leather: Race, Gender and Sexuality in the Colonial Contest*, London: Routledge.

McGrath, J. (1981) (intro.) *The Cheviot, the Stag, and the Black, Black Oil*, London: Methuen.

Mda, Z. (1995) "Theater and Reconciliation in South Africa," *Theater* 25 (3): 36–45.

Mdhluli, S.V. (1933) *The Development of the African*, Marianhill Mission.

Merrington, P. (1997) "Masques, Monuments, and Masons: The 1910 Pageant of the Union of South Africa," *Theatre Journal* 49: 1–14.

Mesthrie, R. (2002a) "South Africa: A Sociolinguistic Overview," in Mesthrie (ed.) *Language in South Africa*, 11–26, Cambridge UP.

Mesthrie, R. (2002b) "From Second Language to First Language: Indian South African English," in Mesthrie, *Language in South Africa*, 339–55.

Meyer, P.J. (1942) *Demokrasie of Volkstaat?*, Stellenbosch: Afrikaner Nasionale Studentenbond.

Middeke, M., G. Homann and P.P. Schnierer (eds.) (2015) *The Methuen Guide to Contemporary South African Theatre*. London: Bloomsbury.

Midgley, H.P. (1993) "Author, Ideology and Publisher: Lovedale Missionary Press and Early Black Writing in South Africa," M.A. thesis, Rhodes University.

Millin, S.G. (1924) *God's Step-Children*, London: Constable.

Millin, S.G. (1954) *The People of South Africa*, London: Constable.

Minogue, K. (1995), "Cultural Cringe: Cultural Inferiority Complex and Republicanism in Australia," *National Review* 47 (25): 21–22.

Mkhabela, S. (2001) *Open Earth and Black Roses: Remembering 16 June 1976*, Johannesburg: Skotaville.

Mlambo, A. (2014) *A History of Zimbabwe*, Cambridge UP.

Mngadi, S. (1997) "'Africanization'—or the New Exoticism," *Scrutiny2* 2 (1): 18–22.

Modisane, W. (1986 [1963]) *Blame Me on History*, Johannesburg: Ad Donker.

Mofokeng, J. (1996) "Theatre for Export: The Commercialization of the Black People's Struggle in South African Export Musicals," in G. Davis, A. Fuchs (eds.) *Theatre and Change in South Africa*, Amsterdam: Harwood.

Mofokeng, S. (1996) "The Black Photo Album: 1890–1950," *National Arts Festival Program*, 80–81, Grahamstown Foundation.

Moleba, E. (2016) "Marikana Youth," M.A. thesis, Wits University.

Moodie, T.D. (1975) *The Rise of Afrikanerdom: Power, Apartheid, and the Afrikaner Civil Religion*, Berkeley: University of California Press.

Morris, A. (1999) *Bleakness and Light: Inner City Transition in Hillbrow*, Johannesburg: Wits UP.

Morris, G. (2016) "Magnet Theatre 'Intervenes' in Khayelitsha," in Lewis, Krueger (eds.) *Magnet Theatre*, 223–42.

Morris, G. (2017) "Dinosaurs Become Birds: Changing Cultural Values in Cape Town Theatre," *Theatre Research International* 42 (2): 146–62.

Moss, G. (2014) *The New Radicals: A Generational Memoir of the 1970s*, Johannesburg: Jacana.

Motsei, M. (2007) *The Kanga and the Kangaroo Court: Reflections on Jacob Zuma's Rape Trial*, Johannesburg: Jacana.

Mountain, A. (2004) *Unsung Heritage: Perspectives on Slavery*, Cape Town: D. Philip.

Mphahlele, E. (2002) *Es'kia: Education, African Humanism, Social Consciousness, Literary Appreciation*, Cape Town: Kwela.

Mudimbe, V.I. (1988) *The Invention of Africa*, Bloomington: Indiana UP.

Mutwa, C.V. (1974/75) "*Umlinganiso*—The Living Imitation," *S'ketsh*: 30–32.

Muyanga, N. (2016) "A Conversation with Neo Muyanga [Krueger]," in Krueger Lewis (eds.) *Magnet Theatre*, 77–82.

Naidoo, M. (1997) "The Search for a Cultural Identity: A Personal View of South African 'Indian' Theatre," *Theatre Journal* 49: 29–39.

Nakasa, N. (1959) "The Life and Death of King Kong," in Chapman (ed.) *The Drum Decade*, 166–77.

Nandy, A. (1983) *The Intimate Enemy: Loss and Recovery of Self under Colonialism*, New Delhi: Oxford UP.

Naudé, S.C.M. (1950) "The Rise of The Afrikaans Theatre," *Trek: South Africa's Literary Magazine* (April): 8–10.

Ndebele, N. (1994) *South African Literature and Culture: Rediscovery of the Ordinary*, Manchester UP.

Ndlovu, D. (1986) "Introduction," *Woza Afrika!*, ix–xxviii, New York: Braziller.

Ndlovu, S.M. (2006) "The Soweto Uprising, Part 1," *The Road to Democracy in South Africa*, vol. 2: 217–350, Pretoria: UNISA Press.

Ngũgĩ Wa Thiong'o (1986) *Decolonising the Mind: The Politics of Language in African Literature*, London: James Currey.

Nkosi, L. (1972) (intro.) *The Will to Die*, London: Heinemann.

Nkosi, L. (1983) *Home and Exile and Other Selections*, London: Longman.

Nora, P. (1989) "Between Memory and History: *Les Lieux de mémoire*" M. Roudebush (trans.), *Representations* 26 (Spring): 7–21.

O'Meara, D. (1983) *Volkskapitalisme: Class, Capital, and Ideology in the Development of Afrikaner Nationalism*, Johannesburg: Ravan.

O'Meara, D. (1996) *Forty Lost Years: The Apartheid State and the Politics of the National Party, 1948–1994*, Johannesburg: Ravan.

Orkin, M. (1991) *Drama and the South African State*, Johannesburg: Wits UP.

Orkin, M. (1995) (ed., intro) *At the Junction: Four Plays by the Junction Avenue Theatre Company*, Johannesburg: Wits UP.

Parker, P. (1996) "South Africa and the Common Purpose Rule in Crowd Murders," *Journal of African Law* 40 (1): 78–102.

Parker, W., L. Dalrymple, E. Durden (2000) *Communicating Beyond AIDS Awareness*, 2nd ed., Pretoria: Dept. of Health.

PET Newsletter, S. Variava (ed.), Johannesburg: n.p.

Peterson, B. (1993) (intro.) *And the Girls in Their Sunday Dresses*, Johannesburg: Wits UP.

Peterson, B. (2000) *Monarchs, Missionaries & African Intellectuals: African Theater and the Unmaking of Colonial Marginality*, Trenton, NJ: Africa World Press.

Phillips, H. (2012) *Epidemics: The Story of South Africa's Five Most Lethal Human Diseases*, Athens: Ohio UP.

Phillips, R. (1930) *The Bantu Are Coming*, New York: Richard Smith.

Pickard-Cambridge, C. (1989) *The Greying of Johannesburg*, Johannesburg: SAIRR.

Polley, J. (1973) *Die Sestigers*, Cape Town: Human Rousseau.

Posel, D., J. Zeller (2015) Language Shift or Increased Bilingualism in South Africa (UKZN; http://www.jzeller.de/pdf/Shift.pdf).

Purkey, M. (1993) Introduction, *Sophiatown*, Johannesburg: Wits UP.

Purkey, M. (2008) "Market Voices; Interview with L. Kruger," *Theater* 38 (1): 18–30.

Purkey, M. (2013) "Artistic Director's Report," *Market Theatre Annual Report*, Johannesburg: Market Theatre.

Rabie, J. (1985) "Is dit ons erns—in Afrika?" *Skrywer en Gemeenskap*, Pretoria: HAUM.

Rambally, A. (ed.) (1977) *Black Review 1975/76*, Durban: Black Community Programs.

Ramphele, M. (1991) *Bounds of Possibility: The Legacy of Steve Biko and Black Consciousness*, Cape Town: D. Philip.

Ravengai, S. (2015), "Embodiment, Mobility and Encounter in Jonathan Nkala's *The Crossing*," in Fleischman (ed.) *Performing Migrancy and Mobility in Africa*, 77–96.

Read, J. (comp.) (1991) *Athol Fugard: A Bibliography*, Grahamstown: National English Literary Museum.

Rive, R. (1989) *Advance, Retreat*, Cape Town: David Philip.

Roach, J. (1996) *Cities of the Dead: Circum-Atlantic Performance*, New York: Columbia UP.

Roberge, P. (2002) "Afrikaans: Considering Origins," in Mesthrie (ed.) *Language in South Africa*, 79–103.

Roberts, S. (2015) "The 'Pioneers," Middeke et al. (eds.), *Methuen Guide*, 17–41.

Routh, G. (1950a) "The Johannesburg Art Theatre," *Trek* (September): 25–27.

Routh, G. (1950b) "The Bantu People's Theatre," *Trek* (October): 20–23.

Sachs, A. (1990a) "Preparing Ourselves for Freedom," in I. de Kok and K. Press (eds.) *Spring is Rebellious*, 19–29, Cape Town: Buchu.

Sachs, A. (1990b) *Protecting Human Rights in a New South Africa*, Cape Town: Oxford UP.

Sachs, B. (1959) *Personalities and Places*, Johannesburg: Kayor.

Sagan, L. (1996) *Lights and Shadows: The Autobiography of Leontine Sagan*, L. Kruger (ed.), Johannesburg: Wits UP.

Salverson, J. (2001) "Change on Whose Terms? Testimony and an Erotics of Injury," *Theater* 31 (3): 119–25.

Sampson, A. (1983) *Drum: An African Adventure and Afterwards*, London: Hodder & Stoughton.

Samuel, R. et al. (1985) *Theatres of the Left: Working Class Theatre in Britain and the United States, 1880–1935*, London: Routledge.

Sanders, M. (2016) *Learning Zulu: A Secret History of Language in South Africa*, Princeton UP.

Saragas, A. (2017) *Strike a Rock* (DVD), Johannesburg: Elafos Productions.

Sassen, R. (2015) "Physical Theatre," in Middeke et al. (eds.) *Methuen Guide*, 77–95.

Scarry, E. (1985) *The Body in Pain: The Making and Unmaking of the World*, Oxford UP.

Schach, L. (1996) *The Flag is Flying: A Very Personal History of Theatre in the Old South Africa*, Cape Town: Human Rousseau.

Schadeberg, J. (comp.) (1987) *Fifties People of Johannesburg*, Johannesburg: Baileys African History Archive.

Schauffer, D. (1994) *In the Shadow of the Shah*, Durban: Asoka.

Schechner, R. (1985) *Between Theater and Anthropology*, Philadelphia: University of Pennsylvania Press.

Schneider, R. (2011) *Performance Remains: Art and War in Times of Theatrical Reenactment*, New York: Routledge.

Schwartz, P. (1988) *The Best of Company: The Story of Johannesburg's Market Theatre*, Johannesburg: Ad Donker.

Schwartz, P. (1997) (ed., intro.) *Born in the RSA; Four Workshopped Plays*, Johannesburg: Wits UP.

Segatti, A., L. Landau (2011) *Contemporary Migration to South Africa*, Washington DC: World Bank.

Sekhabi, A. (2015) "Interview with G. Homann," in Middeke et al. (eds.) *Methuen Guide*, 341–63.

Sellkow, T.A., T. Mbulaheni (2013) "Sugar Daddy Relationships and Conspicuous Consumption among University Students in South Africa," *Agenda: Empowering Women for Gender Equity* 27 (2): 86–98.

Sepamla, S. (1973) "The Mdali Black Arts Festival," *S'ketsh* (Summer): 42–43.

Sepamla, S. (1981) "Towards an African Theatre," *Rand Daily Mail* (April 2): n.p.

Shell, R. (1994) *Children of Bondage: A Social History of the Slave Society at the Cape, 1652–1838*, Hanover, NH: UP of New England.

Shepherd, R.H.W. (1935) *Literature for the South African Bantu*, Pretoria: Carnegie Corporation.

Sichel, A. (2015) "Paul Slabolepszy," in Middeke et al. (eds.), *Methuen Guide*, 163–75.

Sieg, K. (2015) "Pitfalls of Decolonizing the Exhibitionary Complex of Brett Bailey's *Exhibit B*," *Theatre Research International* 40 (3): 250–71.

Simon, B. (1974) "Education Through Respect," *The Leech* 44 (2): 84–85.

Simone, A.M. (1994) "In the Mix: Remaking Coloured Identities," *Africa Insight* 24 (3): 161–73.

Simone, A.M. (1998) "Globalization and the Identity of African Urban Practices," in H. Judin, I. Vladislavić (eds.) *Blank___: Architecture, Apartheid and After*, 175–87, Rotterdam: Netherlands Architecture Institute.

Skjelten, S. (2006) *A People's Constitution: Public Participation in the South African Constitution-Making Process*, Midrand: Institute for Global Dialogue.

Skota, T.D. (ed.) (1931) *The African Yearly Register. An Illustrated National Biographical Dictionary of Black Folks in Africa*, Johannesburg: Esson.

Skurski, J., F. Coronil (1993) "Country and City in a Colonial Landscape," in Dworkin (ed.) *Views beyond the Border Country*, 231–59.

Slosberg, B. (1939) *Pagan Tapestry*, London: Rich & Cravan.

Small, A. (1961) *Die Eerste steen*, Cape Town: HAUM.

Small, A. (1985) "Die Skryfambag en apartheid," *Skrywer en Gemeenskap*, Pretoria: HAUM.

Smit, B. (1985) "Skrywe—'n Ambag?" *Skrywer en Gemeenskap*.

Smith, J. (1990) *Toneel en Politiek*, Bellville: UWCP.

Soja, E. (1997) "Six Discourses on the Postmetropolis," in S. Westwood (ed.) *Imagining Cities: Scripts, Signs, Memory*, 19–30, London: Routledge.

Solberg, R. (2011) *Bra Gib: Father of South Africa's Township Theatre*, Pietermaritzburg: UKZNP.

Stead, R. (1984) "The National Theatre Organization, 1947–62," in T. Hauptfleisch (ed.) *The Breytie Book*, 63–77, Randburg: Limelight.

Steadman, I. (1985) "Drama and Social Consciousness: Black Theatre on the Witwatersrand to 1984," Ph.D thesis, Wits University.

Steadman, I. (1990) "Toward Popular Theatre in South Africa," *Journal of Southern African Studies* 16: 208–28.

Steadman, I. (1995) "Introduction," in Maponya, *Doing Plays for a Change*.

Stein, P., R. Jacobson (ed.) (1986) *Sophiatown Speaks*, Johannesburg: Junction Avenue.

Sutherland, A. (2013) "Dramatic Spaces in Patriarchal Contexts," in H. Barnes (ed.), *Applied Drama and Theatre as an Interdisciplinary Field*, 177–85, Amsterdam: Rodopi.

Taylor, D. (2003) *The Archive and the Repertoire: Performing Cultural Memory in the Americas*, Durham, NC: Duke UP.

Thomas, A. (1972a) "Interview with Adam Small," *S'ketsh* (Summer): 33–34.

Thomas, A. (1972b) "Kanna Hy Kô Hystoe," *S'ketsh* (Summer): 26.

Thompson, L., rev. L. Berat (2014) *History of South Africa*, 4th ed., New Haven, CT: Yale UP.

Tucker, P. (1997) *Just the Ticket: My 50 Years in Show Business*, Johannesburg: J. Ball.

Turner, V. (1982) *From Ritual to Theatre*, New York: Performing Arts Journal.

Vail, L., L. White (1991) *Power and the Praise Poem: South African Voices in History*, Charlottesville: UP Virginia.

Vandenbroucke, R. (1986) *Truths the Hands Can Touch: The Theatre of Athol Fugard*, Johannesburg: Ad Donker.

Van der Kolk, B., O. van der Hart (1995) "The Intrusive Past: The Flexibility of Memory and the Engraving of Trauma," in C. Caruth (ed.) *Trauma: Explorations in Memory*, 158–81, Baltimore, MD: Johns Hopkins UP.

Van Graan, M., T. Ballantyne (eds.) (2003) *South African Handbook on Arts and Culture 2002*, Cape Town: D. Philip.

Van Niekerk, M. (1994) *Triomf*. Cape Town: Quellerie.

Van Onselen, C. (1996) *The Seed is Mine: The Life of Kas Maine, African Sharecropper, 1894–1985*, Cape Town: D. Philip.

Verwoerd, H.F. (1966) *Verwoerd Speaks: 1948–66*, A. Pelzer (ed.), Johannesburg: Afrikaanse Pers.

Vilakazi, B.W. (1942) "Some Aspects of Zulu Literature," *African Studies* 1 (4): 270–74.

Visser, N. (1976) "South Africa: The Renaissance that Failed," *Journal of Commonwealth Literature* 9: 42–57.

Visser, N., T. Couzens (1985) (eds., intro) *Collected Works of H I.E. Dhlomo*, Johannesburg: Ravan.

Von Kotze, A. (1989) "The Struggle for Workers Theater in South Africa," *Brecht Yearbook* 14: 157–67.

Walder, D. (1985) *Athol Fugard*, New York: Grove.

Walder, D. (1993) (ed., intro.) Fugard, *Township Plays*, Oxford UP.

Watson [Shariff], P. (1998) "Dialogue, Gender and Performance: Producing a Rural Comic Beyond the Learner Paradox," PhD thesis, Wits University.

Weeder, M. (2004) "The Forced Removal of the Prestwich Dead," in A. Olifant et al. (eds.) *Democracy X: Marking the Present, Presenting the Past*, 26–31, Leiden: Brill.

Wenzel, J. (2009) *Bulletproof: Afterlives of Anticolonial Prophesy in South Africa*, University of Chicago Press.

Wilentz, E. (ed.) (1960) *The Beat Scene*, New York: Corinth.

Williams, R. (1973) *The Country and the City*, London: Chatto & Windus.

Williams, R. (1979) *Politics and Letters: Interviews with New Left Review*, London: Verso.

Williams, R. (1995) *The Sociology of Culture*, University of Chicago Press.

Witz, L. (2003) *Apartheid's Festival: Contesting South Africa's National Pasts*, Bloomington: Indiana UP.

Worden, N., C. Crais (eds., intro) (1994) *Breaking the Chains: Slavery and its Legacy in the Nineteenth Century Cape Colony*, Johannesburg: Wits UP.

Zuma, J. (2016) *State of the Nation Address*: http://www.gov.za/speeches/president-jacob-zuma-state-nation-address-2016-11-feb-2016-0000.

Index

Lightning Source UK Ltd.
Milton Keynes UK
UKHW022131150120
357028UK00003B/184/P